THE RENAISSANCE
ESSAYS IN INTERPRETATION

THE
RENAISSANCE

ESSAYS IN INTERPRETATION

André Chastel
Cecil Grayson
Marie Boas Hall
Denys Hay
Paul Oskar Kristeller
Nicolai Rubinstein
Charles B. Schmitt
Charles Trinkaus
Walter Ullmann

METHUEN
LONDON AND NEW YORK

First published in Great Britain in 1982 by
Methuen & Co. Ltd
11 New Fetter Lane, London EC4P 4EE

Published in the USA by
Methuen & Co.
in association with Methuen, Inc.
733 Third Avenue, New York, NY 10017

English translation © 1982 Methuen & Co. Ltd
The original edition was first published in Italy,
under the title *Il Rinascimento: Interpretazioni e Problemi*,
© 1979 Guis. Laterza & Figli Spa, Roma-Bari

Printed in Great Britain at the University Press, Cambridge

British Library Cataloguing in Publication Data

The Renaissance.
1. Renaissance – Europe   2. Europe – Civilization
I. Chastel, André   II. Il Rinascimento. *English*
940.2'1   CB428

ISBN 0-416-31130-X

TO EUGENIO GARIN

CONTENTS

1

HISTORIANS AND THE RENAISSANCE DURING THE LAST TWENTY-FIVE YEARS

DENYS HAY

NYONE surveying the problem of the Renaissance in the last twenty or thirty years must be astonished at the tenacity with which the categories established by Jacob Burckhardt have survived criticism. *Die Kultur der Renaissance in Italien* came out in Basle in 1860 and over a century later its main argument remains virtually unchallenged. True, Burckhardt's synthesis had been built on foundations which went back to the Renaissance period itself, to Petrarch and his successors, long before Vasari gave 'Rinascita' its definition as applied to the fine arts. How the concept of the rebirth of classical norms began to take over education and literature, both in revived Latin and Greek as well as in the vernaculars, has been told in the authoritative pages of Wallace K. Ferguson's *The Renaissance in Historical Thought*.[1] What Burckhardt (and Georg Voigt at much the same time, though on a much narrower front)[2] did was to extend the concept of the Renaissance from the arts and belles-lettres to the wider world of society and of history in its broadest sense. Voigt explained how the humanities at the time of Coluccio Salutati were adopted by the Florentines; Burckhardt's essay began with a substantial survey of Italian history, which he entitled 'The state as a work of art' (though the phrase remains somewhat gnomic). In the rest of his modestly written book, Burckhardt applied as thoroughly as he could the aphorism invented by Jules Michelet: that the Renaissance witnessed 'the discovery of the world and of man'.[3] This meant for Burckhardt that the Renaissance ushered in attitudes which would change the whole world, first of all in Italy and then elsewhere, to inaugurate that 'modern' world, with its attitudes to natural phenomena, moral and religious questions, as well as to public affairs and the creative work of artists and writers. In the main it is within the context of these ideas that students of the Renaissance still move; indeed it is probably true to say that the basic tenets of the Burckhardtian position are more dominant, more unchallenged, today than they were before the two World Wars.

It is not the intention of this study to analyse the evolution of Renaissance studies before 1939. Yet something must be said of the criticism encountered by Burckhardt and his disciples before then, if we are properly to appreciate the diminution, even the disappearance for all practical purposes, of such criticism in recent decades. However, in view of Professor Ferguson's full survey there is no need for an elaborate description of the attacks directed at Burckhardt's position. Perhaps the criticisms may be reduced to two broad headings. There were those who argued that the Renaissance which started in Italy in the fourteenth and fifteenth centuries was only one of several such episodes in the cultural development of Europe, so that 'Renaissance' should be regarded as a generic name for successive but disparate returns to, or recoveries of, Classical Antiquity. On the other hand there were some who denied that anything had happened in Italy which deserved to be regarded as special and important.

The first group of critics were in general the more impressive and productive. As a result of their labours medieval studies were greatly enriched by research into the 'Carolingian' renaissance and the 'twelfth-century' renaissance. The former was for long regarded, and rightly, as a somewhat fugitive moment in which a mere handful of scholars, following Alcuin's inspiration, were involved.[4] Unquestionably many of the men involved had some public influence; their activities led to the preservation of many ancient manuscripts; and the writing of the period was to inspire, albeit mistakenly, the belief that the clear minuscule lettering in which these texts were copied was antique, in this way leading them to be treated as models for the humanist hands of the fifteenth century and later.[5]

The 'twelfth-century' renaissance was only slightly more appealing to a wider public, and in some ways was to have less far-reaching consequences, at any rate so far as later cultural events in Italy were concerned. Associated with the schools of Chartres and Paris, with Latin writers like Bernard and Theoderic of Chartres and with the English prelate, John of Salisbury, we have the impression of a learned coterie cultivating Latin letters for each other's benefit, detached from the rough and tumble of real life as led by the mass of their contemporaries. Charles Homer Haskins' admirable study, *The Renaissance of the Twelfth Century*,[6] restricts its subject to the 'complete development of Romanesque art and the rise of Gothic; the full bloom of vernacular poetry, both lyric and epic; and the new learning and the new literature

[2]

in Latin'.[7] Haskins' book, however, ends with a chapter called 'The beginnings of universities', and with Paris and Bologna and their multiplying offspring, we enter a new intellectual environment in the thirteenth century. This has been characterized, most persistently and ferociously by Giuseppe Toffanin, as a world of 'science' or legalism.[8] The metaphysicians and the theologians, the teachers of the sacred text and the professors of canon and civil law, came to dominate higher education, and drove literature and the humanities into the by-ways of education, into the most dingy and the most disreputable corners of the groves of academe. The result (so runs the argument) was that the emotional and moral solvent of the ancient classics was frozen for three or four generations, inaccessible to serious and sensible men. That the thirteenth-century university had little time for poetry and letters is incontestable. Yet we should remember that – despite initial resistance by the hierarchy in Paris – Aristotle was better known, if only in Latin versions, in the thirteenth century than at any time before the sixteenth; that the jurists of Italy in the thirteenth century were to form the most influential of the admirers of Petrarch and the 'new learning' a hundred years later; and that the notarial art and the *ars dictaminis* secured the practice if not the idealization of good literature.[9]

The 'Carolingian' and 'twelfth-century' renaissances were thus supported by a very small, though influential, group, and so had little widespread patronage, unless one includes (as Haskins did) the development of Gothic art and architecture. All in all, we must be grateful for the useful distinction which Erwin Panofsky made between the 'Renaissance' and 'renascences' in western art in the book so titled.[10] He applied his analysis to the arts but it seems to me equally relevant in the spheres of learning and literature. There were moments when classical motifs, ideas and texts attracted attention among a few *cognoscenti*, but these were relatively evanescent[11] and in no sense dispose of the originality, social relevance and influence, profound and long lived, of the cultural changes of the Italy of the fourteenth and subsequent centuries, destined to dominate the cultural values of the western world almost to our own day.

The faint criticisms encountered by Burckhardt reduced, or attempted to reduce, the concept of renaissance to a mere recurrent type of revived interest in the antique. The other criticisms, while they cannot be so neatly associated, all in the end denied in effect that there was an Italian Renaissance at all – or at any rate that it had any significance. This was partly attempted by stressing that the 'modern world', which Burckhardt had seen the Renaissance ushering in, was in practice permeated with medieval concepts. Such was the argument of literary critics like Douglas Bush and E.M.W. Tillyard,[12] parallel in its way to the argument advanced much earlier, that even in the thirteenth century 'humanism' was influential: it was argued by H. Thode that the key figure in the evolution of the Italian Renaissance and the modern world was St Francis of Assisi.[13] A different line was pursued by some historians of both the Roman and the Protestant persuasions. Almost from the start reformers had seen the striking innovations in teaching as a mere episode in the recovery of ancient purity, an incident only to be commemorated in the new (or old but revived) churches. That Melanchthon was a sound Latinist in the new manner and Calvin could be regarded as a humanist of stature seemed to clinch the matter. Who 'laid the egg that Luther hatched' but Erasmus himself, prince of the new learning? Besides, the great ages of Roman literature corresponded with the great ages of the early Church. For many a Protestant school-child, certainly down to my own day in Britain, the importance of the Renaissance lay in its being a prelude to the far more important Reformation: witness the titles of the first two volumes of the *Cambridge Modern History*: I. *Renaissance*, II. *Reformation*. These came out in 1902. That they were planned by the Roman Catholic Lord Acton merely reinforces the hold that the connection I have outlined exercised in northern Europe at this time.

These assumptions were, however, less drastically opposed to the significance of the Renaissance than those which effectively sought to obliterate the concept or deny its validity altogether. Of those who were prepared to challenge the basic notion of individualism, or rather the cult of the individual as Burckhardt himself would have termed it, none was more persistent than that great French philosopher and man of letters, Etienne Gilson. His challenge was repeatedly delivered, but in no place more movingly than in *Héloïse et Abélard*, only the last of a series of criticisms.[14]

> Avant de trouver une formule pour définir le moyen âge, il faudrait en trouver une pour définir Héloïse. Je conseillerais ensuite d'en chercher une pour définir Pétrarque. Ceci fait, que l'on en cherche une troisième pour définir Erasme. Ces trois problèmes une fois résolus, on pourra procéder en toute sécurité à définir le Moyen Age et la Renaissance. Trois plus deux font cinq impossibilités.[15]

I will say a word later on Gilson's position.

The other main attack, less witty, less shrewd and, in my judgement, less relevant, came from the historians of science. If Gilson had in a sense produced a syllogism which sought to demonstrate the irre-levancy of categories by finding evidence (in a sense) for all attitudes at all times, so the historian of science presented the following argument:

> The Renaissance is supposed to lead to the Modern World;
> The modern world is based on physical science;
> There was no humanist interest in physical science;
> Therefore there was no Renaissance in Italy in the fourteenth and fifteenth centuries.

The most vociferous purveyor of such syllogistic propositions, if not perhaps the most subtle, was the late Lynn Thorndike, at length in his *History of Magic and Experimental Science*,[16] and more briefly on several other occasions. But he did not stand alone. Some similar presuppositions colour the large-scale work of Pierre Duhem.[17] George Sarton's view was that 'from the scientific point of view, the Renaissance was *not* a Renaissance'.[18] And many other writers took a not dissimilar line, or at any rate reinforced the view that medieval men were as concerned with the 'discovery of the world' as their Renaissance successors.[19] One has a lingering suspicion that with this approach the writers have allowed the modern dominance of the natural sciences to lead them to exaggerate the influence of the few professors at Paris, Oxford and elsewhere who speculated on cosmological theory, the concept of motion, and so on.

There is, clearly, an imperative need for historians not to become tyrannized by their artificial abstractions. There is nothing God-given about terms like 'Renaissance', 'modern', 'Risorgimento' or any similar expressions. Historians should all be 'nominalists', to use medieval scholastic terminology: and this is really the position adopted by Johan Huizinga, which in its very different way is as subtle and sophisticated as Burckhardt's.

> The soul of Western Christendom itself was outgrowing medieval forms and modes of thought that had become shackles. The Middle Ages had always lived in the shadow of Antiquity, always handled its treasures, or what they had of them, interpreting it [Antiquity] according to truly medieval principles: scholastic theology and chivalry, asceticism and courtesy. Now, by an inward ripening, the mind, after being so long conversant with the forms of Antiquity, began to grasp its spirit.[20]

After the Second World War these debates and doubts seem stilled and the framework of Burckhardt, modified here and there, as it was to be later, still held firm. Like a well-made ship, his survey survived the winds of criticism.[21] But, before we consider the developments in

Renaissance historiography since 1950, it is essential to note some very important works which fall just before, or in, or just after the war years, and whose influence as a result had a delayed effect. They are chiefly to be associated with three men, whom I name here in what I believe to be their order of seniority by age: Hans Baron, Paul Oskar Kristeller and Eugenio Garin. The first two had been German citizens and, when one notices with some astonishment the relative absence of significant German or Austrian Renaissance scholarship after 1945[22], as contrasted with the rich talent devoted to Reformation studies, one must recall that remarkable *diaspora* of scholars from these countries which has enriched scholarship in this as in other fields, especially in the USA. Some of the names of such writers will occur in what follows.

Baron's first major work on Bruni's history appeared in German in 1928, but to my mind even more influential were the pieces published in English in 1939–40. In many ways these revolutionized Renaissance scholarship by introducing a link, closer than that forged by Burckhardt or anyone else, between public life and public literature. Even more important than the essay on Bruni are 'Cicero and the Roman civic spirit' and 'Franciscan poverty and civic wealth', both peculiarly pregnant with ideas which were to enrich succeeding scholars. 'Civic humanism' in a very real sense derives from these essays its modern acceptance as a 'term of art', as one of those 'nominalist' concepts which we could nowadays ill dispose of – a term, indeed, which is being liberally appropriated for other periods and circumstances.[23] Baron's name will figure again below, but he deserves priority here, not only because of his age.[24]

Kristeller probably entered the arena of Renaissance scholarship somewhat later (1929) than Baron and his influence has been quite different. Far from offering a novel concept of 'civic humanism' he has proceeded with the double dedication of a philosopher and bibliographer who has concentrated his main interests on the fifteenth century. This had made its impact before the war: *Supplementum Ficinianum . . . Opuscula inedita et dispersa* came out in two volumes in Florence in 1937. His name, like Baron's, will occur later in this survey.

Finally, Eugenio Garin, to whose work this collection of essays bears witness, produced his study of *Giovanni Pico della Mirandola*, also in Florence, in 1937. Like Kristeller, his university function was to teach philosophy. Like Baron and Kristeller his prolific contributions continue; all three act as a bridge between the pre-war and post-war worlds of Renaissance scholarship.[25]

In the last twenty-five or thirty years the continued leadership of the three scholars just mentioned has ensured inescapable continuities between pre- and post-war activity in Renaissance research. It is not as though 1939 and war had not been a troublesome possibility for years, and an emotional impact of fear or desperation had already begun, one suspects, to influence scholars long before the invasion of Poland. That so many Germans and Austrians were obliged to live abroad doubtless explains to some extent (as I have said) why post-1945 Renaissance scholarship is less evident in Germany than it had been earlier. A small indication of this is the absence, so far as I know, of any journal in German expressly devoted to the Renaissance, such periodicals being found in France (or Switzerland), America and Italy. That is not, of course, to say that the German Renaissance has been totally neglected. But significant works seem mainly to have been produced by scholars outside Germany – one thinks of the writings of Foster, Strauss and Spitz. The point is worth stressing, since Burckhardt had a thoroughly German training (he was a pupil of Ranke and Kugler) and the elaboration of his essay (ein Versuch, as he subtitled his book) by later Germans, for whose erudition he expressed little sympathy, suggested that Germany was likely to witness a continued development in this field of history.[26]

As I stated above, the survival of Burckhardt's main categories seems no longer at risk. The work of demolishing or denying them has been abandoned in favour of detailed analysis, criticism and correction, and above all elaboration. This has been made possible largely by adapting a view of the Renaissance as a fairly prolonged period in time. Despite his tendency to draw his evidence from three centuries somewhat indiscriminately, despite the lengthy historical Part I, which runs from Frederick II to Charles V, I do not believe that Burckhardt intended to view the Renaissance as a substantial period. He intended the cultural changes which he investigated and illustrated to constitute a watershed in time rather than an epoch in world history. The Renaissance inaugurated the modern world, made the Italian the 'first-born among the sons of modern Europe'. Individualism, the cult of fame, the revival of Antiquity, 'the discerning and bringing to light' of 'the full, whole nature of man', the production of a new society, in which talent, intellectual or political, could enable anyone to rise into the upper classes – this I believe to be the essence of Burckhardt's picture of the Renaissance. As the English historian G.P. Gooch remarked in his *History and Historians in the Nineteenth Century*,[27] 'as Riehl loved the peasant, Burckhardt loved the élite'. The picture Burckhardt painted was, we should remember, far from optimistic. The exciting changes just mentioned went with, if they did not positively involve, a decline in

[7]

religious sentiment. Yet if superstition increased, among a chosen few an enlightened pantheistic paganism developed. The book ends thus:

> Echoes of medieval mysticism here flow into one current with Platonic doctrines, and with a characteristically modern spirit. One of the most precious fruits of the knowledge of the world and of man here comes to maturity, on whose account alone the Italian Renaissance must be called the leader of modern ages.[28]

This brief summary of *Die Kultur der Renaissance in Italien*[29] and the quotation of its last lines will indicate to the reader how faithfully the areas of life and learning identified by Burckhardt have been further elaborated, and especially in recent decades. A glance at the contents of this very volume will provide easy confirmation that this is the case. They will emphasize also that the word is now, in practice, regarded as a period of time.

The Swiss historian has thus encouraged the acceptance by historians of a new epoch, which has, I suppose, had most influence in the United States, where every large university history department may be depended on to have one or more Renaissance specialists. So in the western world we have currently four eras: ancient, medieval, Renaissance, modern (all, indeed, but especially the latter, vulnerable to further subdivisions such as 'early modern', 'contemporary'). I do not propose to say more on the question of periodization, but to accept this treatment of the Renaissance as a fact. There have been many discussions of the matter, one of the best and most well-known being by Delio Cantimori.[30]

Thus we apply the term Renaissance freely, perhaps more outside Italy than inside that country, to everything that happened between about 1350 and 1600 – politics, science, and of course the fine arts, literature and learning. This can and sometimes does cause confusion between the older Vasari–Michelet–Burckhardt scheme, where the emphasis is on the inspiration of Classical Antiquity and innovation, and the new position. For example, it is hard to detect anything humanist in the bulk of the literature released by the printing press from the mid-fifteenth to the mid-sixteenth centuries; and one could say something similar about much northern European art and architecture. It is perhaps because there are difficulties like these that scholars have devoted themselves in the last generation to pursuing detailed researches rather than embarking on the reformulation of vast interpretative theories which in any case produce their own terminological quandaries. A Renaissance *convegno*, more particularly in the USA, usually issues in a collection of papers dealing with any

[8]

aspect of the period, regardless of its connection with humanists or the humanities. The titles of books themselves (again this is best observed outside Italy) use Renaissance as a generic term for all the occurrences of several centuries.[31] Among the positive advantages of this is that non-Italian writers are not tempted to avoid the discussion of cultural change within the social and political context. One can read the whole of Luigi Simeoni's in many ways admirable *Le signorie*[32] without being allowed to admit that the massive changes in the Italian milieu which we describe synoptically as the Renaissance deserve a place in his text; in fact Simeoni at the very start of his book expressly dismisses the Renaissance as having any effect on the public life of the nation. The matter, however, deserves the sort of careful discussion Chabod gave it,[33] and in any case it is integral to any total view of Italy in the fourteenth and fifteenth centuries if only because many of the narrative sources are steeped in humanist style and impregnated with humanist assumptions of an ideologically significant kind. One must, however, not exaggerate the difference between Italian and non-Italian practice. If non-Italian historians regularly admit art and learning, science and philosophy, into their general surveys of the Renaissance it is often not as an essential element in the narrative, but somewhat peripheral, even merely decorative. Much the same criticism might be levelled at the treatment accorded to the Renaissance in the new *Storia d'Italia*, edited by Einaudi; there the issue is virtually ignored in the first, key volume, and it is discussed at length but in an entirely distinct section in the second volume.[34]

Despite Burckhardt's invitation to associate history *simpliciter* with cultural history the only outstanding exponent of this approach seems to me to be Hans Baron. This is apparent both in his pre-war essays and in even more explicit fashion in his *Crisis of the Early Italian Renaissance*,[35] in which he advanced the argument that it was the political threats to Florentine liberty, chiefly by the Visconti, which precipitated the conscious reception of the new style, in substance republican and in inspiration classical, by the ruling classes of the city on the Arno. There is no doubt of the influence this thesis has exerted; like all magisterial pronouncements it has been paid the compliment of severe criticism.[36] But besides those for whom Baron's arguments seem unpersuasive, there are in addition others who, quite independently, see no need to enlarge the concept of the Renaissance beyond the limits it had for Voltaire. I may instance my old friend Roberto Weiss who viewed the Renaissance and its humanist propagators as simply a story of recovering ancient texts, collecting classical manuscripts and so on, and not even to any significant extent drawing attention to the effects of the humanities on secondary-school curricula. Nor would Baron regard his work in this particular sense as breaking new ground. His *Crisis* is dedicated to Walter Goetz, 'who taught me that history should be a study of both politics and culture'. One of the most promising developments in this regard is the attention increasingly being paid to Italian political speculation at this time, or, to use Burckhardt's somewhat enigmatic words, 'the state as a work of art'.

This last phrase, with its suggestions of nineteenth-century pragmatism, hardly lends itself to the messy realities of Italian and European politics in the fifteenth or sixteenth centuries. But Nicolai Rubinstein, Felix Gilbert and William Bouwsma, among others, have shown how rewarding can be the investigation not only of what happened, but of what the best minds of the day thought ought to happen.[37] I name these three scholars not at random but because their works have, as it were, crossed my path; I am well aware that there are many others but obviously I cannot attempt a systematic bibliography of this or any other aspect of my subject. The new emphasis on political thought, while it naturally gravitates to individual thinkers such as Valla, Guicciardini and their theorizing contemporaries,[38] also leads to a straight discussion of political and administrative history.

Here the effort and the results in late times have been truly remarkable. It is almost invidious to single out single writers from the mass of researchers whose time has been devoted (without always specific reference to the Renaissance) to the fourteenth and fifteenth centuries. A large number are Americans, benefiting from generous support from foundations in the USA and abodes with and near good libraries at I Tatti and the American Academy in Rome. Perhaps the most stimulating work is one which crosses easily from speculation to action; certainly Chabod referred to it in such terms. I am speaking of Rudolf von Albertini, *Das florentinische Staatsbewusstsein im Übergang von der Republik zum Prinzipat*.[39] In this remarkable work the men of letters act, so the speak, as *metteurs en scène* for the play itself.

To the actors in the public drama a great deal of work has been devoted. The books and articles of so many Americans come to mind – Brucker, Becker, Martines, Molho, for example[40] – that an Anglo-Saxon like myself tends to forget the formidable activities of Italian political historians themselves, scholars such as Berengo, Cognasso, Ridolfi, Valeri, the contributors to the new collective histories such as Einaudi's venture and the substantial volumes devoted to the history of Milan, Naples and Padua.[41] Is it too much to say that co-operation on this scale would not have been easy to secure half a century ago? Would *stranieri* like the Florentine Garin or the Valdaostan Chabod have written substantial portions[42] of the Treccani degli Alfieri volumes on Milan? To an outsider this seems to be a wholesome development in Italian historiography, and one obviously not confined to the Renaissance period. If Italian political history at this time cannot be treated as a unified story (and here I stand whole-heartedly behind Simeoni), or only at the expense of reality,[43] then at least the experts can collaborate on a topical basis within a regional framework.

In this activity there is, perhaps, an undue emphasis placed on the history of Florence as the very type and model of Italian political and cultural evolution. Florence is in fact a most eccentric feature of peninsular political life, and indisputably has a critical place in the artistic changes of the early Renaissance and even perhaps keeps its interest into the mannerist period. There are the manuscripts in the Laurentian and dozens of other libraries, public and private and, above all, the town has in its Biblioteca Nazionale the biggest, best organized and most efficient of the scholarly 'public' libraries[44] of Italy. This it remains despite the terrible effects of the floods of 1966. (The absence of any other effective national library with complete holdings of all books published in Italy and of any library with all important works, not just on Italian history, published abroad, remains one of the disgraces of Italian academic provision and, if only incidentally, one of the main impediments to a rational survey of Italian history, cultural or otherwise.)

A rough and ready impression of the prominence of Tuscan and especially Florentine studies in recent Italian research may be obtained from the space allocated to it in *La storiografia italiana negli ultimi vent' anni*, in which Tuscany occupies about a fifth of the section devoted to regional studies in the later Middle Ages.[45]

Another reason for Florentine studies taking the lead in historical research is, of course, the existence of state and other archives. The former are vast and, despite damage over the years, including the floods mentioned above, comprise an astonishingly rich repository covering both the period of the commune and the principate. The *fonds* in the Archivio di stato, together with the many other public and private collections of papers in the city, as well as those in Lucca, Pisa, Siena, Prato and other towns of the region, act as magnets both for seasoned scholars, some of whose projects are of great importance,[46] as well as for younger men and women. These records were virtually unused either by Burckhardt, or by his contemporaries. Yet not very long after, in 1896, R. Davidsohn was to begin his demonstration of the riches to be mined in the records. The neglect of archival material was not due to its

[11]

inaccessibility, especially in Tuscany. It was much more due to the deep-seated tradition that narrative history was based on narrative sources and the only additional matter regularly admitted (mainly through the practice and precept of Ranke) were those 'narrative' documents, diplomatic dispatches and *relazioni*, the latter particularly valuable in Venice from the early fifteenth century. Admittedly Italian state archives, extraordinarily varied and valuable as many of them were, were also often in a very confused condition and were only treated scientifically as the present century got under way.[47] The result was that Italian archives (as is more or less the case with those in other countries) were jungles penetrated by largely untrained antiquarian-minded persons, interested more in the details of some individual's biography or questions of the topography of estates than in the examination of political or social development as such.[48]

How dramatically this situation has changed! The advent of economic history as a sophisticated discipline in its own right has had profound effects on the use of archives, reinforced as it occasionally was and is (especially in Italy) by Marxist ideological assumptions, convincing researchers that their work was in some mysterious way encouraging the revolutionary process. The serried volumes of taxation records began to usurp the place of the serried volumes of diplomatic records in the priorities of historians. This can be illustrated in scores of works by Italians and foreigners. Elio Conti (for example) has devoted years of study to the cadastral records to explain rural Tuscan land-holding.[49] Scores of others have followed him to the records of the *catasti* , as for instance Lauro Martines in his survey of the income of humanists at the turn of the fourteenth and fifteenth centuries, or Richard Goldthwaite in his investigation of the wealth of four Florentine families.[50] In recent years increasing attention has been paid to the structure of the Italian family: for example, the work of David Herlihy and Christiane Klapish-Zuber, especially *Les Toscans et leurs familles*.[51] Many other scholars are at work in this field.

Economic history has been pursued, of course, all over the peninsula and not just in Tuscany. It is difficult to identify typical works without appearing to neglect others of equal value. Genoese trade and banking has been the province of Jacques Heers; Venetian shipping and trade have been studied pre-eminently by F.C. Lane and Alberto Tenenti; for Rome we turn to the masterly volumes of Jean Delumeau, centred on the mid-sixteenth century but ranging backwards in time.[52] But in this area surely Tuscany still has a lead. There are the successive studies of the late Raymond de Roover on the Medici bank and Bowski's work on Sienese public finance.[53] Economic considerations also play a large part in the 'straight' history, uniting political, social and cultural elements displayed in many of the writings of Gene A. Brucker.[54]

Many of these monographs are intricate and technical and assume a degree of sustained effort on the part of the reader, e.g. in the understanding of the credit and exchange arrangements of a world which dealt in money which was both paper (almost but not quite in our sense of the term) and metal (genuine metal needing to be assayed), and a mixture involving paper transactions based on the genuine gold and silver of the coins: all very hard for those of us who hardly recall a time when money was more than tokens. Fortunately some admirable general economic historians have surveyed the Renaissance era.[55] It is however fair in this context to stress that these writers on general economic history are not concerned in any direct sense with the Renaissance as such, as Lopez had been in his essay referred to above,[56] with the exception of Sapori, who contributed (albeit in an indirect manner) to the debate on periodization.[57] The fact is that in broad terms the flowering of Italian genius in the arts and in letters corresponded with a period of economic recession.

If economic historians have enriched our understanding of the background to the Italian Renaissance by investigating rural economy and mercantile practice, one must perforce be more cautious of the findings of those scholars who have moved from the known to the hypothetical in the ocean of figures afforded by Italian record material. One may describe this as a movement from the abacus to the computer, or as a signal tribute to the school of *Annales* and the influence of Fernand Braudel. I say a 'movement', for the outstanding figure in this world of calculation as far as Italy is concerned is the above-mentioned American, David Herlihy, whose earliest work was an extremely good account of the history of Pisa in the years of her decline as a great power.[58] This was written (as other admirable essays by him)[59] before the mirage of mathematical exactitude enveloped him as it did so many others. One has the impression that this odd phase is passing away and that at all events it had not attracted any significant Italian adherents; they remained content with older methods of dealing with figures. There is no evidence to suggest, for instance, that Beloch's population calculations, which become firm only as we move from the sixteenth to the seventeenth century, have been supplemented by modern research, however sophisticated.[60] Figures were compiled for specific occasions: they cannot usually be made to serve purposes other than those for which they were at first assembled.[61]

I have touched on some of the salient innovations of recent years, assuming that – although Italians have been slower to adopt the

[13]

convention than others – we must accept the Renaissance now as a period of time, in which all that happens falls fairly under scrutiny. But, this accepted, it is remarkable how conservative what might be called 'Renaissance' scholarship has remained, faithful to its centuries-old association with the fine arts, education, belles-lettres and ethical problems, all in association with *Die Wiederbelebung des classischen Altherthums*, to use Georg Voigt's title (1859). This is very clearly seen in the work of Eugenio Garin himself. His prodigious output follows in the tradition of scholarship in which the recovery of Antiquity and the perfection of a revived Latin as a means of communication is firmly rooted; to these interests we must add philosophy, about which a word in a moment. His general study *L'umanesimo italiano: filosofia e vita civile nel Rinascimento*, first appeared in German (Berne, 1947), then in Italian (Bari, 1952). In 1957 there appeared *L'educazione in Europa* (also published in Bari), to be read with his large anthology of Renaissance texts on the subject.[62] *L'umanesimo italiano* has been his most influential book so far, not least in the English-speaking world, where a translation appeared in 1968 in Oxford. It is worth remarking that in this book he reached many conclusions similar to those of Hans Baron. But Garin's chief fame is, surely, the discovery of new texts and the meticulous editing of old ones. Here his signal contribution to the series 'La letteratura italiana: storia e testi', *Prosatori latini del quattrocento*,[63] has become indispensable to all teachers and students of the Renaissance. But it would be absurd to list Garin's editorial work, beyond reminding the reader that his influence in this sphere is very considerable as one of the joint editors of *Rinascimento* since 1962 (and now its sole editor). (The multitude of Garin's books, articles and reviews as a whole were listed down to 1969 in the *Bibliografia* published by Laterza in that year to mark his sixtieth birthday.) This insistence on textual scholarship is the most authentic inheritance of the Renaissance, taking us back to Poggio, Salutati, Niccoli and their peers. Garin's work in this type of scholarship is, I believe, not only in the *tradizione rinascimentale* but represents the interests of many scholars in Italy since the war. One thinks of scores of editors and commentators: Spongano, Branca, Bonfantini, Panigada and Perosa are names that spring to mind. Nor must we forget the foreign scholars who have contributed to editorial work on Italian Renaissance texts: B.L. Ullman's edition of Salutati's *De laboribus Herculis* (Zurich, 1951); Cecil Grayson's edition of L.B. Alberti's *Della famiglia* (Bari, 1960–6), Raymond Marcel's edition and translation of Marsilio Ficino's *Commentaire sur le banquet de Platon* (Paris, 1956). The moment one writes down a few names one is conscious that they are but a small sample of the many who have contributed. In the long list it is surely certain that here at least Italians are the most numerous, still maintaining the great tradition of textual criticism and publication that runs, almost unbroken, from Muratori to Remigio Sabbadini and onwards. All in all, we are now infinitely better provided with reliable texts of Italian authors from the mid-fourteenth to the mid-sixteenth century than was the case before the Second World War, and much of the credit for the work itself and for encouraging others to embark on it belongs to Garin. His philosophical interests are dealt with elsewhere in this volume, by Paul Oskar Kristeller. It may however be noted that they too include editorial work on Pico della Mirandola and other speculative writers of the period.

The preponderant literary (and artistic) emphasis of recent works on the Renaissance may also be seen by glancing at the contents of the three main journals devoted to Renaissance studies – *Rinascita* and its sequel *Rinascimento* (since 1950), *Bibliothèque d'humanisme et Renaissance* (since 1941) and *Renaissance Quarterly* (since 1967 and since volume 28 incorporating the annual *Renaissance Studies*).[64] It is, of course, the case that many important communications are made to other periodicals: the big national historical reviews, for example, and those exclusively devoted to the arts and literature. But specialization prevails: a trend found in every branch of knowledge, alas with many detrimental effects, such as a parochialism of scholarship, a narrowing of cultural horizons and an encouragement to pedantic points of marginal interest. But it exists and therefore many a paper which would have been published in the *Giornale storico della letteratura italiana* fifty years ago now appears in *Rinascimento*. I do not mean that its quality is thus diminished, only that the specialisms that bedevil our lives make it exceedingly hard to encourage even the attempt to take a sympathetic interest in a subject as a whole rather than some period or aspect of it. Perhaps I speak here as a benighted Briton, condemned to much teaching and never having enjoyed much leisure for research, but nevertheless Italian professors do *some* teaching (and many of them a good deal), and not all Americans get support for lengthy sojourns abroad. The problem of a narrowing of our general view of literature, the arts, society and politics is, therefore, I fear, a growing one.

The dichotomy is particularly noticeable in the field of culture and may be vividly illustrated by the relative neglect of the new humanist attitudes, and techniques of communication ('poetry'), in countries other than Italy. In a sense, as I said earlier, I believe it to be true that the late Roberto Weiss simply did not believe in any *generalized* spread of the humanities: he saw the collection of manuscripts, the schoolmaster, the sonnet even, as happening in the England of the fifteenth century, but did not ask why *then*, save that the missionaries, so to speak, came from Italy; the Renaissance spread like the pox – by contagion.[65] The approach of another student to another part of Europe was, I consider, much more fruitful. I refer to the many studies devoted to the humanities in France from the fourteenth to the seventeenth centuries composed with enormous erudition and no little wit by another old friend, alas also recently deceased, Franco Simone. His researches did try to establish, and in my view succeeded in establishing, which of Petrarch's works were 'digestible' in the France of the early Renaissance, and went on to establish norms for both literature and history, in their interreactions, over succeeding centuries.[66]

Greatly as social and political history has influenced the study of cultural history in the Renaissance period – and this could have been driven home much more forcibly by adducing more names of recent scholars who have made great use of documentary material[67] – there yet remain areas where intensive research is still needed. Perhaps the most significant of these is the cultural and spiritual history of the Church in Italy during the fourteenth and fifteenth centuries. Many of the great writers and artists were clergy and the bulk of their work one may guess was devoted either to moral issues or to ecclesiastical subjects. All were at any rate technically Christians, despite Burckhardt's conviction that the period saw a rise in scepticism and irreligion, a point to be heavily emphasized by Pastor in his distinction between the 'Pagan' and the 'Christian' Renaissance. Admittedly it is extremely difficult to know what are a man's innermost convictions. This is obviously the case with the creator of mute buildings and pictures. But it is far from being a great deal easier when one is dealing with written views. Obviously there are identifiable extremes. For cases in point one could instance the severe condemnation of the new styles and assumptions in Giovanni Dominici's *Lucula noctis* or the firm repetition of the old case for 'poetry', in Boccaccio's *Genealogia deorum gentilium*, or in Salutati, the specific object of Dominici's treatise. But it is often extremely difficult to determine when or whether a writer is expressing his own views, and this is especially so in dialogues, that favourite form of Renaissance literature based on a technique of exposition beloved by Antiquity. What exactly does Petrarch mean when, at the end of the *Secretum*, he admits the truth – the absolute truth – of St Augustine's strictures and then refuses to act upon them, at any rate for the foreseeable future? What exactly do we infer of Valla's own position from the views put into the mouths of interlocutors in his *De libero arbitrio*?[68] Or, to take what might appear at first sight a perfectly plain problem, what was Boccaccio's personal attitude to the question of sexual morality?[69] Was Platina's *vitae pontificum romanorum* a humdrum narrative or, at any rate occasionally, a deliberate attempt to urge the need for a reformed Papacy?[70]

Church history in Renaissance Italy has been neglected until recently. However, the *Rivista della storia della chiesa in Italia* has made a remarkable contribution since 1946; and other periodicals of great interest are springing up, such as the more episodic *Ricerche per la storia religiosa di Roma* (since 1977). But a good deal of work has also certainly been put into the edition of texts and we may cite as examples the splendid editions which have appeared of the sermons of Bernardino da Siena and Bernardino da Feltre.[71] There has also been much recent work done on the confraternities and movements of popular devotion prior to the sixteenth century[72] and such study is probably a more rewarding entrée into the religious milieu than the analysis of men of great devotion like the famous Observant preachers already mentioned, or even those friars whose political influence was demonstrably considerable, like the Dominican Savonarola. For the confraternities brought together both the simple and the learned, the rich and the poor. What we need, I feel, are more works such as the remarkably suggestive work of Alberto Tenenti, *Il senso della morte e l'amore della vita nel Rinascimento*[73], in which, as the reader will recall, he contrasts the literature and symbolism of death and of holy dying in Italy and northern Europe and, in greatest detail, in Italy and France. It is notable that Tenenti is a historian, not a literary critic. Quite apart from the largely 'un-literary' nature of his written evidence, he is less likely to fall into the trap which awaits the biographer, of assuming a coherence and continuity of position in his hero, a fault which flaws many studies of individual men of religion. The historian of religious sensibility must read between the lines; must try to see the effects of popular manifestations (here the great public spectacles of Italy, and especially of Rome, await a historian who is alive to their significance in the political and spiritual spheres)[74] and the influence of growing literacy and the printing press. On this last point it is worth repeating parenthetically the complaint voiced earlier regarding Italian libraries, here relating it to the absence of any adequate catalogues of Italian printed books, save what is provided by the *Indice generale degli incunaboli* and the *Gesamtkatalog der Wiegendrucke* (as far as they go) for incunables, and those catalogues which emanate from the only library with a complete catalogue, the British Library References Division, formerly the British Museum Library.[75] This is very sad considering how many incunables and also books printed in the sixteenth and seventeenth centuries are to be found in Italian libraries.

If it seems that religion in its broadest sense – popular and learned piety, patronage, finance of buildings and church decorations and cult developments – is deserving of greater study than it has yet had from Italian and other scholars, there is one area where activity has been intense. I refer to the Italian reformers. Not only have Antonio Rotondò and Carlo Ginzburg recently produced important studies, but there is now an elaborate series, edited by Luigi Firpo and Giorgio Spini with the assistance of Rotondò and John Tedeschi, *Corpus reformatorum italicorum*.[76] This line of research had its 'first begetter' in Delio Cantimori, whose *Eretici italiani del Cinquecento* appeared first in the form of a collection of documents (1937) and elaborated as a book in 1939 (Florence). One of the most illuminating results of these enquiries shows how intellectual (or, if you will, non-popular) these developments were, in their attempts to establish widespread diffusion of heterodox views, despite the horrific activities of the Inquisition; and in following up the Italian reformers one is compelled to cross the Alps[77] as with Peter Martyr Vermigli (on whom Philip McNair has written a fine book).[78] The most characteristic form taken by this exported Italian reform was Socinianism, destined to have its full development in a more peaceful period than the stormiest days of the German Reformation, and in places far removed from Italy, notably (in what was to become known as Unitarianism) in Poland, Hungary and England.[79] One has the impression that the historians of the Reformation in Italy, even if in the end it was abortive, are pursuing a more coherent programme than students of the Renaissance as such.[80] This is all the more forcible since the Anglo-Saxon and German tradition is to treat the Renaissance as a kind of preliminary to the serious business of reform. It may be added that Italians are not merely concerning themselves with early evidence of Protestantism (the *Beneficio di Cristo*, B. Ochino and so on) but also with the effects in Italy of what we must learn to call not the 'Counter-Reformation' but the 'Catholic Reformation', which has prompted the excellent writings of Alberigo, Prodi and D'Addario, to name but a few.[81]

Another area which, it may be assumed, would repay detailed study is education. The admirably edited texts which Garin has produced are, like the studies of W.H. Woodward (which have stood the test of time well),[82] based mainly on theoretical expositions rather than on a study of practice. We know a great deal about Guarino and Vittorino, and we know what some of their contemporaries such as Vergerio and Pope Pius II regarded as ideal curricula. But what actually happened in the generality of schools? For educational history illustrating the diffusion of humanist principles we have to turn to students of teaching in northern Europe, where (as in England) the transformation of the curriculum can be dramatically displayed.[83] I am not aware of any comparable work on the schools of Italy and of only a few partial studies of Renaissance universities.[84] The survey of the Italian grammar school in G. Manacorda's incomplete *Storia della scuola in Italia* (Milan, 1914) stops unfortunately before the Florentine Renaissance begins, but some treatment of this problem is to be found in Christian Bec's *Marchands écrivains à Florence 1375–1434*,[85] in his discussion of the 'Formation intellectuelle et culture des marchands'. Much more needs to be done if we are to perceive how the educational changes affected the peninsula as a whole. By the late fifteenth century nearly every Italian scholar wrote in a more or less neo-classical style, just as scholars did in the rest of Europe by 1600 or thereabouts. But how did this come about? Certainly not because the Council of Trent ordered seminaries in all dioceses for priests, for these took centuries to be erected; and certainly not because of the sporadic efforts of Jesuits and Barnabites.

Another gap, perhaps even more surprising, is the study of the effects of the Renaissance on Italian archaeology and historiography. This is, indeed, an area in which Europe as a whole is defective for the Renaissance period. In archaeology the only systematic and scientific work which has been done is concentrated on Rome and tends on the whole to look forward to the new city rather than examine the old: I think of the fine books by T. Magnuson and Redig de Campos.[86] But what is needed is an account of the progressive interest in, and understanding of, Italian classical buildings, from Flavio Biondo (or earlier) onwards. The task would be arduous, for this type of literature is constantly being rewritten generation by generation, and the task in Italy would be compounded by the multiplicity of places where local antiquaries were increasingly at work.

As for historiography, it is sad that we still have to depend, for an overall view, on the work, admirable as it is in many ways, of Eduard Fueter.[87] Fueter is schematic and thorough and, apart from the stimulating survey in Felix Gilbert's *Machiavelli and Guicciardini: Politics and History in Sixteeth Century Florence*,[88] which is much wider-ranging than its title suggests (it includes, for example, a most useful analysis of Pontano's *Actius*), he has, I believe, no rival for the Renaissance period. There are, of course, large numbers of works on the major historians. To go back no further than the 1950s we have 'lives and times' studies by Roberto Ridolfi on *Machiavelli* (1954) and *Guicciardini* (1960). We have some admirable regional studies such as that edited by Agostino Pertusi for Venice.[89] But in general, works such as these tend to neglect the philological element which is surely the basis of the historian's task: his search for and evaluation of his source material, his attempts to date and criticize such material, to gain access to documentary matter and distinguish it from narrative evidence, written or oral. This aspect of historiography has almost entirely been neglected, and not only in Italy. Fueter, to quote a case in point,[90] does not quite ignore Baronius' discussion of sources but he is really concerned to show him as a polemical opponent of the Magdeburg centuriators, whereas his publication of source material surely deserves commendation. We should recall how Valla's celebrated 'De falso edita et ementita Constantini donatione declamatio' lacks anything which we would nowadays regard as historical criticism and we should not attribute the essay so much to his courage (as Fueter does) as to the enmity of his patron Alfonso V to Eugenius IV at that time.[91] Here Fueter falls victim to his quite unreal distinction between the 'schools' of Bruni and of Biondo: the first 'rhetorical', the second 'erudite'. No one who reads Biondo's *Decades* can be under any illusion regarding his erudition, for he merely followed a given source and seldom criticized or compared.[92] It was (and this need surprise no one) in the careful attempts to compare physical remains with classical writings that erudition of the modern sort was to emerge, and with this Fueter is hardly concerned. His plan admits no place for scholarship as such. Mabillon, whose *De re diplomatica* (1681–1704) was surely the foundation of modern scientific historiography, forces his way into Fueter's survey by way of his *Annales ordinis S. Benedicti*, but of Muratori we hear only of the *Annali*, since this is regarded as narrative history; there is not a word of that massive monument, the *Rerum Italicarum scriptores*, which is still used today as a basic tool of research.[93] Admittedly historians, medieval as well as Renaissance, had an axe to grind. The Renaissance historian ground the big axes of powerful rulers: he was often a propagandist and as such played a major role in the studies already alluded to on Italian political thought in the Renaissance. Yet the future of historiography was at stake in the handful of men who published texts, even perhaps when these were forged.[94] Undoubtedly the classical scholars blazed the trail and the historiography of the ancient world was the first to be treated with distinction and sophistication. After all, it fell well within the humanist curriculum.

May I be permitted to add two further desiderata? The first is for a more deliberate and rounded study of Florence in the whole of the fifteenth century. In general, works like Baron's,[95] and Christian Bec's recent and most interesting *Les marchands écrivains: affaires et humanisme à Florence 1375-1434*, tend to end in the 1440s.[96] But works such as Brucker's[97] would be an enormous help if written for the fifteenth, and especially the later fifteenth and the early sixteenth centuries, when they would link up with von Albertini, Cochrane and others, forming a coherent cultural and political survey. There are, indeed, extremely important works such as Nicolai Rubinstein's on the period, but this is not concerned with cultural matters, nor even to any great extent with the political principles which the author had dealt with for earlier and later periods.[98] The absence of a general study of Florence at this time is of particular importance, since it was during the middle and later fifteenth century that the innovations in literature and the arts spread so rapidly to the princely courts of Italy and, later still, penetrated so deeply into the princely courts and societies of the rest of Europe that their consequences, to some degree, are still an important force in modern society. Until the day before yesterday – yes! as recently as that – every scholar and many men of affairs had some Latin, many a great deal, as a direct consequence of the extraordinary elevation of the humanities (as defined by Kristeller) during the earlier, republican, period of 'civic humanism'. It was only when the princes and their courtiers took over the direction of culture from the *marchands écrivains* that Florentine values could be exported.

My reference to Latin leads me to my second plea. It is of a very different sort and perhaps it is now unattainable. I refer to the need for rapid and effective protection and stimulation of the teaching of Latin in all countries where medieval and Renaissance (let alone classical) studies are regarded as significant regions in which to explore the mind of man. Classical languages are in peril and, in this context, I naturally refer to Latin. In Britain and the English-speaking world the decline in the teaching of Latin is dramatic in most places. I understand that much the same is true of even the Romance areas of Europe – France, Spain, even Italy.[99] This is by no means all loss. If a series such as 'La letteratura italiana: Studi e testi', with its facing Italian translations of admirably edited originals, would have been inconceivable before the war, at any rate at a level above the brief anthology, it nevertheless has two good results. First, it makes available to a much wider public the resources of a dead language. Second, the very act of translation reinforces the critical attention the editor pays to his original: I speak from harrowing experience.[100] But these benefits are not much to set against the inability of the average student to understand even the footnotes in the standard works of an older generation, where 'a classical education' could be assumed by writers of serious works.

For a balanced account of the period I have touched on so inadequately in the previous pages, the account of Giuseppe Martini[101] should be consulted, where he had space to summarize many of the works to which I have only been able to allude. In general I believe he is right to stress what he calls the 'linea Baron–Garin' as that which has dominated recent scholarship. In essence this means that students of humanism are finding themselves obliged to take into account the historical background, the political situation, the economic development of their world. One could instance many examples of the fruitful results of this conjunction; indeed many have been mentioned. To these may be added for good measure Garin's own studies (for example, of the chancellor historians of Florence)[102] and the work by Claudio Varese, *Storia e politica nella prosa del quattrocento*,[103] which, incidentally, is one of the relatively few books which makes a gallant attempt to deal with the mid-fourteenth century. In this connection I should like also to mention the most interesting and, I suspect, somewhat neglected social matters discussed by Piero Pieri in *Il Rinascimento e la crisi militare italiana*,[104] which does run down to the 1530s.

There is another reason for consulting the relevant pages in *La storiografia italiana negli ultimi vent'anni*. Both Martini and his collaborator Gigliola Rondinini Soldi deal with a great many *Italian* writers and thus give a more balanced picture than I can, limited as I am to my knowledge of works published outside Italy. Nevertheless the influence of non-Italians on the interpretation of the Renaissance has been profound in the last three decades and my references to non-Italian and especially American scholars could have been greatly extended. Some reasons for this I touch on above when referring to the leadership of Tuscany in the comparative table of research done. But there is, of course, more to it than that. Every country in the world has had a brief period of student trouble in recent years. Italy's universities are both perpetually in student trouble and desperately in need of academic and administrative reform, with particular attention required to organize graduate schools. These as such are rare in the United Kingdom, and in the USA they are often bad. But at their best they prepare young graduates for research in a marvellously systematic way, both by course work and by detailed supervision by a senior teacher. Does it not strike an Italian as absurd that it needed an American, Paul Oskar Kristeller, in his great *Iter italicum*,[105] to identify the unpublished or badly published manuscripts of the Italian Renaissance?

What I am pleading for is an Italian academic system which will produce more men of genius like Garin and not make them so exceptional: my counsel is *reculez pour mieux sauter*. United Kingdom universities seldom run to 'research schools' in any meaningful sense, though we have a right to be proud of the Institute of Historical Research and the Warburg Institute and a few similar graduate centres.[106] But, it may be said, we do encourage students to study the history of *foreign* countries and it is surely a fact that for one Italian studying English or American history there are half a dozen Englishmen and two dozen Americans studying Italian history. The study of other cultures is built into the British and American undergraduate curriculum and extends to postgraduate work.

Yet without the excitements of Italian cultural and political history it is doubtful whether Italy would have attracted so much attention. The end of the ancient Roman world, the slow spread of Christianity, the rise of the communes, the emerging principates, the struggle of Florence with the 'tyrants', the cultural leadership of Italian letters, music and painting from the Renaissance onwards all through the epoch of the Grand Tour, and then the excitements of the Risorgimento and now the excitements of a disintegrating Italy, all make her a wonderful country to concentrate on.

As far as the Renaissance portion of this complicated story is concerned, the indefatigable work of Eugenio Garin gives him a central and commanding place, where his enormous learning is so wide as to deserve the various diverse contributions to this volume. And how many contemporary historians, as opposed to belle-lettristes, have earned in their lifetimes (see p. 14) the distinction of a separately printed bibliography? One knows that it is seriously out-of-date already.[107]

NOTES

1 Cambridge, Mass., 1948. There is an elaborate bibliography, much wider in scope than the title of the book suggests, in Carlo Angeleri, *Il problema religioso del Rinascimento* (Florence, 1952), 163–203. See too the critical bibliography appended by Federico Chabod to his essay, 'The concept of the Renaissance', which I have used in the revised English translation, *Machiavelli and the Renaissance* (London, 1958), 201–47.

2 Georg Voìgt, *Die Wiederbelebung des classischen Altherthums*, reprint (Berlin, 1960); there is a poor and unreliable Italian translation of this by Zippel (Florence, 1888).

3 The title of Part IV of Burckhardt's book and the section in which he touched, *inter alia*, on the natural sciences.

4 For a recent, if partial, study of the period, see Donald Bullough, *The Age of Charlemagne* (London, 1965, rev. edn 1972). When was the expression

'Renaissance' first applied to the scholars and scholarship of Carolingian times? Perhaps in G. Brunhes, *La foi chrétienne et la philosophie au temps de la renaissance carolingienne* (Paris, 1903)? Ferguson, op. cit., argues, p. 45, that the 'Carolingian' renaissance is a concept which goes back to Melanchthon.

5 B.L. Ullman, *Origin and Development of Humanist Script* (Rome, 1960); there is a big and growing literature on this topic.

6 Cambridge, Mass., 1947.

7 Reprint, New York, 1967, 6.

8 G. Toffanin, *Storia dell'umanesimo* (Naples, 1933), frequently reprinted and extended; and in many other works.

9 Paul Oskar Kristeller, *Studies in Renaissance Thought and Letters* (Rome, 1956), 561–7, and in other writings.

10 E. Panofsky, *Renaissance and Renascences in Western Art* (Stockholm, 1960).

11 Some would add an 'Ottonian' renaissance. For F. von Bezold's and F. Schneider's works (1922, 1926), arguing a permanent 'continuity of the classical tradition through the medieval period', see Ferguson, op. cit., 333–4. And cf. also P. Renucci, *L'aventure de l'humanisme européen* (Paris, 1953), with copious references.

12 For Bush see Ferguson, op. cit., 355–6; E.M.W. Tillyard, *The Elizabethan World Picture* (Cambridge, 1944).

13 *Franz von Assisi und die Anfänge der Kunst der Renaissance in Italien* (Berlin, 1885). I avoid discussion here of L. von Pastor's tortuous distinction in his *History of the Popes* between a Christian renaissance (which was healthy) and a pagan renaissance (which was wicked and unhealthy), and of apologetic works such as that by Vladimir Zabughin, *Storia del rinascimento cristiano in Italia* (Milan, 1924). Cf. p. 16.

14 Paris, 1938. For earlier essays by Gilson see Ferguson, op. cit., 335.

15 Op. cit., p. 180.

16 New York, 1923–41.

17 *Le système du monde* (Paris, 1913–17).

18 Quoted by Ferguson, op. cit., 383. See also G. Sarton, *Appreciation of Ancient and Medieval Science during the Renaissance* (Philadelphia, 1955).

19 E.g. Emile Mâle, *L'art religieux du XIIIe siècle en France* (Paris, 1910); N. Pevsner, *The Leaves of Southwell* (London, 1945).

20 Johan Huizinga, *The Waning of the Middle Ages*; I quote from the English translation (London, 1937), 307.

21 The most ponderous contradiction (if that exactly describes it) of the view that the Renaissance was a critical episode is Hiram Haydn's *The Counter Renaissance* (New York, 1950), although he nevertheless regards it as 'a part of the historical period called the Renaissance', a good example of the confusions induced by allowing the periodic concept to get out of hand. A much shorter but more telling examination of some sceptical writers is Paul F. Grendler, *Critics of the Italian World* (Madison, 1969).

22 But not German Swiss, e.g. G. Kisch, W. Kaegi (his life of Burckhardt), R. von Albertini (see, p. 10).

23 For example, one finds recent research devoted to the 'civic humanism' of

the Enlightenment. *Habent sua fata tituli!* Baron's papers are in the *Bulletin of the J. Rylands Library*, XX, and *Speculum*, XIII, both for 1938.

24 For some details see A. Molho and J. Tedeschi (eds), *Renaissance Essays in Honor of Hans Baron* (Dekalb, Ill., and Florence, 1971). His bibliography begins in 1924.

25 For a bibliography of Garin's writings as far as 1969 see p. 14. Kristeller's writings are listed in E.P. Mahoney (ed.), *Philosophy and Humanism. Renaissance Essays in honor of Paul Oskar Kristeller* (New York, 1976), 543–89. Note that Chabod in his bibliographical survey, above, n. 1, devotes section III (pp. 217–19) exclusively to Baron, Kristeller and Garin. In what I have written above I was tempted to add Chabod himself (1901–60), making him a fourth Colossus of the Renaissance field – as in so many of the other areas of his multitudinous interests.

26 At first glance it is paradoxical that the author of the *Cicerone* should have been so hostile to the *eruditi*; in the end he turned back to art history as his main professional concern, but not to erudition!

27 1913.

28 I quote the translation by G.C. Middlemore, 2 vols (London 1878), II, 383. The last phrase in the original runs '*die Renaissance von Italien die Führerin unseres Weltalters*' (ed. Goetz, Stuttgart, 1922), 416, which is perhaps not quite fairly rendered as 'modern ages' by Middlemore.

29 That we should be careful in equating *Kultur* with 'civilization' is demonstrated by Norbert Elias, *Über den Prozess der Civilisation* (Basel, 1939); vol. I of this is available in English as *The Civilising Process* (New York, 1978). I am grateful to Professor E. Midelfort for drawing my attention to this.

30 A *relazione* to the Tenth International Congress of Historical Sciences, Rome, 1955, reprinted in *Studi di storia* (Turin, 1959), 340–65 and in *Storici e storia* (Turin, 1971), 553–77.

31 For instance in the first volume of both the old and the new *Cambridge Modern History*. There is now an illustrated Italian translation of the new *CMH*.

32 In the series 'Storia politica d'Italia', 2 vols (Milan, 1950).

33 Chabod's views were first published in the *Actes du colloque sur la Renaissance 1956* (Paris, 1958).

34 1 (Turin, 1972); 2** (1974) has an essay by Paul Renucci (cf. above, n. 11) on 'la cultura', 1085–466 with, on the Renaissance as such, a subsection entitled 'L'Italia all'avanguardia (secolo xv)', 1210–69. One reason for the subordinate place accorded to the Renaissance in this (in many ways) original and exciting treatment of Italian history is the strong emphasis placed more or less throughout on economic factors, and of course the Renaissance coincided with a marked economic recession in Italy. Cf. Robert S. Lopez, 'Hard times and investment in culture', a lecture given in the Metropolitan Museum, New York, in 1953, and now reprinted in *Six Essays* (New York, 1962). I may perhaps be allowed immodestly to refer to my *Italian Renaissance in its Historical Background* (Cambridge, 1961), translated into Italian with a generous preface by Garin, as *Profilo storico del rinascimento italiano* (Florence, 1966); a new and revised edition of my

book (Cambridge, 1977) will also, I understand, be translated into Italian.

35 Princeton, 1955, in two vols, revised edn in one vol., Princeton, 1966; to be associated with the author's *Humanistic and political Literature in Florence and Venice at the Beginning of the Quattrocento: Studies in Criticism and Chronology* (Cambridge, Mass., 1955).

36 Note especially the book by J.E. Siegel, *Rhetoric and Philosophy in Renaissance Humanism* (Princeton, 1968); and the exchanges between Siegel and Baron in *Past and Present*, 34 and 36 (1966–7).

37 Of Rubinstein's many writings in this area I instance 'Florence and the Despots', *Transactions of the Royal Historical Society*, ser. v, 2 (1952), and 'Florentine constitutionalism and the Medici ascendancy', in *Florentine Studies*, ed. by Rubinstein himself (London, 1968); and see below n. 98. Felix Gilbert's rich researches may be represented by his masterly study of *Machiavelli and Guicciardini* (Princeton, 1965); W. Bouwsma, *Venice and the Defence of Republican Liberty* (Berkeley, 1968).

38 Cf. Gilbert's book referred to in the preceding note; Franco Gaeta, *Lorenzo Valla: filologia e storia nell'umanesimo italiano* (Naples, 1955). I renounce references to other studies of Machiavelli and his speculation save to say that in general I believe great reliance can be placed on Chabod, whose scattered essays on Machiavelli are now gathered together in *Scritti su Machiavelli* (Turin, 1964); cf. above, n. 1.

39 Published in Berne in 1955; there is now an Italian translation (Turin, 1970).

40 In several cases the works I cite could be supplemented by others by the same authors. G.A. Brucker, *Florentine Politics and Society 1343–1378* (Princeton, 1962), and *The Civic World of Renaissance Florence* (Princeton, 1977); M.B. Becker, *Florence in Transition*, 2 vols (Baltimore, 1967–8); L. Martines, *Lawyers and Statecraft in Renaissance Florence* (Princeton, 1968, and cf. below n. 50); A. Molho, 'Florentine public finances', in *The Early Renaissance 1400–33* (Cambridge, Mass., 1971).

41 M. Berengo, *Nobili e mercanti nella Lucca del cinquecento* (Turin, 1965); F. Cognasso, *Storia di Torino* (Turin, 1964) and *L'Italia nel Rinascimento* (Turin, 1965); Roberto Ridolfi, lives of *Savonarola, Machiavelli, Guicciardini* (Rome, respectively 1952, 1954, 1960); N. Valeri, *L'Italia nell'età dei principati* (Verona, 1950); Simeoni, above, n. 32; Piero Pieri, see, p. 22. Since the prestigious volumes of the *Storia di Milano* began to appear in 1953, many other Italian towns and regions have tried to follow suit. As an example I instance the elaborate *Storia di Napoli*, 13 vols (1967–71); others are found for Padua, Piedmont, Genoa and many other urban centres with their dependent areas: see the references in the Valsecchi–Martini volumes referred to below, n. 45. Of a different type is the very thorough and traditional *Storia di Roma*, which contains in its 22 vols an admirable survey, *Topografia e Urbanistica di Roma*, by F. Castagnoli and others (Bologna, 1958). It should again be stressed that the books and authors I have named here are but a fraction of those which would impose themselves if a complete critical bibliography of Italian historians of this period were intended; for one thing I have omitted dozens of important articles in central and regional Italian journals.

42 Garin's contributions are in vols VI and VII, and cover the literary side of Milanese culture in the fifteenth century; Chabod was charged with the composition of vol. IX, but did not live to complete it. His contributions were reprinted as *Storia di Milano nell' epoca di Carlo V* (Turin, 1971).

43 But of course it is sometimes so treated in other works, e.g. Valeri's, above, n. 41.

44 The Nazionale at Florence has about twice as many printed volumes as the Nazionale at Rome. It must be remarked that the system of municipal public libraries which is found in the English-speaking world is virtually non-existent in Italy, outside Milan, although legally encouraged. The concept of 'public library' in Italy is really restricted to great scholarly collections. This is a most striking illustration of the persistence in Italy of humanist values, but one may speculate what effect this undoubted deprivation has had on the intellectual development of Italians; a systematic local provision of reference and general reading on an ever increasing scale, including recent fiction, biographies and 'popular' scholarship, has been a feature of Britain, for example, since about 1850.

45 Franco Valsecchi and Giuseppe Martini (eds), *La storiografia italiana negli ultimi vent'anni*, 2 vols (Milan, 1970). A long section of the regional history of the later Middle Ages by Gigliola Rondinini Soldi is appended to Martini's survey of the Basso medioevo. In order of the number of pages allocated to a region, the provinces order themselves thus: 1. Tuscany (52.5 pp.); 2. Veneto (30.6); 3. Lombardy (21.3); 4. Campania (21); 5. Liguria (21); 6. Sicily (19.5) . . . Rome and Lazio (12). I repeat that this essay does not cover art and architecture, topics which also powerfully draw students to Florence.

46 We may instance the *Lettere* of Lorenzo de' Medici, under the general editorship of Nicolai Rubinstein. Three volumes of this have so far appeared (Florence, 1977), the first two edited by Professor R. Fubini, the third by Professor Rubinstein. Vol. IV (ed. Rubinstein) is about to appear; vols V and VI (Michael Mallett), VII (H. Butters) and VIII (D. Bullard), are in an advanced state of preparation.

47 Cf. the useful survey by P. d'Angiolini and C. Pavone, 'Gli archivi', Einaudi *Storia d'Italia*, 5** (Turin, 1973), 1659-91.

48 The regional surveys already mentioned above (n. 45) illustrate these points, but only to a limited extent given the vast amount of trivial (as well as important) material printed in the numerous local Italian historical journals.

49 Elio Conti, *I catasti agrari della repubblica fiorentina* (Rome, 1966, *et seq.*). On rural history see also many papers by P.J. Jones, e.g. *Cambridge Economic History*, I, 2nd edn (Cambridge, 1966), 340–431.

50 Lauro Martines, *The Social World of the Florentine Humanist 1390–1460* (London, 1963); Richard Goldthwaite, *Private Wealth in Renaissance Florence* (Princeton, 1968).

51 Paris, 1978.

52 Jacques Heers, *Gênes au XVe siècle* (Paris, 1961), a work flawed in my judgement by the relegation of the political narrative, without which the economic analysis becomes obscure, to a perfunctory final chapter; F.C.

[27]

Lane's many works may be represented by his latest and most general, *Venice - A Maritime Republic* (Baltimore, 1973); Alberto Tenenti's writings on Venice include *Naufrages, corsaires et assurances maritimes à Venise* (Paris, 1959) and *Cristoforo da Canal. La marine vénétienne avant Lepanto* (Paris, 1962); J. Delumeau, *Vie économique et sociale de Rome dans la seconde moitié du XVI siècle*, 2 vols (Paris, 1957-9) is also useful for earlier periods, especially on papal finances.

53 Raymond de Roover may be represented by *The Rise and Fall of the Medici Bank 1397-1494* (Cambridge, Mass., 1963); W. Bowski, *The Finances of the Commune of Siena 1287-1355* (Oxford, 1970).

54 *Renaissance Florence* (New York, 1969); *The Civic World of Early Renaissance Florence* (Princeton, 1977); cf. above, n. 40.

55 E.g. G. Luzzatto, *Storia economica d'Italia* (incomplete) (Rome, 1949); Armando Sapori, *Il mercante italiano nel medioevo* (Milan, 1941); *Studi di storia economica medievale* (Florence, 1946) and many earlier works; Yves Renouard, *Les hommes d'affaires d'Italie du moyen âge* (Paris, 1949).

56 Above, n. 34; also Lopez's chapter in *Cambridge Economic History*, II (Cambridge, 1952); having said that, it is fair to add that Christian Bec attributes the inspiration for his *Les marchands écrivains: affaires et humanisme à Florence 1375-1434* (Paris-The Hague, 1967) 'to a hypothesis formulated by Y. Renouard' in a contribution to *Il quattrocento. Libera cattedra di storia della civiltà fiorentina* (Florence, 1954).

57 See Delio Cantimori's contribution to *Studi in onore di Armando Sapori* (Milan, 1957), reprinted in *Storici e storia*, op. cit., 597-609.

58 *Pisa in the Early Renaissance* (New Haven, 1958).

59 E.g. 'Sancta Maria Impruneta: a rural commune in the Middle Ages', Rubinstein (ed.), *Florentine Studies*, 242-76.

60 Karl Julius Beloch, *Bevölkerungsgeschichte Italiens*, II, 2nd edn (Berlin, 1965).

61 For reasoned criticism of what is usually called the *Annales* school, see Robert W. Fogel, 'The limits of quantitative methods', *American Historical Review*, 80 (1975); Alan Bullock, *Is History becoming a Social Science?*, Leslie Stephen Lecture (Cambridge, 1976); and most recently the judicious paper by Professor René Pillorget in *Durham University Journal* (1977), 'From a classical to a serial and quantitative study of history: some new directions in French historical research'. And see the recent work by L. Allegra and A. Torre, *La nascita della storia sociale in Francia: dalla Comune alle Annales* (Turin, 1977). The mention of recent criticism, partly perhaps arising from the tremendous bulk of *Annales*, in no way impugns the significance of all of the authors or all of their contributions, to which I for one have occasionally turned gratefully; the neatest illustration of its influence is the cover and contents of the *Revue historique* in recent years; or the popularity of the title *Annali* or its equivalent, which emphatically does not reflect the continued inspiration of Muratori!

62 Prior to Garin's *L'umanesimo italiano* he had published an anthology of texts on the subject, *Il Rinascimento italiano* (Milan, 1941). On education note also his collection of texts, *L'educazione umanistica in Italia* (Bari, 1949), and *L'educazione in Europa* (Bari, 1957).

[28]

63 Milan, 1952.

64 The *Bibliothèque d'humanisme et Renaissance* was preceded (1934–40) by *Humanisme et Renaissance*; the *Renaissance Quarterly* was preceded by *Renaissance News* (1948–66). Of the non-specialist journals alluded to above perhaps the most important is the *Journal of the Courtauld and Warburg Institutes*.

65 Roberto Weiss, *Il primo secolo dell'umanesimo italiano. Studi e testi* (Rome, 1949), an elaboration and development of his inaugural lecture at London (1947). For his views on humanism in England, see *Humanism in England*, 3rd edn (Oxford, 1957), which is severely restricted to the fifteenth century. His *Spread of Italian Humanism* is entirely literary in a narrow sense and is somewhat disappointing; so too is his contribution on 'Learning and education in Western Europe from 1470 to 1520', *New Cambridge Modern History*, I (Cambridge, 1957), 95–126.

66 Franco Simone's influence was of course exerted to a large extent through *Studi francesi* which he edited from Turin. In many ways his most remarkable work seems to me the early *La coscienza della Rinascita negli umanisti francesi* (Rome, 1949). The insights here displayed were developed further in his *Rinascimento francese* (Turin, 1961) and *Umanesimo, Rinascimento, Barocco in Francia* (Milan, 1968), as well as in many articles. Gilson's influence is evident in all of Simone's work. For his connection with Garin see the *premessa* to the last-named volume.

67 Rubinstein, above, n. 46; E. Fiumi, 'Fioritura e decadenza dell'economia fiorentina', three parts in *Archivio storico italiano*, vols 115–17 (1957–9) and *Storia economica e sociale di San Gemignano* (Florence, 1961). But there are scores more of important studies based on archival studies, as one sees in the titles listed in *La storiografia italiana*.

68 Charles Trinkaus grapples with this sort of problem at several points in his *In Our Image and Likeness*, 2 vols (London, 1970).

69 John Charles Nelson, 'Love and sex in the Decameron', in the Kristeller *Festschrift* (above, n. 25) 339–51.

70 One of the conclusions which my graduate student Richard Palermino seems to be reaching in his study of the work.

71 The first edn by the Fathers of the College of St Bonaventure, 7 vols (Florence, 1950–9); the second edn by Father Carlo Varischi, OFM Cap., 3 vols (Milan, 1964).

72 Of many studies we may recall *Il movimento dei disciplinati nel settimo centenario dal suo inizio*, Convegno internazionale 1960, Deputazione di storia patria per l'Umbria, app. al *Bolletino*, no. 9.

73 Turin, 1957.

74 Cf. Brian Pullan's remarks on processions in Venice in *Rich and Poor in Renaissance Venice* (Oxford, 1971). Contemporary accounts are probably fullest for Rome (where the Jubilee for long was a complication and an encouragement) but they are found everywhere and, it need be hardly said, not just in Italian towns.

75 The chequered career of the *Gesamtkatalog* came to an end with the Second World War; it has subsequently resumed to reach 'Federicis'; Garnaschelli et al. (eds), *Indice generale degli incunaboli delle biblioteche d'Italia*,

began to appear (Rome) in 1943. After 1500 we move into a darker world but the British Museum's short title catalogue for *Italy* (London, 1958) is an immense help, although the Museum lacks a substantial proportion of known titles; cf. also F.J. Norton, *Italian Printers 1501–20* (Cambridge, 1924). The Italian *Primo Catalogo collettivo delle biblioteche italiane* began publication at Rome in 1962, but has not got beyond 'B', with a Dante volume ahead of schedule. The Italian incunables in the British Library are superbly presented in Parts IV to VII of the *Catalogue of Books Printed in the XVth Century now in the British Museum* (London, 1916–35), with the remarkable introduction by J.V. Scholderer in Part VII. This brief note does not by any means exhaust bibliographical aids for the post-1500 period, but over-all they remain sadly inadequate.

76 The first volume to appear, Camillo Renato, *Opere*, ed. A. Rotondò (Florence–Chicago, 1968), is to be followed we hope by many more.

77 Two examples: the studies gathered in A. Rotondò's *Studi e ricerche di storia ereticale italiana del cinquecento* (Turin, 1974); Carlo Ginzburg, *Il Nicodemismo* (Turin, 1970); cf. *Eresia e riforma nell'Italia del cinquecento. Miscellanea I* (Florence–Chicago, 1974).

78 *Peter Martyr in Italy* (Oxford, 1967).

79 John Tedeschi (ed.), *Italian Reformation Studies in Honor of Laelius Socinus* (Florence, 1965).

80 Even the Waldensians are active. Cf. G. Gonnet, *Le confessioni di fede Valdesi prima della riforma* (Turin, 1967).

81 Among the many writings of these scholars I cite only G. Alberigo, *I vescovi italiani al concilio di Trento* (Florence, 1959); P. Prodi, 'Riforma cattolica o controriforma', *Nuove questioni di storia moderna*, ed. L. Bulfaretti (Milan, 1964); A. D'Addario, *Aspetti della controriforma a Firenze* (Rome, 1972). For a recent treatment and text of one of the most notable figures in the wake of these changes see now the *Opere* of Paolo Sarpi, ed. by Gaetano and Luisa Cozzi in the series 'Letteratura Italiana' (Milan, 1969).

82 Below, n. 92.

83 For some references to recent work see my contribution to H. Oberman and T. Brady (eds), *Itinerarium italicum* (essays in honour of Kristeller), (Leiden, 1965).

84 The standard authorities are W.H. Woodward, *Vittorino da Feltre and other Humanist Educators* (Cambridge, 1897), and *Education during the Renaissance* (Cambridge, 1906); and of course Garin's works (above, n. 62), especially *L'educazione in Europa*, 119–21, where he discusses the dispersion of the new methods and ideals in Italian education, but depends, as does Woodward, on the theorists. Yet every Italian town of any size must have had a grammar school by 1500, surely, *endowed* to secure for it more than a precarious existence.

85 Paris, 1967.

86 T. Magnuson, *Studies in Roman Quattrocento Architecture* (Stockholm, 1958); D. Redig de Campos, *I palazzi vaticani* (Bologna, 1967). Roberto Weiss may be consulted for the antiquaries in *The Renaissance Discovery of Classical Antiquity* (Oxford, 1969). But the most thorough and exciting survey is the unpublished Edinburgh doctoral dissertation of Peter Spring

(1973), 'The topographical and archaeological study of the antiquities of the city of Rome 1420–7'.

87 Originally published in German in 1911, it was translated by A. Spinelli as *Storia della Storiografia moderna* (reprinted Milan, 1970); the Italian version is based on the third German edition (1928) which contains a very few additional notes by Fueter; those added by the translator are negligible.

88 Princeton, 1965.

89 *La storiografia veneziana fino al secolo XVI. Aspetti e problemi* (Florence, 1970), especially the contribution of Gaetano Cozzi; cf. also Hans Baron, 'Early Renaissance Venetian chronicles', in his *From Petrarch to Leonardo Bruni* (Chicago, 1968).

90 Ed. ital. cit., 340.

91 Ibid., 144–5.

92 Cf. my lecture, 'Flavio Biondo and the Middle Ages', *Proceedings of the British Academy*, XLV (1959).

93 Fueter, op. cit., 401, 409.

94 I refer to the curious activities of Annius or Nanni da Viterbo (1432–1502) who, so far as I know, still awaits proper study; on Trithemius, his contemporary in Germany, see now the study of Klaus Arnold (Würzburg, 1971).

95 Baron, of course, has concerned himself with later periods, e.g. his study of aspects of Machiavelli's works in *English Historical Review*, LXXVI (1961).

96 Cf. p. 19.

97 Above, n. 40.

98 N. Rubinstein, *The Government of Florence under the Medici, 1434–1494* (Oxford, 1966); see above, n. 37, and also the same author's 'Machiavelli and the world of Florentine politics', in *Studies on Machiavelli* (Florence, 1972). There are a number of articles of great interest dealing with the critical years 1378–1434, e.g. A. Molho, 'Politics and the ruling class in early Renaissance Florence', *Nuova rivista storica*, 52 (1968), 401–20, in which the concept of a 'political class' is usefully discussed, as it is also by Dale Kent, 'The Florentine Reggimento in the Fifteenth Century', *Renaissance Quarterly*, XXVIII (1975), 575–638. But the later fifteenth century in Florence tends to be treated biographically, so to speak, as in the works of Ridolfi ·(above, n. 41); cf. the very interesting book by D. Weinstein, *Savonarola and Florence* (Princeton, 1970).

99 As I understand the matter the classical curriculum used in some countries, including Germany, had statutory authority in secondary and higher education until fairly recently.

100 Polydore Vergil, *Anglica Historia* (London, 1950); Aeneas Sylvius Piccolomini, *De gestis concilii Basiliensis libri ii* (with W.K. Smith) (Oxford, 1967).

101 Above p. 11 and n. 45.

102 Now reprinted in *Scienza e vita civile nel Rinascimento* (Bari, 1965); but in the same collection the essay on 'La cultura fiorentina nell'età di Leonardo' does not introduce political factors.

103 Turin, 1961.

104 Turin, 1952.

105 Warburg Institute and Brill, I (1963), II (1967); a third volume is in preparation.
106 We must all look with admiration tinged with envy at the lavish resources available to French scholars for research at home and abroad in the Centre de recherches scientifiques, VIe section, of the Ecole Pratique des Hautes Etudes.
107 In expressing here admiration and esteem for the recipient of this volume, I should like to associate this essay with the memory of four friends, all mentioned above, who died prematurely: Federico Chabod, Delio Cantimori, Roberto Weiss and Franco Simone. I wish to thank Professor Nicolai Rubinstein for his helpful scrutiny of this essay; errors or misinterpretations are of course my own.

2

THE MEDIEVAL ORIGINS
OF THE RENAISSANCE

WALTER ULLMANN

HE INVITATION to contribute to a volume dedicated to Eugenio Garin and, most appropriately, specifically concerned with the problem of the Renaissance, is at once a privilege and a challenge, for who would not be daunted by the prospect of writing on a topic which is, in more than one respect, the very focal point of the illustrious jubiland's indefatigable and illuminating researches? By its nature this brief sketch can be no more than a small footnote to his massive *oeuvre* with its wide horizons and perspectives. The essay attempts, with however inadequate means, to see the phenomenon of the Renaissance in its genetic-evolutionary character, and it is therefore all the more gratifying to be able to offer the jubiland in a broad outline the result of my own recent research which, I am privileged and happy to say, has a strong affinity with the direction pursued by Garin himself. Seen from the purely historical angle, one of the problems of the Renaissance concerns its intellectual segment – humanism – because the Renaissance manifested itself initially in the rebirth of *humanitas*. The following examination attempts to show that genetically the Renaissance was politically motivated and socially conditioned. Such movements, firmly embedded as they are in the historical process, can never be divorced from their antecedents and do not grow in a vacuum. The problem is therefore also part of the problem of historical continuity and thus touches a nerve-centre of all historical enquiries.[1] The neglect of the integrated effect of historical forces blurs the picture of so variegated a phenomenon as the Renaissance was and prevents its adequate comprehension. Indeed, the evolution of the Renaissance itself presents its own kind of intellectual history, as is indicated in the last section of this essay. May the Olympian of present-day Renaissance scholars accept this modest contribution as a token of profound gratitude.

In its essence the problem of the Renaissance refers to the question,

[33]

what was reborn, what was restored, what was revivified? The commonly advanced view that it was classical literature (and the like) that experienced a rebirth or revival, is, if not tautological, partly commonplace, partly one-sided and quite inadequate to explain so fundamental and complicated a phenomenon as the Renaissance clearly was. It is wholly unrealistic to think that so multifarious a movement could come about as a result of the influence of revived ancient literature. To think in such terms is at best merely begging the question, and at its worst misleading. The understanding of the Renaissance as a historical contingency presupposes that proper attention is paid to society and its underlying assumptions which had deep roots in the historical process. The object of rebirth was nothing else but man himself, *homo*. The resultant *humanism* is, from the strictly historical angle, the initial phase of the Renaissance of which it was an integral part. Man's human*itas* was the seed which was to yield the Renaissance in its virtually inexhaustible multiformity. The revived or resuscitated *homo* and his kernel of human*itas* continued to be the very object of a correctly understood Renaissance.

In order to understand this process it is imperative to think in exclusively historical categories. This requires that the idea of rebirth be placed against the medieval background which, on closer inspection, will be seen to be fully impregnated with the very idea of the Renaissance. It was within the religious precincts of the Middle Ages that the concept of the Renaissance assumed a commanding position in the historical process of the period itself, and indeed gave the age its well-contoured physiognomy. The concept of rebirth was basic in the Middle Ages and resulted in, and makes possible the understanding of, the ecclesiological complexion of society. And it was the latter which determined the status of its members. It was as a reaction against this ecclesiological substance of society that humanism came into its own.

It is certainly one of the most remarkable features of medieval and Renaissance historians that they disregard the consequences of man's own regeneration or renaissance, which he experienced on becoming a Christian. If there is one point that has never been disputed or controverted in the chequered history of Christianity, it is baptism and its effects. There has never been any doubt in any quarter that baptism was a *regeneratio* or a *renovatio*, that is, a rebirth. Nor has it ever been questioned that through baptism man underwent a *secunda nativitas*,[2] for the *generatio* was replaced by a *regeneratio*.[3] The biblical and patristic sources flow richly in this respect.[4] It was the (*homo*) *renatus* and the effects of baptismal rebirth which mattered. For by becoming a Christian, man shed his naturalness, his character of a *homo animalis*

[34]

(to use Pauline terminology) and became a different, that is, a new man, a *homo novus*.[5] Having been reborn he entered a new society. He had to live according to the norms of this new society – the *ecclesia* – so that for him there began a *novitas vitae*.[6] And the society of which the newly baptized became a member was divinely founded (and also had a divinely stipulated form of government). Baptism, therefore, meant, within the public field, the incorporation of natural man into the Church, with the consequence that he was to order his life according to norms which were pertinent to the Church as a divine foundation. Conversely, he was no longer to live according to the norms which he himself as a mere natural being set, but according to those which were given to him.[7] Or seen from a collectivist angle, through baptism a heterogeneous society was transformed into a homogeneous ecclesiological society. The logical conclusion is that society itself, here the Church, determined the life of its members by the laws germane to the character and aim of that society which, having been divinely founded, could therefore function only on its own premises which were not of human but divine provenance.

Baptismal rebirth replaced the natural instincts, those innate forces, those natural propensities which man has in common with the animal world, by norms of an a-natural origin which were rationally fixed, articulated and formulated by those who knew the canon, that is, the rule, of the Church as a divinely founded society.[8] The application of these axioms in the public field involved an entire reorientation of commonly accepted assumptions. The Christian became in every respect a *sub-ditus*, precisely because he had no power to take part in the making of the law that was to govern the new society into which he had been incorporated. And this society, the divinely founded Church, *per definitionem* had nothing to do with nature or its laws: it was founded by a specific act, and had nothing to do with natural growth, or evolution. As a result of his incorporation, itself the sequel to his rebirth, the Christian accepted the norms and laws of the Church, and their formulation was the task of officers specially qualified. In a metaphorical sense law and government of the Church descended from the supreme divinity to lower organs: 'For there is no power but of God'.[9] The Christian was a *fidelis*, where the accent lay on *fides*, hence also the designation of this society as the *congregatio* (or *corpus*) *fidelium* within which the laity and clergy had different functions and offices.[10]

This ecclesiological character of society explains a number of features which are of special relevance in the present context. It is evident that a certain static rigidity distinguished it: everyone should remain in the status to which he was called.[11] This point of view is more easily

[35]

accessible to understanding if due recognition is given to the corporative (or collectivist) form of this society which itself entailed its 'totalitarian' substance. It was the corporateness on the one hand and the totalitarianism on the other which gave medieval ecclesiological society, the Church, its peculiar complexion. And both features are *au fond* bequests of Platonism, however diluted this way have been.[12] Its essential characteristics are not, however, in doubt. For what alone mattered was the Christian norm which was all-embracing and comprehensive in every sense: the atomist or pluralist categorization – such as the religious, moral, political, etc. categories of norms – did not and could not exist within this thought-pattern, dominated as it was by the principle of indivisibility. And in proximity to this thoroughly Platonic bequest stood the principle of unipolarity, according to which reborn man (the *renatus*) pursued one goal only – that of eternal salvation.[13] The path to this end, so it was held, rightfully could be delineated only by those who had special qualifications and therefore knew the canon of the Church by virtue of their superior knowledge. The (baptized) layman had none of these special qualifications.

All this was a practical demonstration of the Platonic cluster of ideas. The totality point of view together with the unipolarity theme and the requirement of charismatic knowledge could hardly lead to any other system than the ecclesiological, which was characterized by monarchic government in the hands of the Papacy. Its government concerned the vital interests of the whole *congregatio fidelium* and was responsible for its well-being and, above all, for its orientation towards its end: the realization of the divinely fixed *telos*. The law as given by the Papacy – or other appropriate ecclesiastical authority – functioned as the vehicle by which the eventual goal was to be achieved.[14] Furthermore, since Christ had promised the society founded by him to have sempiternity, its laws too must have the same character of sempiternity. With this fundamental thesis tallies the other frequently encountered topic that the law itself *animates* society, that is, breathes life into it, whence as early as the Visigothic laws we read that 'Law is the soul of the whole body of the populace'.[15] For just as the human soul was held to be immortal, in the same way the social soul, that is, the law, had assumed this character of immortality or sempiternity.

Considered from this angle the role of the secular ruler within the collective entity of the Church falls into place. Two points warrant some remarks. Firstly, the secular ruler was, by virtue of his baptismal rebirth, incorporated into the Church in a manner no different from that of any other member and stood therefore on a footing exactly identical with that of all other Christians. Secondly, in his function as ruler he had undergone another rebirth or *regeneratio*. For reasons irrelevant in the present context the ruler had, certainly from the eighth century onwards, adopted the designation of *rex Dei gratia*, the significance of which was that he had detached himself from the people or barons. Further, it signified the clearest possible assertion that his power to rule was the result of divine goodwill, of divine mercy (hence also the frequently occurring designations: *per misericordiam* or *clementiam Dei*, or similar terms expressing his humility). It was divine goodwill or grace which was operative and to which obviously nobody could have a right. Moreover, rulership derived from dynastic blood relationship was conclusively set aside as a title-deed to rulership.

In the place of the charisma of blood stepped the charisma of grace. The adoption of the *Dei gratia* title by the rulers was by no means an empty or 'mere' formula, but had deep significance which can be grasped only when due consideration is given to the religious-ecclesiological framework, within which it clearly expressed lack of autonomy on the part of the ruler. That the title itself was simply a shorthand device for what St Paul had said, should long have been recognized: 'by the grace of God I am what I am'.[16] But, and this really is the essential point, since divine grace was involved, the monopoly of the ecclesiastics as mediators of the sacraments came fully into play: they sandwiched themselves, so to speak, between divinity and the king by visibly conferring the divine grace on the latter in the act of unction. The role of the ecclesiastics can all the more easily be grasped since royal anointing was, genetically, merely an extension of post-baptismal anointing[17] which, like baptism itself, was considered a sacrament, and sacraments could be conferred only by the appropriately qualified ecclesiastical officers. The actual biblical model of the royal anointing was in the Old Testament which unambiguously declared that the anointed king became an *alius vir* (he had, in other words, undergone a rebirth). It was this second rebirth which effected a metamorphosis of the king's whole being and made him acquire a status which he did not, and could not, share with anyone else in his kingdom. He formed an estate of his own. He had become the Lord's anointed. He was also a *persona ecclesiastica*, and in the same proportion to which he detached himself from the baronage, his 'natural counsellors', he betook himself into the ecclesiastical camp. In some respects he was an amphibious creature. There is no doubt that the king derived great benefits from his theocratic function. Above all, he was protected in law as well as in dogma and faith to an extent which had all the appearances of a genuine monarchic government, even if it was not absolute.[18]

[37]

Yet this position was bought at a very high price. The anointed
– reborn – king was in a very specific sense tied to the ecclesiastical
hierarchy. The royal promises given on the occasion of his
coronation leave no room for any doubt on this score.[19] He functioned as
the 'Athlete of Christ' or as 'Typus Christi' or as a co-regent with
Christ – expressions which occur in all medieval coronation ordines.[20]
In theory the king's sphere of action was severely restricted. Yet to this
must be added the contradiction which lay in the exercise and practice
of royal government, the so-called proprietary church system, according
to which the owner of the land also claimed and exercised the right to
appoint the cleric who was to serve the church built on the owner's
land. The cleric received the office and benefice from the king. Transposed to the highest governmental plane – that of king or emperor – the
practice meant that important bishoprics were in the gift of the ruler.
How could this practice, which indeed had become a tradition, be
reconciled with the posture which he was to have assumed as a result
of his royal rebirth? Let us not forget that the king was not fully king
until the moment of unction during the coronation service, as
the computation of regnal years amply proves: the unction was
constitutive, and not merely declaratory. Nevertheless, the king acted
in practice as if he still were 'unregenerated', because the proprietary
church system was quite ostensibly the bequest of the ancient, 'natural'
Germanic past.

During the Investiture Contest it was these contradictions between
the theoretical and practical postures which with desirable clarity came
into the open. The appeal to tradition, history, custom on the part of the
king fell flat: the Papacy appealed to the law which it claimed sharply
condemned this very tradition. Pope Gregory VII mercilessly exposed
the inner contradictions of the theocratic king. One is indeed tempted
to say that in no other field than that of government did the tension
between nature and grace stare so glaringly in the face of the observer,
for 'nature' was here represented by the unreflected and unsophisticated
modes of conducting government, whereas 'grace' was represented
by the reborn king, the Lord's anointed, who had in his coronation
promises accepted specific functions and duties within an ecclesiological framework. In other words, Christian and therefore ecclesiological themes were not an emanation of an intuitive religion, but were
highly sophisticated and, by the eleventh century, well thought out and
mature. And it is a truism to say that tradition, when in
conflict with a well-formulated system of thought, is bound to be the
loser. Tradition and custom cave in when confronted with a logically
flawless, constructed system and this was precisely the case in the

Investiture Contest. Ancientness of practices could not confer legality upon them if they were shown by the law of the Church to be illegal. Hence there was only one alternative: either the king was to give up the practices and conduct his government in conformity with the function which his royal rebirth postulated, or he had to face the consequences. *Tertium non datur*. Although the conflict was fought on the plane of government, there was no doubt that what was at stake was the position of the laity within an exclusively ecclesiologically orientated society.[21]

It was indeed the strength of the Papacy that it could appeal to the law which was in ample supply. And it was the weakness of the royal side that it had none of the shining armoury of its papal antagonist. The dilemma which faced the king was how to release himself from the ecclesiological encumbrances and yet function as a Christian king? For on the ecclesiological premises he had no answer to the papal challenge because they precluded any accommodation or adjustment. The theocratic ruler had become the victim of his own, purely voluntarily accepted function as 'the king by the grace of God'. Canossa made a change of the foundations of government imperative if the ruler was to effect a release from the ecclesiological embrace which indubitably had rendered him useful service, but now proved a severe liability. The paradox is plain enough to see: by its repeated, insistent appeal to the law the Papacy itself suggested an escape from the impasse in which contemporary rulers found themselves. For the law that had never died out, at any rate in Italy and in some other intellectually alert regions of Europe, was the Roman law in the shape of Justinian's codification.

The assistance which Roman law from the late eleventh century onwards rendered to contemporary rulers was invaluable. Roman law was held to be the acme of all legal achievement. It was law in every sense of the term and paradoxically in contrast to the ecclesiastical law which though abundantly available was, precisely because of its multiformity, diversity, variety and contradictory character, hardly capable, as yet, of serving as a firm base, because there was not one body of canon law, but a multiplicity of laws. Above all, Roman law was a law made by laymen for laymen. It was a law which embodied the jurisprudential wisdom of republican lawyers as well as the statesmanship of the late Roman emperors. It was a law – notably the Code – which satisfied both jurisprudential and especially governmental requirements, because in it the prototype of monarchical government was classically exhibited.[22]

The utilization of Roman law from the turn of the eleventh and twelfth centuries had three important implications. Firstly, it was primarily the government itself which began to harness the Roman law to its own purposes, and thereby to set afoot the process of its own secularization. Its foundations were to be no longer of the ecclesiological, but of the Roman-secular kind. Secondly, this process of governmental secularization was bound to affect contemporary society which began to loosen its ecclesiological associations, just as the government did. What must be kept in mind is that the function of government was to provide effective leadership. It was concerned not merely with administration or management but with concrete guidance of the people or country under its control, and this concern obviously focused attention on public life. Indeed, what one finds in the twelfth and thirteenth centuries is the partial reversal of the process initiated in the Carolingian age when through governmental measures a whole society was to be collectively reborn on the model of the individual baptismal rebirth.[23] The initiative belonged to the government – in the Carolingian age as well as in the twelfth century. What, counts most in the present context is the third point. Roman law was the first instrument which helped to bring about humanism and Renaissance. For it served as an *exemplum* of hitherto unrecognized magnitude. The fifteenth-century Renaissance cast its shadows back as far as the twelfth century. Differently expressed, it was on the level of government that the process of secularization of its foundations and the desacralization of society began. Without governmental initiative there would neither have been a 'Carolingian' renaissance nor humanism and Renaissance in the later Middle Ages. And there is the further observation which relates to the fructifying effect of Roman law and its professional study: the penetration into its matrix opened up historical perspectives which had hitherto lain hidden beneath the surface. This extremely stimulating effect of Roman law studies should not be lost sight of in the present context. History was first utilized for governmental purposes: its general utilization in wider aspects ensued.

The secularization of governmental foundations withdrew the ruler from the exposed position which he occupied in the ecclesiological framework. This secularization made the ruler 'human', that is, it set aside the *gratia Dei* as the constitutive element of his rulership and title-deed, and in its place stepped the figure of the Roman *princeps*, with the consequence that a new historical dimension was introduced. The German ruler was not 'the king of the Germans', was no longer the *Rex Teutonicorum*, but the *Rex Romanorum*, a rulership which was held to be the stage preliminary to the full Roman emperorship. As a *Rex Romanorum* he claimed to have established a historic link with the late Roman empire. The theocratic side of rulership became now merely attached to the historical component part. The Staufen government from the mid-twelfth century onwards clearly shows this design: to harness the Roman law for governmental purposes and therewith to shift the basis of government materially. The point to be borne in mind is that Roman law was exclusively lay law, was human law *par excellence* and was deeply imbued with Christianity and its norms, notably in the Code. The deep religiosity of the Roman *princeps* was never impugned. Roman law was mundane, secular and had no aspirations towards delineating the path to eternal bliss. Within it there was no room for the view that life was merely a transitory stage. Looked at from this angle, Roman law now in the twelfth century became literally speaking the classical model for governmental purposes, though it was only the first of such models. This influence of Roman law has not yet been adequately assessed within the historical antecedents of the Renaissance and the initial phases of humanism. Roman law was the prototype of human law altogether devoid of any transmundane, transpersonal or other-worldly features. From the genetical point of view, Roman law was one of the most effective begetters of what later became known as humanism and Renaissance.[24] This was the first phase of the Renaissance in its humanist shape – a phase characterized by the manipulation of Roman law by governments. The original impulse came from the government in reply to the papal challenge, and it is this point which needs special emphasis, for it is the first step towards the 're-humanization' of the individual himself whose natural humanity was said to have been neutralized as the result of his baptismal rebirth. There is indeed a parallel between this Renaissance and the 'Carolingian' renaissance in so far as the process of reversal began with the ruler, who himself had in the course of the 'Carolingian' renaissance been reborn through unction and 'clericalized'. Now the reverse was to be witnessed: he was de-clericaliszed and re-humanized by resting his power on purely historical, that is, mundane foundations. In view of this development it is justifiable to maintain that the resultant humanism and Renaissance were originally politically motivated.[25]

In order to comprehend the development adequately, it is advisable to refer briefly, but integratively, to the actual situation in contemporary society which proved itself to be very receptive for the governmental scheme first embraced by the Staufen and shortly afterwards followed by other governments, notably the French. Secularist features were amply in evidence and acted as supportive agents of the secularism promoted by governments, so that here one can speak of a mutually stimulating dependence. It is a truism to say that governmental measures must always be seen in relation to society and the impact they make upon it. Even the briefest sketch must point out that in the twelfth century the lay element had powerfully come to the fore, since in many walks of life a greater participation of the laity in matters involving the public weal was observable. This participation assumed different forms, but common to all of them was the self-assertive reaction of laymen to curialist claims. The rapid growth of the Italian universities is a particularly telling example as the study of Roman law opened up hitherto unperceived horizons for laymen. And in the earliest university Roman law was the only subject taught, lectured upon and studied: at Bologna canon law as a subject of academic pursuit came on the scene in the wake of the study of Roman jurisprudence.

Unwittingly the Papacy with its crusading appeal had also brought the laity to the forefront, since it was the laymen who had to do the fighting, and the subsequent emergence of military orders underlined the rise and importance of the laity. Further, in its fight against simonists and concubinists the Papacy induced a 'strike' by the laity in so far as they exhorted, if not ordered, them to boycott divine services conducted by simonists, etc. On their part the crusades greatly stimulated not only trade with the Levant, but also personal contact with foreign peoples, customs, religions, and so on. The perspectives widened greatly. The town populations were especially affected by this expansion of the layman's vision, whereas in the village communities there had always been the unsophisticated and unreflective application of the ascending theme of government and law in relation to village matters.[26] Where feudal law prevailed there was obviously a very great involvement of the laity in the making and applying of law. Feudal practice powerfully contributed to the harmonization of all social strata, precisely because feudalism presupposed team work and hence promoted social cohesion. The significance of this is that the rigidity and abrasiveness of the rationally and logically flawless system of notions, theses, axioms and principles came to be mitigated greatly. The laity acted in these instances in conformity with their 'natural' insight and assessment, without regard to their status as 'new creatures' It was all rather flexible and given to compromise, above all, because there was little reliance on 'first' principles.

In the intellectual sphere there was – leaving aside the universities – a similarly noticeable awakening in the twelfth and thirteenth centuries. Historiography provides a good example: in many respects it had been an extended biblical exegesis, since the 'universal' histories began with the creation in Genesis and carried the story down to the author's time. The underlying principle was that everything happened 'by the determinate counsel and foreknowledge of God' (Acts 2:23). Man simply carried out – or failed to carry out – a preordained divine plan. He himself was not credited with conceiving the plan. The chronicler 'recorded', but did not explain, hence little attention was paid to individual features, because the 'objectivity' of the record could not take into account personal/individual elements. The title of a work 'Gesta Dei *per* Francos' is revealing and needs no comment on its underlying assumptions.[27] But historiography is only one segment of the prevailing mode of thought before the twelfth century. It is in fact a special application of typology – the king, the bishop, etc., were merely 'types' of office-holders whose contours were 'objectively' conceived within the framework of the law. Hence also the designation of the king as 'Typus Christi', and the disproportionate amount of hagiographical writings which are important, not from the point of view of historical sources *stricto sensu* (they are overwhelmingly worthless), but from the standpoint of typology, because they attempt to throw light on the 'type' of a saintly king, holy bishop, the model duke (*Adelsheiliger*),[28] and so on. In this respect the twelfth century shows vital changes. For instance, Otto of Freising concentrated on the individual as a *persona mundialis* – the choice of terminology is in itself significant – who had his own *individua substantia* and whose *humanitas* somehow partook of his *animalitas*.[29] Man as a natural creature begins to be seen as the moving organ of history. In brief, these are the first signs of a mundanized or 'humanized' historiography, and by employing a Virgilian expression[30] Otto of Freising fixes the task of the historical writer as 'rerum causas cognoscere'. Only a few years later Burgundio of Pisa was to repeat the same idea with the same words.[31] Simultaneously attention begins to be paid to individual traits, and with this went the deployment of observational powers, hitherto dormant, in the search to discover 'rerum causas'.

What is important is that man's *humanitas* as such enters the precincts of writers – hence also the first tentative beginnings of biography and especially autobiography. The age of typology with its rigid objective norms was giving way to an age which acknowledged man's natural complexity. In proximity to biography and autobiography stands the hesitant emergence of a subjective point of view,[32] and the natural evaluation of the actions and measures of kings by employing subjective criteria. It is not therefore surprising that the entry of these criteria into the writings – one has but to think of Ralph de Diceto, Gerald of Wales, Matthew Paris, Philippe of Novare, and a host of others – was accompanied by the growth of vernacular literature

[43]

virtually throughout western Europe. Clearly, the significance of this vernacular growth is partly that the soil was receptive for it, and partly that it expressed the sentiments, feelings, emotions, in fact man's natural thought-processes, in a manner of which Latin was incapable. It was the appeal to, and the appeal from, man's natural humanity which was the secret of the success reaped by vernacular literature. Hand in hand with this went the increase in translations of Latin works into the vernacular. And translations and vernacular compositions made conspicuous the differences within society of customs, habits, and outlook of neighbouring peoples. It was the growing awareness of national differences which fostered the vernacular and was also its effect. The emergence of the concept of nationhood in the twelfth and thirteenth centuries constituted the very antithesis to the hitherto prevailing a-natural universality which, by virtue of the efficacy of the universal faith, disregarded geographical, physical, biological, ethnic and linguistic barriers.[33] To the nationhood corresponded natural man (that is, the unregenerated *homo animalis*). The strength of the common ecclesiological bond that held (universal) society together was considerably affected by the phenomenon of the nation which was little else but natural man writ large – it was, seen purely historically, a rebirth or restoration of the tribal groupings under a different name which had been absorbed into the all-embracing society, the Church, but which now regained its character in a different guise.

The influence of this national feature can be observed in the growth of territorial sovereignty (the *Rex Francorum* was to become the *Rex Franciae* or the *Rex Anglorum* to change into the *Rex Angliae*, and so on) and above all in the literature which began to depict the different national characteristics of the French, the Germans, the Italians, etc. – witness Alexander of Roes.[34] In turn this stimulated the observational powers, as is proved by the ambassadorial reports from distant lands as well as the intrusion of the purely physical elements into theological and philosophical discussions. Here, precisely at the turn of the twelfth and thirteenth centuries, the Arab influences demand special attention. It is the beginning of the naturalist-physical trend, but still within the theological framework. Alfred of Sareshel (Alfredus Anglicus) is a conspicuous example: he operated with the *animalitas* of man in which the *anima* as well as the *animal* were joined. He clearly realized the function of the arteries' pulsation, the heart, the lungs, the digestion and the cerebral operations. Alan of Lille can be added as another example of this new orientation. That the natural sciences began to make their debut in the thirteenth century can therefore cause no surprise, and it is in this context that the receptivity of the soil for Aristotle's philosophy can be fully appraised. The very term *scientia naturalis* came to denote this new intellectual pursuit of physical phenomena, a pursuit which tallied perfectly with the newly received Aristotelian theses. Not the least important aspect of this literally speaking new cosmology was what has been most appropriately called 'the secularization of time',[35] a concept that clearly showed that the unity of the present and future life was broken. Time could and should be measured exactly: it was a this-worldly, mundane, humanly comprehensible unit and entity. The concept of timelessness belonged to transmundane, transcendental categories of thought.[36] Hand in hand with this humanization went progress in medicine, notably anatomy and surgery. The Black Death itself greatly stimulated medical research and above all public sanitation. It is rarely noticed that painting and drawing came to be seen as means of research in order to penetrate into the laws of nature, and this is particularly true in regard to anatomical drawings which slowly begin to emerge and indicate extraordinary powers of observation: at the end of this development stands Leonardo who in a superb manner shows what service drawings and paintings can render to the anatomical knowledge of man.

Here is the point where at least a passing reference should be made to artistic productions in the twelfth and thirteenth centuries, because they persuasively demonstrate the same feature: naturalism and concentration on the humanity of man. It is well known that the fine arts were particularly strongly dominated by typological representation – in sculpture, portraiture, illuminations, etc. Here the gradual change to an individualized art is quite remarkable, especially from the first half of the thirteenth century onwards. This change might well be epitomized by the dictum 'From deity to humanity' or 'bringing God down to earth'. Real and naturally seen people replaced the type. It is certainly no coincidence that the new Orders of the Friars particularly strongly stimulated this development. Stories had to be told in a realistic manner, a postulate which tallied of course with the demands of vernacular literature. Landscape painting made its debut – the most natural of all natural subjects at long last won its rightful place. Hence the artist could give free rein to his talents by deploying his own reflections, his own evaluations and assessments: the Gospel stories were rendered differently by differently motivated artists according to the (subjective) picture they themselves had mentally formed. Curiosity began to be a motivating force. Matters which had been hidden from man's vision, simply because they were natural, were now explored. Consequently, the great interest the animal world evoked – Frederick II's menagerie of hitherto unknown creatures

[45]

(monkeys, camels, leopards) is just one of many examples; the Frenchman Villard de Honnecourt's sketch-book contained a drawing of a lion from life.[37] A new dramatic naturalism emerged. Once more Italian examples abound. Niccolò Pisano, Giotto, Duccio, are just a few instances of superb thirteenth-century artistry. Anonymous craftsmen in distant lands pursued exactly the same aim – some of the corbels in Westminster Abbey in London show first-rate observational powers by the artist, as well as his skill in depicting the individual features of his subjects. An important consequence of this new trend was the attempt to preserve one's own glory and status for posterity by artistic means, such as busts or statues, which is not only a symptom of the aversion from typology but also the exact parallel to autobiography.

It has been necessary to provide a glance at phenomena which seem only remotely to have any relevance to the 'problem of the Renaissance'. But appearances may be deceptive. For if we accord due consideration to the intimate link between the secularization of government and the secularism observable in society at large and their mutual supplementation and fructification, we have taken a mighty step forward in order to comprehend (more adequately than has hitherto been the case) the change, as well as the impact of the change, which the absorption of Aristotelian themes involved. The feature common to the secularization of governmental foundations and the secularist social manifestations was the emphasis on the mundane, on the natural, on the human aspects, and the corresponding diminution of the importance accorded to the divine, the other-worldly, if not exclusively religious, elements. These secularist features in government and society furnished the substructure, and were in actual fact the effective presupposition for the doctrinal and theoretical reversal that resulted from the Aristotelian reception. Without this substructure it would be wellnigh impossible to explain the readiness for Aristotelian themes and the rapidity with which they entered into all branches of intellectual activities. No theory or doctrine, however well propounded, argued and articulated, can have any hope of being accepted if society itself is not ready for it.

In more than one respect the 'philosopher' had shown in theory what in practice was already either attempted or actually done. He provided the theoretical justification for giving natural, human, purely mundane elements a standing which they had not had in the traditional thought-patterns, largely orientated as they were by Platonic influences. By positing nature as one of the fundamental instruments of his philosophy, Aristotle effected a veritable revolution, and this revolution affected the focal point of all Christianity – the theme of baptismal rebirth. We may recall that through baptism the natural humanity of man was, metaphorically speaking, washed away by baptismal waters which transformed the *homo animalis* into a *nova creatura* that lived a *novitas vitae* according to norms which were of divine, a-human provenance. It has been seen that thereby the status of the reborn individual was fundamentally changed, and the consequences of this change came to be most conspicuously and fully displayed in the public field, that is to say in government and thereby in the creation of the vehicle by which government could be carried out, the law. The descending theme of government and law reigned supreme.

In view of the actuality of the historical situation and the secularization of governmental foundations, the fertility and readiness of the soil for the reception of Aristotelian naturalism can assuredly cause no surprise. He provided the *pièces justificatives* for what had already been seen to be done in practice. He provided the articulate rationale of the hitherto inarticulate premises which were found in all layers of society and in variegated fields. In particular, it was his *Politics* which became immediately relevant. It was the mature expression of a world order conceived in physical terms. In it the operational element was that of nature which made man a political animal who took part in the shaping of his society by employing his own natural abilities. His own society was the state, in itself as much a product of nature as man himself is.[38] Here once again we can observe how much familiarity with a terminology assisted a new thesis, for all literate men were conversant with the *homo animalis* of St Paul.[39]

The Aristotelian 'political animal' was the instrument which in the thirteenth century effected the restoration or resurrection or rebirth, the renaissance of the very man of nature whose baptism was said to have been neutralized, if not wholly eliminated. Indeed, this is what Eugenio Garin has called in a different context the 'rehabilitation' of man.[40] It was to all intents and purposes the restoration of *homo ut homo*.[41] On the plane of doctrine this was a justification of what was observable in the (briefly sketched) different intellectual, social, artistic, feudal and other activities and what was *au fond* the presupposition of the secularized foundations of government. This rehabilitation or restoration or rebirth of man as a natural creature was – at any rate in the public order – the re-humanization of the (Pauline) *nova creatura*. Thereby he had reacquired a status which through baptismal rebirth he had lost. This reacquistion applied evidently primarily to the public field in which the subject had no legitimate function other than to obey the decree lawfully given to him by superior authority. The effect of the renaissance of natural man was that baptismal rebirth was partially put into reverse. Within the secular-mundane public order, this renaissance postulated full attention of man as a natural product, as a man of flesh. In other words, physical-carnal generation as well as baptismal regeneration through grace were accorded full and legitimate standing. Man's *humanitas* now came into its own again. After centuries of hibernation, unadulterated natural man had acquired an appropriate place in the cosmological order.

The segment primarily if not exclusively affected was the public sphere, and so the repercussions of this Aristotelian reception were profound. To begin with, there was a dual ordering of ideas – as indeed Thomas Aquinas was explicitly to define this state of affairs. One order was concerned with the mundane, secular, visible world – the political order proper. Here it must be stressed that the concept of the 'political', for which neither Roman law nor the antecedent governmental literature provided any space for deployment, had now fully entered the thought-pattern of thinkers and writers. And it was the political order which rested on the natural, secular and mundane foundations and provided its own criteria of assessment, evaluation and insight. The other order was supernatural in the literal meaning of the term, and its criteria followed divine revelation, commands and norms. The significance of this new standpoint was that the ancient Christian and largely Platonic thesis of the totality receded into the background, with the consequence that in the place of unipolarity (the sole end of man was eternal salvation and bliss) stepped bipolarity (one end of man's legitimate aspiration was this-worldly, mundane, pursuing its own physical well-being; the other was transcendental and other-worldly, transmundane). To this bipolarity corresponded the Aristotelian distinction between the good man and the good citizen. The former related to ethical, the latter to political, norms. Ethics and politics were conceptually cleanly separated. The morally good man need not be a politically good citizen, and vice versa.[42] Indeed, Aquinas, perhaps the best interpreter of Aristotle, elaborated this principle of bipolarity maturely.[43] Ethics, religion and politics began to form distinct categories of thought and conduct and were autonomous, though by no means antagonistic to each other. They complemented and supplemented each other. What is relevant and needs pointing out is that, with the rebirth of *homo* as a being demanding full recognition, in his private capacity the individual was seen acting in accordance with ethical norms (to which now in the thirteenth century were added religious precepts) and in his public capacity he acted in accordance with political principles, and had become a fully fledged citizen.[44] The citizen was in the public sphere what (natural) man was in the ethical. It was not so much the individual as man, but his function as citizen which initially made the deepest impact. The attention which was lavished on the citizen, characterized the second initial phase of the Renaissance. For want of a better term I call this second phase 'political humanism'. In this the Renaissance found its earliest concrete and tangible manifestation: it was the 'proto-renaissance'.

Political humanism became the chief topic of the 'new' learning from the second half of the fourteenth century onwards. A large part of its attraction and rapid dissemination can be explained by familiarity with the terminology employed. For instance, there was the concept of the citizen. Every king, emperor, duke, etc. issued his charters or letters *civibus Remenensibus, Sarisberiensibus, Mediolanensibus, Coloniensibus*, etc. though in actual fact and theory they were his subjects, but what mattered was linguistic identity and consequently familiarity with the concept which not merely facilitated the emergence of political humanism, but rather conditioned it. Nevertheless, linguistic identity does not imply identity in meaning. This political humanism as the 'proto-renaissance' brought about the concept of the state as an autonomous, independent, self-sufficient entity because it was a product of nature just as much as (natural) man was. And the state was composed of citizens. In the previous ecclesiological phase there was no conceptual possibility of arriving at this notion of the state, precisely because there was solely the all-embracing ecclesiological unit of universal dimensions. The further consequence was that the Church itself in course of time experienced a de-mundanization and was to be confined in its activities to non-secular, a-natural, matters of faith. After all, it professedly had nothing to do with nature and operated exclusively in realms outside and above nature.

It is therefore highly significant that this phase of the 'proto-renaissance' was characterized by the emergence of the state as the collectivized unit of the citizens who answered natural criteria, *as well as* by the (continued) existence of the Church whose subjects were *fideles* answering supranatural postulates. The principle of bipolarity had found concrete expression in the state and in the Church, where previously there was but one unit within which the principle of unipolarity alone was operational. Furthermore, in the antecedent age there was, according to the principle of unipolarity, only one criterion,

[49]

the religious, whereas now there were two, the political (or secular or mundane or human or natural) as well as the religious. It was still the faith which was the material ingredient of law within the proper supernatural sphere, while in the state what counted was the citizens' consent which conferred enforceability on the law. Hence now the very birth of the new *scientia politica* as the science that dealt with political matters, hence also the very coinage of *politizare* (derived from Aristotle's *politeuesthai*) because there was no equivalent term in the Latin vocabulary, and when there was no term, one can reasonably be certain that there was no need for it. But now this need was very conspicuous, because the citizens by giving consent to law – and therefore taking part in government – must engage in politics, must discuss and hammer out political issues and have, therefore, need to *politizare*. Most modern languages employ this term in this very sense: *politicare, politicise, politisieren, politiser*.

Lastly, through the restoration or rebirth or rehabilitation of natural *homo*, his *humanitas* simultaneously came into the horizon of writers and thinkers. Man's *humanitas* was separated from *divinitas*, so that even in the 'proto-renaissance' there were the *studia humanitatis* next to which there were the *studia divinitatis*. Terminology once more proved to be of crucial importance. The very term *humanitas* had long been familiar to literate men, though it was almost exclusively employed within ecclesiological precincts. Nevertheless, Roman law too was perfectly familiar with the term, and wholly independently from any theological or christological issues. And familiarity with Cicero's specific distinction between *humanitas* and *divinitas* contributed to the ease with which the new cosmology shaped the thought-processes of the thirteenth and fourteenth century thinkers.[45] The heightened role allocated to *humanitas* arose from the social instinct that was implanted in man: this is exactly what Aquinas had called the *instinctus naturae*[46] which was inapplicable to the Church, but all the more applicable to the state which consisted only of mere humans, hence the need to concentrate on their *humanitas*. What emerged in the late thirteenth century was a human cosmology in which (unregenerated) man played a decisive, though by no means an exclusive, role. In other words, the Renaissance found its earliest expression in connection with the renaissance of the citizen as the integral member of the state, so that humanism became in this second phase of the Renaissance a segment of scholarship that concerned itself with matters of the rehabilitated humanity in the context of political science, in the context of the citizen's standing and function within the state. The latter was nothing but the former writ large. The citizen was the political expression of rehabilitated natural humanity.

At this juncture it is perhaps advisable to stress that the *studia humanitatis* were not concerned with grammar, rhetoric, syntax and the like, but, as the term and the contrasting *studia divinitatis* persuasively demonstrate, with man's innermost being, with the human substance of unregenerated man, and, in this second phase of the Renaissance, with him in his public, political status as a citizen. In his corresponding private capacity he was to receive the attention which was his due at a much later date. But in whatever capacity his *humanitas* was studied, it was understood not to include grammar and other topics as these belonged to elementary schooling and not to humanity. It is therefore quite misleading to render the term *studia humanitatis* by 'study of the humanities', which is supposed to embrace grammar, rhetoric, poetry and classical pursuits, as if humanity concerned itself with no more than these subjects. The *studia humanitatis* (and one should note that the plural referred to studies, not to humanity) focused attention not on these trivial matters but on *humanitas* itself, on the being of man, precisely what had previously not evoked much interest. The 'study of the humanities' belongs to the modern age, not to the age of humanism.

The new cosmology in which unregenerated man, the natural self of man, occupied the centre can perhaps best be shown by the change of wind that affected the very concept of history and hence of historiography.[47] It was Petrarch who demonstrated this change most convincingly. To him the age between the collapse of the Roman empire in the west and his own time was 'a dark night', and to Leonardo Bruni the preceding seven centuries were 'a dark age',[48] not indeed because little was known, but because in the dark age or night it was not man himself who directed the path of history. It was baptismally reborn men, the *novae creaturae*, who were moved (or were said to have been moved) by divinity and by norms not of their own making, who 'shaped' history. Not without justification were they compared with chess figures. Petrarch's and Bruni's views are symptomatic of the new orientation. The disregard of the 'dark age' was warranted because motivations, norms, laws, principles and evaluations belonged to the ecclesiological set which had no natural or human paternity. It was the absence of the *human* element and of human motivations which explains this view of the 'dark ages'. But to Petrarch and Bruni, history was the story of natural-human men: humanity stood at its core. It was humanly motivated measures, acts, developments and deeds capable of a human-natural explanation and rational-mundane comprehension, which counted as the essence of history, and not those which were set in motion by supranatural forces through men who acted (or were said to act) on criteria of an a-human provenance. Citizen-centred humanism called for citizen-centred history.[49]

This humanist view of history has far greater significance than it has been credited with by modern scholarship. For how was a society that contained only citizens, that is, a society wherein politics occupied a central place, to be governed, manipulated, organized and arranged? Further, the rebirth of the citizen postulated a framework for society and for its organization and constitution for which no pattern was available that could serve as a model.[50] Of course, Aristotle and his synthesizer and harmonizer, Thomas Aquinas and his followers, propounded well-marshalled and argued theories entirely in conformity with the capacity of the reborn political man – the citizen – but this was pure theory and as yet a mere postulate. What was more immediately important was a practical example which could serve as a model for governing a state composed of citizens. The ascending thesis of government and law proposed by John of Paris and Marsilius, *et alii*, had to be supplemented by the practical and concrete example: pure theory had to be given flesh and blood. What lay nearer to hand than ancient Rome? Indeed, it was Petrarch himself who exclaimed: 'For what is all history, other than praise of Rome?'[51] One is here tempted to say that in the same way as ancient Greece and Rome stood at the cradle of the medieval world and changed the earlier medieval outlook, so ancient Greece (epitomized in Aristotle) and Rome (epitomized in Ulpian) were to give the modern world its specific physiognomy which, paradoxically enough, radically differed from the ancient, notably Roman, universalism.

The regress to ancient Rome became the more pressing, the more the Humanist thesis itself advanced. It is one of the most remarkable features in Renaissance studies that the role of Roman law as the primeval mirror of society and government has hardly been recognized. Roman law was the first – and perhaps most influential – model relating to government and society which was not derived from ecclesiological premises. Roman law was the classic *exemplum*, to use a medieval and a Renaissance term. It presupposed a society entirely composed of citizens. Dante's invocation of the universal Roman empire as a model for the comprehensive *societas humana* or the *civilitas humana* which, to him, was nothing but the collectivized *humanitas*, meant that in the ancient Roman empire there could be seen a state that transgressed physical, linguistic, ethnic and biological barriers and formed one unit held together by the law made by humans and manifested the *potentia ipsius humanitatis*.[52] Dante indeed paved

[52]

the way to the consultation of the ancients, and in a quite specific way he directed attention to Roman law. Every law student was familiar with the *lex regia* according to which the Roman people had conferred all power on the prince.[53] Dante's friend, the great jurist and poet, Cino da Pistoia, had written *'imperium a Deo, imperator a populo'*.[54] And Petrarch's friend, Cola di Rienzo, in a spectacular manner rediscovered the 'original' *lex regia*. He produced the bronze tablet on which was inscribed the actual text of this *lex*. Hardly any more convincing model or source of a model could be shown. It was, moreover, the same Cola who re-enacted the rebirth of a Roman tribune of the people by the *lavacrum regenerationis* which was the exact counterpart to the baptismal *lavacrum regenerationis*, the baptismal cleansing.[55]

Viewed dispassionately there can be no doubt that the search for models or *exempla* gained momentum as the fourteenth century advanced, and this search concerned patterns directly relevant to political (and social) matters. It was these for which the search was conducted, because it was within the political precincts that there was a veritable vacuum and a very real need for *exempla*, in order to find out how to organize and how to govern a society that was based on the *potentia humanitatis*. In ancient Rome only citizens, that is unregenerated men, dominated the scene, as was abundantly made clear in the *Corpus Iuris Civilis* which provided the pattern for legal and constitutional questions, whereas for public political life there was no better guide than Cicero. Cicero was a stylist, but also a jurist, a philosopher, an epistolographer, an orator, a moralist and much else besides, yet all these were overshadowed by his role as a *politicus*. A closer study of his influence reveals that it was in his rediscovered works (such as in his *Ad Atticum*) that the significant terminology of *libri politici* and the *theses politicae* were prominently displayed. No doubt, he served as a personal model *in rebus politicis* (ἐν τοις πολιτικοίς), and as such he characterized himself. Assuredly, Cicero was only one of the authors of Antiquity who was studied. What needs pointing out is that by studying ancient writers fourteenth-century man attempted to penetrate into and acquire concrete knowlege of the workings of an exclusively 'human' society, and politics, the new category of thought relative to the ordering of unregenerated society, was of especial concern. The ancients revealed the mechanics of politics, and that is why Roman law was a lynchpin of the initial phases of the Renaissance, and the jurists became the most conspicuous representatives of this 'proto-renaissance' in the fourteenth century. Law manifested the working of *humanitas* to a degree which no other social phenomenon did. The jurists, that is, the civilians, were the first who, from the twelfth century onwards, scientifically pointed to the way in which the emancipation of the subject from tutelage was to be achieved with the help of the Roman law, for here there was not only the *civis*, but also the *consensus* in the law-creative process. Without realizing it, such jurists as Accursius, Cinus, Bartolus and their *sequaces* were pacemakers of humanism.[56] In other words, *humanitas* was separated from *divinitas* to which entirely different criteria applied. Civic as distinct from ecclesiologically motivated conduct, and political as distinct from conduct based on faith and grace was what now mattered, and again it would be merely rhetorical to ask where else but in ancient Rome could pure, civic, political life be observed.

In parenthesis we may recall that an exactly parallel feature could be witnessed in the Carolingian period when society was to be reborn: here, too, was the attempt to reshape or remodel or recreate a raw society into an exclusively Christian one. This social rebirth was modelled on the individual baptismal rebirth. Hence knowledge of the axioms and theses germane to Christianity was to be acquired by assimilating and applying the teachings of the patristic authors, such as Cyprian, Ambrose, Jerome and Augustine, because Christianity was not a 'natural' or intuitive religion.[57] From the late thirteenth century onwards exactly the same process can be seen at work, only in a reverse order. The models were not the patristic writers, but the ancient authors: Quintilian, Seneca, Cicero, Livy, and so on. They served as vehicles which depicted a thoroughly humanly conceived society, because they were wholly uncontaminated by Christianity, ecclesiology, etc. They were studied in their totality, and not, as hitherto, merely for grammatical-didactic purposes of prose composition. Of course, most of the ancient authors had in any case been preserved, copied and known in the preceding centuries, but their function was different then from the one which they now served. The point of reference had since changed, for whereas formerly these same authors had the limited function of serving as models for the composition of Latin prose, so that their function was confined to form, now they were read for the sake of their substance and their matter. Their opulence and their function as the media of instruction for civic and political cohabitation was only now fully recognized (hence their great appeal) because, despite an embarrassing abundance of medieval literature relative to government, there was precious little in it from which one could glean how a civic-human society was to be governed or organized. It is the change of perspective which distinguished the use of ancient authors in the high Middle Ages from that made of them in the initial phases of the Renaissance.

This consultation of the ancients became indeed all the more pressing as scholarship most competently and powerfully propounded the humanist theme within governmental precincts. Precisely because the *homo naturalis* was restored or rehabilitated or reborn, and was the very object of the new *scientia politica* in the shape of the citizen, there was what might well be termed an avalanche of scholarly writings dedicated to the resuscitated *humanitas* in the political field. There was nothing comparable in literary quantity and quality within the study of ethics or for that matter within any other intellectual sphere.

Only a few representative examples can here be mentioned in the briefest possible manner. In one way or another they all were adherents of the Aristotelian-Thomist pattern of thought. There was, for instance, John of Paris in the very early years of the fourteenth century, for whom the *humanus*-qualification was the essential operational element within the orbit of public government and society. Consequently, it was the 'consensus *humanus*' which was the material ingredient of the law and through which government assumed legitimate power, so that it was a mere 'rex *humanus*' who ruled. The basic presupposition in John's concise system lay in what he called the 'virtus naturae *humanae*' through which the 'principatus politicus' came into being, and this was for him the 'principatus populi'. This was the *democracia*,[58] which provided for all matters relevant to social and public life. The *tota vita* of the citizens or the *commune bonum civium* was the object of government and came into its purview when the 'virtus naturae humanae' had a free rein. The employment of the totality point of view within the precincts of citizenship and 'democracia' will not escape appropriate attention. Precisely because John rested his system on nature (and not on any supranatural) considerations, he modestly did not postulate the 'best' form of government, but restricted himself to the *diversae politiae* which might prevail according to climatic, geographical and other physical elements. Property within this framework was no longer an issue of grace.[59] It was restored to its original natural habitat: it was a natural human right to acquire property. What the citizens had thus acquired by their own human labour, effort and industry, they could freely dispose of. Property (as so much else) was fetched down from its heavenly environs to this world: it was a purely mundane issue.[60]

Very similar observations can be made about John's contemporary, Pierre Dubois, who sharply advanced the theme of bipolarity and to all intents and purposes constructed, on the natural-human level, the thesis of national and territorial sovereignty, and advocated the secularization of Church property. The clerics' vocation was not to deal with purely human concerns, but to care for the supranatural well-being where property was irrelevant. Therefore, with the help of the Roman law and the realization of the late Roman emperor's monarchic powers, he proclaimed the true sovereignty of the king by ascribing to him full powers to legislate on all matters, including sacred ones, in the cause of the defence of the faith. 'Did not Moses deal with sacred matters when he gave the laws?' is one of his characteristically brilliant thrusts. Legislative omnipotence was, he claimed, in the interest of the *utilitas communis* which was earth-bound, secular and mundane.[61]

Although setting out from similar premises, Marsilius of Padua made *humanitas* the corner-stone of his theory. Basing himself exclusively on the concept of the citizen and hence also on the concept of the state as the *universitas* or the *congregatio civium* (the contradistinction to the *congregatio fidelium* at once springs to mind and clarifies the advance that has been made), he cannot attribute any enforceable character to a rule or law which is not of exclusively human origin. The 'legislator *humanus*' (where the accent decidedly lies on the *humanus*) is the sole source of the law. Further, it is the consent of the citizens – and not the faith of the subjects – which is the material element of the law, hence the invocation of the Roman law principle 'what touches all must be approved by all'. The state is not merely the citizen writ large, but above all humanity in an abstract legal sense. All this, as can easily be seen, was the effect of human rebirth or renaissance which had taken place in this phase of the 'proto-renaissance'. The necessary sequel was the decisive postulate of the bipolarity in regard to the individual's end: a mundane, human as well a transmundane, a-human end. The human legislator had full control over all citizens, including the clergy. The process initiated in the first phase of the Renaissance – the secularization of government – found its culmination here.[62] That the book was soon translated into the Florentine vernacular can hardly cause much surprise,[63] and is indeed persuasive evidence for the thesis that 'political humanism' was the hallmark of the 'proto-renaissance'. And in view of the need for *politizare* stressed by Marsilius and others, it is clear that public discussion rapidly advanced – especially in the vernacular[64] – and propaganda now came fully into its own. Political humanism was the most direct sequel to the rebirth of the citizen whose full potentiality was powerfully advocated and propounded by Marsilius. Participation in the creation of the law and in government was clearly the end to be aimed at.

These specimens make abundantly clear the readiness of the soil for the application of humanist theses in the field where they mattered on the one hand, and on the other the deep inroads which this very application made upon political reality. The inherent force in the maxim (based on Roman law) that the king in his kingdom was an emperor, that is, had the same autonomous position which the late Roman emperor had in relation to legislative powers, came now to be fully recognized,[65] and the significance of this is only heightened by the concomitant emergence of the national territorial state as a natural autonomous entity. It stood in stark contrast to the ecclesiological, universal unit. The acknowledgement of the *natio* – commonly etymologically explained by a reference to *nasci* – presupposed that ethnic, linguistic, geographical or other physical features were given their due, precisely what was denied to them within the universal ecclesiological framework. This, in conjunction with the notion of the state, ostensibly led to the perforation, disintegration, fragmentation of what was once one undivided whole. This dismemberment acted as a contributory cause, and as an effect, which further stimulated humanist pursuits in the correctly understood sense. Ordinary humanity at all relevant times used the vernacular as its medium of communication and not the artificial, stilted Latin of the learned circles, and it was the vernacular literature that now began to grow mightily in quantity and quality in all parts of Europe. Additionally, the fourteenth century was also the time when the actual situation fostered political humanism. There was the Avignon Papacy followed by a disastrous schism; there was the Hundred Years War between England and France; there was civil war with consequent restlessness and disorder in Germany; there were the first signs of workers' rebellions in the Flemish woollen industries and among the peasants in England, not to mention the unrest among the labourers themselves; there was the great natural science revolution which as the fourteenth century advanced occasioned earnest questionings and raised doubts where previously there had been the certainty of faith; there were national universities gradually ousting the established seats of learning and bringing in their train a new picture of the world. In short, the traditional world order seemed to dissolve and the traditonal landmarks to disappear.

Sensitive contemporary minds clearly perceived this development and assessed its probable effects accurately before it gathered momentum. Perceptive thinkers rebelled against the threatening tide of humanism and reacted, literally speaking, against it, precisely at the level at which humanism had shown itself to be particularly dynamic and dominant – at the political level. Pope Boniface VIII's *Unam sanctam* was aimed at arresting precisely this disintegration. Operating as he did with the traditional baptismal rebirth idea, the decree invoked all the ecclesiological universalist ideas which had served their purpose

[57]

so well in the preceding ages: it was a clarion call to uphold the principle of universality, unipolarity and totality by the rigid application of the descending theme of government and law.[66] Dante pursued exactly the same purpose in his *Monarchia*, only with different means. He too perceived the disintegrating effects which the national state was to produce, and therefore passionately advocated the re-establishment of a world order on a universal scale for which the ancient Roman empire was to be a model. His plea was for the utilization of the experience and the history of Rome. This ancient empire was a unit that had worked well and was, indeed, providentially chosen as the entity within which Christ was born and to which he had brought peace. It was the unregenerated Roman empire and its monarchy – not the one which had existed since the ninth century and had applied the idea of baptismal rebirth on a global scale – which should serve as a pattern for the 'genus *humanum*, for the 'civilitas *humana*' and for the 'universitas *hominum*'. It was to be the *exemplum* from which contemporaries could and should draw inspiration (and not one which should be imitated). This ancient empire merely preportrayed the universal state postulated by Dante.[67]

In his opposition to the disintegration effected by the application of humanist principles, Giles of Rome made baptismal rebirth the kernel of his doctrine (a somewhat remarkable turn to be taken by an author who had proved himself a thorough-going Aristotelian). Possibly it was precisely his familiarity with Aristotelian Thomism which made him realize the consequences of this point of view better than some of his contemporaries. It is therefore most significant that in his tract[68] Giles carefully avoided the very pillars of the new humanist cosmology, that is, the concepts of the state, citizen and politics, and stressed instead the crucial role of baptismal rebirth for governmental purposes and all matters in the public field. Hence it was axiomatic to him that only baptismally regenerated men might own property, govern, and hold public offices, because all these were issues of divine grace, the very core of baptismal rebirth. The significance of this standpoint is that although at his time there were in any case only baptismally regenerated men, nevertheless according to the humanist thesis no baptismal rebirth at all was necessary to govern or to own property, etc. Understandably he put the emphasis on unipolarity since within his system there was no room for different ends and aims, no room for citizenship, or an autonomous and independent state. This polemical literature of the early fourteenth century is persuasive evidence of the very character of the initial phase of humanism: it was politically motivated and had nothing to do with the classicizing kind of humanism which took its place later in the fifteenth century. Indeed, the opponents of a new scheme sometimes highlight its essence much better than its own advocates, because they apprehend the implications more directly than men of later generations with whom the effects of the immediate impact had largely worn off. A good example of the turn of the fourteenth and fifteenth centuries is the fiery, anti-humanist Cardinal Johannes Dominici: he had no quarrel whatsoever with the 'revival of the classics', or the imitation of classical writings, or aestheticism and the like, but concentrated his fire on the real issues of humanism, that is, its secular-mundane-human aspects which involved an entire re-orientation and intellectual revolution, with far-reaching consequences in the social and political fields.[69] Here too there is a passionate advocacy of the cherished and time-honoured principles of totality, unipolarity and universality.

Since citizenship as a social and political concept was new, the search for a better understanding of the citizen's function and status continued apace and came to be grouped under the heading of the *studia humanitatis*. They and the *studia divinitatis* were complementary to each other – not exclusive – and focused attention on different sets of norms which corresponded to the manner of living. The *vita activa* and *contemplativa* expressed the same thing seen from a different angle. Once more this was no new nomenclature but had a very distinguished ancestry.[70] These concepts were previously meaningful within the ecclesiological context and were orientated by the exclusively religious set of norms. Now, however, each assumed a function of its own, and each had its own set of values. The *vita activa* and *contemplativa* fitted the principle of bipolarity perfectly, whereas in the earlier dispensation they were both firmly embedded in the ecclesiological frame-work of unipolarity. For the *vita contemplativa* there had been a superabundance of precepts and exhortations in the writings of medieval authors, but for the *vita activa* (of the citizen) there was a very real dearth of models. The search, or rather the study of these, became not merely a fashion, but was in fact a necessity, because the *vita activa* extended from the political field to the totality of the mundane-human way of living and conducting oneself: it was to be its own fulfilment and did not merely constitute a *vita transitoria*.[71] Hence the significance of the *exempla* of antiquity which prompted, not imitation, but creative assimilation, accommodation and adjustment to conditions in the fourteenth century. This is exactly why (as we have seen) John of Paris spoke of the *tota vita* of the citizen that mattered politically, and we shall presently see that this totality thesis made a very triumphant

[59]

re-entry in later Renaissance thought.

It stands to reason that within this context history was bound to assume a major role. It was the history of Rome (especially as epitomized in Livy) and of Antiquity in general which ranked highest.[72] Salutati expressed this perfectly when he adduced the *scientia rerum gestarum* as an essential instrument which was capable of teaching – hence the constant stress on *instruere et docere* – and this in turn explains the popularity enjoyed by Cicero and Seneca.[73] Understanding of *humanitas* was increased by the study of history, because politics was *humanitas* activated in a civic sense. This explains the preponderance of active 'politicians', jurists, chancellors, etc. in the initial phases of humanism, such as is instanced by Salutati, Bruni, Conversino, Vergerio, Palmieri and a host of others. The *studia humanitatis* embraced the whole spectrum of man's, and therefore the citizen's, activity and referred to natural and autonomous norms which did not stand, as in an earlier age, in relation to religious ends.[74] The point to be stressed is that the *exempla* invoked and studied were only the means to an end and not an end in themselves. The *studia humanitatis* were to demonstrate the quality of living that was called *bene vivere* (this was not understood in any hedonistic or materialistic sense, or as bourgeois epicurianism) in the pursuit of the *vita activa* or *civilis*.[75] The *studia humanitatis* came to be subsumed under the heading of 'education in the service of the citizen', and this concept of the *bene vivere* later culminated in Machiavelli's *civile vivere*.[76]

The *studia humanitatis* came to change their function in time and there were good reasons why the study of the *exempla* became an end in itself. The *studia humanitatis* came to assume the function with which they have been commonly credited. A very large part of the explanation lies in specialization. The study of the *exempla* had so far been an auxiliary science, but as with many auxiliary sciences, it began to dissociate itself from its original purpose and become detached from its original point of reference. Finally it assumed a standing of its own with corresponding premises, criteria and norms: what had been merely relative, because it was useful to the citizen's education and to politics, became now a science of its own. The *studia* became, as time went on, less and less associated with the state, with the citizen or with politics. Specialization of disciplines had set in, and these were related to purely literary, cultural, aesthetic and similar pursuits. Since the original point of reference – politics – was left behind, Renaissance humanism began to burgeon forth in all its multiformity. This was a process not at all unfamiliar in the Middle Ages. In the eleventh and twelfth centuries, for example, there was no separation of the various branches which constituted theology, but as a result of deeper penetration into its matrix and the greater availability of sources, the various parts of theology – the *communauté des matières* – assumed a status of their own: canonistics, liturgy, philosophy, theology in the narrow sense, and so on, became specific branches of scholarship, and even they in their turn produced specialized offspring such as procedural, matrimonial, criminal studies in law, or moral, pastoral, fundamental theology, soteriology, and so on. Indeed, the same development occurred when in the fourteenth century jurisprudence and politics parted company.[77]

The depth of interest and the intensity which the *studia humanitatis* evoked and the insights which they supplied, evidently sharpened the literary sense and made scholarly productions of antecedent ages now seem barren and 'illiterate' and appear to bear witness to a 'barbarous age'.[78] Indeed, medieval Latin left a great deal to be desired when compared with its classical parent. The heightened literary sense began to develop its own norms, began to point to the inadequacy of current Latin compositions and postulated a purification of the language (as well as an imitation of classical Latin). But since such authors as Cicero were purveyors of Greek thought, the need arose to translate Greek into Latin – hence the frequency of Greek works in Latin guise from the fourteenth and fifteenth centuries onwards.[79] It was still the early humanists who were the pacemakers – Salutati or Bruni at once spring to mind.[80] Chairs were founded to study Greek, and Greek scholars such as Chrysoloras gathered eminent men around themselves who were to be instructed in the Greek idiom. There was obviously a mutual benefit to both Latin and Greek since translations promote the sense of language, syntax, structure, and so on. By detaching themselves from their original function, the *studia humanitatis* were concerned primarily with linguistic, aesthetic and educational problems and the relevant models. Obviously, the pursuit of the correct Latin style and structure was a highly specialized task and demanded intense concentration and focus, so much so that the original purpose of consulting the ancients faded into the background and eventually into oblivion.[81]

It is worthwhile saying in the present context that these humanist efforts – characterizing as they did the third and final phase of the development of the Renaissance and its humanist segment – were the prerogatives of an élite of scholars and were far removed from the broader strata of society. The Latin which they cultivated had little bearing on everyday life, in fact, in view of the growth of literacy as a result of newly founded schools, colleges and universities and other educational establishments, the impact of Latin – purified or unpurified – was of no consequence and was in relative terms less than it had been in previous ages. Furthermore, learned books, *Summae* and glosses, quite apart from official documents, differed no whit from their predecessors as far as language and presentation were concerned. While this observation is generally true, it has special relevance to those scholars who were declared followers of the new kind of humanism, and yet in their own professional works and pursuits their language, exposition and tenor were wholly indistinguishable from their predecessors. For instance, Franciscus de Accoltis, one of the famous jurists of the mid-fifteenth century, professor at Bologna, Siena and Florence, was a very typical humanist in philological matters and yet his juristic commentaries on the *Digestum vetus* and the *Codex* betray not a shred of any kind of philological expertise and linguistic refinement. The same can be said about Marianus Socinus who taught at Siena university.[82] On the other hand, what had begun, almost imperceptibly in the fourteenth century, flowered in the fifteenth: vernacular literature flooded even the hitherto 'privileged' precincts. Religious tracts for instructional uses were written in the vernacular and this was quite apart from catechisms written in the Volgare, and translations of the Bible, as well as the ubiquitous passion plays, in all European regions. None of these 'popular' literary works shows any sign of what is held to be unadulterated humanism.

There is a cluster of problems intimately associated with the Renaissance which deserves a few remarks in the present context. No doubt is permissible about the dependence of Renaissance humanism, in its initial phases, on Aristotle, with a corresponding decline of Platonic influence. In several respects one could say that the 'proto-renaissance' was Aristotelian-inspired and stood in sharp contrast to the traditional medieval outlook,[83] itself the application of Plato's framework which was characterized by unipolarity, totality and universality, whereas atomization was germane to Aristotle's way of thinking. Hence the early Renaissance scholars, that is, the humanists, were decidedly inclined towards republicanism (in contradistinction to the prevalent medieval form of monarchic government). Virtually all the noted chancellors of Florence in the last decades of the fourteenth and the early decades of the fifteenth centuries presented the republican theme with varying degrees of emphasis.[84] The theoreticians of the state were republicans (though this republicanism is by no means identical with democracy) in the sense that all citizens had the same status and function or rights in regard to participation in the government of the republic. Yet the observer cannot disregard the development in the later decades of the fifteenth century, when more and more theoreticians became averse to the republican form of government and began to direct their gaze towards its monarchic counterpart. What is certainly also noteworthy is that Plato's star began to rise again, so much so that his philosophy – in the Academy at Florence represented by Marsilio Ficino and the *Theologia Platonica* – became dominant once more, with the consequence that Aristotle was not only relegated to the background, but in actual fact became a symbol of the medieval barbarous scholasticism, tainted as it was with the worst intellectual excesses: Aristotle became the target of attack.[85] To make the picture complete, simultaneously there developed in Italy the city tyrannies – instanced in Florence by the Medici, in Rimini by the Malatesta, in Ferrara by the de Este, in Urbino by the Montefeltre, and so on and so forth. In the language of the theory of the state, this was monarchic absolutism in contrast to the earlier republicanism. At the end of the road stood Niccolò Machiavelli.

Here I can only indicate the signposts of this development. Two writers of the later fifteenth century should be singled out: Francesco Patrizi and Giovanni Pontano. Indeed both these authors would once more show that the original core of the Renaissance was political. Both can serve as classic instances that the law was the vehicle of government and was even then still considered the articulate and dynamic kernel of the Renaissance movement. Both also show the rising tide of Platonism and the diminution of Aristotelian influence. Let us begin with Patrizi who in course of time was to become professor of Platonic philosophy.[86] His earlier work, *De institutione reipublicae*, seeks to demonstrate that the state – his *societas civilis* – was man's work introduced for the sake of (common) utility by nature (*duce naturae* is a rather significant term) since man was far more of a *sociale animal* than were bees, ants, cranes and suchlike species.[87] The beginning of the state lay in the family which was the *seminarium civitatum*.[88] Although Patrizi does hold that the monarchic form of government was the most ancient as well as the most natural form, as evidenced by the bees,[89] he nevertheless is unambiguous in his view that the very idea of citizen postulates participation in government.[90] In a 'people's state' – the *popularis respublica*[91] – law-creative power and the power to appoint public servants rested with the multitude of citizens. This was then a state in which ἰσονομία, that is, 'an equality of right, as it were holds sway' so that 'all things are to be administered rightfully amongst all'.[92] Here also the definition of Florentinus, the classical jurist, came to full fruition,[93] hence he considered that the best

[63]

form of government in the state was republican 'which is mixed together from all kinds of men'.[94] Only in a republic does law alone hold sway and therefore bring about equality of citizens and stability of the social order.[95] And he adduced another great Roman jurist, Pomponius, who called the law a mutual compact in the state.[96]

Whereas the *De institutione* cannot claim much originality, his later work, *De regno et regis institutione*, ostensibly designed to supplement the earlier tract, deserves some consideration because it shows a remarkable gravitation towards the monarchic or élitist form of government and, in contradistinction to the earlier work, frequently invokes Plato, whom he called *divinus praeceptor* or *philosophorum summus*.[97] Here he is outspokenly against any identification of the *plebs* with the *populus*: only citizens are members of the latter.[98] To him a kingdom was a *paternum imperium* and here too he considered the family as the basic structure, seeing in it the model for a paternalistic form of government in the shape of monarchy. The government's chief task is the promotion of the *utilitas communis*[99] which can efficiently be procured only by one ruler whom he designates *pastor omnium*. He becomes the custodian of what is good within the state,[100] and is significantly enough called *quasi animatum ius* which no doubt re-echoes the *lex animata*.[101] The further the book proceeds, the more enthusiastic its author becomes for the monarchic theme. For him there is nothing more natural than monarchic rule – *naturale imperium unius regis* – a rule which also reflects the monotheistic theme within mundane environs.[102] The king has care of all the subjects' interests with a paternal circumspection. The very concept of equality, which he had praised in his former work, now fills him with disgust, because it involves counting by numbers and thus gives preference to quantity at the expense of quality, which means that there is no difference in the vote between the most dimwitted peasant and the most illustrious, intelligent man. This, he exclaims, is not equality, but rather inequality: 'in which [equality] there is no greater inequality than what seems to be equality itself'.[103] The monarch, on the other hand, exercises unbiased judgement[104] and is immune to corruption, because he already has everything he needs (a veritable Dantesque argument, though Patrizi was probably unaware of it). His monarch is advised to model himself on the Roman laws which breathe wisdom and have been the patterns for the world for so many centuries.[105] Monarchic rule presupposes stern obedience to the law which, according to Plato, he claims, is also imposed by nature. Disobedience is *maximum crimen* because it perverts *rerum ordinem*.[106] One might well detect a note of cynicism when he asserts that it is much easier to rule those who find themselves in adverse circumstances than those whom good fortune has exalted.

These views of Patrizi need no comment. What does deserve an observation is the total absence of any contemporary reference and the virtual neglect of any religious or ecclesiastical theme within his political conceptions, as set forth in this work. Very occasionally he does refer to religious ceremonies but then only because they promote the cult of divine majesty and teach us *pie et sancte vivere*[107] so that we may attain *plenam felicitatem perpetuam sempiternamque*. This may possibly approximate a purely ritualistic standpoint which does not attach great weight to substance and contents of religious norms. In this work ritual precepts seem to have become means to an end and as such had the function to habituate man to certain thought-processes and consequent actions.

Not only a revival of Platonism in the strict meaning of the term, but above all a 'renaissance' or rejuvenation of the totality point of view – the very theme which was cast off in the immediately preceding period – and its accompaniment, the unipolarity thesis, are some of the characteristics of Pontano's work: with him the sole and supreme criterion of public action is the good of the state. Old themes reappear in a different garb. He based himself fairly and squarely on the concept of nature which in his thought was quite unsophisticated. The concept simply referred to the physical order, such as 'the movements of heaven and the starts, what is the order of things, and what their measure',[108] for by acquiring knowledge of the physical world we acquire knowledge of matters 'which have lain hidden and unknown to all ages before us'.[109] Although the natural laws which prevail in the physical world are common to man and beast, the enquiry should mainly concern itself with the discovery of what nature itself prescribes:

> Now there are, amongst those things which are governed by the laws of nature, certain things common to men and animals: as, the desire for offspring, the search for food, the avoidance of storms and heat. But one must estimate, not what or how much man has in common with animals, but what it is which nature herself prescribes.[110]

It certainly is a remarkable step forward when on this foundation Pontano axiomatically states that by virtue of (carnal) birth there exists an inborn duty to live together and preserve society itself. This duty includes above all observance of, and obedience to, the laws. The postulate of a stern obedience to the law is in its results identical with the former (ecclesiologically based) conception, though the grounds of this postulate are wholly different: 'Justice is to be preserved and the

[65]

laws obeyed, so that, since we are born to associate in numbers and to behave socially, we may fulfil our task.'[111]

Pontano's aversion from any kind of republican government and his advocacy of monarchy can hardly cause much surprise. In demonstrating this he employs the kind of anthropomorphic metaphor which St Paul had set forth in a different context. The state, according to Pontano, consists of many parts, but not all parts are equally suitable for governing: 'A state is nothing other than an association of men gathered together according to law: some are born to obey, others – because they are superior in intellect and excellence – to rule.' This is an ingenious amalgamation of Ciceronian and Aristotelian arguments. Bakers, sausage-makers and cooks 'and the sort of men who are occupied in sordid employments and whose minds are those of slaves' should, according to Aristotle, be classed as slaves, and had no right to participate in government, for the simple reason that they were not fit to do so.[112] He nevertheless faces up to the problem of reconciling liberty with the demand for obedience to the ruler's laws – one is almost tempted to see in the heading of the relevant chapter a precursor of Rousseau: 'whether, since man is born free, he ought to obey a master?'[113] He replies that liberty does not mean licence to do and not to do what one likes – 'this is not only not liberty, but something utterly the opposite of liberty'[114] – and in obeying the law a postulate of nature comes to fruition. The more we obey kings and public servants the greater our freedom will be: 'It is abundantly proved that though we are born free, still we must obey kings and magistrates: and we are then most free when we are most obedient to them'.[115] He insists (and this is the gist of his doctrine) on obedience not to 'superior authority' but rather to the laws which emanate from it. Law to him is the vehicle of government and this is, *au fond*, the reason why obedience to it can be unquestionably demanded.

Pontano believes that the monarchic form of government can be observed in the natural world and demonstrated by rational argument. He calls nature '*optimam* prudentissimamque artificem'.[116] Hence it is '*naturalissimum*' that a king as monarch governs. This is so in the cosmos where God is alone and sits in judgement, he the governor and director of all. The animal world proves this too beyond a shadow of doubt, and once more the bee symbol is adduced to show that there is but one governor in a well-ordered community.[117] All mute animals and beasts have according to nature their leaders.[118] But in addition to this there are rational arguments that men act 'for the sake of some good' – '*boni alicuius gratia*' – and the greatest good is the state 'by whose grace indeed all men do all things'. Nevertheless, in order to achieve this highest good, a *'dux'* is necessary to indicate the way, and for Pontano reason provides this leadership.[119] The monarch or *'dux'* is simply personified reason. In a roundabout way the ancient allegory of soul and body reappears: 'as the mind gives orders in man, as the head of the family gives orders in the household'; hence in a community, such as the state, it is the monarch who directs the path.[120] His ruler is self-sufficient – again shades of Dante – and therefore cannot have any motives for aggrandizement. This is in fact Pontano's main deduction from historical observations, for, according to him, when there is a plurality of rulers, the result is often tyranny, 'as amongst the Corinthians, the Miletians and the Athenians'[121] who initially had kings, 'as Cicero relates'. And when there are several who govern, the states 'suffer almost continually from revolutions'. To him, consequently, it is clear that the well-being of the state and its preservation, the safety of its subjects and the maintenance of order and peace is better taken care of by one rather than many.[122] The king is *pater patriae*[123] in whose hands the security of the state lies, for it is his will that makes law: he is the speaking law because his decision embodies the will of the master.[124]

The sternly monarchic point of view emboldens Pontano to advance some theses which certainly foreshadow, if not anticipate, some of Machiavelli's arguments. It is Pontano's recurring theme that by executing the leader's orders the liberty of the fatherland is best protected. The monarch must be free in the exercise of his will, with the implication that the supreme principle guiding his government and law must be the common interest. If the common interest conflicts with probity, Pontano suggests that, in the interest of public utility and public well-being, probity may be sacrificed to the latter: priority belongs to public welfare. 'In such a case, considerations of utility might be so powerful that an honourable man would prefer to avoid the issue, but without regret and without serious reproach.'[125] Clearly the formula provided is flexible. This is the application of the *raison d'état* within the Renaissance thought-pattern. Furthermore, he protests that deceit and falsehood are *'duo turpissima vitia'*, but he nevertheless declares that in the interests of king and kingdom truth may well become the victim if time and circumstances so demand: 'But although truth must always be observed, nevertheless events and time might occasionally press so strongly that it should be kept in complete silence.'[126] This is especially the case in time of war when the safety of king and country are at stake. It is common prudence, he holds, that in such conditions the ruler does not immediately appear to be lying, since this is the action of a wise man, one who weighs utility and necessity against truth and falsehood.[127] The government must always consider what the result of its actions will be. In all its simplicity the teleological principle is expressed thus: 'to be referred to their purpose', which he exemplifies by killing, which is prohibited yet is allowed and indeed prescribed by law 'that crimes shall be punished and good men shall be secure in the state'.[128] The end justifies the means, or seen from a different angle, one might be tempted to say that 'reason of state' or the *salus publica* as the *suprema lex* has made its triumphant entry into the world of political axioms. Nevertheless, in some ways this entry may well appear as the re-establishment or reincarnation of familiar medieval theses and principles.[129]

Since the custodians of the laws are the public servants – the *magistratus* – they can demand obedience from the subjects in the interest of the state. Pontano says that they are to be wondrously honoured by the citizens because they bear *maiestatem*. Indeed, they are '*publici patres*' for they perform the tasks of the state.[130] It is not difficult to see that in this way the well-tried hierarchical principle of medieval parentage reappears in a different context but with identical meaning. It prevails between various grades of public officers and between them and the subjects, for, he declares, it is necessary that some should be greater, others lesser, but above all of them there is one chief and most powerful magistrate whom the rest obey.[131] From this standpoint the resurrection of the descending theme of government and law follows logically. As bearers of public power, public office holders have power of life and death: 'Who shall doubt that they are to be honoured more than fathers? For they are considered sacrosanct and have the power of decision between life and death.'[132] Pontano believes that only by implementing these principles can public tranquillity and liberty be guaranteed.

It is no exaggeration to maintain that, by propounding this system, the monothematic thought-pattern which characterized pre-Renaissance thinking experienced a veritable restoration within a purely mundane orbit. What mattered previously was eternal bliss and salvation of which the Church was the chief medium and custodian, but after a period of transitional coexistence in which bipolarity was advocated, the wheel had come full circle: monothematic unipolarity and totality had returned, though the reference was not to eternal bliss, but to the *salus patriae vel regni*. Is it really surprising that no lesser man than Marsilio Ficino translated Dante's *Monarchia* for the benefit of some Florentine citizens? And no surprise can be caused by Ficino's making Dante drink from Plato.[133] What is certainly remarkable is that Dante underwent, so to speak, a change of personality and identity. The editor of his *Monarchia* in the sixteenth century assures his readers that its author should not be confused with 'that celebrated old Italian poet', because he was a wholly different man, 'a philosopher, a very acute and learned man, once a good friend of Angelo Poliziano'.[134] A schizophrenic transmutation was to make Dante palatable for the new outlook.

As Pontano abundantly shows, what mattered from the late fifteenth century onwards was the political principle pure and simple: it dominated thought as well as action. Indeed one can here speak of a politocentrism which was the hallmark of Niccolò Machiavelli, as has most recently been shown.[135] That politocentrism may possibly be one of the reasons why the origin of the state and of governmental powers evokes little interest in Pontano. Here too he moves in very good company. In his magisterial way Eugenio Garin has commented on Pontano's *De Principe* which 'already manifests concepts and impulses to which Machiavelli was to give unparalleled rigour'.[136]

What was common to the pre-Renaissance and the Renaissance was a very marked gravitation towards authority which was epitomized in the demand for obedience. That, indeed, seems to me a possible explanation for the eclipse which Aristotle suffered and for the popularity which Plato enjoyed. It may also explain why republicanism degenerated so easily into petty tyrannies as the earlier Aristotle was replaced by Plato's wholeness standpoint with a concomitant aversion to republicanism. The development of Renaissance thinking in the fifteenth century presents a situation which is not without its inherent contradictions, and yet harbours the germs of dialectical evolution. After a detour, thinkers and writers arrived at the same monarchic point of view which the high Middle Ages had advocated. Pontano is a particularly persuasive instance of using classical examples as pattens for the revived Platonic totality thesis, with its corollary of unipolarity. As a matter of fact, the situation in the ecclesiastical field was not at all dissimilar to that in the political sphere. The early decades of the fifteenth century reverberated with the enthusiastic application of a full and sonorous conciliarism, that is, the application of the ascending theme of government and law as well as the Aristotelian *epieikeia*, with the consequence that the subordination of the Pope to the general council became an axiom. But within a few decades the monarchic system of the Papacy was fully restored, and of the conciliarists barely a handful battled on, only to be totally submerged by the monarchic tide in the second half of the fifteenth century. What might well be considered a paradoxical accompaniment of Renaissance thought (and practice) was the rapidity and fierceness of the Inquistion which raged with unabated fury within exactly the same chronological

[69]

framework.[137] Casting our glance further afield, did not the Platonic upsurge in fifteenth-century Oxford under John Colet, who was thoroughly familiar with Marsilio Ficino's theses (and who in fact had made abstracts of Ps. Denys and incorporated them in his own works) and in the sixteenth century the influential and active Cambridge Platonists[138] fit into the same scheme of things? And are not the Utopian idealists of the subsequent generation – Thomas More, Francis Bacon, James Harrington, to mention just a few of the English Renaissance – rather characteristic exponents of maxims inspired by Plato?[139]

There is indeed urgent need to clarify the mutual connection between these various manifestations. The question which the enquirer has to face is, was the revival of Platonism conditioned by the actuality of the situation, or was the relationship the other way round, or was there no connection? Are there no intellectual links between the Henrician system of government in England and the contemporary Platonist developments? Another cluster of problems concerns the Roman law itself. Had it not itself provided a double front? For on the one hand there was the *lex regia* according to which the monarch derived his power from the Roman people, and on the other hand there was in the same body the stern monarchic descending theme of government. In this context the very concept of law in the sense of *ius, diritto, droit* and *Recht* would seem to require some attention, because humanist jurisprudence assuredly came to develop a concept of law that differed in material respects from that which was commonly held in the antecedent period. Further problems of the Renaissance obtrude themselves. It has long been recognized that in the preceding age the individual, subjective personality was overshadowed by the objective norm, hence the exuberance of typological productions in the arts, literature and historiography. From the late fourteenth century onwards this objective cosmology began to give way to a subjective assessment of, and a correspondingly heightened attention to, the individual personality, with the consequence that the idea of law itself – a most conspicuous symptom of the objectivist standpoint – came to lose a great deal of its dominating position and was eventually replaced by the individuality of man. It was the *persona* who now became the central figure (one is tempted to speak here of a personality-centred outlook) which in its turn substantially affected the historical process and historiography itself: the law came to be relegated to a secondary, if not tertiary, place in the hierarchy of social values. In proximity to the rising tide of vernacular literature stood the contemporaneous development in music. Music certainly began to be a medium of expression and convey sentiments and emotions which had hitherto found little outlet. The analysis of the relationship between the vernacular and music is indeed an urgent task within the framework of the problem, scope and extent of the Renaissance.

Special significance attaches itself to the problem of how far the expansion of educational facilities in the fourteenth and fifteenth centuries – one has but to think of the numerous new academic foundations, newly established schools, etc. – and pedagogy in general reflected the Renaissance movement. To be specific, how far did pedagogic and educational measures exercise a vertical and horizontal influence (if by the former is understood the progressive gradual schooling of larger sections of the population by the provision of greater educational facilities, notably at the grass roots of society, and if the latter referred to the extension in regional respects to embrace countries and cities)? Were the quite astonishing educational advances possibly facilitated by the vernacular, and did medieval élitism act as a challenge because it made educational attainments a virtual monopoly of the clergy? Another cluster of problems concerns the explanation of the poor response in fifteenth-century England to the newly released forces.[140] Since humanism seized the whole spectrum of man's *humanitas* and therefore comprehended the totality of human life in all its various manifestations, segments, expressions and aims, the need for an integrative approach to the solution of these manifold problems seems self-evident. Government, society and its members, the individuals, must be seen in the totality of their interrelations, and not in their atomized, sectional and isolated aspects. Human society as such provides the meaning and function of, as well as the place for, man's humanity. But while these questions concern the final phase of the Renaissance, similarly crucial problems confront the enquirer in its initial phases, and here it is the indisputably genetic link with the ecclesiological substratum of the Middle Ages which stands in the forefront, and this is what I have attempted to elucidate in this modest contribution. For, on the present occasion, to invite attention to these specific problems of the Renaissance is a duty of all researchers who wish to honour the jubiland, to whom they are profoundly grateful for the numerous, immeasurably illuminating insights with which he has supplied them in his works over the years.

[71]

NOTES

1 None has more convincingly pointed to this feature than Garin himself in his fundamental *Medioevo e rinascimento: Studi e ricerche* (Bari–Rome, 1954; new edn, 1973).

2 Cf. for instance Ambrosiaster (ed.), *Corpus scriptorum ecclesiasticorum latinorum (CSEL)*, 82.236. Before baptism there was *homo tantum*; for the *renovatio*, see p. 104: the Christian 'walks in a new way of life'; *Quaestiones veteris et novi testamenti*, ibid., 50.298, cap. 113: the reborn enters a '*novellus populus*'; and cap. 127, p. 408: 'For to be born again is to be renewed, and he who is renewed is made again' ('*renasci enim renovari est et qui renovatur instauratur*'). Further, Augustine in his *Sermo* 121, in J.P. Migne, *Patrologia Latina (PL)*, 38.679ff.; id., *Expositio in Epistolam ad Romanos*, ed. in *CSEL*, 84.174, lines 12ff. ('*renovatio in baptismo est*'); also his *De baptismo*, ed. ibid., 51.194 and 255ff.; *De Genesi ad literam*, ed. ibid., 28.197ff. stressing that '*renovabimur etiam in carne*'. See also Hilary of Poitiers, ibid., 65.119, line 15 and p. 201, line 15; further Pope Gelasius I in *Avellana*, ed. ibid., 35.419, line 7 and p. 426, line 13, also p. 425, line 8: the Arator, who was most widely read in the Middle Ages, ed. in *CSEL*, 72.142, lines 1147ff. For Pseudo-Isidore see Ps. Melchiades, cap. 6–7, in P. Hinschius, *Decretales Pseudo-Isidorianae* (reprint, Aalen, 1963), 245ff.

3 Augustine, *Sermo* 121, *PL*, 38.679ff.; 'The first birth is of man and woman, the second birth is of God and the Church' ('*Prima nativitas ex masculo et femina, secunda nativitas ex Deo et ecclesia*').

4 St Paul, I Cor. 2:14ff.; II Cor. 5:17; Gal. 6:15; Ephes. 4:23; Col. 4:10; St John 3:4–6; for some patristic views see n. 2 above.

5 Ephes. 2:15; 4:24. See also Tit. 3:5; I Pet. 2:3.

6 Rom. 6:4

7 For literature cf. W. Ullmann, *Medieval Foundations of Renaissance Humanism* (London, 1977), 14 n. 1.

8 In a wider sense this substitution of the instinctive propensities and forces by rationally conceived norms signifies the emancipation of natural man from his purely animal instincts and reflects a highly sophisticated thought, in itself the sign of an advanced cultural standard. The emancipation refers to the individual's liberalization from mystical 'dark' uncontrollable powers by his subjection to rules and norms which emanate from a rational plan. It is, in other words, the replacement of the natural purely instinctive urges by intellectually comprehensible measures. Baptismal rebirth is, within a religiously understood society, the dominance of the intellect and ratio in the place of mere natural instinct, inclination, insight, proclivity or evaluation. And, after all, all cultural measures and efforts have this aim.

9 Rom. 13:1ff. For the descending (and ascending) themes of government and law, cf. W. Ullmann, *Principles of Government and Politics in the Middle Ages*, 4th edn (London, 1978), 19ff. The theme of incorporation is very frequently stressed, cf. for example at the height of the Carolingian renaissance the third council of Valence, anno 855, cap. 5, J.D. Mansi (ed.), *Conciliorum collectio*, 15 (Venice, 1770), cols 5–6: 'We believe that

we must assent most strongly to this, that the whole host of the faithful shall be regenerated by water and the holy spirit, and by this truly embodied in the Church . . . a true regeneration' ('*Firmissime credimus tenendum, quod omnis multitude fidelium ex aqua et spiritu sancto regenerata ac per hoc veraciter ecclesiae incorporata . . . vera regeneratio*'), so that by persevering in the faith the Christian comes 'to the fulness of salvation and to the receiving of eternal bliss' ('*ad plenitudinem salutis et ad perceptionem aeternae beatitudinis*'). From the high Middle Ages, Alanus ab Insulis may be cited as an example: *Liber de planctu naturae*, in *PL*, 210.431ff., at col. 445D where the problem is dealt with in the context of grace and nature. Nature says: 'Man is born by my action, born again by the authority of God . . . by me man is given life to die, by Him he is brought again to life . . . I do not know the nature of this (second) birth' ('*Homo mea actione nascitur, Dei auctoritate renascitur . . . per me homo procreatur ad mortem, per ipsam recreatur ad vitam . . . ego Natura huius (secundae) nativitatis ignoro naturam*').

10 See especially I Cor. 12:4ff.; Ephes. 1:23; 4:10–11, 16; Rom. 12:4.

11 See I Cor. 7:20: 'Let every man abide in the same calling wherein he was called.'

12 For the medieval neo-Platonism, see especially Tullio Gregory, *Platonismo medievale: Studi e ricerche* (Istituto storico italiano per il Medio Evo, 26–7) (Rome, 1958). Cf. also E. Gilson, *La philosophie du moyen âge des origines patristiques à la fin du XIVe siècle*, 3rd edn (Paris, 1947), 265ff.; Endre v. Ivanka, *Plato christianus* (Einsiedeln, 1965), 309ff. and 476ff. For a wider context cf. also U. Mann, *Das Christentum als absolute Religion* (Darmstadt, 1971), 5ff., 68ff., 202ff.

13 For the three basic themes – totality (wholeness), unipolarity and universality, see the Introduction to my *The Papacy and Political Ideas in the Middle Ages* (London, 1976).

14 This point of view touches on the famous Sohm thesis; see J.N. Bakhuizen van den Brink, 'Ius ecclesiasticum', *Medelingen der koninklijke Nederlandse Akademie van Wetenschappen*, 31 (1968), especially 34ff.

15 *Mon. Germ. Hist. Leges Visigothorum*, i.2.2.: '*Lex est anima totius corporis popularis.*' For the background see W. Ullmann, *Papst und König*, Salzburger Universitätsschriften: Dike, vol. III (1966), 37ff.; id., *Law and Politics in the Middle Ages* (Cambridge, 1975), 47ff.

16 I Cor. 15:10. For the historical background see W. Ullmann, *The Carolingian Renaissance* (London, 1969), 71ff. (for the explicit use of the Pauline phrase by the Burgundian king Boso in the ninth century: '*Ego Boso Dei gratia id quod sum*'). For an example from the twelfth century cf. Henry V: '*Heinricus Dei gratia id quod sum*' (in *Codex Udalrici*, Ph. Jaffé (ed.), *Bibliotheca rerum Germanicarum*, V (reprint, 1965), no. 94, p. 182). The descending theme of government is particularly clearly expressed in the dependence which lower royal officers demonstrated by referring to the king's grace: '*Ego Thomas Brittonus . . . Dei et regia gratia dominator castelli . . .*', F. Nitti Vito (ed.), *Codice diplomatico Barese*, V (Bari, 1902), no. 81, p. 139); further examples ibid., no. 82, p. 141; no. 88, p. 152, etc.

17 For this see L. Mitchell, *Baptismal anointing*, Alcuin Club Publications

no. 48 (London, 1966), 121, 129ff.

18 This is the tutorial function of the ruler (the ruler as *tutor regni*) who has the *tutamentum regni*; cf. Ullmann, *The Carolingian Renaissance*, 122ff., 177ff.

19 See Ullmann, *Principles*, 140ff.

20 Especially clearly expressed in the sword formula: 'so that you may deserve to reign without end with the saviour of the world, whose appearance you bear' (*'quatinus cum mundi salvatore, cuius typum geris, sine fine merearis regnare'*), but also in the consecratory prayer *'Deus, Dei filius . . .'*, in the enthronement prayer, *'Sta et retine . . .'*, and also in *'Prospice'*.

21 This is the deeper meaning of Gregory VII's statement that the lowest exorcist stood on a higher level than an emperor; see his Reg. 8.21, ed. E. Caspar, 555.

22 Cf. Ullmann, *Medieval Foundations*, 34ff.

23 For the social character of the Carolingian renaissance, cf. Ullmann, *The Carolingian Renaissance*, 5ff.

24 The soil had of course been long prepared by the Vulgate which had employed a good many Roman law terms, about which see W. Ullmann, 'The Bible and principles of government in the Middle Ages', *Settimana Spoleto*, 10 (1963), 181–227 (now reprinted in Collected Studies I, *The Church and the Law in the Earlier Middle Ages*, London, 1975, ch.2). Above all it was the Roman *ius publicum* in the shape of Ulpian's definition which was to prove a decisive instrument in the hands of rulers who knew how to manipulate it.

25 Ulpian's formula later gave rise to the terminology of the *Rex in regno est imperator* which signified his full territorial (and national) sovereignty: he functioned in the same way as the late Roman emperor had. For some observations cf. Ullmann, *Medieval Foundations*, 49ff., 119ff., 128.

26 Some details in Ullmann, *Principles*, 283ff.; id., *Individual and Society in the Middle Ages* (London, 1967), 53ff.

27 A good example of an earlier age is Notker of St Gall, reporting on Charlemagne: *'Tunc sanctus ille (scil. papa) divinam constitutionem secutus . . . Karolum Romam venire postulavit'* (Mon. Germ. Hist. Scriptores, II, 743, lines 12ff.).

28 For this type see *Lexikon des Mittelalters*, I (Munich, 1977), col. 148, with bibliography. For some observations cf. J. Koch, in W. Lammers, *Geschichtsdenken und Geschichtsbild im Mittelalter* (Darmstadt, 1965), 321ff.; G. Wolf, 'Das 12. Jahrhundert als Geburtsstunde der Moderne und die Frage nach der Krise der Geschichtswissenschaft', *Miscellanea Medievalia*, 9 (1974), 80ff.; also Ullmann, *Medieval Foundations*, 64ff.

29 Cf. preceding note.

30 *Georgica*, 2.490 (ed. Loeb Classical Library, 150).

31 In his dedicatory letter to Frederick I of the translation of Nemesius of Emesa, see G. Verbeke and F.R. Moncho, *Néméius d'Emèse* (= *Corpus latinum commentariorum in Aristotelem Graecorum*, supplementary vol. I, Leiden, 1975). The title of the work was : *De natura hominis*. See E. Garin, 'La *dignitas hominis* e la letteratura patristica', *La Rinascita*, 1 (1938), 102ff., especially 112ff. on Nemesius.

32 Cf. the very pertinent observations by J. Szöverffy, 'Bruch mit der Tradition' in K. Bosl (ed.), *Gesellschaft, Kultur, Literatur: Beiträge Luitpold Wallach gewidmet* (Stuttgart, 1975), 209–22; especially 219ff.; note also the introductory remark concerning terminology.

33 For some antecedents see J. Ehlers, 'Karolingische Tradition und frühes Nationalbewusstsein in Frankreich', *Francia*, 4 (1976), 213–35 (here also further literature). For the background of the emerging awareness of nationhood cf. the relevant studies in H. Beumann and W. Schröder (eds), *Nationes: Historische und Philologische Untersuchungen zur Entstehung der europäischen Nationen* (Sigmaringen 1978), especially H.-D. Kahl, 'Einige Beobachtungen zum Sprachgebrauch von *natio* im mittelalterlichen Latein', 63–108; H. Beumann, 'Die Bedeutung des Kaisertums für die Entstehung der deutschen Nation', 317–66; and M. Richter, 'Mittelalterlicher Nationalismus: Wales im 13. Jahrhundert', 463–502.

34 H. Grundmann and H. Heimmel (eds), Alexander, *Memoriale* (Weimar, 1949), 48; also his *Notitia saeculi*, ed. ibid., 84ff.

35 See J. Leclercq, 'Zeiterfahrung' in *Miscellanea* (see n. 28), 1ff., especially 16.

36 Cf. also Ullmann, *Medieval Foundations*, 82.

37 For this see C.H. Haskins, *Studies in the History of Medieval Science*, 3rd edn (London, 1960), 254ff.

38 For some details see Ullmann, *Principles*, 231ff.; also id., *Individual and Society*, 115ff. Such statements of Aristotle as 'Nature does nothing in vain' or 'Nature does nothing superfluous' or 'Nature behaves as if it foresaw the future' and many others of the same kind, fell, in view of their teleological import and direction, on very fertile soil.

39 I Cor. 2:14.

40 E. Garin, *L'educazione in Europa 1400–1600* (Bari, 1957), 32ff.

41 See M.A. Hewson, *Giles of Rome and the Medieval Theory of Conception* (London, 1975), 39ff.

42 This bipolarity will in course of time give way to multipolarity and eventually bring about the modern pluralist society.

43 See the quotation in Ullmann, *Principles*, 247ff. Further, L. Lachance, *L'humanisme politique de S. Thomas d'Aquin* (Paris–Montreal, 1965), 349ff.; also, Ullmann, *Individual and Society*, 120.

44 Ullmann, *Individual and Society*, 102ff.

45 For Cicero cf. his *De divinatione*, 2.80 (ed. Loeb Classical Library, p. 462).

46 Cf. Ullmann, *Medieval Foundations*, 97ff.

47 See n. 27.

48 Cf. Ullmann, *Medieval Foundations* 113ff.

49 For an illuminating characterization of 'History' within Renaissance precincts, see Garin, *Medioevo e rinascimento*, 192ff.; especially 201ff. Cf. 204: 'With humanism the detailed search begins for the face of the individual: it becomes essential to seek out the appearance of a man' ('Con l'umanesimo comincia la ricerca precisa del volto di ognuno: diventa essenziale ritrovare l'aspetto di un uomo').

50 This is exactly the same in the so-called Third World today which relies on

the developed industrial countries to supply it with expert consultants and literature to help build its own communities.

51 *'Quid enim aliud omnis historia quam Romana laus?'* See T.E. Mommsen, 'Petrarch's conception of the Dark Ages', *Speculum*, 17 (1942), 226ff.

52 For some observations cf. Ullmann, *Principles*, 261ff. In this context see also A. Buck, 'Dante und die Ausbildung des italienischen Nationalbewusstseins', in *Nationes* (see n. 33), 489–503; Ullmann, *Law and Politics*, 278, for editions and literature; further 'Dante's *Monarchia* as an illustration of a politico-religious *renovatio*', in *Traditio-Krisis-Renovatio: Festschrift für Winfried Zeller* (Marburg, 1976), 101ff. (reprinted in Collected Studies III: *Scholarship and Politics in the Middle Ages*, London, 1978, ch.8).

53 Dig. 1.4.1.

54 See the commentary by Cino da Pistoia on the Dig. vetus 1.4.3 no.1.

55 Tit. 3.5. K. Burdach and P. Piur, *Der Briefwechsel des Cola di Rienzo* (Berlin, 1912), Ep. 28, p. 112, line 68.

56 About the role of the jurists see Roberto Weiss, *The Dawn of Humanism* (London, 1947), 5; and for 'humanist jurisprudence' see especially E. Garin, *L'età nuova: ricerche di storia della cultura dal XII al XVI secolo* (Naples, 1969), 235–60, with incisive passages from, and comments on, civilians and canonists alike, especially 247ff. See further for the later period H.E. Troje, 'Humanismus und Jurisprudenz', in H. Coing (ed.), *Handbuch der Quellen und Literatur der neueren europäischen Privatrechtsgeschichte*, II (Munich, 1977), 615ff.

57 For details cf. Ullmann, *The Carolingian Renaissance*.

58 *De potestate regia et papali*, ed. F. Bleienstein (Stuttgart, 1969). Literature in Ullmann, *Law and Politics*, 276ff.

59 Cf. Ullmann, *Principles*, 76ff. and 318.

60 With this point of view should be compared the statement made by Pope Gregory VII quoted in Ullmann, *Principles*, 90.

61 Dubois' memorandum to the king, Philip IV; see E. Boutaric (ed.), *Notices et extraits*, 10 (1865), Part 2, no. 30, p. 181.

62 For details, cf. Ullmann, *Principles*, 269ff., 313, 324. That he propounded a political philosophy of humanism, and not a theory of the state, is shown by W. Ullmann in the forthcoming *Atti del Convegno internazionale su Marsilio da Padova* (1982).

63 For full details see E. Garin, *Portraits of the Quattrocento* (New York-London, 1972), 23 n. 9.

64 A good example is the *Songe du Vergier*, in J. Quillet, *La philosophie politique du Songe du Vergier (1378)* (Paris, 1977); ead., 'Songe et songeries dans l'art de la politique du XIVe siècle', *Etudes philosophiques* (1975), 328–49.

65 For some observations cf. Ullmann, *Medieval Foundations* 49ff., 119ff., 128 and for literature see id., *Law and Politics*, 182, 222.

66 Details in *Scholarship and Politics* (see n. 52), chs 6 and 7. Yet it was paradoxically enough his successor, Pope Clement V, who to all intents and purposes laid the theoretical foundations of, and provided the juristic justification for, the sovereign territorial state; cf. W. Ullmann, 'Zur

Entwicklung des Souveränitätsbegriffs im Spätmittelalter', in L. Carlen and F. Steinegger (eds), *Festschrift für Nikolaus Grass* (Innsbruck–Munich, 1974), 9–27. It should be borne in mind that two years before the issue of this basic decree the Council of Vienna in 1511 through the same pope virtually anticipated *Pastoralis cura* and referred to the *regnum Alemanniae*; see ch.28 of this Council, in J. Alberigo *et al.* (eds), *Conciliorum oecumenicorum decreta*, 3rd edn (Bologna, 1973), 383 (= Clementinae V.3.3). For the influence of these views on territorial sovereignty in Henry VIII's reign see W. Ullmann, *Jurisprudence in the Middle Ages*, Collected Studies 4 (London, 1980), ch.12.

67 For some details see *Scholarship and Politics* (see n. 52), ch.8. For a perceptive study of Dante from an unusual angle, see E. Peters, '*Pars partes*: Dante and an urban contribution to political thought', in H.A. Miskimin *et al.* (eds), *The Medieval City* (Yale, 1977), 113–40, especially 115–21.

68 For details, see n. 65.

69 For some observations, cf. Ullmann, *Medieval Foundations*, 165ff.

70 Of the numerous sources only one or two should be mentioned: Augustine, *Enarrationes* in Ps. 51, cap. 6, ed. in *Corpus Christianorum*, 39 (1966), 627; *Civitas Dei*, 8.4; 19.3; Pomerius, *De vita contemplativa*, in *PL*, 59.415ff.; Gregory I, *Moralia*, 6.5.57, in *PL*, 75.761ff.; id., *Homiliae in Hiozechihelem prophetom*, ed. in *Corpus Christianorum*, 142 (1971), 1.5.6, 59 and 261ff.; Alcuin, Ep. 213, in *Mon. Germ. Hist. Epistolae*, IV.355, etc.

71 Which had no value of its own, and became meaningful only in relation to the eventual aim of the Christian.

72 Cf., for example, F. Novati (ed.), Salutati, *Epistolario*, 2 (Rome, 1891), 292, lines 3ff.; knowledge of the past is necessary for 'what is to be done with citizens and with friends, and what is to be done in private or in public' (*'quid cum civibus et amicis quidque privatim vel publice sit agendum'*); further ibid., 72, lines 6ff.: 'One must produce examples: both sacred and secular writings overflow richly with clear testimonies and examples' (*'Oportet exempla proponere: plane quidem et ubertim tam divinae quam saeculares litterae . . . testimoniis exuberant et exemplis'*). Numerous other passages can be cited.

73 Cf. Cicero, *De oratore*, 2.36 and 1.5: 'Moreover, all antiquity, all weight of precedent, must be adhered to, nor should the science of jurisprudence or civil law be neglected' (*'Tenenda praeterea est omnis antiquitas, exemplorum vis, neque legum aut iuris civilis scientia negligenda est'*). *Epistolae ad Lucilium morales*, 6.5, etc.

74 Hence it is that aretalogy begins to assume a complexion different from that which it had in the antecedent age. The concept and meaning of virtue is obviously a reflection of the changed outlook.

75 Leonardo Bruni, *De studiis et litteris liber* in H. Baron (ed.), *Humanistisch-Philosophische Schriften* (Leipzig–Berlin, 1928), 12; E. Kessler, *Das Problem des frühen Humanismus* (Munich, 1968), 209. Bruni advised the consultation of the ancients *die noctuque* (line 6).

76 For some excellent examples see E. Peters, op. cit., 131ff.

77 Cf. Ullmann, *Principles*, 288ff.

78 For this cf. the brilliant observations by E. Garin in his Introduction entitled 'Dante in the Renaissance' to D.B. Thompson and A.F. Nagel (eds), *The Three Crowns of Florence* (New York–London, 1972), ix-xxxiv.

79 For the fertilizing effects of Greek translations into Latin during the fifteenth century, see P.O. Kristeller, *Renaissance Concepts of Man* (New York, 1972), 64ff., 135ff.

80 G. Griffiths, 'Bruni and the university of Rome', *Renaissance Quarterly*, 26 (1973), 1ff., at p. 7.

81 It is above all in jurisprudence that the so-called humanist school made great strides in the attempts to reconstitute or restore the authentic text of the *Corpus Iuris Civilis*. But for reasons which still need an explanation, it was not until the 1630s that at Bourges in France humanist jurisprudence came into its own under Alciatus, the Italian savant who found no echo in his homeland. For details, see H.E. Troje, *Graeca leguntur*, Forschungen zur neueren Privatrechtsgeschichte, 18 (Cologne – Vienna, 1971); id., 'Humanismus und Jurisprudenz', with copius literature and details; cf. also F. Wieacker, *Privatrechtsgeschichte der Neuzeit*, 2nd edn (Göttingen, 1967), 88-93, also 161ff., especially 165-9. But this humanist jurisprudence had lost – like all other humanist writings in this final phase – all contact with government, politics and public law, and confined itself to the exegesis of the law in the narrow meaning of the term.

82 See P. Nardi, *Mariano Sozini: Giureconsulto Senese del Quattrocento* (Milan, 1974); they were colleagues; ibid., 77, 79, 80 n. 41, 109. For Franciscus de Accoltis, see *Lexikon des Mittelalters*, 1 (1977), 75 and *Dizionario biografico degli italiani*, 1.104-5.

83 For the animosity with which some of Aristotle's axioms were received in the universities, cf. *Scholarship and Politics* (see n. 52), ch.6.

84 For this see E. Garin, 'The humanist chancellors of the Florentine Republic from Coluccio Salutati to Bartolomeo Scala', in *Portraits of the Quattrocento*, 1-29.

85 For the philosophical background see E. Garin, 'Aristotelismo e Platonismo del Rinascimento',*La Rinascita*, 2 (1939), 641-71; id., *L'età nuova*, 265ff., and 275ff., for the phases of the 'rinascita di Platone'. The first work to be studied in Italy was indeed *The Republic* (ibid., 271ff., and rich literature, 265 n. 1). For the role of Nicholas of Cusa in the dissemination of Platonism, ibid., 293-317. See further N. Grass in *Gedächtnisschrift für Cusanus* (Innsbruck, 1970), 101ff.

86 See E. Garin, *Italian Humanism* (Oxford, 1965), 197.

87 Franciscus Senensis Patricius, *De institutione reipublicae libri novem* (ed. Paris, 1675), I.3, fol. 13: 'That the civil society which we call 'the state' – for the word 'city' refers only to buildings and walls – was devised for the utility of mankind by the provision of nature seems to me to be unquestionable' ('*Civilem societatem quam civitatem appellamus (urbis enim nomen aedificiis tantum ac moenibus continetur) hominum inventum esse utilitatis gratia duce naturae nequaquam mihi ambigendum esse videtur*'). He continues: 'For man is a much more social animal than bees, ants, cranes, and creatures of that kind, which grow up in herds and look after themselves in herds' ('*Est enim homo sociale animal longemagis.*

quam apes, formicae, grues et eiusmodi genera quae gregatim alantur gregatimque se tuentur').

88 ibid., fol. 13v.

89 I.1, fol. 9: 'Is anyone in doubt that bees have a king, who rules the people by his command and decision?' (*'Regem suum apes habere quis` ambigit qui populum nutu et arbitrio regat?'*)

90 See fol. 16r: 'For I wish him (the citizen) to be able to play his part in public life' (*'Volo enim eum (scil. civem) participem publici muneris esse posse'*).

91 I.4, fol. 16.

92 ibid.: *'quasi iuris equalitas dominatur . . . inter omnes iure omnia administranda sunt.'*

93 Fol. 16v: 'Now a lawyer of Florence said that liberty was a natural characteristic of anything which one wishes to do, provided that it is not forbidden by law or physical violence' (*'Florentinus autem iureconsultus libertatem esse dixit naturalem facultatem eius quod cuique facere libet, nisi quod vi aut iure prohibetur'*).

94 Fol. 18v: *'quae ex omni genere hominum commixta est.'*

95 I.5, fol. 19r: 'I shall call that the best state, in which individuals or groups do not obey the inclination of their own desires, but in which law alone holds sway' (*'Optimam rempublicam appellabo, in qua non singuli aut plures ad nutum suae voluntatis imperant, sed etiam in qua lex tantum dominatur'*). He continues: 'For equality renders civil society stable amongst the citizens, and is most flourishing when everything is directed with equality and justice' (*'Aequalitas namque inter cives societatem civilem stabilem reddit, quae tunc vel maxime viget, cum aequo iure omnia censentur'*).

96 Dig. 1.3.1; *De institut.* I.5, fol. 20r: *'legem communem reipublicae sponsionem.'*

97 *De regno et regis institutione* (ed. Paris, 1567); VII.1. fol. 332r; cf. also I.1, fol. 6v.

98 I.3, fol. 11v: 'For by the name of "the people" all the citizens are meant: "the remaining citizens" are meant when patricians and senators are included' (*'Nam appellatione populi universi cives significantur, connumeratis etiam patriciis et senatoribus caeteri cives significantur'*).

99 I.10, fol. 29v.

100 II.1, fol. 59r: *'rex est custos boni et aequi.'*

101 This is clearly an echo of Justinian's own words. For full information see A. Steinwenter, 'Nomos empsychos', *Anzeiger der Österreichischen Akademie der Wissenschaften*, 83 (1946), 250ff. Cf. also Ullmann, *Law and Politics*, 61, 92.

102 IX.2, fol. 387v: 'For as God moves everything in the universe, the king is said, by a kind of comparison, to do the same in the kingdom which is entrusted to him' (*'Ut enim Deus in universo omnia movet, sic etiam rex in regno sibi permisso per similitudinem quandam efficere dicitur'*).

103 ibid., fol. 388v: *'in qua (scil. equalitate) nihil tam inequale est quam ea ipsa quae videtur esse equalitas.'* Before he says this: 'The opinion of the most stupid and most uncivilized man carries as much weight as that of the most learned and celebrated man' (*'sic ad numerum accedit hebetissimi cuiusque ac rusticani hominis sententia ut acutissimi clarissimique viri'*).

[79]

This utter contempt for quantitative measurements and for the masses is highly significant.

104 *'Integrum semper iudicium.'*

105 VIII.6, fol. 343r: no laws have had greater longevity than the Roman laws. See further IX.2, fol. 388v, where he deals with the replacement of the Roman republic by imperial rule.

106 IX.4, fol. 292v.

107 VIII.10, fol. 372v.

108 Pontano, *De obedientia*, ed. *Opera omnia* (Venice, 1518), vol. I, fol. 10ff.: *'Coeli motus et stellarum, quis [est] ordo rerum et quae [est] mensura.'* For Pontano, cf. V. Prestipino, *Motivi del pensiero umanistico e Giovanni Pontano* (Milan, 1963); F. Tateo, *Umanesimo etico di Giovanni Pontano* (Lecce, 1973); here also further literature. His *De Principe* is edited and translated by E. Garin, *Prosatori Latini del Quattrocento*, in *La Letteratura Italiana: storia e testi*, vol. XIII (Naples, 1932), 1024-63.

109 *De obedientia*, lib. I, fol. 10v: *'Quae omnibus ante nos saeculis incognita latuerint.'*

110 ibid., fol. 10v-11r: *'Sunt tamen ex iis, quae naturae continentur legibus quaedam homini cum belluis communia, ut prolem cupere, ut pastum quaerere temptestatemque vitare et aestus. Sed hoc metiri non decet, quid sit aut quousque commune sit homini cum bestiis, sed quid sit quod natura ipsa praescribit.'*

111 ibid., fol. 11v: *'Iura ipsa servanda sunt et legibus parendum est, ut cum ad coetus colendos societatemque retinendum nati sumus, munus impleamus nostrum.'* He also declares: 'As Cicero says, we are the slaves of the laws, that we may be free' (*'Ut Cicero ait legum servi sumus ut liberi esse possimus'*).

112 *De obedientia*, lib. IV, fol. 28r: *'Et id genus qui in sordidis versantur opificiis et quorum servilis mens est.'*

113 ibid., fol. 27v: *'An homo cum liber sit natus, domino parere debeat?'* In a different context and from a different angle Salutati had touched on this topic: 'It is disgraceful to love ease, since man is born for toil as a bird is born to fly' (*'Ignavum est, cum homo natus sit ad laborem, ut avis ad volandum, otium diligere'*): see the discussion of this recently discovered letter by E. Garin, 'Una epistola di Coluccio Salutati', *Rivista critica di storia della filosofia*, 28 (1973), 451.

114 *De obedientia*, IV, fol. 31v: *'Haec non modo libertas non est, sed vel maxime adversatur libertati.'*

115 ibid., fol. 31v: *'Licet liberi nati simus, tamen et regibus et magistratibus parendum esse ac tum maxime liberos esse nos, cum iis maxime pareamus.*

116 ibid., fol. 29r.

117 ibid.: 'Custom is king amongst the bees, too' (*'in apibus quoque usus est rex'*).

118 ibid., fol. 31r.

119 ibid., fol. 28v: *'Dux autem peritissimus et optimus est ratio.'*

120 We should note that he used here *animus* without distinguishing it from *anima*. He returns (fol. 29r) to the anthropomorphic allegory: 'For, as I have said, amongst the limbs of which the body is composed, there is one more

important than the rest' ('*nam et dixi et in membris e quibus existit corpus unum est quod caeteris praeest'*).

121 ibid., fol. 30r; he continues: 'Sulla too and Marius are to be counted among the very cruellest of tyrants' ('*Sulla quoque et Marius vel inter crudellissimos tyrannos numerandi sunt'*).

122 ibid., fol. 30r.

123 ibid., fol. 35v.

124 ibid., fol. 37v.

125 ibid., fol. 35v: '*Poterit fortasse utilitatis tanta vis esse et tali in causa ut sit aliquando ab honesto declinandum, parum tamen et sine gravi infamia.*'

126 ibid., fol. 36r: '*Licet autem colenda semper sit veritas, poterit tamen tanta interdum vis esse tum rerum tum temporum, ut ea prorsus sit obticenda.*'

127 ibid., fol. 36v.

128 ibid.

129 Cf. W. Ullmann, *The Medieval Idea of Law*, reprint (London, 1968), s.v. 'Public utility'; id., *Growth of Papal Government in the Middle Ages*, 4th edn (London, 1970), 425ff.; id., *Principles*, s.v. '*Utilitas communis*' and '*Utilitas publica*'.

130 *De obedientia*, IV, fol. 40r. This evokes echoes of John of Salisbury's similar point of view, for which cf. W. Ullmann, 'John of Salisbury's Policraticus in the later Middle Ages', now reprinted in his *Jurisprudence*, ch.6, 522, 527. Also in K. Hauck and H. Mordek (eds), *Festschrift für Heinz Löwe* (Cologne – Vienna, 1978).

131 *De obedientia*, IV, fol. 40r.

132 ibid., fol. 40r: '*Quis dubitet vel ampliores illis quam patribus honores habendos esse? Cum autem sacrosancti censeantur et vitae habeant necisque arbitrium.*'

133 Garin, 'Dante in the Renaissance', xxxiff (above n. 78).

134 ibid.

135 E. Guillemain, *Machiavel: l'anthropologie politique* (Geneva, 1977), 260: 'Nous nous permettons d'appeler l'attitude machiavéllienne politocentrisme.' This statement could be applied to Pontano: 'L' existence d'un ordre étatique forme la condition nécessaire pour la naissance de toute valeur. Mais l'ordre étatique lui-même n'est pas une valeur, c'est un fait.' For the raison d'état see also G.A. Pocock, *The Machiavellian Moment: Florentine Political Thought and the Atlantic Republican Tradition* (Princeton, 1975), 369–71.

136 Garin. *Prosatori*, 1021.

137 Cf. H. Grundmann, *Ausgewählte Aufsätze*, 1 (Stuttgart, 1976), 364ff., especially 375ff.

138 Cf. on this H.C. Porter, *Reformation and Reaction in Tudor Cambridge*, reprint (Cambridge, 1972), 418, 422ff. Marsilio Ficino himself had translated Ps. Denys: clearly proof that the work evinced interest among contemporaries.

139 J.K. McConica, *English Humanists and Reformation Politics under Henry VIII and Edward VI* (Oxford, 1965) does not address himself to this topic; cf. 46ff. For Harrington see J.A Pocock, *The Political Writings of James*

Harrington (Cambridge, 1977), especially the tract 'System of Politics', ch.10, 851ff. with the firm emphasis on the reason of state.
140 For some tentative explanations cf. Ullmann, *Medieval Foundations*, 181, 185ff.

3

THEMES FOR A
RENAISSANCE ANTHROPOLOGY

CHARLES TRINKAUS

ULTURAL anthropology, or the comparative study of the vast varieties of human cultures encountered in the new and old worlds since 1492, developed into a scientific discipline in the post-Darwinian late nineteenth century. But its scholarly origins can be traced back to the late Renaissance descriptions and speculations in Italy, France and elsewhere. Beginning in the fourteenth century there had been an efflorescence of writings on the nature and status of man as a divine creation and within the scale of being, loosely designated as 'the Renaissance philosophy of man'.[1] It is this Renaissance forerunner of the discipline of anthropology, particularly in its religious context, that will be the subject of this essay.

Renaissance conceptions of man derived from a number of intellectual traditions of which two were critical: the revived ancient conception of *humanitas* (or Greek *paideia*) which formed the core of the *studia humanitatis* and the humanist movement,[2] and the Christian medieval tradition of discussions of *conditio hominis* under the complementary titles of *De miseria humanae conditionis* and *De dignitate humanae conditionis*.[3] It was the combination of these two traditions – one classical, one Christian – which gave the characteristic form and content to Renaissance treatises on man and which differentiated the Renaissance philosophy of man from its predecessors. This in turn was closely linked with, if not a central ingredient of, a Renaissance '*theologia rhetorica*'.

HUMANITAS AND GENUS HUMANUS

By *paideia* or *humanitas* ancient Greeks and Romans meant what we today would regard as the 'culture' acquired by growing up in a particular society. However, they thought of these terms as referring to a generic human culture rather than their own peculiar one[4] and the education which instilled *paideia* or *humanitas* was, again, *the* education and not simply their own. Moreover, they denied that what Asians and barbarians acquired through their own *mores* was culture. Rather, by taking over Greek or Roman ways, they believed that any people could acquire universal *paideia* or *humanitas*. We tend to find that ancient education was aristocratic or plutocratic and so regard it as offensive to our notion that culture and education should be universal. It was not so much that the ancients wished to confine culture to the upper classes, but that they believed its acquisition in some way differentiated and elevated its possessor over the mere practitioner of manual labour or the mechanical arts, even including those of painting, sculpture, architecture and musical performance. Culture was for most of its proponents and theorists in antiquity, and in the Renaissance as well, something that was superimposed on the natural characteristics of mankind. It was the product of nurture and convention rather than of nature, though some individuals were considered to be better endowed by nature with the gift of acquiring culture.

The assumption that men existing in their age might learn how to acquire the *humanitas* and culture which the ancients knew how to possess was basic to the Renaissance notions of the revival of antiquity, however specified. This meant that the contemporaries of the humanists who composed the *vulgus* were without culture. Indeed, the notion that the men of the Middle Ages were, if not barbarians, barbaric in their lack of culture, derives from the classical conception of *humanitas* which the humanists found in Cicero, Quintilian, Aulus Gellius and their other sources. Inherent in the humanists' admiration for *humanitas*, however, with its *Homo sum: nihil humani alienum mihi puto*,[5] and its universality, was a recognition that there was a difference between one way of speaking, feeling and thinking and its appropriateness to a given situation and another. The very ancient sophistic emphasis on the subjectivity and relativity of ideas and values, which despite his social rigidities was manifested even in Cicero (especially in the *Academica*), and even more in Quintilian with his reservation of the *status controversiae quale sit* to the orator, gave rise to a comparative and relativistic view of vocabulary, meaning, syntax, composition, style, even language as has recently been shown. There was not one point where culture was at its peak or a single classical moment. Time, place and circumstances determined the multiple particular qualities that were appropriate. *Propria* became more valid as a criterion than *vera* and recaptured some of the Gorgianic *kairos*. Not only did human culture come to be seen as variable and relative, but man himself began to be seen as infinitely plastic and socially adaptable.[6]

Listen to Pontano, in his *De sermone*, on how discourse manifests the social character of the virtues:

> Just as reason, herself, is the guide and mistress for directing actions, so speech is the administrator of all those things which, conceived in the mind, and activated by thinking, are dragged forth into the public world, since, as it is said, we are born sociable and must live together. Wherever speech is greater and more frequent, there is a richer supply of all those things in which life is lacking (since need is given as a companion to all men at their birth). Through speech life itself is made far more adaptable as well as more capable both of acquiring virtues and of attaining happiness.[7]

Developing his conception of the virtues as the bonds of society directly out of his study of rhetoric, Pontano distinguished between two basic types of rhetoric. First there is the 'oratorical art' by which men may become civil leaders 'in the most populous cities and in the greatest enterprises'.[8] Here the traditional formal rhetorics – forensic, legislative and epideictic – come into use. There is also, however, a more general function of speech which in the daily discourse of life creates and manifests the variety and differences of individual and collective culture.

> For we are not speaking at all about that part of rhetoric which is called the oratorical strength and skill or the rhetorical art, but only about that common speech by which men approach friends, and carry on their daily business in gatherings, conversations, family and civil meetings and customs. For this reason those who are engaged in such matters are commended according to a quite different criterion than those who are called orators.[9]

Thus Pontano asserted that culture is not only attained by cultivation of the high language arts among the élite of society, but is also made up of the daily intercourse of all men in their societies, thus rendering the meaning of culture closer to modern anthropological usage. He moved on to an exposition of the variety and diversity of the use of speech in different and among different peoples. At this point, in a lengthy but compelling and definitive passage, he established the principle of cultural relativism which so many humanists derived from their studies of history and language:

> Nor indeed does nature depart from herself in this matter or from that

[85]

variety and dissimilitude which are characteristic of her. Since the manner of speaking of some persons is severe and somewhat sad, of others joyful and gay; of one the talk is smooth and fancy, of another crude and harsh; also this one reveals in his speaking the customs of the city but that one those of the country, there is the type who would like to seem witty and affable and the contrasting kind who would be severe and rigid and the one who is especially truthful and hostile to all pretence, to whom no dissimulation or what is called 'irony' in Greek is pleasing. Therefore the type of speech strongly seems to follow both the nature of the speaker and also his customs. Why is this? Because peoples and nations, either by their very nature or by established custom and usage, approve and hold in high value what others elsewhere disapprove, and some are more taciturn and others, on the contrary, more loquacious. Boastful speech delights the Spaniards, colourful and complicated language the Greeks; the talk of the Romans was grave, that of the Spartans brief and rough, the Athenians fulsome and stilted, the Carthaginians and Africans shrewd and sly, as was said of their nature. Thus it happens that one kind of colloquy is more highly approved in one place and less so in another.[10]

For Pontano social existence required two central virtues – urbanity and veracity. These were manifested by men's manners of speaking and, following Aristotle, he saw these as desirable means between extremes. Urbanity is what may be called 'an especially admirable solace and lightening of the cares and burdens of labours honourably undertaken'. Veracity is what may be called 'that which so characterizes man himself that through it human conciliation may be established, trust flourish in the city, our actions and transactions become linked together, and our promises and teachings observed'.[11]

Although Pontano formally followed Aristotle's relativistic moral casuistry, he was also indebted to the more morally neutral analysis of Cicero which placed the virtues in a graduated spectrum (as we know Lorenzo Valla also did in opposing the Aristotelian mean). But Pontano's own insights seem closer to the kind of personification of the political modes presented by Plato in the ninth book of the *Republic* (which Pontano was not likely to have been following). For he saw that certain characterological types emerge from the involvement of a man in the nexus of the possible moral-rhetorical relations available in society. Opposite to the man of veracity, or truth, himself a central and necessary character-type in Pontano's thinking, come all of the graphically portrayed types of deceivers such as the 'adulators, and those who make a merchandise out of words whenever they use pleasing and flattering speech'.[12] Also opposite to the urbane man, but from a different direction, is the quarrelsome and contentious man whom Pontano described as follows:

> And as some use this gift of speech conceded by nature for reconciling friendships, for consoling and comforting others in their troubles, labours and griefs, others, the contentious, use or abuse it rather in the opposite way, arousing hatred and stirring up quarrels as well as sowing the seeds of discord. . . . They are certainly odious kinds of men, and very similar to flies, as they seem entirely born for uproar, annoyance, disquiet and for disturbance and weariness of life![13]

Although his concern was with the accurate description and subtle definition of the terms used to denote such characters, it is clear that he saw the various modes of using language arising out of the social experience of mankind as crystallized in certain personal cultures or moral linguistic structures. Individual styles of speaking correspond to specific ways of relating to other persons. The array of combinations of *verba* and *res*, the language and concepts, which these different but typical social experiences and stances of human culture present, were understood and explained as *humanitas* by Pontano – something a modern anthropologist might call 'culture' in our own very different modern sense.

But *humanitas* was also a specific virtue, and the *habitus* of the *vir humanus*. Pontano discussed the differences between *comitas*, *popularitas* and *humanitas* as variants of *urbanitas* or *facetitas*. These virtues comprise the range and variety of attitudes and behaviour characteristic of men who seek to enliven and console their fellows and bring them into pleasant and enduring companionship. It is evident from Pontano's and other humanists' usage of *humanitas* and *humanus* in their writings that the word often occurs in the context of the quality or the mode of human relationships, so that the notion of the 'humane' as an aspect of the 'human' was not totally excluded from the Greek and Latin notions of *paideia* and *humanitas* as cultural or educational concepts. This we will claim despite the frequent humanist citation of Aulus Gellius' pronouncement that Latin *humanitas* does not mean Greek *philanthropeia* but *paideia*. What Pontano at least meant by *humanus* is shown in his description of a friend, the philosopher Giovanni Pardo:

> He was humane toward every kind of human life and action . . . he did nothing proudly, nothing arrogantly; in his approach, his speech

and his behaviour he presented himself as an equal to everyone; he took it badly when he saw anyone being insolent to another person; the accidents of friends and citizens weighed heavily upon him; he consoled the suffering, helping them as much as he was able, visiting them, assisting them, giving his direct help; he stood by anyone at any time as a gracious and affable companion.[14]

As to the general qualities of *humanitas* and *comitas*, which also are called *civilitas* by some:

> *Humanity* differs from *comity* in several ways. For whoever is moved by other persons' injuries, inconveniences, captivity, grief, poverty, banishment and other ills, him we call 'humane', yet not in any sense 'companionable'. . . . But there is in both qualities a certain kind of communality of living in deeds and transaction which we would like to call either 'facility' or 'tractability'.[15]

Humanitas might then be said to be a Renaissance cultural ideal which sought through the *studia humanitatis* to pursue those studies which might most contribute to human and civil well-being. But *humanitas* was also construed to be a broad but identifiable conception of man characterized by sympathetic concern for the well-being of other individual humans and for the general well-being of the civilization or culture which sustained men's common life. Both of these conceptions of *humanitas* were rooted in the ancient humanist myth of the origins of civilization through the language arts. It was put forth as such in Cicero's *De inventione*, or in Protagoras' tale in Plato's dialogue of the gifts of reverence, justice and the liberal arts given by Zeus to primitive man. Giannozzo Manetti, praising the language arts as evidence of the greatness of human inventiveness, gave his own version of this myth:

> For when primitive man and his ancient successors became aware that they could not live for themselves alone without some kind of mutual exchange and reciprocal influence, they invented a certain subtle and acute art of speaking so that, by using their tongues to shape words, they could make known to all those listening their hidden and intimate thoughts. After this, when by the passage of time men had multiplied in an amazing way and populated the different regions and provinces of the globe, it became necessary for script to be invented. . . . Hence such various kinds of languages, such various types of letters, are seen to have come into existence and spread.[16]

[88]

Thus the notion of the linguistic disciplines fulfilling essential moral and social functions for the common life of mankind was deeply embedded in *humanitas* – the root term and concept of humanism. Culture and moral responsibility were inseparably connected.

A different, but also paradigmatically humanist, view of the formation of human character and society may be found in the *Epistola: De nobilitate et distinctione humani generis* of Antonio de Ferrariis, Il Galateo, composed *c.* 1488.[17] Pontano considered Il Galateo to be his best example of the man of comity. According to Il Galateo, the Latins and Greeks had divided mankind into civilized cultures (their own) and all others, whom they had called by that fetid term, 'barbarians'. Il Galateo preferred to call the others *externi*. But these others also used contemptuous terms for foreigners. Some peoples divided men according to social status rather than ethnic culture, into nobles and commoners, but Il Galateo's own view, following Cicero and Plato, was to consider the *optimates* not as a social class but as a group distinguished by their *mores*, meaning that they possessed not just morally neutral and different customs but goodness, so that for him the distinction between the more civilized and morally superior and those who are barbarian or morally inferior occurs within one nation and not between various nations. Thus other peoples have, as equivalents of the Greek *philosophi* and the Latin *sapientes*,

> gymnosophists, magi, Chaldeans, priests, prophets. Among the Arabs also in more recent times many excellent men distinguished themselves in the studies of wisdom. We Christians have had at one time our own kind who followed after true wisdom and taught it to us – the Apostles and the Evangelists.[18]

Thus for him the true and essential distinction between men is based upon the principle by which men are separated from animals, namely mind and reason. Men, indeed, differ from each other so much and have such different customs that they even seem to differ in species: 'And the very name man is equivocal and is not given the same meaning by everyone, for instance in the case of man as depicted and true man.'[19] Differing from Pontano's structuring of the modes of human behaviour according to the necessities of the civic order and of private advantage, Il Galateo establishes a universal criterion according to a fixed hierarchy of being. He is, however, aware of a tension between these two ordering principles of human culture.

The more men prevail in the use of the mind, according to Il Galateo, the more they are participants of *verae humanitatis*. But some of the worst men possess family, wealth, fame, office, power, physical

[89]

strength, beauty, agility, eloquence, the favour and grace of the people or the friendship of princes. Hence he divided all peoples into philosophers on the one hand and the plebeians or *vulgus* on the other; this division corresponding not to their external circumstances at all but only to their degree of education and moral goodness. He depicted these two kinds of men, portraying them as two mutually related types and reflecting in this the humanists' frequent insecurity and sense of moral superiority rather than Pontano's social functionalism. The *philosophus*, but not the *vir civilis* who seeks to please the *populus*, is the true aristocrat born only for himself and the immortal gods. The *philosophus*, in a conflation of Christian saint and Stoic sage, is totally honest, open, self-sacrificing and humble, whereas the men of the *vulgus* only pretend to serve the virtues and conceal their deep selfishness; 'they think it most beautiful to show off their wisdom, to display their most saintly customs, to conceal their crimes'.[20]

How do men fall into these two moral classes? Again, he suggests all customs are relative. What is fitting for one kind of man is not for another. Yet these two contrasting patterns emerge from *educatio* in our own modern sense of the word 'education'. Il Galateo offers a brilliant description here, not unlike the one Plato put into the mouth of Protagoras, of the way in which all aspects of upbringing are educational. 'Education is large and very potent in human affairs, and those first foods offered to tender souls are of great moment in all of life'.[21] Plato was thankful he was a Greek not because the Greeks were a superior race but because they had superior *mores et studia*. It is so easy for the young to admire the scurrilous and spurn the teachings of philosophers; just as patients resist the prescriptions of their doctors so they ignore the pleas, the praise and the blame of the philosophers, even though they are held to be *sapientes* by the *vulgus*:

> But since nothing is easier than to deceive oneself and nothing more divine in life than to know oneself, since we are men, we are deceived many times, but never are we more proud and arrogant than when we correct and condemn the counsels and actions of those of whom we scarcely deserve to be students.[22]

Il Galateo was not a frustrated schoolmaster but a member of a distinguished noble family. What he projects in this *Epistola* had long been a humanist stereotype: the opposition of the scholar to the vulgar self-interest of the men of affairs and of the common people. It is a version of the discussions of true nobility that had evolved since Dante's *Convivio*.[23] In Galateo's version the humanist, himself, is given the blessing of having achieved true humanity. For it is really the humanist whom Galateo calls 'philosopher' – the teacher of youth by praise and blame and society's moral guardian.

Particularly significant was Galateo's linkage of learning with piety. Christ's life was not *civilis* but truly *philosophica*. The *docti* are the true Christians and those of the beatitude, 'Blessed are we when men revile us and when we are persecuted for the sake of righteousness'. Such are we, the *sapientes*, 'when the vilest plebeians judge us to be insane'. But the plebeians, 'conscious of their own stupidity and malice', speak as follows: 'They – the *sapientes* – are the ones we sometimes have held in contempt. . . . We, the irrational ones, thought their life insane and their end without honour. Lo how they are reckoned among the sons of God! . . . Therefore we have departed from the way of truth.' The barbarians are those leading a brutish life whatever their race, class or family. The nobles are the virtuous men even if of barbarian or servile origin. 'For who, unless he was ignorant of human affairs and of true nobility, would call Horace plebeian or ignoble?'[24] So also Virgil, Cicero, Demosthenes, Socrates, Aristotle, Plato, Theophrastus, Hippocrates and Homer were truly noble though of humble origin.

For Galateo, as for Petrarch, *otium* was a high value:

> How great and how blessed is the life of leisure whenever it is present to any degree, those who are not philosophers would not know. . . . Leisure among the wise is held to be blessed, but among the barbarians, that is among uneducated men and those of the lower classes, as lazy idleness worthy of contempt and shame. Therefore only philosophers labour that they may rest and be at leisure, ordinary people, indeed, labour daily so that they may labour and suffer the more.[25]

There is in this position a summing-up of a major type of humanist thinking about man and his position in society – one which links classical learning and the type of the Roman sage with the holy man of Christianity. A new conception of lay piety, if not of lay sainthood, was quietly forged through this synthesis of Stoic sage and Christian martyr. In its stress on *otium* it contrasted with the attitude of an Alberti, a Valla, or a Manetti as described below – but not with their sense of moral righteousness and superiority. One should not, however, see this humanist concept of *otium* as totally one of withdrawal. Pontano speaks of the 'urbane' man as aware that

> just as idleness and all sorts of quiet are granted us for the sake of relaxing and so that the return to labours and affairs may not be sodden, for the same reasons jokes, sayings, wit, charm and humour

are granted and not so that life, our thoughts and all our studies should be placed in them or so that we might appear to be wasting away in leisure and idleness.[26]

CONDITIO HOMINIS

Another Renaissance ideal, that of *operosità* (the opposite of *ozio* or leisure), found its roots more in the patristic exegesis of Genesis 1:26, where creative man is seen as made in the image of God the creator. Though Petrarch with his twofold *otia* (*religiosum* and *litterarium*) may seem to have founded the humanist myth of the Stoic-Christian sage, he managed to convert it into a more activist and creative notion of his own role as moral midwife, and in this he necessarily projected a different and more positive image of the condition of man. It is to this second Renaissance humanist myth of creative man, with its Christian roots (but also combined with Protagorean-Ciceronian conceptions) that we now turn. We shall reserve for a third section our discussion of some of the more radical religious and cultural implications that underlay the more diffuse treatments of *humanitas* and *conditio hominis*.

Viewing the literature on the *conditio hominis* theme from Petrarch to the late sixteenth-century defences of the humanities, one should first emphasize its rhetorical character. Although its substance was central to Renaissance thought and of great historical importance, its form and function was also characteristic. Petrarch's declarations on the misery of the human condition were meant to be monitory and those on the dignity of man consolatory. Despite the hazards arising from his constant revisions, a development may be traced from the self-expressive and self-analytical lyricism of the *Canzoniere* and the profound dramatization of his personal conflicts in the *Secretum*, to a more directly active and hortatory kind of writing in the *Invectivae* and the *De remediis* and the later versions of the *De viris illustribus* – not that Petrarch ever abandoned an earlier practice altogether or stopped attempting to modify it! What he comes to is rhetorical history, on the one hand, and what may be called *theologia rhetorica*, on the other. Although Petrarch's contribution to Renaissance historical consciousness is admittedly very important, only the latter will be treated here. If in the *De ignorantia* he embraced 'the words that move and sting' of Latin rhetoric, it was in the context of what he had called his *homiliae* in the *Contra medicum* or in the way we should characterize the speeches of *Ratio* in the *De remediis*, that is, as lay literary sermons. It is exactly in this that the humanists' revival of antiquity, and their response to contemporary moral, psychological and social conditions, intersect.[27]

The *De remediis* is a highly fragmented work, yet has an amazing range and sweep of content. Its two books are divided into 122 triumphs and 132 despairs. Some are grand and some petty, but they are not merely miscellaneous, for Petrarch follows certain conventional structures: a review of the course of life; a catalogue of goods and evils according to the standard Aristotelian categories of soul, body and externals; the various high and low social states; the rewards and punishments of political power and weakness; the satisfactions and annoyances of family and friends. Authenticity of reportage breaks through the conventionality of the categories. Though short and sometimes stereotypical, his qualitative familiarity with the life of his world is patent. It is indeed the actual conditions of men in his time that he is depicting, abstracted into his 254 commonplace situations of elation and sorrow. What he offers by way of counselling in the *persona* of *Ratio* is again the idealization of the reciprocal polarities of human existence (what I have elsewhere called a 'double-consciousness'). The wise man, who now need no longer be the sage but can be the ordinary man, should know that misery lurks behind every prosperous condition and this should temper his triumph; he also should know that, whatever his wretchedness, disappointments and suffering, as a man he occupies a place of great dignity and great future hope in the universe. The picture of the human world which emerges is not that of a capricious fortune or an accident-dominated scene, but of a structural duality or ambiguity in all of life's circumstances. The advice Petrarch offers is how to cope with the emotional hazards of life. It is the message of the possibility of attaining moral identity and autonomy, and a serenity and calm under all conditions. *Ratio* does not bring salvation, but it brings the sense of having a soul and being a person in the world that opens the possibility of faith and hope and to which there may come grace. But we shall discuss that later.

What Petrarch contributed to his readership, which extended through nearly four centuries, was a sense of dignity and sanity that was compatible with piety, and he did this for a period of history in which the struggle for power, wealth and prestige was becoming frantic, and the deprivations desperate. His consolatory-monitory rhetoric did nothing to sedate the harshness of events, but offered a pattern of rationality in personal attitude and behaviour that perhaps helped to preserve civilization, and gave a moral theodicy for religious faith in the midst of the horrors of the age which he, himself, had so well depicted.

Petrarch also contributed a specific pattern for the statement of the dignity of man which was repeated with variation and amplification in the ensuing treatises on this theme.[28] The pattern was traditional and medieval in part. The human species, created by plural act of the Trinity in its image, received a soul with memory, intellect and will mirroring the divine Trinity of Father, Son and Spirit, as in the Augustinian exegesis recapitulated by Peter Lombard. Man was placed over the other species and walked erect in token of his contemplation of the divine and his effort to regain his similitude to God through virtuousness. Through Christ's incarnation he could take pride in his potentiality for divinization and look forward to immortality. He was protected by guardian angels, and through his superior powers of intellect not only ruled the beasts but created civilization.

Petrarch's own statement, itself one of his lay sermons of the *De remediis*, did not have the 'free-standing' literary autonomy of later Renaissance treatises. It brought the Christian message from the over-refined abstractness and technical language of scholastic theology, found in the more ontologically oriented thirteenth century and in the more critical and dialectical fourteenth-century, to the level of the ordinary man. For him the dignity-of-man theme was complementary to that of human misery, and he seems to have been encouraged to project the former as a complement to the latter by a letter from a Grand Prior of the Carthusians (*Senili* XVI. 9). In this case, and in that of the first formal literary treatise on *The Excellence of Man* by Bartolomeo Fazio in 1447, monastic figures such as the Grand Prior and Antonio da Barga (once Prior of the Olivetan house of San Miniato in Florence), seem to have provided the incitement. It is also probable that Giannozzo Manetti's much expanded treatment of 1453 had an earlier version inspired by the same Antonio da Barga.[29] In all three instances Pope Innocent III's *De miseria humanae conditionis* was in the background. As the then Cardinal Deacon Lotario da Signa said to Peter, Bishop of the church of Porto and Santa Rufina:

> If indeed your paternity should urge it, Christ willing, I will describe the dignity of human nature; for just as through the one (the *De contemptu mundi*) the elated is humbled, so through the other (the *De dignitate humanae naturae*) the humble is exalted.[30]

Both Petrarch and Fazio professed to fulfil Lotario's unfulfilled offer. Manetti, on the other hand, polemicized directly against him. More importantly, both Petrarch's and Fazio's treatments of the dignity-of-man theme are bound together with the complementary *de miseria* one, and both are directed toward moral counselling and rhetorical efforts

[94]

toward consolation and monition. The topical format of Petrarch's *De remediis* may be compared with that of Pope Innocent's famous work. The popularity of both throughout the late medieval and early modern period was enormous (judging by Maccarrone's listing of manuscripts and editions to 1600 for Lotario and Nicholas Mann's compilation of *De remediis* manuscripts, with Fiske's listing of editions).[31] These two clearly Renaissance works had deep medieval roots running back at least to Pope Gregory's *Book of Pastoral Care* with its compilation of the modes for counselling the arrogant and the despairing. But with it the still surviving Roman Stoic influence became tangible, and Petrarch's renewal of it in more explicitly rhetorical and Senecan terms was patently also a return to patristic Christianity. Its form, function and content were the cure of souls by the therapy of the word, both divine and human, though Petrarch's aims were existential as much as salvational.

The question then arises of how much the renewal of authentic understanding of ancient rhetoric contributed to a transformation of the medieval-Christian theme of the *conditio hominis* from a consolatory context to the assertion of a powerful vision of the capacities and cultural dominance of man. Actually, it seems to have led more to a deepening of a consolatory rhetoric in a lay and existential context (though clearly Christian in its content), whereas the enhanced vision of the powers of man, contemporary in origin, found inspiration in the traditional exegesis of Genesis 1:26–8.

Petrarch had put forth a very strong statement of confidence in the curative powers of rhetoric, drawn from both Cicero and Seneca and reviving in his *De remediis* the para-medical, or at least mental-hygienic, aspect of rhetoric. This function has been neglected by scholars who have tended to see only the forensic, political, epideictic and literary-theoretical sides of rhetoric. Yet it seems to have flourished among the Greek sophists and even to have had some links with Hippocratic medicine, was reflected in Plato's and Aristotle's concern with *catharsis*, and experienced a revival in Roman Stoicism.[32] A sequel to the consolatory usage of the dignity-of-man theme for the cure of souls, was the Ficinian combination of certain humanist conceptions of the power of language with a new metapsychic and theurgic conception of the cosmos on which a therapeutic 'spiritual magic' was based. Further study of both are needed.[33]

Neither Boccaccio, Salutati nor Valla, who contributed so much to the formation of a humanist philosophy of action and will, wrote directly on the dignity-of-man theme, although they made scattered references to the concept. While Salutati's *De seculo et religione* has

[95]

certain affinities with the *de miseria* theme, his *De nobilitate legum et medicinae* is an affirmation of the role of human will and reason in regulating the affairs of men. As a humanist Boccaccio seems to have had a major concern with building bridges between his earlier medieval literary culture and the Petrarchan classicism he admired, but he certainly shared Petrarch's admiration of man's moral autonomy and his expectation that, under given circumstances, it could become realized. In his *Repastinatio dialecticae et philosophiae* Valla developed the central analogy of the dignity-of-man theme, that between the persons of the Trinity and the faculties of the soul, into the theoretical base for his opposition of ˙Quintilian's rhetorical categories of sub-stance, quality and action to Aristotle's naturalistic epistemology and ontology. They all moved, in other words, toward the activist, creationist vision of human dignity that was to challenge the older, more traditional employment of the theme for consolatory rhetoric. We shall speak further of Valla and Salutati in our discussion of a *theologia rhetorica*.

Besides this distinction of a consolatory and a celebratory treatment of the dignity theme, best exemplified by Petrarch and Manetti respectively, another important distinction was that between the versions which stressed the theological features of man's dignity, with immortality as its ultimate attainment, and the versions which, while retaining the former ingredients, add to them an emphasis on man's worldly achievements and powers. Admittedly these two distinctions overlap, and it would be wrong to characterize either polarity as 'transcendent/immanent' as all four emphasize man's deification. But the second type of each distinction finds man's potential divinity exemplified by his operative reconstructing of this world, besides retaining the gift of immortality. One finds Manetti breaking away from the conception that man's dignity is the rhetorical complement of man's misery: directly combating Lotario's topics, he stressed that man can achieve dignity and also escape misery. Fazio, da Barga and Brando-lini, on the other hand, keep misery as the normal condition of earthly existence. Counter to the establishment of the theme of dignity, in separation from the polemic against misery, there was also a corresponding selection of the miserable and pessimistic aspects of man's existence promulgated in separation from, and even opposition to, any notion of dignity and autonomy. Poggio Bracciolini in his pessimism most clearly and self-consciously represents this tendency.[34]

A cynical doubter of the effectiveness and sincerity of both the politically powerful and the professionally pious, Poggio saw misery everywhere as the inherent condition of life after the fall of man.

Seemingly Stoic in his attitude, he was essentially sceptical of the affirmative and reconstructive rationalism of Stoicism as well, perhaps in a deeper and more violent sense than his enemy Valla. Right reason cannot alleviate human misery which is universal and overwhelming but it can contribute to an idealistic illusion of goodness in those favoured few with sufficient material goods to practise charity. Human motivation is ineluctably sinful whatever its nominal conception of itself: grace alone can redeem. Moral action, even for worldly ends, is a Pelagian illusion.

Poggio's view of human motivation and behaviour brought him closer in his outlook to some of the darker views of the Reformation than almost any other pre-Reformation humanist, even though – despite all his anti-clerical jibes and his contempt for the mendicant orders – he thought of himself as fully orthodox and religiously conservative. He lacked Petrarch's and Fazio's confidence in reason and rhetoric. These lacked for him the potency and charm so many of his contemporaries saw and admired. Poggio thus represented a voice of doubt concerning the basic values of his own culture and was close in this to the cynical despair which, as Eugenio Garin has recently shown, expressed a persisting side of Leon Battista Alberti's consciousness.[35]

The strongest contrast existed between the views of Manetti, who developed the optimistic side of Petrarch's bipolar remedies, and Poggio's total rejection of consolatory rhetoric and of every bridge between earthly behaviour and salvation. Curiously, however, those humanists who seem to have gone furthest in emphasizing the creative or the civic sides of man's eminence and his manifestation of a divine image, followed Stoic, Ciceronian or Aristotelian lines of argument – curiously because, as is well known, Lorenzo Valla polemicized throughout his career against Stoicism and Aristotle and made a point of preferring Quintilian to Cicero; and Valla's only nominally Epicurean anthropology strongly encouraged bold human actions and the assertion of man's creative powers over the natural and historical worlds.[36] Valla's opposition to the classical mentors, however, was more tactical than fundamental; for him they represented the tokens of an allegiance to a regrettable, unnecessary and incorrect reliance on classical philosophical precedents by Christian thinkers, both old and contemporary. Yet in certain ways both Poggio and Valla found themselves on the same side in their scepticism concerning the views of classical philosophy on the condition of man. Both also relied ultimately on grace to guide man's behaviour, regarding the play of natural motives as almost too powerful to be directed rationally. One may also note a similar ambivalence in Petrarch, although less emphatic. For these three important figures man's capacity to manifest the divine image through his direction of nature and creation of a human world of second nature, was more problematical than it was for Manetti, Morandi and, in certain of his writings, Alberti. Alberti's ambivalence might be mentioned precisely here, as he does not elect one or the other of the polar themes on the condition of man but takes emphatically each position at various and clearly overlapping times. Nevertheless we shall use his more constructivist writings, with Manetti's and Morandi's, to illustrate this important humanist stress on human creativity and productivity as a realization of man's potential divinity, but we do not forget the brilliant yet puzzled passages in which Eugenio Garin explores Alberti's ambivalence and even his stance against the argument for the dignity of man.

Whatever Manetti's debts to Bartolomeo Fazio or Antonio da Barga, and despite his bald and lengthy citations of Cicero, Lactantius and so many others, his treatise, none the less, reveals independent and powerful thought.[37] His caution and dependence on citation occurs primarily in his first two books where he dealt with the excellences of the body and soul. In the second book on the soul he followed the medieval not the Augustinian order in naming the divine image of the Trinity in man as intellect, memory and will, and, in keeping with the analogy, emphasized man's intelligence but slid easily over memory and will. This was, perhaps, an unintended reversion to the scholastic Aristotle in a Christian context, but he interpreted intelligence in a clearly Renaissance mode as the operation of human inventiveness and creativity throughout human history – man's 'many, great and remarkable instruments or machines marvellously invented and comprehended'.[38]

These civilizing works of man were classified in an ascending hierarchy: navigation, building, painting, sculpture, poetry (which begins the *altiora et liberaliora*), history, oratory and jurisprudence, philosophy, medicine, astronomy and theology. He offered examples from all these categories, and all are ancient ones except those from the first four, the mechanical arts, which come before the higher liberal arts. For these he gave as examples the Portuguese and Italian navigations into the glacial and the Moorish oceans, Brunelleschi's dome, Giotto's paintings and Ghiberti's bronze doors.

Manetti stressed operational intelligence in book two, preparing the way for his third book on the whole man where he fully asserted his own characteristic encomium of man as possessing all the qualities that we like to believe were most admired in the Renaissance. Man's divine creation determines his thought. What, then, of the making of man? he asked. Should we not say that he was most beautifully and admirably and divinely made? But why did God make man? Was it in order to achieve a work of true perfection? The questions are traditional, transmitted to him by the Olivetan Prior, Antonio da Barga. But the rhetoric, as da Barga hoped, is new. Thus he asked in what manner God made man, and answered 'God created man as the most beautiful, most ingenious, most wise, most opulent and finally most powerful' of creatures.[39]

The concept of man as the guardian of the original creation and the creator of the second nature of the human world is reflected in Manetti's treatment of each of these categories. Man's beauty is best shown in his own sense of beauty which leads him to beautify the world with his works:

Finally, what should we say about mankind who, established as cultivators of the earth, does not permit it to be rendered wild by the cruelty of beasts nor to be made into wasteland by the harshness of plants; mankind by whose works fields, islands and shores are made into countrysides and cities and brightly shine? Indeed, if we were able to see all this with our eyes, just as in our minds, what a marvellous spectacle would appear to those of us living and looking.[40]

Man's ingenuity of inventiveness – the prime quality itself – is manifested in his lengthy listing of the works of man:

Everything after that first, new and rude creation of the world seems to have been invented, constructed and perfected by us by means of a certain, singular and special sharpness of the human mind. They are ours, that is human, because they are seen to have been made by men.[41]

There follows his lengthy listing. Then:

These things, certainly, and other things as many and as great, can be examined everywhere, so that the world and all its beauties seems to have been first invented and established by Almighty God for the use of men, then received by them and rendered much more beautiful and much more ornate and far more refined.[42]

Man's wisdom is expressed in his capacity to order and govern the world and himself, and this itself has led to the knowledge and understanding of the true God and His providence. Man's riches consist in all the parts of nature at his disposal (which are listed and classified at great length). Does this not suggest to us that the great work in natural history of the early modern centuries, especially its explorations and cataloguing of nature, is rooted in this Renaissance conception of man and his role in the world? Finally, Manetti asserts, man's power consists in both his natural and supernatural capacities.

If this was the quality or mode of man's creation, then his function or duty, it follows, is to understand the universe given him by God and to operate in it – *intelligere et agere* – as Garin so effectively argued years ago. All that Manetti previously said of man's excellences has led up to this Renaissance insight, firmly based on Genesis 1:28 – 'Be fruitful and multiply, and replenish the earth, and subdue it; and have dominion over the fish of the sea, and over the fowl of the air, and over every living thing that moveth upon the earth' – which he had cited a little earlier. Manetti's position is clear enough:

> So we think and believe the equally right and simple, as well as unique, office of man is such that the world, and especially those things which we see established in this whole earthly sphere, was made for his sake and that he has the knowledge and ability to govern and administer it. He could not do this at all unless he was fully able to perfect and fulfil the task by action and understanding.[43]

This is perhaps as explicit a statement of modern European man's conception of his earthly purpose as being to dominate and control the natural world as one could hope to find at this distance from the Renaissance (when we see today so many of our contemporaries standing appalled at what seems to be the historical consequences of this point of view, so much more strongly asserted and acted upon in the centuries after Manetti's own).

Manetti optimistically observed:

> Therefore man while alive becomes an inhabitant of the world, and piously dying, he is made into a possessor of heaven, and in this way, both in this present life and in the future one and, indeed, in every time, he is held to be happy and blessed.

But then, as if aware of the perils more recently seen in this position, he added the following warning:

> And from this so great and so sublime dignity and excellence of man, as though from the very root, envy, pride, indignation, lust for domination, and ambition, as well as other disturbances of the soul of this sort, not unjustly arise and flow. For whoever thinks himself to have been made so worthy that he seems to excel and dominate all created things certainly will not suffer to be surpassed by others, which is the vice of envy, but worse, longs most of all to excel others,

which is thought and believed to be the proper vice of pride and ambition. But if, perchance, it happens that anyone is spurned, or neglected and despised, he is offended to such an extent that he will pursue his humiliators as none other than his capital and bitterest enemies and certain specific violators and detractors of his excellences strenuously even unto death. And I, considering this again and again, and wishing to describe and define man, have explained him, not wrongly in my opinion, as an animal filled with indignation.[44]

Unable, perhaps, fully to accept the moral and religious implications of this condemnation of man as *homo indignabundus*, Manetti went on to claim that it would not be fitting and agreeable for man, who was created in such excellence, to remain perpetually damned. Hence God sent His Son to take on human flesh and suffer the ignominious death of the Cross to redeem mankind. But even if our first parents had not sinned, Christ would have descended, not to redeem mankind, but 'in order that man through this humble assumption of human flesh might be marvellously and unbelievably honoured and glorified'.[45] Many learned and holy men seem to have believed this, he added, perhaps referring here to Duns Scotus' famous doctrine that the Incarnation was predestined and the elect elected before the creation of Adam, so that salvation was not due to the Advent, but he named no names. More to the point, he asserted the doctrine of man's deification as the final completion of man's dignity, which lacked nothing else 'except that through admixture with divinity itself it would not only become conjoined with divinity in that person of Christ but also would be made one and the same with the divine nature'.[46]

How difficult it is to classify Manetti as a thinker according to any of the existing intellectual traditions! He ranged through so many classical and Christian sources – Aristotelian, Stoic and Ciceronian, patristic and medieval – and even within these groupings paid his respects to different and opposing levels and views. In the end he seem to have woven out of his amazing erudition a fabric that integrates as warp and woof the Christian creation myth in Genesis 1 of man's role as governor and provider over the natural world in the 'image' of divine providence, with the classical rhetorical (Protagorean-Ciceronian) myth of man as the creator of peace, order and civilization through the invention of the liberal arts, and especially language, in the midst of the savagery of the primitive generations of mankind which bound them to their *bestialitas* and kept them from realizing their *humanitas*. But into the fabric formed of the conjunction of these two traditions Manetti poured the

[101]

dye of his own experience as a Florentine merchant, citizen and admired governor and orator, who in his own pride of achievement and humanistic study (*agere et intelligere*) carried these classical and Christian visions of man into a conceptual and rhetorical definitiveness that went far beyond their original more fragmentary projection. In this way Manetti made his work into a paradigm of the Renaissance genre of the dignity of man.

A brief comment may also be made about Benedetto Morandi's less well-known treatise *De felicitate humana*, in which progress and human civilization is also stressed. Morandi's thinking remained far more encased than Manetti's within traditional Aristotelian terminology, as would not be unexpected in Bologna, still a stronghold of scholastic education despite an increasing humanistic presence. It was the Aristotelian who clashed with the far more conservative, though humanistic, physician, Giovanni Garzoni. Morandi, in brief, argued that the conditions of human existence in this world, quite apart from the higher beatitude of the next life (which he did not deny), could be considered generally favourable to mankind. Although they varied with time, place and culture, these conditions of life are the result of the operation of human industry upon nature, and they lift mankind far above what the natural gifts of animals can give them. The latter, 'compared to the things which human industry invented, are most sordid and abject. And it would have been needless for nature, who does nothing otiose, to have conferred them on man, since by his inventiveness and reason man prepares better things for himself than nature grants to the brutes'.[47]

It did not trouble him that man's superiority was that of *homo viator*:

> Nor do I regard mortals as miserable because the most benign Creator-God said to man, 'In the sweat of thy brow shall ye eat your bread'. In these words he tacitly warned man that not in robbery but in sparing the goods of others, not in enfeebling leisure but in always doing something, he should live his life. And if hands, feet, tongue, eyes and the other organs of the body have their proper functions, will the whole man have none? Therefore what does it profit a man to know, to feel, to believe, to wish, to remember, to compare past with present and through that judge the future, if there was nothing to be done by man?[48]

Again, he rejected the fall of man as a cause for human misery:

> That mortals are not miserable due to the Fall of our parents contaminating all posterity is shown by the words which pious

[102]

Mother Church for that reason sings, namely, 'O happy guilt which merited to have so great and such a Redeemer', speaking of our saviour Jesus Christ.[49]

As for man's creation in God's image, this too did not seem to make him miserable:

> Certainly the human mind can by no reasoning understand that God made man in his image and made him lord of all things which are in the air, on the land or in the sea, possessed of all the disciplines and a little less than the angels . . . so that at length man would be miserable and calamitous and the divine efforts, the nativity and passion and resurrection of Christ for the salvation of man, would be in vain.[50]

Life for man was a struggle, but in this struggle man made a decent existence for himself. Like Manetti's *intelligere et agere*, Morandi offers something he calls *actio studiosa*. But Garzoni, his opponent, says:

> 'Labour is unending'. Hence there is greater merit in fighting than in yielding ground. . . . Philosophers say that the first perfection is that he is learned in the good arts; the second they place in studious action. The wise man, moreover, if he is leisurely differs not at all from the slothful, or at least the somnolent. . . . Therefore he will be happy when he is engaged in studious action.[51]

Leon Battista Alberti wrote no specific treatise on man. Yet, as Garin has argued, all his moral essays deal with the condition of human existence. In the discourse of his uncle Lionardo in the second *Libro della famiglia*, and in his work of old age, *De iciarchia*, Alberti expressed a philosophy closely akin to Manetti's and Morandi's. We must be aware, however, that the constructivist vision of human possibility in these works is matched by his complementary pessimism and despair concerning man's lot and his powers, which Garin has so brilliantly expounded. Although the humanistic genre of the dignity of man dealt predominantly with the theological origins, status and destiny of man in general, with where man stood in comparison with animals and divinity and with what was characteristically human, *humanitas*, Alberti in these two works focuses on the historical reality of the process of becoming a man of dignity. Here and now, in the midst of, and against the current of, the enormous mass of human recalcitrance to anything but man's immediate gratification, Alberti projects his vision. It is true that in the treatises not all men reached the level of dignity of which the species was capable, and that Alberti is offering his idealization of the dignified man as he viewed him in early manhood and again in ripe old age. But like Poggio he despaired of most men and thus presented but the dialectical possibility of another mode of existence, which gives still another humanist version of the ideal of the activistic life. In both works the evils of *ozio* are opposed by *operosità*. The true conception of man, as of all life, in Lionardo's view and in Alberti's in *De iciarchia*, is that he should be constantly acting: 'Therefore it seems to me, and I so believe, that man was certainly not born to pine away in indolence but to stand up and do things'.[52]

Lionardo proceeded to support this view by presenting a series of traditional *topoi* from the genre of the dignity of man. It would be stupid to argue that the divine force of man's soul, mind, intellect, judgement, memory, virtues and passions, 'with which he overcomes the strength, swiftness and ferocity of any other animal, were given for not wishing to work much'. He did not like Epicurus' view that 'in God supreme happiness consists in doing nothing'. Anaxagoras' stress on man's erect posture for studying 'the marvellous works of God', and that of the Stoics, who held man is by nature 'the contemplator and activator of things', pleased him more. He liked Protagoras' opinion that 'man is the measure of all things'. He could, if he wished, quote other ancients and many sayings of our theologians. Especially pleasing was Aristotle, 'who demonstrated that man is happy like a mortal god in understanding and acting with reason and *virtù*'.[53] Here, again, is the Aristotelian *intelligere et agere* used by Manetti.

The many beautiful and useful things placed in the world to fill man's needs prove his divine origin:

> Here add to this how much man must render service to God in order to satisfy Him with good works for the gift of such great powers which he has given the soul of man, something which is far beyond the scope of other earthly animated creatures.

There follows his depiction of the greatness of man's nature given him by God:

> Nature, that is God, made man as composed of a celestial and divine part, something that is most beautiful and most noble beyond anything mortal . . .

possessing a beautiful and agile body, keen senses, discourse and judgement for learning all necessary things, the mental qualities needed for investigating and understanding all things, the moral restraint necessary for living with other men.

[104]

God also established a strong bond in human souls to hold human society together – justice, equity, liberality and love, with which a man can merit gratitude and praise among other mortals, and pity and mercy before God.

God strengthened the breast of man so that he could sustain every labour, adversity and turn of fortune, so that he could overcome difficulties, conquer suffering, and not fear death. With

firmness, stability, constancy and strength, and with contempt for perishable things . . . with justice, piety, temperance, and with every other perfect and highly laudable action.

Finally, he concluded:

I am persuaded, therefore, that man was not born to sorrow in leisure but to become active in magnificent and large affairs, with which one can please and honour God, in the first place, and, through having the use of perfect virtue in oneself, acquire the fruit of felicity.[54]

We cannot follow his long amplification of the importance of virtue and *operosità* and finally of *onestà* in this book. Nor can we, because of space, discuss *De iciarchia*, where this image of the operative man comes through even more strongly from Alberti in his own *persona*. The vision of man as born to manage himself, the world of nature and mankind is asserted by Alberti as an ideal of how man should strive to live well, greatly and humanly in his own environment of the Renaissance city. Yet Alberti's example also reveals the dissidence and tension in urban culture between this optimistic, constructivist view and Alberti's cynical observations of man's wolf-like behaviour to his fellows and the rest of nature.

Held though it was with much ambivalence, a new conception of man was clearly emerging in the Renaissance out of a synthesis of the Stoic view found in Cicero's *De natura deorum* and Augustine's Trinitarian anthropology. Man, in this view, was emphatically active, operative, directive and managerial. Aristotle's three categories of production, action and speculation also exerted a less precisely conceptualized influence. There were also elements of detachment and passivity in Stoic thought and of asceticism and other-worldliness in Augustine. Yet it is remarkable how these three – Manetti, Morandi and more ambiguously Alberti – along with other thinkers of the period, drew upon their own sense of the values embedded in Italian urban culture to construct a vivid and empirical conception of man as a creator. However rhetorical and self-serving of their own way of life this conception was, it none the less succeeded in projecting the basic structure and motivation of Renaissance anthropological thought in a vision of man making his own history and triumphing over nature and fortune. The elements of historical realism that emerge in this transformed literary genre, prompted by so much concern with how Christian man can cope with the actualities and complexities of late medieval society, should not be obscured by the clearly religious modalities that characterized this way of thinking. Yet it is essential that the religious framings of Renaissance anthropological thought are not eliminated but fully appreciated. We turn now to an examination of them.

THEOLOGIA RHETORICA

The views put forth in the humanists' discussions of *humanitas* and treatises on the condition of man had profound theological presuppositions and implications, not always clearly articulated but loosely present. It would have been impossible in an intellectual movement generated within the historical context of late medieval Christian Europe for it to have been otherwise. Indeed, a fundamental motivation for the revival of ancient thought and letters was a need to discover a convergence between Christian religious beliefs and the cultural and intellectual problems generated by life in the Italian cities. The availability, both immediate and researched, of the thought and expression of antiquity made it inevitable that ancient culture would provide models and insights for the identification and communication of contemporary problems. But these could be conceived in no other framework than Christian.

Let us take, for example, the case of Petrarch. His sensitivity to the needs of his contemporaries for a more responsible management of their emotional responses to the pressures of urban living than scholastic and canonistic culture provided, led him straight to Seneca's *Epistulae* and Cicero's *Tusculans*. It also led him to find the Christian solution, not in scholastic theology, but in that most poignant ancient confrontation of classical and Christian value, the *Confessions* of St Augustine. And led him to his first great formulations in the *Secretum* and *De vita solitaria*, and to the more profound meditation of the experiential problems of sin, free will, justification and grace found in the *De otio religioso*.[55] The Stoic anthropology of divine rational mind immanent in each individual who is at the same time distracted by the false images of reality imposed by the senses is adapted to Christian ends. The role of the sage pointing to the true and rational way is transformed into that of the saint counselling the deep meditation of death, hell and the horrors of sins. In this way a Christian structuring of reality replaces the superficial lure of sensuality in which the ordinary man, including Petrarch himself, feels trapped. Scholars have fussed over Augustinus' Stoicism, but for Petrarch the greater emotional profundity of Christian experience, mediated by the *Confessions*, triumphs over Stoic rationalistic formula.

The *De otio religioso* sees him in the role of religious counsellor and takes his reader (monastic or lay) through the drama of despair at human insignificance and fear of perdition to the great emotional relief of salvation *gratia sola*. Petrarch's is our first, and perhaps best, example of a humanistic *theologia rhetorica* which defines the elements of Christian theology as embedded in the experience and feelings of living individuals. We might today call it 'existential' if the misplacement of such borrowed terms were not both unnecessary and confusing. But if the direct pastoral confrontation of confessor and confessant is crucial in the medieval Christian experience, Petrarch's literary employment of the situation is a vivid, and for him more experientially valid and hence 'true' statement of Christian doctrine, which scholastic theology as 'science' had succeeded in removing from the context of everyday Christian living.

Yet Petrarch, despite his insights into the affective nature of faith, remained ambivalent·on the issue of reason, even leaving *Ratio* as spokesman in imitation of Seneca in the later *De remediis*. His endorsement of *gratia sola* of the *De otio* certainly placed salvation beyond reason, beyond free will, but not entirely beyond will. The ambiguity of the role of will in rhetoric is inherent, as appeals to reason were part of the Ciceronian-Senecan tradition taken up from the Stoics. Yet will was seen as affective and non-rational, and rhetoric as such seeks to move, and to move towards action carrying out a transformed inner purpose or will, as Augustine affirmed in the *De doctrina Christiana*. An Augustinian position necessarily sees the ultimate moment of conversion as supra-rational resolution of conflicting wills, which Petrarch recognized in the *Secretum*. Petrarch's endorsement of Latin rhetoric over Aristotelian science in *De ignorantia* also put him on the side of will – 'It is better to will the good than to know the truth'.[56] One need not see any Franciscan or Scotist influence in those humanists who endorse the primacy of the will, because in so many ways their own rhetorical arts and purposes demand it. However, the Augustinian influence from the OESA (*Ordo fratrum eremitorum sancti Augustini*), from Dionigio da Borgo San Sepolcro, from Luigi Marsili and others, is not to be dismissed.

Salutati exhibited much of the same ambivalence about will and reason as Petrarch had.[57] But he also made far-reaching statements of the primacy of the will in human existence and its command over both the intellect and the senses. He seems to have been confronted by some of the same moral and theological dilemmas as the nominalist scholastics of the fourteenth-century faced, although there is no doubt that he chose a different path. The problem again for him was one of exhortation both to himself and his fellows, as against the need felt by Ockhamists (whose influence in Italy, and especially in Florence, was still meagre in Salutati's day) for careful analysis of the logical inconsistencies in theological statements and between them and the scriptures. We should recognize that both rhetoric and dialectic in the fourteenth and fifteenth centuries could lead to a new kind of theology containing a new anthropology. There was perhaps in the case of both types of intellectual practitioners, a common dissatisfaction with the heroic efforts of the twelfth- and thirteenth-century paladins of a theological 'science' to bind Christianity to Hellenic, and primarily to Aristotelian, metaphysics.

Salutati, perhaps more than most humanists, wrote specifically about theological questions. Though he did not sermonize, he addressed consolatory and hortatory letters to his friends and justified his viewpoint in his treatises. Will became uppermost in the context of deciding to embark on a certain way of life, to cultivate certain virtues. Salutati affirmed the primacy of the will most emphatically in *De nobilitate legum et medicinae* (one of the most important of the many important humanist statements made available by Eugenio Garin).[58] The principle of man acting upon the world in keeping with, and justified by, God's command in Genesis 1:28–30, underlies Salutati's forceful statements:

> The first action does not even come into the intellect without the counsel and command of the will. The natural desire of knowing is not an attribute of the intellect but of the will. . . . Although the soul may be nobler than exterior things, intellection is a movement from them into the soul, whereas in what is volition the movement is from the soul into things themselves.[59]

Nothing moves in the soul unless the will commands:

> whose strength is so great and its rule over the other powers of the soul so mighty, that even though the instruments of the senses are the recipients of the sensible species (images), the effect of such a reception scarcely proceeds further without the orders of the will.[60]

These statements occur within the conventional Aristotelian

epistemology from the *De anima* he presents, and although, like some of the Ockhamists, he emphasized that man can only know particulars, he clearly retained the notion of the 'real existence' of genera and species preserved within the individual object. In epistemology he was no nominalist here, though later he endorsed a poetic epistemology of the metaphorical character of all human knowledge and statement concerning God and spiritual beings. On the other hand, it is interesting that Ockham most definitely played down the Scotist emphasis on the primacy of the will and insisted upon a bivalence of these two functional aspects of the soul, whereas it is the humanist, prompted by the needs and implications of rhetoric, who carries voluntarism further. Humanism and nominalism are not fully congruous.

Salutati's conception of his intellectual role and purpose is also to be seen in the relatively late directly theological treatise, *De fato, fortuna et casu*. Strongly Augustinian and also apparently influenced by such thirteenth-century figures as Aegidius of Rome, Salutati affirmed a conception of man as highly active, operating in a world of contingencies – natural, economic, social and political. At the same time he sought a mode of harmonizing man's will with divine providence and the network of natural causation, identified and elaborated by philosophy with divine freedom – each of them problems of central concern to contemporary nominalist theology. Theological in format, the treatise's literary form and position were humanistic, especially in its drive to assert man as co-operator with God in making and directing the universe, a viewpoint that supports and is totally consistent with the later, more literary genre of the dignity of man. Salutati saw the humanist's role as one of providing leadership in binding the *studia humanitatis* and the *studia divinitatis* (his name for the older theological writings) into a mutually supporting unity and certainly had a conception of *humanitas* as concerned with the nature and destiny of mankind in this world and the next.

The work of Lorenzo Valla[61] was of fundamental importance in projecting a Christian-rhetorical conception of man – one which marked a break of the most radical kind from both the medieval Hellenic-Aristotelian metaphysics, and from the naiveté and sentimentality of the Renaissance humanist hope of synthesizing a classical *praeparatio evangeliae* with conventional Christianity. The recent important studies of Valla by Fois, Di Napoli and Camporeale all affirm this.[62] It is difficult to have any certainty as to exactly where Valla's doctrines led historically: whether to Erasmus, or Luther, or the more radical anti-Trinitarian and Socinian heresies, if genuinely to any of them. There seems no question of his own desire, at least, to be a loyal and orthodox Catholic Christian as this was conceived in the fifteenth century. We know that in his own lifetime, Valla was considered doctrinally dangerous (if not a heretic) but at the same time was befriended by cardinals and popes. We also know that he was in post-Tridentine disrepute, admired by Luther, followed by Erasmus in some respects but rejected in others, cited on the Trinity by Servetus, and so on. We cannot deny that there was a reformist impulse in him, and that he wished to straighten out the thinking and doctrinal confusion of his contemporaries, but in this aim he did not depart far from his friends Nicholas of Cusa, the German cardinal, Bessarion, or Pope Nicholas V, or possibly from certain other humanists such as Alberti or Manetti. He had perhaps more in common with Giovanni Gioviano Pontano, the young Neapolitan humanist he seems to have befriended but who rejected and criticized him. Pontano thought of Valla as following only one line of authority, his own, but also recalled his personal kindness. For Pontano he was the perfect example of a *homo contentiosus*.[63] I believe that in all three judgements Pontano was right. Valla was totally anti-Aristotelian, but in many instances primarily for the sake of opposing the scholastics' great authority. Pontano was strongly pro-Aristotle, for he recognized the very strengths of practical insight into human behaviour and linguistic usage that Valla stubbornly ignored. But in the final analysis Pontano's position was as fundamentally anti-metaphysical as Valla's. Or, at least, both men thoroughly undermined the topical metaphysics of Hellenism, preferring an historical conception of thought as springing from cultural experience and linguistic usage. Whatever historical precedents there are here for contemporary analytical linguistic philosophy, or for historicism in general, the implications of his drastic linguistic critique of the nature and origins of human culture for the Christian religion were crucial for Valla. He might well have claimed that his critique itself grew from the implications of Christianity, specifically of its creationist vision of God, with man in the divine image making and shaping his own culture on the model of God creating nature. But on the other hand the Christian Gospel was scripturally based and linguistic, a message presented to us by Christ and his apostles, coming from God but in form a literary text to be understood grammatically, rhetorically, historically and poetically.

Clearly Valla's philological and grammatical studies of classical texts and the New Testament have been stressed by scholars because (*pace* Manetti) he was the founder of biblical humanism and exerted a profound (though contradictory) influence on Erasmus and Luther, as well as on the Latin cultures. However, Valla's anthropology – his

[110]

conception of human thought and action and of the relation of man's status to that of the animal and the divine – simultaneously led to his seizing upon all that he thought was valid in ancient thought and a transformation of medieval-Renaissance thinking about man into a radically new perspective. The ancients generally conceived of man as part of a graduated scale of animal, human and divine with each segment overlapping with the next. Man was, in his physiology and lower psychology, animal, in his intellectuality or spirituality, semi-divine and potentially divine. But Antiquity also offered an alternative conception through the rhetorical tradition. Valla grasped the anthropological implications of the rhetorical tradition which were rooted in Greek sophist (Gorgian–Protagorean) thought. These were in Valla's view the subjectivity of man, the impossibility of the individual transcending his own perceptions except by interpreting another's and incorporating these into his own, and the primarily affective and voluntarist character of this condition, which reduced thinking and communication to provisional convention between two or more humans, all of which made it impossible for mankind to differentiate itself from animal kind on the basis of its psychic and intellectual powers. In many of these powers the animals also excelled. In this way Valla carried the sophistic argument farther than the ancients and destroyed the presupposition of natural hierarchy on which classical ontology was based.

Moreover, Valla's and the sophistic conception of the human condition rendered the concept of nature, or the natural, otiose, since the concept itself was seen as a human product. Men differentiated themselves from animals in so far as they utilized their capacities, which differed from animals only in degree and not in kind, to gain a greater quantity or intensity of pleasure and to avoid pain and trouble more effectively. Man was not animal in body and semi-divine in spirit; he was animal both in body and spirit. Man was not born (i.e. naturally) divine; he encountered phenomena which he interpreted as manifesting divinity. The ancient philosophers (and those Latin rhetoricians influenced by them) inflated man's mental and spiritual powers into something godlike, but this Valla believed was illusory. Instead, man, if he had faith, believed that accounts of God given by men in the scriptures were true and that man had at his beginning as a species encountered his Creator directly and had retained a dim recollection of this afterward. According to Valla faith was not generically different from knowledge since all knowledge and truth was simply any man's sincere affirmation that he thought something was true, and therefore truth itself was a faith that a certain judgement was correct. A man of

[111]

faith would, after the coming of Christ and the founding of his Church reported in the New Testament, have a far greater knowledge of divinity than those ancients who lost their initial knowledge of God but, dimly recalling it, sought to make themselves gods by transcending their own animal natures through the veneration of intellect and virtue. A Christian who believed that God had returned as Christ would also believe that immortality and resurrection awaited mankind after death. It was only by faith in the truth of Christianity, as revealed in the scriptures, that man could differentiate himself from the animal generically and could then anticipate the possibility of immortality, beatitude and deification in the afterlife.

Such, summarily stated, is Valla's Christian vision of man and God as put forth primarily in his *De vero bono*, but supplemented by readings of his *Repastinatio philosophiae et dialecticae* (first redaction).[64] What he offered, if I have read him correctly, was a resolution of the problem of double consciousness inherited from Antiquity, wherein Petrarch and other humanists, and notably Il Galateo as described above, wrestled with the contradictions between a knowledge of the world gained from personal and shared historical experience, and another one derived from an ultimately divinely inspired intellection of an absolute and rational truth.

This double consciousness, clearly enunciated in Plato's confrontation of Protagoras and Socrates of the *Theatetus*,[65] continued through the syntheses and contrasts of rhetoric and philosophy of the pagan and Christian Latin thinkers on into the Renaissance. There the notion of a lower truth of rhetorical verisimilitude sufficient for politics and everday life, and a higher truth of philosophy, rational demonstration or mystical intuition necessary for orthodoxy and science, was sometimes incorporated into more conventional humanist thinking, but more often it was utilized by scholastic philosophers to subordinate rhetoric, and the understanding of daily life and political affairs, to their own so-called higher learning. Valla in fact reduced the latter to the former.[66] There is no truth but what is subjectively entertained as true, and our collective faith is Christianity.

In doing so, without direct knowledge of the sophists or *Theatetus* (though with minute and precise knowledge of the Latin texts drawing upon them), Valla affirmed the same preference for will over intellect which Petrarch somewhat ambiguously declared in his 'It is better to will the good than to know the truth' and 'Therefore they wander far who put their time into knowing, not loving God'.[67] But Petrarch's and also Salutati's emphasis on the primacy of will, thoroughgoing as we have seen the latter to be, fell short of Valla's radical denial of any autonomy to thought and his simultaneous subordination of ratiocination to verbal usage and to affect.

Valla, moreover, broke sharply from the tradition of scholastic discussions of the problem of human nature. Will, of course, had been brought into it from an Augustinian rather than an Aristotelian provenance. But Valla went further than either Franciscans or Augustinians, or earlier humanists, in his development of Augustinianism. Making no effort to discover a mode of reconciliation with the Aristotelian hierarchy of vegetative, sensitive and rational souls, he fully assimilated the conception of man as an image of the Trinity, consisting, as Augustine had expounded, of the coequal trinity of memory, intellect and will. Yet for Valla it was clear that primacy was given to affect, to non-rational will, even though he formally kept the equistasis of the three faculties. In the end his transformation of Augustinianism, in which the passions were made equally licit with intellectual virtues and the latter equally culpable, determined his position. In *De vero bono*, just as Augustine saw the pagan virtues as splendid vices, Valla made pagan passion (his eroticized 'Epicureanism' of Vegio or Beccadelli) into Christian charity, and pleasure into beatitude. The pagan world, in which Stoic debates Epicurean on behalf of *honestas* or *voluptas*, is transcended in the Christian one where the heroic virtue of fortitude is the same as charity and the means to Christian fulfilment; divine love of God for the sake of the passion of love is the end. But means and end differ only in time; both are charity, one in the present, the other future; or the first passing and the second becoming eternally present.

However, in Valla's Renaissance version, trinitarian man becomes creative and activist. Virtue is *fortezza/carità* because man is a force (*vis*) acting upon the world. Virtue is infused into man by grace but effused out of man. It is therefore not a *habitus*. Rather prudence, the intellect, the arts and all the disciplines are slowly acquired by training, and are habits. Man is born with his passions but painstakingly acquires his intellectual skills. Man with his trinitarian nature is likened to a flame:

> Just as a flame seizes and devours and renders into ashes the material by which it is fed, so the soul is nourished in learning and hides what it perceives within itself and transfigures it in its own heat and light, so that it paints others rather than being painted by others. And as the sun paints its image in polished and smooth things and does not receive their images in itself, so the soul, advancing into exterior things by its own light, projects and depicts a certain image of its memory, intellect and will.[68]

Man, therefore, is part of nature in sharing the same kinds of capacities with animals. But in so far as he discovers that his trinitarian nature is of divine origin and is in the image and likeness of God, man transcends his nature and diverts his pursuit of pleasure from the limited things of this life to the eternal pleasure of beatitude. In this he simultaneously creates a higher Christian culture and transcends nature, or becomes divine. Pagan man sought to create culture with the acquisition of virtues as his chief end of life, but in this he remained one with nature and the animals, and all his creations (as in fact ancient philosophers believed) are merely extensions of nature. Only Christian man becomes a true creator in this world by fulfilling his divinely assigned role of providential manager of nature.

Three closely related themes – free will, pleasure, deification – are also involved in humanist discussions of providentiality, and for all three, which were widely discussed by other humanists, Valla provided a paradigmatic clarity and relevance of interpretation. Humanists not only affirmed the power of will but discussed the necessity of *liberum arbitrium* as an inherent quality of will. Rhetoric assumes this freedom of choice, for otherwise its appeals are futile. Will became a problem both in the context of secular actions and in that of salvation. In the former there was never any question of man's providential freedom to govern nature or human affairs, the only obstacles being physical recalcitrance, fortune and human incapacity to act wisely due to the complexity of man's psychic nature. However, it has to be assumed that by rhetorical appeal he could be aroused to clarity of perception and thought, and propriety of action in the secular realm. The real debate occurred over the question of whether man could attain salvation by the merits of his freely chosen actions or psychic states. Here we cannot review the vast question of ecclesiastical discussions of which many humanists were well aware. And although their importance is obvious we are compelled by reason of space to omit treatment of Petrarch and Salutati. Because they qualify more as formal philosophers than humanists, we also do not deal with Ficino and Giovanni Pico della Mirandola and the entire development of Platonism and Hermetism.

Whereas Petrarch and Salutati had emphasized grace and providence but also necessarily affirmed human freedom of choice, Valla's famous position seems even more contradictory. But it is not. Freedom of the will is asserted as an undeniable quality of human experience, which is the first great source of truth for Valla. But divine foreknowledge and predestination are also affirmed on the basis of his faith in the Pauline passages in Romans. The scriptures were, of course, the other great source of truth for Valla. It was clear to him that they were contradictory, but because man's understanding was limited to experience and faith he could not resolve their contradiction but had to accept them both as a *mysterium*.[69] He was closer to Petrarch in standing on experience and faith and avoiding philosophical complexities, but was not unsympathetic to Salutati's desire to affirm a vision of God and man, despite the *ventosa sophistica* of dialectical theology.

Pleasure and sensuality were also subject to humanist praise and blame, particularly as far as the pursuit of pleasure seemed to divert man from God and salvation, and reduce him abjectly to an animal state. Hence a variety of opinions is to be found among the humanists which, again, we cannot deal with here. Valla was not the only one to endorse pleasure as central to human experience, but let us see how he interpreted it in its secular and religious contexts.

Valla's position was important because he stressed, in his antiphilosophism, the continuity between the psychic natures of animals and men when outside the realm of salvation. The power of will and of affectivity which he stressed, he saw as closely linked to the senses. *Voluptas*, as the gratificatory goal of animal/human life in Books 1 and 2 of *De vero bono*, is made the equivalent of love and charity in Book 3. Love of God is the ultimate pleasure, but not for the sake of God but because God is the efficient cause of human pleasure and of the human capacity to love. God creates the lovable objects of the world and the human capacities of sensory recipience and loving – *amatio*.

> In God both of these concur, for He produced us from nothing, fit for enjoying good things, so that we ought to love him more than ourselves, and He supplied those very goods which we perceive. Moreover God is these goods Himself, but is distinguished from them by a certain property. For our beatitude is not God Himself but descends from God, as the joy which I take in seeing brightness, or hearing a mellow voice, is not the same as the brightness or the voice, but these things offered to my senses cause me to enjoy. Thus from the vision and knowledge of God, beatitude itself is generated. It should also be noticed that although I say pleasure or delight is the only good, nevertheless, I love not pleasure but God. Pleasure itself is love, but what makes pleasure is God. The recipient loves, the received is loved; loving (*amatio*) is delight itself, or pleasure, or beatitude, or happiness, or charity, which is the ultimate end and on account of which all other things are made.[70]

This is clearly a crucial passage, since Valla speaks as a Christian but endorses pleasure, and by his great power of penetrating to the heart of an experience, sees the identity of pleasure and charity or love. Pleasure of loving is both the ultimate human experience and the great motivator of human thought and action.

Another important humanist theme was that of 'deification'. In the context of image-and-likeness theology, salvation was traditionally seen as *theosis* or *deificatio*, for through this man regained his lost original dignity and even, through Christ's work of redemption, surpassed it. The conception gained a special significance in the Renaissance through its linkage with the new vision of man's creativity on the model of divine creativity. The special qualities of man expounded by Manetti found a more explicit parallel in Ficino's list of the qualities of divinity which men emulated in their eagerness to attain deification. These can be found in the first eight chapters of Book 14 of his *Theologia Platonica* – 'That the soul attempts to become God we show by twelve signs according to the twelve gifts of God.' But, as indicated above, we shall not carry our analysis into Renaissance Platonism but simply allude to the tremendous importance of the deification theme in figures such as Ficino and Pico, and perhaps even more in Nicholas of Cusa's conception of man as the creator of culture in the image of God as Creator of reality.[71]

Valla set forth his own vision of deification in his sermon on the Eucharist and in his imagined journey of a soul to Christ in *De vero bono*.[72] But more importantly, one should see in his treatment of affect and virtue an embattled conception of human energy that approaches the notion of divine power. An admirer of combat and struggle, a *miles Christianus* who considered his life and writing as in the service of the Church Militant, his identification of *fortezza* and *carità* as *virtù* in its purest form combines elements drawn from Homeric *arêtè* and from medieval Christian *virtus*. Each pointed toward divinization, the hero emulating the gods by his fortitude, the Christian through his charity manifesting the infusion of divine grace. Though Valla spurned the notion of a *habitus gratiae*, the acquisition of virtue, which he saw as poured in and poured out, remained inexplicable. If acquired, it betokened strength of mind, for to sin is to be conquered by weakness toward that which a man should conquer. Fortitude is the ardour of love which renders animals fierce in the protection of their young, but:

> as we speak more magnificently and aptly, this is why the Apostles, receiving the Holy Spirit, which is the charity of the Father and the Son, were made strong for preaching the Word of God, which previously the Lord had promised to them.[73]

Filled with the Holy Spirit, the *miles Christianus* battles for the right, and in this struggle he approaches the beatification of the other life.

Valla represents, then, the most thorough synthesis of certain patristic-Christian, principally Augustinian, ideas with classical language and rhetorical theory. Within this synthesis of rhetorical and Pauline perspectives, Valla developed a philosophy of man that assimilated the widespread striving for power in Renaissance culture. This power has usually been portrayed by historians as secular and political. Yet it was also a generic human power which not only searched for a certain religious licitness in its possession but was, in its very form and conception, drawn from the Christian tradition of man as created in the divine image. Just as hero or saint was held to approach divinity, so true power was conceived as divine power. This striving for religious and religiously sanctioned power is related as an historical phenomenon to the amazing efflorescence of magic in this period, both natural and spiritual.

But to the humanists power also had a more empirical and naturalistic basis. Language, words and discourse had come to be grasped as something greater than a medium for communicating mental concepts and logical demonstrations. The humanist investigators of classical poetry and rhetoric discovered that language possessed both charm and potency that was activistic and moved men in an organized struggle for existence. Although their classical sources were permeated with philosophic rationalism, the more thorough students of rhetoric – notably Valla and Pontano – discerned the irrational power elements even in the rhetorical writings of Aristotle, Cicero and Quintilian. It was possibly for this reason that Valla was so insistent that ancient rhetoric and grammar had much to offer Christians as means for the promotion of Christ's cause, whereas the ancient philosophical schools were the seedbeds of disunity and heresy. In his own conception of language (he constantly speaks of *vis verbi*) and of the central place of *virtus* (read as 'force' or 'power') in man's existence, there is a recovery of that ancient sophistic recognition of rhetoric as an instrument of power like a magical charm or a potent drug administered by a physician such as is found in Gorgias' *Defence of Helen*. Petrarch, also, argued forcefully for the curative power of language both in his *Contra medicum* and his *De remediis*.[74]

If the above is a valid interpretation of humanist thought, it suggests at the very least that the 'potency' of Renaissance humanism cannot be comprehended in the view of it as a pedantic group of classicizing literary scholars. Indeed the literary and philological studies of the humanists led them to important insights concerning the historical character of human thought and culture. It suggests, furthermore, that the humanists' conceptions of man and his role in the universe had, not

[117]

at all surprisingly, a profound rapport with the basic trends of Renaissance Italian political, economic and social history and even more with its artistic, cultural and religious history. Finally, one might argue that in the depth, sharpness and range of understanding of their views of human nature and its societal, political and religious ramifications, the humanists clearly laid the foundations for early modern discussions of man, such as have provided a basis for modern anthropological thought. One thinks of Hobbes and Descartes, of Vico and Mandeville among others. But we should also not forget that we should view their anthropological-religious thought anthropologically, and within that context we cannot avoid recognizing how much of the characteristic attitudes and motivations of the men of the Renaissance themselves this body of writing contains – unless, perchance, we have in fact constructed our own neo-Burckhardtian conceptions of Renaissance culture from it!

NOTES

1 Modern study of Renaissance philosophy of man (or philosophical anthropology) begins with Giovanni Gentile, 'Il concetto dell'uomo nel Rinascimento', of 1916, reprinted in his *Il pensiero italiano del Rinascimento* (most recently Florence, 1968), and with Ernst Cassirer, *Individuum und Kosmos in der Philosophie der Renaissance* (1927), Eng. trans. by Mario Domandi (Oxford, 1963). Both were neo-Burckhardtian and neo-Hegelian or neo-Kantian. For more modern studies see Eugenio Garin, 'La "Dignitas Hominis" e la letteratura patristica', *La Rinascita*, I (1938), 102–46, and many of his other writings; P.O. Kristeller, *Renaissance Concepts of Man and Other Essays* (New York, 1972); Giovanni di Napoli, ' "Contemptus Mundi" e "Dignitas Hominis" nel Rinascimento', *Rivista di filosofia neoscolastica*, XLVIII (1956), 9–41, and his *L'immortalità dell'anima nel Rinascimento* (Turin, 1963); Charles Trinkaus, *In Our Image and Likeness: Humanity and Divinity in Italian Humanist Thought* (London–Chicago, 1970) (hereafter cited as *IOIAL*) and 'The Renaissance idea of the dignity of man', *Dictionary of the History of Ideas*, IV (New York, 1973), 136-47. Extensive further bibliographies in Kristeller, Di Napoli, Trinkaus.

2 See Werner Jaeger, *Paideia: the Ideals of Greek Culture*, 3 vols (Oxford, 1939–44); Henri-I. Marrou, *Histoire de l'éducation dans l'antiquité*, 6th edn (Paris, 1965), 151–60 ('La civilisation de la "Paideia" '). For *humanitas* and Renaissance see Kristeller's classical statement, 'Humanism and Scholasticism in the Italian Renaissance', *Byzantion*, XVII (1944/5), 346–74, reprinted in *Studies in Renaissance Thought and Letters* (Rome, 1956), 553–83 and elsewhere. Also see Gioacchino Paparelli, *Feritas, Humanitas, Divinitas (L'essenza umanistica del Rinascimento)* (Naples, 1973).

3 See Garin, Di Napoli, Trinkaus as above.
4 See Jaeger, op. cit., I, xiii-xxix, for important discussion of ancient conception of culture and way differs from modern relativistic anthropology.
5 Cf. Paparelli, op. cit., 124–6.
6 Thus the Renaissance emphasis on *humanitas* as a product of custom and
education, rather than nature, introduced an explicit relativism into the
universalism received from Antiquity. See S. N. Stever, *Philology and
Historical Thought in Early Italian Humanism* (Ann Arbor, University
Microfilms, 1976. Diss. Univ. of Michigan).
7 G.G. Pontano, *De sermone libri sex*, ed. by S. Lupi and A. Riscato (Lugano,
1954), I.i.3: '*Ut autem ratio ipsa dux est ac magistra ad actiones quasque
dirigendas, sic oratio illorum ministra est omnium quae mente concepta
ratiocinandoque agitata depromuntur in medium, cum sociabiles, ut dictum
est, nati simus sitque vivendum in multitudine; quae quo maior est ac
frequentior, eo in illa huberior est copia eorum omnium quibus vita indiget,
quando nascentibus hominibus inopia data est comes; qua re vita ipsa longe
aptior redditur atque habilior tum ad assequandas virtutes tum ad
felicitatem comparandam.*'
8 ibid., I.iii.1: '*populosissimis in civitatibus amplissimisque in
administrationibus.*'
9 ibid. I.iii.2: '*Sed nos hac in parte de ea, quae oratoria sive vis facultasque sive
ars dicitur, nihil omnino loquimur, verum de oratione tantum ipsa
communi, quaque homines adeundis amicis, communicandis negociis in
quotidianis praecipue utuntur sermonibus, in conventibus, consessionibus,
congressibus familiaribusque ac civilibus consuetudinibus. Qua a re alia
quadam hi ratione commendantur quam qui oratores dicuntur atque
eloquentas.*'
10 ibid., I.iv.1–2: '*Nec vero natura in hoc quoque a se ipsa discessit aut ab ea,
quae sua ipsius propria est, varietate ac dissimilitudine. Cum aliorum
sermones severi sint ac subtristes, aliorum iucundi et lepidi, huius blanda sit
elocutio atque ornata, illius inculta et aspera, atque alius in loquendo prae se
ferat urbis mores, alius vero ruris, est videri qui velit facetus et comis, contra
qui austerus et rigidus, qui maxime verus omnique a simulatione alienus,
secus autem cui dissimulatio placeat aut ea quae Graece est "ironia". Itaque
loquendi genus tum cuiusque naturam tum etiam mores sequi potissimum
videtur. Quid! quod populi gentesque, sive nature ab ipsa sive ab institutione
et usu quodque alia alibi magis probantur suntque in pretio maiori, aliae
taciturniores sunt, contra loquaciores aliae! Magniloquentia delectat
Hispanos, fucatus ac compositus sermo Graecos, Romanorum gravis fuit
oratio, Lacedaemoniorum brevis et horrida, Atheniensium multa et
studiosa, at Carthaginiensium Afrorumque callida et vafra, de natura
illorum sic dicta. Quo fit, ut genus colloquendi alibi aliud magis probetur aut
minus.*'
11 ibid., I.vii.2: '*quae susceptorum laborum honestum sit levamen
relaxatioque maxime laudabilis a curis ac molestis . . . quae hominem
ipsum ita constituat ut per eam constet humana conciliatio vigeatque in
civitate fides, penes quam actionum nostrarum omnium ac negotiationum
vinculum existat ac promissorum doctorumque observatio.*'

12 ibid., I.vii.1: '*adulatores et quasi verborum mercaturam faciant, oratione ubique utuntur secunda et blanda.*'

13 ibid., I.xviii.1–2: '*Et quam alii a natura concessam elocutionem exercent in conservanda hominum societate, in conciliandi amicitiis, in solandis demulcendisque molestiis, laboribus ac moeroribus aliorum, ea ipsi in adversum utantur vel abutantur potius ad odia contrahenda litesque excitandas ac serenda discordiarum semina.* . . . *Odiosum sane genus hominum et muscarum maxime simile, ut nati hi omnino videantur ad turbas, vexationes, inquietudinem vitaeque ad universae turbationem ac taedia.*'

14 ibid., I.xxx.3: '*quacumque in actione ac vitae genere humanum:* . . . *nihil superbe agit, nihil arroganter; in incessu, in sermone, in consuetudine aequalem se cunctis exhibet; aegre fert ubi in quempiam agi viderit insolentius, fert gravate et amicorum et civium adversos casus; solatur moerentes, laborantibus qua potest succurrit, adest, opitulatur, operam suam confert; astat ubique comes ei mansuetudo ac facilitas.*'

15 ibid., I.xxx.4: '*a comitate non uno modo differt humanitas. Etenim, qui aliorum moveatur damnis, incommodis, captivitate, orbitate, inopia, exilio malisque aliis, humanum hunc dicimus, nequaquam in hoc tamen comem.* . . . *Inest tamen utrique quaedam quasi communitas vivendi quacumque in actione ac negocio, sive eam facilitatem vocare volumus sive tractabilitatem.*'

16 G. Manetti, *De dignitate et excellentia hominis*, ed. by E.R. Leonard (Padua, 1976), III.20; 78: '*Nam cum primi illi homines et vetusti eorum successores sine mutuis quibusdam et vicissitudinariis favoribus per se solos nequaquam vivere posse animadvertent, subtile quoddam et acutum loquendi artificium adinvenerunt ut per linguam intercedentibus verbis abstrusa queque atque intime mentis sensa cunctis audientibus innotescerent. Cum deinde, tractu ut fit temporis, genus humanum mirum in modum multiplicaretur ad diversas orbis regiones provinciasque incoleret, necessarium fuit ut elementarum caracteres invenirentur* . . . *Unde tam varia linguarum genera et tam diverse litterarum figure emanasse et profluxisse cernuntur.*'

17 *Epistole*, critical edn by A. Altamura (Lecce, 1959), 104–20.

18 ibid., 104–5: '*gymnosophistae, magi, chaldei, sacerdotes, vates. Apud Arabes etiam, nostrae aetati proximis saeculis, multi et excellentes viri in sapientiae floruerunt. Nos Christiani habuimus quondam nostros, qui veram sapientiam secuti sunt, quam et nos docuerunt, apostolos et evangelistas.*'

19 ibid., 105: '*et hoc nomen homo aequivocum esse et non secundum eandem rationem de omnibus praedicari, ut de homine picto et de homine vero.*'

20 ibid., 106: '*pulcherrimum putant ostentare sapientiam, ostentare sanctissimos mores, occultare scelera.*'

21 ibid., 108: '*Magna in rebus humanis ac potentissima res est educatio, primaque illa pabula teneris animis adhibita multum habent in tota vita momenti.*'

22 ibid., 110: '*Sed quum nihil facilius sit quam seipsum fallere nihilque in vita divinius quam seipsum cognoscere, saepenumero, cum homines simus,*

[120]

fallimor; sed nunquam superbius aut arrogantius quam cum eorum, quorum vix discipuli esse meremur, consilia atque actiones corrigimus atque damnamus.'

23 Cf. my *Adversity's Noblemen, The Italian Humanists on Happiness* (New York, 1965), 47–63 and *passim;* Francesco Tateo, 'La disputa della nobiltà', in *Tradizione e realtà nell'Umanesimo italiano* (Bari, 1967), 355–421.

24 Op. cit., 112: *'beatos nos esse cum maledixerint nobis homines et cum persecutionem patimur propter iustitiam. . . . cum vilissima plebs nos insanos iudicaverit. . . . conscia stultitiae et malitiae suae, . . . "Hi sunt, quos habuimus aliquando in derisum. . . . Nos insensati vitam illorum existimabamus insaniam, et finem illorum sine honore. Ecce quomodo computati sunt inter filios Dei! . . . Ergo erravimus a via veritatis . . ." . . . Quis enim, nisi inscius rerum humanarum et verae nobilitatis, Horatium plebeium aut ignobilem appellaverit?'*

25 ibid., 111: *'Quae quanti sit et quam beata, siqua est, vita otiosa, qui philosophi non sunt non noverunt. . . . Ocium apud sapientes beatum habetur; apud barbaros, hoc est apud indoctos et plebeios, ut ignavum contemptui ac dedecori. Soli igitur philosophi . . . laborant ut quiescant et ocientur; populares vero laborant quotidie, ut magis et magis laborent et agantur.'*

26 Pontano, op. cit., I.xii.4: *'perinde ut cessatio omnis quiesque conceditur relaxandi gratia utque reditus ad labores ac negocia non sit gravis, sic iocos, dicta, sales, lepores facetiasque concedi, ne vitam cogitationesque nostras omnis studiaque in iis collocasse aut in ocio desidiaque aut in marcescentia potius nos appareat.'*

27 *IOIAL*, part II, 'The human condition in humanist thought', provides background for this section but the treatment is independent, more considered and, I hope, more developed. My discussion of Petrarch is based on more extended treatment in my *The Poet as Philosopher, Petrarch and the Formation of Renaissance Consciousness* (New Haven, 1979), but, again, it considers Renaissance anthropological thought in general.

28 Cf. *IOIAL*, 179–80, 190–6.

29 Cf. *IOIAL*, ch.V for da Barga.

30 Lotharius Cardinalis, *De miseria humanae conditionis*, ed. by Michele Maccarrone (Lugano, 1955), 3: *'Si vero paternitas vestra suggesserit, dignitatem humane nature Christo favente describam, quatinus ita per hoc humilietur elatus ut per illud humilis exaltetur.'*

31 Maccarrone, x-xx; Nicholas Mann, 'The manuscripts of Petrarch's *De remediis*, a checklist', *Italia medioevale e umanistica*, 14 (1971), 57–90; W. Fiske, *Francis Petrarch's Treatise De remediis utriusque fortunae, Text and Versions, Bibliographical Notices*, III (Florence, 1888).

32 Cf. P.L. Entralgo, *La Curación por la Palabra en la Antigüedad Clásica* (Madrid, 1958), Eng. trans. L. Rather and J. Sharp (New Haven, 1970).

33 Cf. D.P. Walker, *Spiritual and Demonic Magic from Ficino to Campanella* (London, 1958), ch.I. See now G.W. McClure, *The Renaissance Vision of Solace and Tranquillity* (Ann Arbor, University Microfilms, 1981. Diss. Univ. of Michigan).

34 See *IOIAL*, 258–70 for Poggio arguments.

35 In his 'Studi su Leon Battista Alberti', in *Rinascite e Rivoluzioni: Movimenti culturali dal XIV al XVII secolo* (Rome-Bari, 1975), 133–96.

36 Cf. Salvatore I. Camporeale, *Lorenzo Valla, Umanesimo e teologia* (Florence, 1972), ch.I; Mario Fois, *Il pensiero cristiano di Lorenzo Valla* (Rome, 1969), ch.XIII.

37 The discussion of Manetti which follows, while dependent on *IOIAL*, cap. VI, 230–58, develops further an emphasis on human creativity. For his text I now follow the recent edition of Elizabeth R. Leonard, *Giannozzo Manetti, De dignitate et excellentia hominis* (Padua, 1976). Cited as 'Leonard'.

38 Lib. II, paragraph 36; Leonard, 57–8(paragraph numbering is by Leonard): '*plera magna et ingentia vel facinora vel machinamenta admirabiliter inventa et intellecta.*'

39 III, 11; Leonard, 71: '*Deus . . . hominem formosissimum, ingeniosissimum sapientissimum, opulentissimum ac denique potentissimum efficeret*'.

40 Quoting Cicero, *De nat. deorum*, II, 39; III, 12; Leonard, 73: '*Quid denique de humano genere dicemus? qui quasi cultores terre constituti non patiuntur eam nec immanitate beluarum efferari nec stirpium asperitate vastari, quorumque operibus agri, insule littoraque collucent distincta terris et urbibus? Que quidem omnia, si ut animis sic oculis uno aspectu videre et conspicere possemus quale et quam mirabile spectaculum nobis ita viventibus et conspicientibus appareret.*'

41 III, 20; Leonard, 77: '*cuncta queque post primam illam novam ac rudem mundi creationem ex singulari quodam et precipuo humane mentis acumine a nobis adinventa ac confecta et absoluta fuisse videantur. Nostra namque hoc est humana sunt, quoniam ab hominibus effecta cernuntur.*'

42 III, 21; Leonard, 78: '*Hec quidem et cetera huiusmodi tot ac tales undique conspiciuntur ut mundus et cuncta eius ornamenta ab omnipotenti Deo ad usus hominum primo inventa institutaque et ab ipsis postea hominibus gratanter accepta multo pulchriora multoque ornatiora ac longe politiora effecta fuisse videantur.*'

43 III, 45; Leonard, 91: '*sic pariter rectum et simplex atque unicum offitium suum tale esse existimamus et credimus, ut mundum eius causa factum ac presertim cuncta que in hoc universo terrarum orbe constituta videmus gubernare et administrare cognoscat et valeat, quod nequaquam nisi cum agendo tum intelligendo penitus perficere et omnino adimplere poterit.*'

44 III, 55–6; Leonard, 97: '*Proinde et homo vivens mundi incola fit et pie moriens celi possessor efficitur, ac per hunc modum et in hac presenti et in futura vita semper et omni quidem tempore felix beatusque habetur. Et ex hac igitur tanta ac tam sublimi hominis dignitate et excellentia velut ab ipsa radice invidia, superbia, indignatio, dominandi libido et ambitio, atque cetere huiusmodi animi perturbationes non iniuria oriuntur et profluunt. Nam qui se se ita dignum factum fuisse considerat, ut cunctis rebus creatis preesse ac dominari videatur, profecto non modo ab aliis superari non patietur, quod est invidie, sed potius ceteros excellere vel maxime concupiscet, quod superbie et ambitionis proprium vitium existimatur et creditur. At si forte contigerit ut aliquando spernatur, negligatur, et contemnatur, usque adeo indignatur ut contemptores suos non secus quam*'

capitales ac acerrimos hostes ac proprios quosdam excellentiarum suarum violatores et detractores enixe usque ad necem persequatur. Quod ego etiam atque etiam considerans atque hominem noviter describere et diffinire volens, ipsum animal indignabundum mea quidem sententia non iniuria explicavi.'

45 III, 58; Leonard, 98: 'ut hominem per hanc humilem humane carne susceptionem mirabiliter et incredibiliter honoraret glorificaretque.'

46 III, 59; Leonard, 98: 'nisi ut ea per admixtionem cum ipsa divinitate non solum coniuncta in illa Christi persona cum divina, sed etiam ut cum divina natura et sola efficeretur.'

47 Urb. lat. 1245, f. 28r; Ottob. lat. 1828, f. 176r.: 'comparata his quae humana invenit industria, sordidissima et abiectissima sunt. Ea etiam contulisse homini naturam supervacaneum fuisset, quae nihil agit otiosum, quoniam ingenio et ratione sibi meliora parat homo quam quae brutis natura concessit.' Cf. IOIAL, 281, 438 n. 33.

48 ibid., f. 22v; f. 127r: 'Nec miseros esse mortales autumno, licet Creator benignissimus Deus homini dixerit, "In sudore vultus tui visceris pane tuo." In quibus verbis tacite monuit, non praedandum, rebus parcendum alienis, non otio marcescendum sed agendum semper aliquid. An si erit manus, pedes, linguae, oculi caeterorumque corporis organorum munus proprium totius hominis nullum erit! Quid igitur illi profuit intelligere, quid sentire, quid opinari, velle, memorari, quid praeterita cum presentia conferre ac per ea futuris iudicare si nihil agendum homini fuerat!' Cf. IOIAL, 281, 438 n. 34.

49 ibid., f. 20r; f. 169v: 'De parentum nostrorum labe omnem posteritatem inquinatem quod non sint mortales idcirco miseria, hoc satis sit dixisse quod pia mater ecclesia propterea canit, videlicet, "O felix culpa quae tantam ac talem meruit habere redemptorem." de Jesu salvatore nostro intelligens.' Cf. IOIAL, 288, 441, n. 48.

50 ibid., f. 25v; f. 174v: 'Profecto nulla ratione humanum capere ingenium potest quod Deus hominem ad imaginem sui dominumque rerum omnium, quae in aere, quae in terra, quae in mari sunt, compotum disciplinarum omnium et paulo inferiorem fecerit angelis . . . ut demum miser et calamitosus esset homo, irritique forent divini conatus, nativitas Christi, passio et resurrectio pro salute humana.' Cf. IOIAL, 289, 441 n. 50.

51 ibid., ff. 15v, 16v; 166r-v: 'At dicet labor est indeficiens. Maius hinc stat meritum pugnanti quam cedenti locum. . . . Primam hominis perfectionem philosophantes esse dicunt quod sit bonis artibus eruditus, secundam vero in actione studiosa collocant. Sapiens autem si fuerit otiosus nihil a segni vel saltem dormiente differt. . . . Felix erit igitur dum fuerit in actione studiosa.' Cf. IOIAL, 286, 441 n. 48.

52 I libri della famiglia in Cecil Grayson (ed.), Opere volgari, I (Bari, 1960); De iciarchia, ibid., II (Bari, 1966). Passage I, 131: 'Pertanto cosi mi pare da credere sia l'uomo nato, certo non per marcire giacendo, ma per stare faccendo.'

53 ibid., I, 131-2: '. . . colle quali l'uomo vince la forza, velocità e ferocità d'ogni altro animale . . . esserci date per nolle molto adoperare. . . . in Dio somma felicità el far nulla. . . . maravigliose opere divine. . . . speculatore e

operatore delle cose. . . . l'uomo essere modo e misura di tutte le cose. . . . el quale constitui l'uomo essere quasi come un- mortale iddio felice, intendendo e faccendo con ragione e virtù.'

54 ibid., I, 133–4: *'Aggiugni qui a queste quanto l'uomo abbia a rendere premio a Dio, a satisfarli con buone opere per e' doni di tanta virtù quanta Egli diede all'anima dell'uomo sopra tutti gli altri terreni animanti grandissima e prestantissima. Fece la natura, cioè Iddio, l'uomo composto parte celeste e divino, parte sopra ogni mortale cosa formosissimo e nobilissimo. . . . Statui ancora Iddio negli animi umani un fermo vinculo e contenere la umana compagnia, iustizia, equità, liberalità e amore, colle quali l'uomo potesse apresso gli altri mortali meritare grazia e lode, e apresso el Procreatore suo pietà e clemenza . . . fermezza, stabilità, constanza e forza, e spregio delle cose caduche . . . con giustizia, pietà moderanza e con ogni altri perfetta e lodatissima operazione. Sia adunque persuaso che l'uomo nacque non per atristirsi in ozio, ma per adoperarsi in cose magnifice e ampie, colle quali e' possa piacere e onorare Iddio in prima, e per avere in sé stessi come uso di perfetta virtù, così frutto di felicità.'*

55 For the ensuing discussion of Petrarch see my *IOIAL*, ch.1 and *The Poet as Philosopher*, chs 3–5.

56 *'Satius est autem bonum velle quam veram nosse.'* In G. Martellotti et al. (eds), *Prose* (Milan–Naples, 1955), 748.

57 For a fuller discussion see *IOIAL*, ch.2.

58 Ed. E. Garin (Florence, 1947), cited as 'Garin'.

59 Garin, 192: *'etiam ad intellectum non perveniat actus primus sine consensu vel imperio voluntatis. Naturale quidem sciendi desiderium · non est intellectus sed voluntatis. . . . licet anima sit nobilior exterioribus rebus a quibus intelligere motus est ad animam; et in hoc quod est velle sit ab anima in res ipsas.'* Cf. *IOIAL*, 64, 349 n. 37.

60 Garin, 184: *'cuius quidem tanta vis est tantusque super alias anime potentias principatus, quod etiam licet sensuum instrumenta recipiunt sensibilium species, talis receptionis effectus sine voluntatis iussibus ulterius vix procedat.'* Cf. *IOIAL*, 67, 350 n. 46.

61 For fuller discussion see *IOIAL*, ch.3.

62 For Fois and Camporeale see n. 36 above. G. Di Napoli, *Lorenzo Valla, Filosofia e religione nell'Umanesimo italiano* (Rome, 1971).

63 Pontano, op. cit., I. xviii. 6.

64 Cf. my earlier discussion in *IOIAL*, ch.3, *passim* and 146–50, 167–70. While Comporeale, Fois, Di Napoli and myself all have different emphases, we seem to approach a consensus as to Valla's great importance as a religious thinker.

65 See *The Poet as Philosopher*, ch.2, and my 'Protagoras in the Renaissance, an exploration', in E.P. Mahoney (ed.), *Philosophy and Humanism* (Leiden, 1976), 119–213.

66 I believe that the scholarly study of this debate of humanists and scholastics over 'truth' is only now beginning. But see J.E. Seigel, *Rhetoric and Philosophy in Renaissance Humanism* (Princeton, 1968), ch.5; and C. Vasoli, *Studi sulla cultura del Rinascimento* (Manduria, 1968), 257–344.

See also my 'The Question of Truth in Renaissance Rhetoric and Anthropology' in *Renaissance Eloquence: Studies in the Theory and Practice of Renaissance Rhetoric*, James J. Murphy (ed.) (Berkeley and Los Angeles forthcoming).

67 *Itaque longe errant qui . . . in cognoscendo, non amando Deo tempus ponunt.* See n. 56 above.

68 Urb. lat. 1207, f. 76v: '*sicut flamma ignis materiam qua ali apprehendit, devorat, et in prunas convertit, sic anima alitur discendo et ea quae percipit in se recondit, suoque calore ac sua luce transfigurat ut ipsa potius pingit alia quam pingatur ab aliis. Et ut sol in rebus politis ac levibus imaginem suam pingit non illarum in se accipit, sic anima fulgore suo in exteriora prodiens memoriae, intellectus, voluntatisve velut quandam obiicit, et depingit imaginem.*' Cf. *IOIAL*, 164, 386 n. 147.

69 Cf. *IOIAL*, 165-8.

70 Ottob. lat. 2075, f. 2194; *De vero falsoque bono*, ed. by M. de P. Lorch (Bari, 1970), 114: '*In deum haec ambo concurrunt, qui et nos producit ex nihilo, aptos bonis fruendis, ut se plus quam nos amare debeamus; et haec ipsa suppeditavit bona. Haec autem bona Deus ipse est, sed quadam proprietate distinguitur. Nam beatitudo nostra non est ipsemet Deus sed a Deo descendit, ut gaudium quod capio videnda claritate, aut audienda suavi voce non idem est quod claritas aut vox, sed haec sensibus meis oblata faciunt ut gaudeam. Ita ex visione et notitia Dei beatitudo ipsa generatur. Illud quoque animadvertendum, licet dicam voluptatem, sive delectationem esse solum bonum, non tamen voluptatem amo sed Deum. Voluptas ipsa amor est quod autem voluptatem facit Deus. Recipiens amat; receptum amatur; amatio ipsa delectatio est, sive voluptas, sive beatitudo, sive felicitas, sive charitas; qui est finis ultimus et propter quem fiunt cetera,*' Cf. *IOIAL*, 138, 376 n. 86.

71 '*Quod anima nitatur Deus fieri, ostendimus signis duodecim secundum duodecim Dei dotes.*' Cf. Marsilio Ficino, *Théologie Platonicienne de l'Immortalité des Ames*, ed. R. Marcel (Paris, 1964), II, 246-79. I.e. 'God is and man strives to be (1) one, true and good; (2) everything; (3) the creator of the universe; (4) above all; (5) in all; (6) always. God does and man strives to: (7) provide for all; (8) administer justly; (9) persevere with fortitude in his state of being; (10) deal temperately and smoothly; (11) live richly and joyously; (12) see, admire and worship himself' (*IOIAL*, 487). For Nicholas of Cusa see Pauline Moffitt Watts, *Nicolaus Cusanus, A Fifteenth-Century Vision of Man* (Leiden, 1982), chs 3, 4 and 5.

72 See *IOIAL*, 144-6, 633-8.

73 Urb. lat. 1207, f. 73v: '*ut magnificentius ac pro materia aptius loquamur hinc est quod apostoli accepto spiritu sancto qui est caritas patris et filii effecti sunt fortes ad loquendum verbum Dei, id quod autem Dominus eis futurum promiserat.*' Cf. *IOIAL*, 160, 385 n. 139.

74 Cf. *The Poet as Philosopher*, chs 4 and 5.

4

THE RENAISSANCE
IN THE HISTORY OF
PHILOSOPHICAL THOUGHT

PAUL OSKAR KRISTELLER

INCE the publication, more than a century ago, of Jacob Burckhardt's essay on the civilization of the Renaissance in Italy, the problem of the Renaissance* has been at the centre of a wide and often confused debate. If we eliminate the term 'renaissance', used by Burckhardt, and before him by Michelet, many aspects of this debate can be traced through the eighteenth century to as far back as the fourteenth or fifteenth centuries.[1] The controversy even boasts its own historiography, and although it may have seemed to ebb in the past few decades, there have nevertheless been several interesting contributions,[2] and it may be said that the most varied opinions still have their proponents and that there is still no generally accepted over-all view. The long war has not been settled by victory; it has merely given way to an armistice imposed by exhaustion and boredom. In my acceptance of the invitation to express and, perhaps, to repeat my opinion on the subject, there is no intention of raising polemics. My only wish is to pay homage to a dear colleague and old friend with whom, at least on this particular point, I believe I am in agreement.[3]

If the post-Burckhardtian debate on the Renaissance has often been barren and muddled, it is due above all to two factors. First, Burckhardt's position on several points has been misunderstood; and second, discussion has been conducted using poorly defined generic terms. The historic and descriptive method has often been polluted with value judgements not shared by everyone, and the tendency to confuse the concepts and phenomena of the past with more or less similar counterparts belonging to the present, has led to the formulation of biased or even anachronistic interpretations. I shall do my best to avoid making such mistakes, but I cannot be sure of success.

[127]

It is my belief that an historical period of such complexity cannot be described in a simple definition. Either this definition is too broad, in which case it may be applied to other historical periods and is therefore no longer solely characteristic of the Renaissance, or it is too narrow and thus may describe some aspects of the Renaissance while necessarily excluding others. A historical period has its own particular physiognomy, and the attempt to identify that physiognomy must proceed one step at a time. If there is a definition to be formulated, that formulation must come at the conclusion of our study and not at its outset. We cannot hope to begin with a definition, or with a complete concept; all we may use is a regulative idea, in the Kantian sense of the term. We must set ourselves the task of understanding and interpreting the entire period by examining each of its aspects, not only those we most like.

One of the most difficult aspects inherent to our problem is that of the length and chronological boundaries attributed to the Renaissance; this is indirectly related to the whole question of historical periodization. If we were to combine the latest date proposed for the beginning of the Renaissance with the earliest date proposed for its conclusion, we would give the period a timespan of twenty-seven years. Inversely, if we were to choose the earliest date proposed for its beginning and the latest date for its termination, we would give the period more than four hundred years' duration. Of course, this does not even take into account those who deny that the Renaissance ever existed and consider 1500 to be the year in which the Middle Ages gave way to the Modern Age. I confess that I cannot agree that historical periodization has such an absolute or objective value. The entire question depends on one's point of view, and certainly some outlooks give the twelfth or eighteenth centuries greater importance than the fifteenth in the history of western culture. It is true that the fifteenth century marked the beginning of many developments which survived until relatively recent times, but the vantage point of those, such as Burckhardt, who could still see the Renaissance as the precursor to a present age, cannot help but differ from that of modern scholars, who must see the period as a precursor to a more recent past which has itself reached a conclusion. Furthermore, the ever-growing tendency to look beyond the limits of western Europe when examining the history of human civilization has clearly shown that the Renaissance occupies a relatively limited space in the over-all picture. It would seem best to concentrate on quality rather than quantity, and define the Renaissance as European civilization from 1300 or 1350 to about 1600. In referring to European, and not merely Italian, civilization, I touch upon yet another of the issues which has caused discussion and misunderstanding. Burckhardt spoke only of Italy, but he assumed that Italian developments later spread to the other European countries. Successive scholars pointed out that each country's Renaissance culture had grown from its own indigenous medieval roots. Of course these roots existed, but it must be kept in mind that they existed in Italy as well, and that the Italian influence on the other countries cannot be denied.

Thus the conception of the Renaissance varies according to the chronological limits we assign it, and it takes on national and even regional characteristics. Not only did Italy, Spain and England differ from each other, but Florence, Venice and Naples varied considerably as well. Moreover, the entire conception of the Renaissance changes greatly when seen from the different viewpoints of the various aspects of civilization, such as political, economic or ecclesiastical history, historiography, literature, music or the arts, the exact or occult sciences, philology and paleography, jurisprudence and medicine, theory and practice of education, theology or philosophy. Part of the confusion surrounding the debate on the Renaissance has come from the fact that scholars have usually spoken from the viewpoint of their own specializations; typically the opposition to Burckhardt has not come so much from scholars belonging to his own fields of art and literary history as from historians of the sciences and of economics, who operate in fields into which he never ventured. Consequently, it seems to me that the attempt of the present volume, to study the problem of the Renaissance from the separate points of view of several sectors of science and culture, could contribute greatly to a clarification of the problems and concepts which traditionally make up the debate.

The task of defining philosophy seems still more difficult than the problem of the Renaissance, and every thinker or school offers a different definition. Like the history of the other aspects of culture, the history of philosophy is usually written from the point of view of one particular philosophy; in building a case for the argument that certain thinkers from the past have been its precursors, each point of view usually gives little attention to thinkers or problems which are not related to it. Our goal should be to create a history of philosophy which comprehends everything which has at any time been considered a part of philosophy. In widening our perspective, such an aim could make us aware of problems and ideas worthy of our attention. Of course, it must be clear that philosophic thought may be seen in two lights: first, in its strictly technical and professional sense; and second, in a broader sense which goes beyond professional philosophy to include the largely philosophic thought found in the writings of poets, men of letters,

[129]

theologians and scientists. The historian of philosophy must shed light on the development of professional philosophy, but if we are to understand Renaissance thought we must examine it in the broader sense, with particular attention to humanism, or we run the risk of defining philosophy in a way which would preclude its existence in the fifteenth century or, for that matter, in the twentieth.

It must also be noted that, throughout the history of philosophy, variations have been seen not only in the doctrines and in the very concept of philosophy itself, but also in the relations between philosophy and other branches of thought and culture. No matter how distinct medieval philosophy was from theology, it none the less had a special relationship with that branch of thought, thus distinguishing it from ancient or modern philosophy; likewise, modern philosophy, from René Descartes to the present, has had a similar close relationship with the natural sciences. Thus it may be said that Renaissance philosophy had a special relationship with the arts, and with historic and philological studies, and that it is impossible to understand the sense of Renaissance philosophy if this particular feature is ignored and the criteria pertaining to medieval or modern philosophy are applied instead.

Apart from the problems inherent in the separate concepts of the Renaissance and philosophy, it is particularly difficult to apply the concept of the Renaissance to the history of philosophy, or to speak of 'Renaissance philosophy'. Historians of the philosophy of this period, up to Carriere, Fiorentino and Dilthey, have not always used the word 'renaissance' in their titles, nor have they always clearly applied Burckhardt's concept to philosophy.[4] Ernst Cassirer and Giovanni Gentile were among the first to deal explicitly with Renaissance thought and philosophy.[5] The fact is that the concept is ambiguous: we may only speak to a certain extent of a body of philosophical thought as belonging to a period which for other, mostly artistic or literary reasons, we are accustomed to calling the Renaissance. Or we may make the implicit, if somewhat ambitious, claim that what confronts us is an expression in the field of philosophy of the same Renaissance 'spirit' we have encountered in its artistic, literary and perhaps political manifestations. But it is my belief that we must be content with the first – and more modest – concept at the outset, inasmuch as it does not lend itself to any misunderstanding. If we insist on adopting the second as well, it must be treated again as a Kantian regulative idea, and we must simply hope that the progress of our studies brings us closer to such a concept.

The history of ancient philosophy was a favourite subject of the

[130]

ancient philosophers and grammarians; we may follow its development from Aristotle to Sextus Empiricus and Diogenes Laertius (to name only those sources which have survived until our times). Since the eighteenth century, historians of philosophy have dealt primarily with ancient philosophy, but they have also discussed medieval and modern philosophy.[6] After the first half of the nineteenth century, medieval philosophy was studied mainly by Catholic scholars; after 1879, it received a great impetus from the flourishing of neo-Thomism. Only in the present century has Renaissance philosophy become the subject of specialized studies. Apart from an intrinsic interest in particular movements and thinkers, one of the principal goals of modern study must be to explain the interval which separates the scholastic philosophy of St Thomas Aquinas and William of Ockham from the modern metaphysics of Descartes and Spinoza.

To characterize Renaissance thought, one could begin with an examination of certain doctrines or, more correctly, of certain themes and problems which were often discussed, such as the dignity of man, the immortality of the soul, fate and fortune, wisdom and so forth. Or one could point out those famous thinkers who have been the object of many studies, such as Petrarch, Valla, Nicholas of Cusa, Ficino, Pico, Leonardo da Vinci, Pomponazzi, Machiavelli, Montaigne and many more. But I prefer to describe the most important movements of the period, despite my awareness that the label does not explain the doctrine, and that an individual thinker can never be reduced to the definition of one movement, or even of several movements, to which he may belong.

Humanism, the intellectual movement which in many respects is the most characteristic of the Renaissance, is riddled with debate and controversy regarding its length, meaning and value only slightly less complex than that regarding the Renaissance itself. Among Italian historians, humanism was often identified with quattrocento culture and kept separate from the Renaissance which was considered a cinquecento phenomenon; it is only recently that this habit may have begun to disappear.[7] For English-speaking peoples, the word 'humanism' comprises the two Italian concepts of *umanesimo* and *umanismo*; this has led to great confusion because the vague, moralizing sense of contemporary humanism is undoubtedly applied to Renaissance humanism and it is often forgotten that although Renaissance humanism did insist upon human values, it none the less pursued these values by concentrating on a classical, humanistic culture which is usually overlooked in our century. I have often insisted, and must do so again, that Renaissance humanism is clearly

[131]

related to the *studia humanitatis*, a scheme which comprises grammar, rhetoric, poetry, history and moral philosophy, and is sharply distinguished from the liberal arts of the Middle Ages and from the fine arts of the modern age. Just as 'grammar' was meant to be the study of classical Greek and Latin language and literature, and 'rhetoric' and 'poetry' consisted of the study of classical writers of poetry and prose as well as of the practice of composition in both prose and verse, so the *studia humanitatis*, of which the humanists were masters, included, among other things, classical philology, literature (Latin as well as vernacular), historiography and moral philosophy. Although they were a part of the study and university curriculum of the Renaissance, as they had been in the late Middle Ages, the other philosophical disciplines, such as logic, natural philosophy and metaphysics and also theology, jurisprudence, medicine and mathematics, were excluded from this scheme. Thus humanism is not the entire picture of Renaissance knowledge or thought; it is merely one well-defined sector. The only one of the philosophical disciplines included as a part of the *studia humanitatis* is moral philosophy; all the others are left out. On the other hand, apart from moral philosophy, the *studia humanitatis* included many studies which have nothing to do with philosophy in the strict sense, such as philology, literature and history. Several of the humanists, such as Petrarch, Salutati, Bruni, Valla, Leon Battista Alberti and many more, made important contributions to moral thought, and also directed their attentions to history, literature and philology. Many other humanists, however, dealt with poetry, rhetoric, philology or history and never once made the slightest contribution to moral or philosophical thought. In its entirety, humanism is an association of intellectual interests which does not correspond at all to the combinations to which we are accustomed in our world. Those who write the history of humanism as the history of thought, and particularly of moral thought, are certainly describing the aspect of humanism which we historians of philosophy consider to be the most important. But they are overlooking the other important and characteristic contributions made by humanism – to classical studies, to historiography, to literature in prose and verse – not to mention the two practical contributions which carried the greatest influence: humanist education, which survived until recent times; and humanist script, which has only now eliminated the last traces of so-called Gothic script.

Although I am insisting on the limited role played by humanism in the over-all philosophic and erudite picture of the Renaissance, I do not mean to deny the importance of the role played by humanism in the history of thought. But we must distinguish between the direct contribution made by humanism in the area of the *studia humanitatis* and especially of moral thought, and the indirect contribution made outside this area and by those scholars who, although they were not pure humanists as we have tried to define them, none the less had a humanist education and combined the humanist influences with other professional traditions which were, for the most part, medieval. Neither Ficino, Pico, Pomponazzi nor Patrizi was a 'humanist', but it would be an error to deny that there is an element of humanism in the rich and complex thought of each of these men.

The moral doctrine of the humanists has come down to us in a vast assortment of treatises and dialogues, orations and letters. Although this wealth has been studied with care and attention by Baron and Garin, Tateo, Trinkaus and many others,[8] it still calls for further study, inasmuch as critical editions have yet to be published for many of the important texts; likewise, there are still many little-known or neglected texts whose importance cannot yet be ascertained. The first thing to be examined are the themes to which the humanists directed their treatises. They are often the same themes which are found in ancient and medieval philosophical literature, especially of the popular variety: supreme good; virtue and pleasure; fate, fortune and free will; man's dignity and his misery; nobility and riches and their relation to virtue. The humanists spoke of the relation between intellect and will; they often favoured the will. They spoke of the duties and advantages of the different forms of life, often comparing them: the solitary or monastic life v. family life; arms v. letters; the contemplative life v. the active life, medicine v. jurisprudence; republic v. monarchy. They defended the importance of their studies against the criticism of the schoolmen and theologians, or even attacked scholastic philosophy as abstruse and useless. These themes and subjects are interesting, but they are neither profound nor rigorous, if measured according to the criteria of ancient, modern or even medieval philosophy. The conclusions are often ambiguous, and even the various theses of Petrarch, Bruni or Valla do not constitute a systematic thought or a collection of doctrines which could generally be accepted by the other humanists. Rather than specific doctrines, they shared general attitudes characterized by the cultural ideal which was based upon the study of Latin and Greek classics. This ideal was the foundation of studies and of elementary and secondary schooling. The humanists also shared the conviction that Antiquity had been superior to more recent times and that the movement should therefore strive to achieve a rebirth of letters, studies and thought. Although opposed to scholastic theology and philosophy,

[133]

the humanists did not oppose Christianity. They felt that the reawakening of the ancient classics implied a concomitant reawakening of the Christian classics, as embodied in the Bible and the Church Fathers. But the intense study of ancient literature and philosophy led to the secularization of studies and culture, and Alberti, along with other humanists, wrote moral treatises of a secular content in which the religious faith of the author was no less hidden than in the *De Consolatione Philosophiae* of Boethius.

The humanists' stylistic and philological habits are no less important than their ideas and attitudes. Not only did these habits give character to the literary, erudite and moral works of the movement, but they had a profound influence on the philosophical disciplines and on other fields not a part of the *studia humanitatis*. The *quaestio* and the commentary were gradually replaced by the treatise and the dialogue, by the speech and the epistle, and finally, by the essay. Elegant Ciceronian prose or, at least, prose inspired by the classics, replaced the dialectic reasoning of the schoolmen, not only in the structure of the periods but also in terminology, and the result was often a loss of precision. Abstract generalization gave way to personal opinion and individual experience. The use of sources and their ideas reflected a wider and deeper knowledge of Latin and especially Greek texts. The poems of Lucretius, so rarely copied or quoted during the Middle Ages, now enjoyed wide popularity and so made known the atomistic cosmology of Democritus and Epicurus. The philosophical writings of Cicero, well known to medieval culture, were now studied as a means to gain more insight into the Stoic, Epicurean and Academic doctrines. In addition, a real flood of Greek philosophical texts was studied in the original and translated for the first time into Latin: these texts included many of the works of Plato, Proclus and the commentators of Aristotle; the principal work of Sextus Empiricus; all of the works of Theophrastus, Epictetus, Marcus Aurelius, Plotinus and the other neo-Platonists; as well as the popular works of Isocrates, Plutarch and Lucian; and the lives of the philosophers by Diogenes Laertius, which included important texts from Epicurus. Even writings such as those of Aristotle, which had been translated and studied in the Middle Ages, were studied in the original Greek and translated again, thus lending themselves to new interpretations. The effect was to make the entire treasure trove of ancient philosophy more accessible to the western world than it had been since the days of ancient Rome; it may even have exceeded that level. This recuperation resulted in serious efforts to recreate an authentic or modified form of Stoic, Epicurean and sceptical philosophy; to purify the Aristotelian and neo-Platonic doctrines known to the Middle Ages; and to apply eclectic reasoning to all problems, with liberal reference to all available ancient (or pseudo-ancient) sources. Moreover, the philological method and textual and historical criticism were gradually developing, and their philosophical benefits turned up in the works of Ermolao Barbaro and Poliziano. This fifteenth- and, to an even greater extent, sixteenth-century development created a ferment in its variety of ideas, which were chosen from many sources and then rearranged, dissolving the precise, rigid concepts established by late scholasticism. Although this phenomenon did not give immediate rise to a new, clear and firm synthesis, it did prepare the way for the more precise and durable work of Galileo and Descartes.

The influence of humanism went beyond the *studia humanitatis* to touch every level of Renaissance culture. Humanist classicism made its way first into neo-Latin literature and later into the vernacular literatures, sculpture, as well as architecture. When the ancient models were missing, as in the cases of painting and music, the gap was filled by speculation and some pseudo-ancient examples. In the realm of jurisprudence, the critical and historical method was applied to the sources of Roman law, especially by the sixteenth-century French.[9] Both Protestant theology and its Catholic counterpart used the methods of humanism in their textual criticism of the Bible and of the Greek and Latin Fathers, and in their studies of ecclesiastical history.[10] The field of medicine was enriched by the original texts and by new translations of Hippocrates, Galen and other Greek writers,[11] just as the mathematical sciences were enhanced by the previously unknown writings of Apollonius, Diophantos and Pappus and by the little-known works of Archimedes.[12] The physical and biological sciences, still considered part of natural philosophy, were improved by the original texts and by new or more exact translations of Aristotle and his Greek commentators, as well as of Theophrastus and others. The works of Aristotle, Plato and the neo-Platonists, as well as the apocryphal writings of Hermes, Zoroaster, Orpheus and others, contributed to metaphysics. Logic was subjected to various attempts of humanistic reform, from Valla to Ramus and Nizolius, all of whom tended to associate logic with rhetoric.[13] In each of these areas, humanism furnished the ferment, the methods, the style and the classical sources, rather than the content or substance, which were supplied partly by medieval traditions and partly by new experiences and observations, such as those gained in the New World.

The first signs of Italian humanism can be found in the early trecento, and even as far back as the late duecento, when its grammatical and rhetorical (more than philosophical) connections to the Middle Ages were still visible. Although the first full blossoming took place in the quattrocento, it should not be forgotten that the movement remained active, especially in the disciplines of rhetoric, Latin poetry, historiography and classical philology, straight through the entire cinquecento and into the early seicento. Bembo, Vida, Vettori and Sigonio were only four representatives of a movement which was still lively and productive. On the other hand, although the origins of humanist culture were Italian, the movement was by no means limited to Italy. As early as the fourteenth century, it had spread to France, Germany and Bohemia; in the next century, it reached the rest of Europe. It was in the sixteenth century that the great non-Italian humanists worked: Reuchlin, Erasmus, Budé, Vives and Sir Thomas More were only a few of the most illustrious of these. There were variations in style, and there were contrasts due to the different countries and moments in time, but the same fundamental traits existed: a deep classical culture, a sense of criticism and history, a literary elegance, eclecticism, an interest not only in moral and pedagogic problems but in political and religious ones as well, an aversion to scholasticism and an indifference to the professional traditions of the university disciplines. By the end of the century, we find Lipsius, the great renovator of Stoic philosophy, and Montaigne, the vibrant, cultured moralist, whose classical references and highly personal style combined the best features of humanist culture, despite the fact that he wrote his *Essais* in French rather than in Latin, which he had learned well as a youth. And finally we come to the great French and Dutch scholars such as Turnèbe and Scaliger, who developed the classical philology of the humanists and transmitted it to successive centuries.

I cannot share the opinion which has occasionally claimed that humanist culture was suppressed by the religious movements of the sixteenth century, or that the humanists, as a group, favoured one religion, whether Protestant or Catholic. Humanist culture as such was neutral with regard to certain theological or even philosophical doctrines, and each humanist was free to formulate his opinions according to his own convictions and inclinations. We find humanist scholars and men of letters, as well as men reared in the humanist culture, among the Catholics, Protestants and heretics of the sixteenth century. Perhaps Luther, certainly Melanchthon, Calvin and many Jesuits were well steeped in the humanist culture of their time, and it was thanks to them that the humanist school became so firmly established in all the Catholic and Protestant countries that it managed to survive until the first decades of our own century.

Although it is true that humanism was probably the most lively and novel element in Renaissance intellectual culture, especially in fourteenth- and fifteenth-century Italy, and although its influence gradually spread out to touch every area of the culture of the period, it would none the less be an error to think that the intellectual life of the period could be reduced to humanism alone. The fact is that there were many traditions and movements with differing origins and interests, and every one of them either rivalled or simply coexisted alongside humanism. Our picture of the period would be incomplete – even distorted – if we were to repeat the oft-committed error of ignoring the existence and the importance of these other movements, or even of treating them as the mere residue of a medieval tradition which had run dry. Humanist culture managed to conquer the secondary schools and to take over the university instruction of grammar, rhetoric, poetry, Greek, and often moral philosophy. However, at the same time, instruction continued in the other disciplines, whose origins went back to the twelfth and thirteenth centuries, when the universities were founded; the scholastic, i.e. university, tradition of these subjects was never interrupted during the period in question, but was merely modified by the influence of humanism. This phenomenon has been more clearly understood in the past few decades, but much research should still be carried out on university documents and learned literature in both printed and manuscript forms. The same problem exists with regard to theology, jurisprudence, medicine and mathematics, but we must limit ourselves here to the philosophical disciplines which, at that time, also included the physical and biological sciences.

Consideration of these rather fundamental facts is essential to the comprehension of the importance and vitality of Aristotelianism, whose position in Renaissance thought was distinct from that of humanism. Whether we assign more importance to Aristotelianism or to humanism depends on our criteria. If we choose to emphasize the technical and professional, i.e. university, tradition of philosophy, then it must be acknowledged that this tradition was represented during the Renaissance by Aristotelianism, and that the humanists' contributions to philosophy, however interesting and influential, were essentially those of dilettanti and outsiders. This does not detract from the importance of those contributions, just as it cannot be denied that there were other moments in the history of philosophy when philosophical thought was modified or transformed by external impulses which were extraneous to the technical and professional tradition of the preceding period. But historians of Renaissance thought would be committing an

[137]

error of judgement if they were to take the humanists' invectives against contemporary scholasticism at face value, without examining the other side of the coin, as many historians of literature and even of philosophy have in fact done. As Renan and then Duhem both remarked, the late medieval Aristotelians adopted a rationalistic method, studying many problems of logic and physics in such a way that they appeared to be the predecessors of free thought and modern science.[14] From this angle, the humanists' contributions appear less illustrious; it is occasionally written that the progress of the sciences was delayed at least a century by the movement. The only way to escape from this dilemma is to realize that it is not only in our own century that there have been two, or rather, several cultures, and that we cannot expect the scholars of one culture to contribute to the progress of another; throughout the ages, there have always been many differing opinions with regard to the same problem and, what is more, there have always been competition and rivalry between the scholars of different themes and problems.

The vast Aristotelian literature produced from the thirteenth century to the seventeenth and beyond, is rooted in university and scholastic teaching.[15] It includes commentaries on the writings of Aristotle and on some of the complementary texts, such as the logical works of Porphyry, Gilbertus Porretanus and Peter of Spain and Averroes's treatise of physics, *De substantia orbis*; these commentaries reflect the practice of the *lectura*. Only some of these texts have survived to the present day; a large number, at least of those from the later period, have still not been studied. Often they only exist in the form of lecture notes, which were occasionally edited by the professors themselves, but were usually the exclusive work of students who had attended the lectures. They usually begin with a general introduction, one issue of which includes an analysis of to which part of philosophy the text in question belongs. This type of commentary, based on the study of the text chosen for instruction, gradually appeared in all the other disciplines taught at the universities, from theology to jurisprudence, medicine and mathematics. Each of these had its pre-scholastic tradition, which may be traced back through the grammatical commentaries of the twelfth century and of the early Middle Ages to the ancient Latin commentaries of Servius and Boethius and finally to the Greek commentaries on Aristotle and other writers.[16] The other literary form of Aristotelian philosophy and the other scholastic disciplines is the *quaestio*, or the collection of questions. The *quaestio* has its own precise, almost schematic structure, which corresponds to another important practice in university instruction, the *disputatio*. The collections, and the questions themselves, were often edited by the professor and it was rare for a student to edit them directly.

All the commentaries and questions shared the same text, its terminology in the officially adopted Latin translation, and the series of problems treated in the order of the text. But there was remarkable variety in the choice of problems and in their treatment. The texts were often given different or contrasting interpretations, and discussion led to problems and solutions which were often quite removed from the Aristotelian text. This may be easily explained by the fact that the commentator had two aims: first, to explain Aristotle's text and, second, to elucidate the true, valid doctrine of his own subject, on the basis of the authoritative Aristotelian text. The writing of Aristotle is difficult in Greek; it certainly is no easier in even the most literal Latin translation. Furthermore, the original text is fragmented and full of gaps, with more or less explicit contradictions apparent among the various passages. Then there are specific problems, or certain aspects of one problem, which interested the commentator and to which the text gives only an ambiguous answer or no answer at all. Thus the commentator who wanted to teach his subject felt authorized to reconcile the apparent contradictions in the text and to fill in its gaps, using criteria which he and his listeners accepted. This method has been used at all times by the interpreters of authoritative texts. Most of the time, the commentators believed they were being faithful to Aristotle's thinking, but occasionally one of them was brave enough to contradict Aristotle, on the basis of other theological or scientific authorities, or on the basis of his own opinions, which he believed to be well founded. In any event, the Aristotelian comments and questions offer a great variety of interpretations and positions and even when these do not agree with the interpretation we believe corresponds most exactly to the original passage, they still give us insight into the commentator's position, which may be philologically inexact, but whose philosophical interest is not marred by its invalidity. However, we should not limit ourselves to examining the position or thesis of the commentator, as usually happens; we should study the arguments and reasonings with which he attempts to support that thesis. It is these lines of reasoning which often illuminate us on his characteristic way of thinking and sometimes reveal the unsuspected sources of his thought.

The Aristotelian literature has come down to us from the universities and the other schools of higher learning in all the countries of the Latin world.[17] The thirteenth- and fourteenth-century philosophical literature of Paris and Oxford is quite well known, thanks to the research of medievalists; the same is true for fourteenth-century literature from central Europe's new university centres such as Prague, Cracow, Vienna and Heidelberg. The developments of the fifteenth and sixteenth centuries have been less thoroughly explored. Despite the temporary prohibition of the nominalist school in the fifteenth century, the Parisian school continued to flourish; it was active throughout the sixteenth century, as can be seen from the printed editions of old and new scholastic texts. At least one professor of Aristotelian philosophy could be found at the new Collège Royal side by side with the humanists and mathematicians: Francesco Vimercato, whose connections with Italian Aristotelianism should be further examined.[18] Little is known about late Aristotelianism in the English universities, perhaps because private and individual education at the colleges had come to play a more important role than public university instruction. During the second half of the sixteenth century, John Case did gain some fame as an Aristotelian commentator. In fifteenth-century German universities, Aristotelianism was strong and productive, but recent studies have favoured the theology, rather than the philosophy, of the German nominalists, as well as their influence on the thinking of Luther.[19] During the sixteenth century, it was Melanchthon who established the teaching of Aristotelian philosophy in the universities of Protestant Germany and this tradition was still solidly entrenched in the seventeenth century and later.[20] In the universities of Spain, Portugal and their American colonies, Aristotelian instruction held an important place alongside theological instruction. Moreover, Aristotelian instruction can be found in the *Studia* of the Dominicans and other religious orders as early as the thirteenth century; along with humanistic and mathematical instruction, it appears regularly in sixteenth- and seventeenth-century Jesuit colleges.

If I have chosen to speak last of Aristotelianism in Italy, it is because, from the very beginning, it took on different characteristics from the Aristotelianism of other countries. This contrast lies not in the choice of texts or in the method for their explanation, but in the different relationship which existed between Italian Aristotelian philosophy and the other university disciplines, due in turn to the distinct structure of the Italian universities. Montpellier was the only university outside of Italy which was not made up of the four faculties of theology, jurisprudence, medicine and philosophy (and the arts), with philosophy serving principally as a preparation for theology, the predominant discipline. Like Montpellier, the School of Salerno had still not acquired the organization typical of the other universities, although the two were actually older than the rest. Instruction at Salerno centred around

[140]

medicine; Aristotelian philosophy was introduced in the twelfth century as a necessary complement to theoretical medicine, and perhaps not even as a separate discipline. From Bologna on, the other Italian universities began as schools of Roman and canon law, where the fundamental discipline was supplemented with preparatory courses of grammar and rhetoric. During the thirteenth century, the instruction of medicine was established in Bologna and elsewhere, and the faculty of medicine, which included Aristotelian philosophy, grammar and rhetoric, and mathematics, came to be independent from the faculty of law; often the two rivalled one another. None of the Italian universities had a separate faculty of theology, and the teaching of theology in Italy was always limited to the schools of the religious orders and to the rare and sporadic university courses given under the aegis of the faculty of medicine and the arts. This type of development gave rise to the secular character of Italian Aristotelianism, associated, from the twelfth to the eighteenth century, with the study and instruction of medicine, and never with theology. It is correct to speak of secular Aristotelianism, rather than of Paduan Averroism, as did Renan and his followers. In fact, we have come to see that the concept of Averroism is ambiguous and that the doctrine of the unity of the intellect which was considered characteristic of Averroism was not held by many of the thinkers who are often called Averroists. Furthermore, it has been shown that secular Aristotelianism was not peculiar to Padua; in fact, it first flourished in Bologna before it appeared in Padua, and it can be found in all the Italian universities, while the university of Padua played its important role during the period in which it distinguished itself in all the disciplines, i.e. in the late fifteenth century and in the sixteenth century after 1525.[21]

Italian Aristotelianism, from the twelfth to the fourteenth centuries, has been studied by Nardi, Grabmann, Anneliese Maier, Sofia Vanni Rovighi, Celestino Piana and others, but is still a field for vast further study.[22] We know even less of the quattrocento Aristotelian philosophers, despite monographs on Paolo Veneto, Giovanni Marliani, Caetano of Thiene and Nicoletto Vernia.[23] Studies should be completed on these authors and on others who are even less well known. This task should fall, above all, to historians of logic and physics: in fact, we know the natural philosophers of the school of Paris and the logicians of the school of Oxford were copied, studied and later printed in fifteenth-century Italy. Considering the remarkable contribution that these two fourteenth-century schools made to logic and physics, it seems quite strange that the fifteenth- and sixteenth-century Italian Aristotelians, who purposely took up these studies in a period when they had been more or less abandoned by their northern centres, have not received more attention from scholars of these subjects. We are better informed on the cinquecento Italian Aristotelians, thanks to the solid reputation of Pomponazzi, as well as to the works of Nardi, Randall and their followers.[24] We are now beginning to see that Pomponazzi was not an Aristotelian humanist but a scholastic thinker of particular importance, who was intimately associated with a university tradition which had flourished several centuries before his time and which would continue to flourish for at least a century after his death. We have learned to appreciate contemporaries of his, such as Achillini and Nifo, as well as successors such as Zabarella and Cremonini,[25] but even amongst their works there are still numerous writings and problems which should be explored. There are several other thinkers too who were as famous, or only slightly less famous, in their day, but who have yet to be studied.

This Aristotelian school, particularly its Italian branch, is characterized by an impressive vitality and by a variety of problems. Although firmly established upon its own tradition, it none the less benefited from a useful exchange of ideas with its numerous external associations. Pomponazzi was an Aristotelian commentator but was indebted to the humanists of his time for his knowledge of many classical texts such as those of Plato, Plutarch and the commentator Alexander of Aphrodisias. His philosophical doctrine is Stoic rather than Aristotelian on several fundamental questions. Humanist and Platonic elements are also found in other Aristotelian thinkers of the cinquecento; the thought of Zabarella, one of the best Aristotelian commentators of all times, is admirable not only for its philosophical acumen, but also for its familiarity with the Greek text of Aristotle, which made Zabarella, among other things, the heir to the humanist Aristotelianism foreshadowed in Petrarch and culminating in Ermolao Barbaro. Furthermore, as many scholars have remarked, Galileo was influenced, if not by their doctrines and method (which he opposed), then at least by the themes and problems and occasionally the terminology, of several sixteenth-century Aristotelian philosophers whom he had read as a youth and who, for their part, had transmitted the non-Aristotelian doctrines of the fourteenth-century Aristotelians, such as the theory of impetus.[26]

Thus it must be concluded that, despite the fact that the physics of Renaissance, and particularly Italian, Aristotelianism was refuted by Galileo and other seventeenth-century scientists up to Newton, and that its metaphysics was abandoned by Descartes and his rationalist and empiricist successors down to Kant, the movement none the less deserves respect and further study and should be recognized, at least in the area of philosophy, for the place it occupied alongside humanism, as a strong and widespread element in the culture of the period.

Like humanism and Aristotelianism, Platonism, the third great movement of the Renaissance, is still in need of much research and a great deal of clarification. Quattrocento Florentine Platonism has often been interpreted as a mere part or appendix of humanism, because its representatives were in fact steeped in humanist culture, and because they studied and translated the Platonic and neo-Platonic texts. It is true that they did attempt to revive ancient Platonism, albeit with different ancient elements, just as other humanists had tried, or would try, to resuscitate the Stoic, Epicurean, sceptic and other doctrines. On the other hand, Renaissance Platonism often opposed late medieval scholastic Aristotelianism, and this contrast was accentuated by the reference to the anti-Aristotelian Platonism of Pletho and his Byzantine followers. None the less, we have learnt that there was a strong Platonic and neo-Platonic movement in the Middle Ages, based upon the translations of several texts from Plato and Proclus, on Boethius and other Latin Platonists, and above all on St Augustine and on the extremely widespread texts which circulated under the name of Dionysius the Areopagite.[27] Moreover, as we have seen, Aristotelianism in the Renaissance was possessed of remarkable strength, making it anything but a barren residue of the late Middle Ages. And finally, it has been shown that the Platonism of both Ficino and Pico was in no way anti-Aristotelian; it was profoundly permeated with and influenced by scholastic philosophy. It gave great space to cosmological and metaphysical problems which never attracted the thought of the humanists. As compared to the sources and influences of the past, it must be acknowledged that its synthesis was original, in its entirety and in many of its separate elements.[28] These reasons make it imperative to consider and treat Renaissance Platonism as a movement unto itself, distinct from Aristotelianism and humanism.

Renaissance Platonism did not take its strength from the tradition of instruction, as did Aristotelianism, which dominated the teaching of philosophy and the sciences in the universities and religious colleges, or humanism, which dominated the secondary-school and the university instruction of the *studia humanitatis*. In the late sixteenth century, Francesco Patrizi occupied chairs of Platonic philosophy in Ferrara and Rome, where he tried in vain to replace Aristotelian philosophy with the Platonic in university teaching. For several decades, Pisa hosted courses of Platonic philosophy held by scholars who also taught Aristotelian philosophy and were thus willing to search for compatibility in the two schools. The Platonic Academy of Florence, under Ficino, was certainly

[143]

an influential nucleus for the discussion and divulgation of Platonist-related doctrines, but its organization was loose and it lasted a mere three decades. In the sixteenth century, when academies began to spring up in all the Italian cities as extra-university centres of literary culture, Platonic love became a frequent subject of lectures and conferences which dealt with some of the sonnets of Petrarch and Bembo. But this cannot be called a real teaching of Platonic philosophy.[29] Renaissance Platonism owed its strength not to the schools, but to the fact that the three most important quattrocento thinkers – Nicholas of Cusa, Ficino and Pico – were, if not pure Platonists, then at least highly affected by Platonism. Like the texts of Plato and the neo-Platonists, the works of these three men were widely read in the late fifteenth century and in the sixteenth century, in both manuscript and printed form. Their many interested readers were not only professional philosophers; they were poets, men of letters, scientists, theologians, scholars and dilettantes.

In speaking of Platonism, it is important to understand that this is not the tradition of the pure doctrine of Plato, as modern scholars after Schleiermacher have tried to construe it. It is a wide and complex movement which combines the most authentic Platonic doctrines with neo-Platonic and pseudo-Platonic ideas from various periods and origins.

Every thinker who is called Platonic represents his own synthesis of Platonic, extraneous and original elements, which must all be carefully examined; it is quite possible to find two thinkers who are correctly identified as Platonic or Platonizing, but who share no common doctrine. It cannot be postulated that the earlier of two thinkers called Platonic must have influenced the later, unless there are clear connections in doctrine, terminology or text. In this case, as in many others, the labels written by modern doxographers do not lend themselves to an algebra or alchemy of ideas.

Nicholas of Cusa, probably the most original and profound fifteenth-century thinker, has been the object of many recent studies, particularly in Germany, but the critical edition of his works is still incomplete.[30] The sources of his thought and culture include scholastic philosophy – Scotism and nominalism in particular – and the mystic and neo-Platonic movement of the Middle Ages, plus a deeper familiarity with Plato, Proclus, the (pseudo-)Dionysius and others, both in the original Greek and in many new humanist translations. His interests in mathematics and astronomy have attracted the attention of historians of science. His language is extremely difficult; his themes and terminology change from one work to the next, and it is not always easy to decide if this is due to differing development or accentuation, or if it derives from more fundamental changes in doctrine. In treating the general and specific concepts of reason as simple abstractions, he discloses nominalist tendencies. But when he defines God as an infinite essence and the coincidence of opposites, and interprets the world and all of its parts as distinct manifestations and contractions of a simple divine archetype, explaining our knowledge of God as the continual approximation of our intellect to the infinite, this clearly shows Platonic and neo-Platonic overtones, and in particular, the influence of St Augustine and the Areopagite. Nicholas of Cusa was closely associated with the humanist world, but the roots of his thought are different, and the influence of his works was felt less in his own times than in the sixteenth century, when it reached its peak, for example in Lefèvre d'Etaples, Charles de Bovelles and Giordano Bruno.

Marsilio Ficino and his Platonic Academy represent the most important centre of Renaissance Platonism. By publishing the first complete Latin translation of the works of Plato, and the first version of Plotinus, Ficino made these central texts available to all western readers; the addition of an introduction and commentaries also determined the way these texts would be read and understood for several centuries to come. Ficino's *Theologia Platonica*, presented as an authoritative synthesis of Plato's metaphysics, was accepted as such both in its day and later. In fact, although his synthesis included many elements which were extraneous to Plato, i.e. neo-Platonic, Aristotelian and Epicurean, Augustinian, Thomist and others, it none the less was able to leave its successors a rich and solid metaphysical alternative to conventional Aristotelianism. Ficino's acceptance of the apocryphal writings of Hermes Trismegistus, Zoroaster, Orpheus and Pythagoras as documents attesting to an ancient and pre-Platonic wisdom, gave him the means to present the Platonic tradition as an almost unbroken chain, a form of perennial philosophy which was distinguished from Hebrew and Christian religious tradition, but in fundamental agreement with it. Encouraged by his neo-Platonic and Hermetic sources, but also by his familiarity with medical literature, he accepted and propagated certain forms of astrology and magic. Many sixteenth-century thinkers liked his central ideas on the contemplative life, on the immortality of the soul, on natural religion, on Platonic love, on the innate ideas of man which derive from the archetypal ideas of the divine intellect, on a universe permeated by the Soul of the World and unified by the thought and appetite of the rational and human soul; the influence of these ideas was reinforced by the Platonic, neo-Platonic and Hermetic authority which seemed to support them.[31]

While it is true that Ficino's young friend Giovanni Pico della Mirandola, who tragically met with an early death, felt the influence of his friend and of his Platonism, he cannot be characterized as merely Ficinian or even Platonic. Pico's humanist education was enriched by a masterful familiarity with the scholastic philosophy he had acquired in Padua and Paris; he always tried to absorb numerous scholastic doctrines into his own thought and to defend the scholastic philosophers from the attacks of the humanist Ermolao Barbaro. As a youth, Pico also studied magic, but in his last and longest book he firmly attacked judiciary astrology, supporting his position with arguments from astronomy, philosophy and theology. One of the first western scholars to learn Hebrew and Arabic, he took an interest in the untranslated writings of Averroes, in the rabbinical commentaries on the Bible and, most of all, in cabalistic literature, which he believed he could reconcile with Christian theology. The Christian cabalist movement of the sixteenth century, which includes Reuchlin and many others, originates in Pico's works, as does the cabalistic element in late Renaissance syncretism.[32] In the same way the Hermetic, Chaldaic and magic element can be traced back to Ficino.

The history of sixteenth-century Platonism still requires extensive research. The Platonic tradition which existed in Florence and Pisa after Ficino, began with Francesco da Diacceto and was carried on by Francesco Verino the Second and others.[33] There were other scholars and commentators of Plato, such as Sebastiano Fox Morcillo, Jacques Charpentier and Petrus Tiara. There was a tradition of comparing Plato and Aristotle , beginning with Pletho, Bessarion and their Byzantine and Italian followers and adversaries, and continuing through the sixteenth century up to Jacopo Mazzoni and others.[34] The doctrine of Platonic and divine love was adopted, developed and disseminated by many poets and theologians; it became the subject of a series of treatises on love, including Ficino's commentary on Plato's *Symposium*, Pico's commentary on a *canzone* by Girolamo Benivieni, the works of Bembo, Castiglione, Diacceto and Leone Ebreo, up to the *Eroici Furori* by Bruno.[35] As for the theologians, there was Giles of Viterbo, with his still unpublished commentary on the Sentences *ad mentem Platonis*[36] and Agostino Steuco, first to adopt the title of *philosophia perennis*.[37] Then there are the many thinkers who are not usually considered Platonists, but who were influenced by Platonism on various interesting points: Erasmus, Sir Thomas More, Lefèvre d'Etaples, Charles de Bouelles, Symphorien Champier, Agrippa, Postel, Bodin, Telesio, Bruno, Kepler and Galileo himself.[38]

We should briefly mention the cinquecento thinkers whose

contributions are original, particularly in natural philosophy, although they were more or less affected by humanism, Aristotelianism and Platonism.[39] It should be kept in mind that complete originality does not exist, so that we are speaking of relative originality, which may consist of nuances rather than spectacular claims. Moreover, as the originality of wrong ideas is worth little, it is often more valuable if true doctrines which have been known for some time, but doubted for the wrong reasons, are repeated in a new form or context.

The cosmology of Cardano, Telesio, Patrizi and Bruno has to its credit the attempt to replace traditional Aristotelian cosmology with a new construction based on new principles. Patrizi tries to replace the four Aristotelian elements with four new principles which he calls space, light, heat and dampness (fluor). Using the strictly empirical epistemology which impressed Bacon, Telesio names heat, cold and matter as the first principles of nature and tries to contradict Aristotle to prove that empty space precedes the bodies which occupy it, just as empty time exists before the motions which measure it. Giordano Bruno's first metaphysical principle is an infinite, which is both form and matter at the same time and produces all the specific beings as particular manifestations of its own essence; his conception seems to lie half-way between Nicholas of Cusa's and Spinoza's. Bruno's cosmology proposes an infinite universe made up of finite worlds, among which is our solar sphere. He makes explicit use of the ideas of Lucretius and Copernicus and gives us the conception of an immense universe, which quite closely approaches the conceptions of modern astronomy.

I hope this rather superficial summary of fifteenth- and sixteenth-century thought has been useful in illustrating some aspects of our problem. The period was characterized by a great abundance of ideas, some new, others ancient and long forgotten; ideas of an intrinsic interest which were helpful both in dissolving the synthesis of the preceding period and in preparing the way for the following one. The science of Galileo, Kepler and Newton was based on a new concept: the idea of applying mathematics and experiments to the physical sciences. The empiricist philosophy of Bacon neglected the mathematical aspect but formulated a programme of empirical and inductive science. The philosophy of Descartes used the model of the new mathematical physics to formulate a certain, precise, rationalistic metaphysics. None of these developments belongs to the Renaissance, but I believe that they all presuppose the philosophical and cultural developments of the previous two or three centuries, which we have discussed here.

The direct influence which Renaissance thought had on metaphysics, epistemology and the modern sciences came to a halt with the era of Galileo and Descartes. But in the shadier areas of modern philosophy, the influence continued in the form of many secondary, almost invisible movements. The empirical rationalism of Pomponazzi and the Aristotelians should not be confused with the free thought of later centuries, but it certainly was there that it found its continuation and further development. Although the element of magic in Platonism was abandoned by philosophers and scientists, it continued to fascinate poets and occultists until the nineteenth century and later, just as pagan mythology continued to inspire the imagination during the Christian centuries. Moreover, Platonic metaphysics and epistemology left their marks on the idealist tradition, i.e. in Descartes and Spinoza, in the late Berkeley and up to Leibniz, Kant and Hegel. Nor do I think this tradition is extinct. Many scholars like it, and even if the most influential thinkers of our time do not agree with them, I do. Finally, just as modern aesthetics is related in several areas to Renaissance poetics and rhetoric, so humanism has left to later centuries the inheritance of classical philology and historical criticism. These disciplines were perfected in the nineteenth century and have been applied to many new sectors of cultural history in our own century. They continue to flourish and to bear new and important results but, despite the efforts of Croce, Gentile, Dilthey, Rickert and Cassirer, they have still not made inroads into the conscience of philosophers, who ought to find this a fertile field for logic, epistemology and for a comprehensive philosophy of culture.

Like the philosophy of other periods, Renaissance philosophy contains many ideas of an intrinsic and permanent worth and interest. If we insist upon trying to show that these thinkers were the predecessors or precursors of certain modern or contemporary movements, their importance will never be demonstrated. What seemed modern yesterday is no longer so today, and what seems modern today might not be so tomorrow. A thinker who belongs to the past does not seem to gain much by association with a modernity which is *passé* or outmoded. It would seem safer to treat the thought of the past, whether that of the Renaissance or of some other period, as a treasure trove of ideas which are always fruitful when studied, even though they may not lend themselves to repetition without some modification, and even though they merely contribute to the themes and alternatives of the philosophical and human discourse, which we adopt and perpetuate, and which we hope our successors will continue as long as our culture manages to retain the tiniest breath of authentic life – a thing which at this moment is not beyond doubt, but also not beyond hope.

Translated from the Italian by Kristin Jarratt.

NOTES

* It is best to quote once and for all: *Bibliografia degli scritti di Eugenio Garin* (Bari, 1969); 'Bibliography of the Publications of Paul Oskar Kristeller', in Edward P. Mahoney (ed.), *Philosophy and Humanism* (Leiden-New York, 1976), 54-89.

1 Wallace K. Ferguson, *The Renaissance in Historical Thought* (Boston, 1948); H. Weisinger, 'Renaissance accounts of the revival of learning', *Studies in Philology*, XLV (1948), 105-18, and other articles; P.O. Kristeller, 'Studies on Renaissance humanism during the last twenty years', *Studies in the Renaissance*, IX (1962), 1-30; Tinsley Helton (ed.), *The Renaissance* (Madison, 1961); A. Buck (ed.), *Zu Begriff und Problem der Renaissance* (Darmstadt, 1969).

2 F. Masai, 'La Notion de Renaissance', in *Les Catégories en Histoire* (Brussels, 1968), 57-86; Walter Ullmann, *Medieval Foundations of Renaissance Humanism* (London, 1977).

3 E. Garin, *Rinascite e rivoluzioni*, 2nd edn (Rome-Bari, 1976).

4 M. Carriere, *Die philosophische Weltanschauung der Reformationszeit*, 2nd edn (Leipzig, 1887) (1st edn, Tübingen, 1847); F. Fiorentino, *Il risorgimento filosofico nel quattrocento* (Naples, 1885); W. Dilthey, 'Auffassung und Analyse des Menschen im 15. und 16. Jahrhundert', in his *Gesammelte Schriften*, II (Leipzig-Berlin, 1929), 1-89, published for the first time in *Archiv für Geschichte der Philosophie*, IV-V (1891-2).

5 E. Cassirer, *Das Erkenntnisproblem in der Philosophie und Wissenschaft der neueren Zeit*, bk 1: *Die Renaissance des Erkenntnisproblems* (Berlin, 1911), 19; *Individuum und Kosmos in der Philosophie der Renaissance* (Leipzig-Berlin, 1927); G. Gentile, *Giordano Bruno e il pensiero del rinascimento* (Florence, 1920); 3rd edn, *Il pensiero del rinascimento* (1940); *Studi sul rinascimento* (Florence, 1923; 2nd edn 1936). The series 'Renaissance und Philosophie', edited by A. Dyroff, published 16 volumes from 1908 to 1916.

6 J. Brucker (*Historia critica philosophiae*, vol. IV, Leipzig, 1766) speaks at length of philosophy, *A restauratione literarum ad nostra tempora*; W. G. Tennemann (*Geschichte der Philosophie*, vol. IX, Leipzig, 1814) deals with *Wiederbelebung griechischer Philosophie*; G. W. F. Hegel (*Vorlesungen uber die Geschichte der Philosophie*, vol. III, held 1829-30; printed in vol. 19 of *Sämtliche Werke*, ed. H. Glockner, Stuttgart, 1929) begins one section (p. 212) with *Wiederaufleben der Wissenschaften*; V. Cousin (*Histoire générale de la Philosophie*, Paris, 1861, 311-63) dedicates one lesson of his course to the *Philosophie de la Renaissance* (evidently after Michelet rather than Burckhardt); Johann Eduard Erdmann (*Grundriss der Geschichte der Philosophie*, Berlin, 1866) dedicates one section to the 'Renaissance', in which he deals with the rebirth of the Greek systems; another to the philosophers of nature, from Paracelsus to Bacon; and a third to the political philosophers, from Machiavelli to Hobbes.

7 G. Saitta, *Il pensiero italiano nell'Umanesimo e nel Rinascimento*, 3 vols (Bologna, 1949-51); E. Garin, *La cultura filosofica del Rinascimento italiano* (Florence, 1961).

8 H. Baron, *The Crisis of the Early Italian Renaissance* (Princeton, 1955; new edn, 1966); *From Petrarch to Leonardo Bruni* (Chicago, 1968); E. Garin,

L'Umanesimo italiano. Filosofia e vita civile nel Rinascimento (Bari, 1952); *Der italienische Humanismus* (Berne, 1947); F. Tateo, *Tradizione e realtà nell'Umanesimo italiano* (Bari, 1967); Charles Trinkaus, *Adversity's Noblemen*, (New York, 1940); *In Our Image and Likeness*, 2 vols (Chicago, 1970); Eugene F. Rice, *The Renaissance Idea of Wisdom* (Cambridge, Mass. 1958); G. Di Napoli, *L'immortalità dell'anima nel Rinascimento* (Turin, 1963); E. Grassi, *Verteidigung des individuellen Lebens: Studia humanitatis als philosophische Überlieferung* (Berne, 1946); E. Kessler, *Das Problem des frühen Humanismus: Seine philosophische Bedeutung bei Coluccio Salutati* (Munich, 1968); *Petrarca und die Geschichte* (Munich, 1978); P. O. Kristeller, *Renaissance Concepts of Man* (New York, 1972). For literary repercussions: A. Buck, *Die humanistische Tradition in der Romania* (Hamburg, 1968); *Die Rezeption der Antike in den romanischen Literaturen der Renaissance* (Berlin, 1976). For humanist philology: Silvia Rizzo, *Il lessico filologico degli umanisti* (Rome, 1973). For humanist archeology: R. Weiss, *The Renaissance Discovery of Classical Antiquity* (Oxford, 1969). For humanist script: B. L. Ullman, *The Origin and Development of Humanistic Script* (Rome, 1969); Albinia de la Mare, *The Handwriting of the Italian Humanists*, vol. I (Oxford, 1973). For the influence of Stoicism: L. Zanta, *La renaissance du stoïcisme au XVIe siècle* (Paris, 1914); Jason L. Saunders, *Justus Lipsius; The Philosophy of Renaissance Stoicism* (New York, 1955); G. Abel, *Stoizismus und frühe Neuzeit* (Berlin, 1978). For the influence of scepticism: Richard H. Popkin, *The History of Scepticism from Erasmus to Descartes* (Assen, 1960); Charles B. Schmitt, *Cicero Scepticus*, (The Hague, 1972). For humanist pedagogy, reference to the well-known volumes of W. H. Woodward and Garin is sufficient.

9 Donald F. Kelley, *Foundations of Modern Historical Scholarship* (New York, 1970); D. Maffei, *Gli inizi dell'umanesimo giuridico* (Milan, 1956); G. Kisch, *Humanismus und Jurisprudenz* (Basle, 1955); *Erasmus und die Jurisprudenz seiner Zeit* (Basle, 1960).

10 P. Polman, *L'élément historique dans la controverse religieuse du XVIe siècle* (Gembloux, 1932); Charles L. Stinger, *Humanism and the Church Fathers, Ambrogio Traversari and Christian Antiquity in the Italian Renaissance* (Albany, 1977).

11 P. Kibre, 'Hippocrates Latinus', *Traditio*, XXX–XXXIII (1975–7); Richard J. Durling, 'A Chronological census of Renaissance editions and translations of Galen', *Journal of the Warburg and Courtauld Institutes*, XXIV (1961), 231–305.

12 Paul L. Rose, *The Italian Renaissance of Mathematics* (Geneva, 1975); Marshall Clagett, *Archimedes in the Middle Ages*, vol.I (Madison, 1964); vol. II (Philadelphia, 1977); C. Maccagni (ed.), *Atti del Primo Convegno Internazionale di Ricognizione delle fonti per la storia della scienza italiana* (Florence, 1967); A. C. Crombie, *Augustine to Galileo* (London, 1952).

13 Neal W. Gilbert, *Renaissance Concepts of Method* (New York, 1960); W. Risse, *Logik der Neuzeit* (Stuttgart, 1964); *Bibliographia Logica* (Hildesheim, 1965); Walter J. Ong, *Ramus; Method and the Decay of Dialogue* (Cambridge, Mass., 1958); C. Vasoli, *La dialettica e la retorica dell'umanesimo* (Milan, 1968).

14 P. Duhem, *Etudes sur Léonard de Vinci*, 3 vols (Paris, 1906–13); E. Renan, *Averroès et l'averroïsme* (Paris, 1852). On the matter of free thought, see

[150]

P.O. Kristeller, 'The myth of Renaissance atheism and the French tradition of free thought', *Journal of the History of Philosophy*, VI (1968), 233–43.
15 F. E. Cranz, *A Bibliography of Aristotle Editions, 1501–1600* (Baden-Baden, 1971); Charles L. Lohr, 'Medieval Latin Aristotle commentaries', *Traditio*, XXIII–XXIX (1967–73); 'Renaissance Latin Aristotle Commentaries', *Studies in the Renaissance*, XXI (1974); *Renaissance Quarterly*, XXVIII–XXX (1975–77); P. O. Kristeller, *La tradizione aristotelica nel Rinascimento* (Padua, 1962).
16 E. A. Quain, 'Accessus ad Auctores', *Traditio*, III (1945), 215–64; R. W. Hunt, 'The Introductions to the "Artes" in the twelfth century', in *Studia Mediaevalia in honorem . . . Raymundi Josephi Martin* (Bruges, 1948), 85–112; R. B. C. Huygens, *Accessus ad Auctores* (Leiden, 1970); A. Buck and O. Herding (eds), *Der Kommentar in der Renaissance* (Boppard, 1975).
17 Charles B. Schmitt, *A Critical Survey and Bibliography of Studies on Renaissance Aristotelianism, 1958–1969* (Padua, 1971).
18 Neal W. Gilbert, 'Francesco Vimercato of Milan', *Studies in the Renaissance*, XII (1965), 188–217.
19 Heiko A. Oberman, *The Harvest of Medieval Theology* (Cambridge, Mass., 1963).
20 P. Petersen, *Geschichte der Aristotelischen Philosophie im Protestantischen Deutschland* (Leipzig, 1921); M. Wundt, *Die Deutsche Schulmetaphysik des 17. Jahrhunderts* (Tübingen, 1939); *Die Deutsche Schulphilosophie im Zeitalter der Aufklärung* (Tübingen, 1945).
21 P. O. Kristeller, *La tradizione aristotelica nel Rinascimento* (Padua, 1962).
22 See P. O. Kristeller, 'A Philosophical treatise from Bologna dedicated to Guido Cavalcanti: Magister Jacobus de Pistorio and his questio de felicitate', in *Medioevo e Rinascimento. Studi in onore di Bruno Nardi*, vol. I (Florence, 1955), 425–63 (for other bibliographical indications as well); Z. Kuksewicz, *Averroïsme Bolonais au XIVᵉ siècle* (Wroclaw, 1965); *De Siger de Brabant à Jacques de Plaisance* (Wroclaw, 1968).
23 F. Momigliano, *Paolo Veneto e le correnti del pensiero religioso e filosofico nel suo tempo* (Turin, 1907); M. Clagett, *Giovanni Marliani and Late Medieval Physics* (New York, 1941); Silvestro da Valsanzibio, *Vita e dottrina di Gaetano da Thiene*, 2nd edn (Padua, 1949); Curtis Wilson, *William Heytesbury* (Madison, 1956); P. Ragnisco, *Nicoletto Vernia* (Venice, 1891). For Petrus Mantuanus, see C. Vasoli, 'Pietro degli Alboini da Mantova "scolastico" della fine del Trecento e un'epistola di Coluccio Salutati', *Rinascimento*, ser. II, III (1963), 3–21; Petrus Mantuanus, *De Primo et ultimo instanti*, ed. Theodore E. James, dissertation, Columbia University (1971).
24 B. Nardi, *Saggi sull'aristotelismo padovano dal secolo XIV al XVI* (Florence, 1958); *Studi su Pietro Pomponazzi* (Florence, 1965); John H. Randall, *The School of Padua and the Emergence of Modern Science* (Padua, 1961); *The Career of Philosophy*, vol. I (New York, 1962); A. Poppi, *Introduzione all'aristotelismo padovano* (Padua, 1970); *Saggi sul pensiero inedito di Pietro Pomponazzi* (Padua, 1970).
25 Herbert S. Matsen, *Alessandro Achillini (1463–1512) and His Doctrine of 'Universals' and 'Transcendentals'* (Lewisburg, 1974); Edward P. Mahoney, *The Early Psychology of Agostino Nifo*, dissertation, Columbia University (1967); William F. Edwards, *The Logic of Jacopo Zabarella*, dissertation,

Columbia University (1961); A. Poppi, *La dottrina della scienza in Giacomo Zabarella* (Padua, 1972); L. Maþilleau, *Etude historique sur la philosophie de la renaissance en Italie (Cesare Cremonini)* (Paris, 1881); Maria Assunta della Torre, *Studi su Cesare Cremonini* (Padua, 1968).

26 A. Koyré, *Etudes galiléennes* (Paris, 1939). William A. Wallace discovered the influence of some of the Jesuit commentators in the early works of Galileo.

27 R. Klibansky, *The Continuity of the Platonic Tradition during the Middle Ages* (London, 1939).

28 P.O. Kristeller, *Il pensiero filosofico di Marsilio Ficino* (Florence, 1953); *Studies in Renaissance Thought and Letters* (Rome, 1956), 35–97, 139–50; E. Garin, *Giovanni Pico della Mirandola. Vita e dottrina* (Florence, 1937); A. Rotondò (ed.), *L'opera e il pensiero di Giovanni Pico della Mirandola nella storia dell'Umanesimo*, International Meeting, 1963 (Florence, 1965).

29 P.O. Kristeller, *Studies* (1956), 287–336.

30 Nicolaus de Cusa, *Opera omnia*, ed. Academy of Heidelberg (Leipzig–Hamburg, 1932–77); *Nicolò da Cusa*, Lectures given at the inter–university meeting held in Bressanone in 1960 (Florence, 1962) *Nicolò Cusano agli inizi del mondo moderno* (Bressanone, 1964; Florence, 1970); *Mitteilungen und Forschungsbeiträge der Cusanus-Gesellschaft*, I–XII (1961–77). Space does not permit mention of the numerous books and articles published on Nicholas of Cusa in the past few decades.

31 See above, n. 28. Frances Yates, *Giordano Bruno and the Hermetic Tradition* (London, 1964); D. P. Walker, *Spiritual and Demonic Magic from Ficino to Campanella* (London, 1958).

32 Joseph L. Blau, *The Christian Interpretation of the Cabala in the Renaissance* (New York, 1944); F. Secret, *Le Zôhar chez les Kabbalistes chrétiens de la renaissance* (Paris, 1958); *Les kabbalistes chrétiens de la renaissance* (Paris, 1964).

33 P. O. Kristeller, *Studies* (1956), 287–336.

34 Frederick Purnell, *Jacopo Mazzoni and His Comparison of Plato and Aristotle*, dissertation, Columbia University (1971).

35 John C. Nelson, *Renaissance Theory of Love* (New York, 1958).

36 John W. O'Malley, *Giles of Viterbo on Church and Reform* (Leiden, 1968).

37 Charles B. Schmitt, 'Perennial Philosophy, from Agostino Steuco to Leibniz', *Journal of the History of Ideas*, XXVII (1966), 505–32; G. Di Napoli, 'Il concetto di "Philosophia perennis" di Agostino Steuco nel quadro della tematica rinascimentale', in *Filosofia e cultura in Umbria tra Medioevo e Rinascimento* (Gubbio, 1966), 399–489.

38 *The Prefatory Epistles of Jacques Lefèvre d'Etaples*, ed. E. F. Rice (New York, 1972); Joseph Victor, *Charles de Bovelles* (Geneva, 1978); Charles G. Nauert, *Agrippa and the Crisis of Renaissance Thought* (Urbana, 1965); Paola Zambelli, *Di un'opera sconosciuta di Cornelio Agrippa* (Castrocaro, 1965), and other essays which ought to be published in one volume; William J. Bouwsma, *Concordia mundi, The Career and Thought of Guillaume Postel* (Cambridge, Mass., 1957); Jean Bodin, *Colloquim*, translated and annotated by Marion L. D. Kuntz (Princeton, 1975).

39 H. Védrine, *Les philosophes de la renaissance* (Paris, 1971); P. O. Kristeller, *Eight Philosophers of the Italian Renaissance* (Stanford, 1964).

5

POLITICAL THEORIES
IN THE RENAISSANCE

NICOLAI RUBINSTEIN

HE TRANSLATION, in the mid-thirteenth century, of Aristotle's *Politics*, and the acceptance of many of its fundamental principles and themes by St Thomas Aquinas, have long been considered a turning-point in the evolution of western political thought.[1] The naturalness of political life, the teleological function of secular society, the notions of the common good and of distributive justice, and the theory of the mixed constitution, were all ideas which were enthusiastically absorbed by political thinkers during the following decades and adapted, in various ways, to fit contemporary conditions and problems. Furthermore, the *Politics* provided, for the first time since Antiquity, a model of a formal political doctrine covering the entire range of political and social life. In both respects the Aristotelian revival affected Europe at large; but it had a specifically Italian dimension. Thirteenth-century Italy provided conditions which were singularly favourable for the reception of the *Politics*. The Italian communes resembled the Greek *polis* in their physical and demographic structure as well as in their republican institutions, while factionalism, social conflicts and revolutions had their counterpart in fourth-century Greece. By systematically analysing such institutions and problems, and, what is more, offering models for the former and possible solutions for the latter, the *Politics* provided a unique key to the new world of urban politics and a guide to face, or even solve, its crises. No such guide had existed before the rediscovery of the *Politics*. By the mid-thirteenth century, there had been independent city republics in Italy for 150 years, and in the case of Venice even longer, yet their impact on political thought had been scant. Before Aquinas, cities as separate political units had no place in the political theories of schoolmen, whose primary concern was to define the duties and functions of princes, the limits of their authority, and, above all, their relationship to the Church in general and the Papacy in particular.[2] This accorded with the legal position of cities in the kingdoms; in so far as they were self-governing, they owed it to royal charters or their equivalent; all the rest was usurpation, as Frederick Barbarossa and his lawyers made abundantly and (from a strictly legal point of view) correctly clear. It was characteristic of the way in which schoolmen ignored these new political realities, that John of Salisbury, who was acquainted with French and Italian cities, found no place for them in his wide-ranging analysis of contemporary society; his organological concept of the state was applied solely to the kingdom; and in it, citizens, unlike peasants and artisans, performed no specific function.[3]

Political thinking among the Italian citizens themselves, in so far as it can be documented, was, before the Aristotelian revival, rudimentary and reflected practical issues of communal policies. The conflicts with the Hohenstaufen emperors gave the notion of *libertas* a specifically civic meaning which sharply contrasted with that attached to the word in the feudal and ecclesiastical spheres. Urban expansionism, as well as social and economic growth, contributed to the development of civic patriotism, and the emergence of internal factions led to an increasing concern with peace and unity as essential foundations of the communal government. The duties of magistrates were spelt out in manuals for the *podestà* in a way which was distantly related to the *specula principum*; these handbooks also included model speeches, which presented the ideal of a peaceful urban society and the duties of the citizen in it.[4] Altogether, the products of the *ars dictaminis* constitute the main sources for urban political thought in this early period, but one would be disappointed if one expected systematic political arguments or analyses from them. Their purpose was didactic, not theoretical. The rhetoric taught by the *ars dictaminis* was an exclusively practical affair: it was left to Petrarch and his humanist successors to revive the Ciceronian model of the union between rhetoric and philosophy.[5] One exception to this was Brunetto Latini, and his counsels on urban government which he included in his *Trésor* were based partly on an abridged version of Aristotle's *Ethics*.[6] He composed this work between 1262 and 1266; St Thomas completed his section of the commentary to the *Politics* in 1272.[7]

A different kind of evidence for çivic political thought in this early period is provided by urban historiography and, generally speaking, by attitudes of citizens to civic history as expressed in contemporary literature. In so far as their principal subject was not a kingdom or the Empire, not a church or a monastery, but a city, urban chroniclers treated the latter as an intelligible political unit whose actions were

[154]

distinct from those of its members, long before civilian lawyers had begun to apply corporation theories to towns as well as to kingdoms.[8] Furthermore, by emphasizing and eulogizing the Roman origins of their cities, they also stressed their links with city-centred Roman Antiquity. In this context Rome was not seen as founder of the Holy Roman Empire but as the founder of Italian cities such as Florence, the 'piccola Roma'. The revival of urban civilization made possible, and not only in Italy, a new perspective of Roman history as the history of a city, and the descendants of Rome were thus able to learn from her vicissitudes. The most popular history of the late Roman republic in the thirteenth century, the *Fet des Romains*, speaks of it as a 'coumun': there were urban communes in France as in Italy;[9] for a Florentine or a Milanese, however, the 'commune' of ancient Rome was also the ancestor of his city. Conversely, the heroes of the Roman republic were no longer confined to their role as exemplars of secular virtues in the earthly city, into which they had been cast by St Augustine, but were seen once more as citizens of a republic. For Brunetto Latini, Cicero was an ideal republican statesman; but he was also the leader of the opposition to Catiline, whose rebellion was closely bound up with the legendary foundation of Florence. It was, however, only in the fourteenth century that Italian historiography became a major source for our knowledge of contemporary political ideas, and in the meantime, the rediscovery and absorption of Aristotle's *Politics* had transformed Italian political thought. This breakthrough began with Aquinas' use of the *Politics* in the *De regimine principum* and in the *Summa Theologica*, but it was only after the turn of the century that Aristotle's political theory was fully assimilated and applied to contemporary Italian conditions and problems. This development may be illustrated by the treatment of monarchical and of pluralistic government in the first book of the *De regimine principum*, composed by Aquinas around 1265, and in Books 3 and 4, written by Ptolemy (Tolomeo) of Lucca about forty years later.[10]

Aquinas follows earlier medieval tradition in considering monarchy the best form of government, but departs from it in the arguments he uses to support his thesis. For his predecessors, the absolute premise of all discussions of government was that it was rule by one: the only alternative to kingship was tyranny, disparities between different types of such government being seen in moral or legal terms, or, in the case of the Empire, in terms of function within the *societas Christiana*. Thus, for John of Salisbury, there are only two kinds of supreme ruler, distinguished by their relation to higher law: the prince, who rules according to it, and the tyrant, who does not. Aquinas, on the other hand, following Aristotle, distinguishes not only between monarchy and tyranny, but also between government by one, by a few, and by many, and it is in this wider and more complex context that he discusses the problem of tyranny. By stating in the first chapter of the *De regimine* that not only rule by one, but also rule by a few and by many, can turn into tyranny as a result of the neglect of the common good, he extends the traditional contrast king–tyrant to the pluralistic regimes of Aristotle's classification of constitutions. This left Aquinas with two forms of government which, besides monarchy, Aristotle defines in that classification as 'true' constitutions, the rule of a few and of many according to the common good. The following chapter of the *De regimine* is thus devoted to the question whether it is 'better . . . for a multitude of men living together to be ruled by one rather than by more than one'; and Aquinas answers, predictably, that 'the rule of one is better than the rule of many'.[11] But that this question could be asked at all, and the superiority of monarchy over pluralistic regimes made the subject of an elaborate argument, constitutes a profound change in the evolution of political thought.

Aquinas argues that 'in nature . . . rule is always by one' and in doing so goes beyond Aristotle by applying Aristotelian naturalism to the form of the state as well as to the state as such. He accordingly concludes that 'it necessarily follows that in human society, the best rule is that of one'.[12] But the superiority of monarchy over all other forms of rule 'is also borne out by experience': past and present events show that provinces or cities which live under pluralistic regimes suffer from internal divisions. What clinches the argument from 'experience' is that, owing to these divisions, as well as to their general instability, pluralistic regimes are more likely to be replaced by tyrannies than are monarchies. 'Past history and contemporary events' prove that tyranny arises 'more frequently . . . in lands which are ruled by many than in those which are ruled by one . . . for when dissension arises in a pluralistic regime, it often happens that one man becomes predominant and usurps for himself control of the people'.[13]

Aquinas does not mention Italy explicitly, but his reference to contemporary events shows unmistakably that he had Italian developments in mind. He explains how the Roman republic, after having long been governed by magistrates, was finally taken over by tyrants as a result of discord and civil war; but similar developments in his own time could only be found in Italy. At the time when Aquinas was writing the *De regimine principum*, despotic rule had begun to assert itself as the alternative to republican government in northern Italian towns, and its success was due to factionalism and civil strife. Ezzelino da Romano, who henceforth exemplified for republicans the tyrant, had imposed his despotic rule in Verona, Padua and other towns during Frederick II's reign. From 1240, the Estensi established a *signoria* in Ferrara. Then, after Ezzelino's death in 1259, the della Scala gradually established their despotic rule in Verona. Between 1260 and 1262, Rolandino of Padua wrote a history of the March of Treviso which in fact was a history of the rise and fall of the da Romano. He sets up Ezzelino's tyrannical rule as 'an example to everyone, that such rule should be rejected': 'Thus we can now clearly behold the extent of horror and abomination wrought by such tyrants in the cities which they rule'.[14] Such a 'servile yoke' must be avoided at all costs, and liberty defended 'until death'. For Rolandino, the positive alternative to tyranny is not monarchy, as for Aquinas, but republican government.

While Aquinas believed that a pluralistic government was more likely to lead to tyranny than monarchy, and that monarchy was a better safeguard against it than pluralistic government, he admitted that for many people the royal office was rendered hateful 'because of the evil deeds of tyrants' so that even those who 'want to be ruled by a king fall into the brutal hands of tyrants, and there are many magistrates who practise tyranny under the guise of regal dignity'.[15] Although Aquinas based his argument on the evidence of Roman history, his terms of reference are not only historical: 'to many people . . . the very name of kingship is odious', '*multis . . . redditur regia dignitas odiosa*'. In the thirteenth century, only in Italy could hatred of tyranny encompass criticism of the royal office itself, but magistrates (*rectores*) turned into tyrants might remind Italians of the autocratic rule of Frederick II's vicars and *podestà*. Aquinas also admitted, though somewhat reluctantly and with express reference to Roman history, that good republican government had certain advantages over monarchies. He not only quoted Sallust's statement on the rise of Roman power after the expulsion of Tarquinius: 'It is incredible to recall how quickly the Roman state grew after it had obtained liberty';[16] but also added, by way of a general observation, that subjects of kings are less inclined to serve the common good than citizens of a republic, since they identify it with the interests of the ruler: experience teaches that a city which is governed by annually appointed magistrates can achieve more than a king who rules over three or four cities. While subjects object even to small exactions by their rulers, citizens willingly bear great burdens 'if they are imposed by the citizen body itself'.[17]

For Aquinas, such advantages could not detract from the superiority of monarchy over all other regimes. Aristotle too had considered monarchy the best constitution,[18] though only in the abstract, and Brunetto Latini, writing his *Trésor* about the same time, could read in the *Compendium Alexandrinum* of the *Ethics* that 'government is of three kinds. . . . And the best of all is the government of kings'. In the *Trésor*, he inverts this order, placing communal government first: 'the third kind is that of the communes, which is by far the best of them'.[19] Unlike Aquinas, the Florentine Brunetto Latini adapts Aristotle's constitutional theory to demonstrate the superiority, not of monarchy, but of communal government. His statement is one of the earliest documents of Italian republican ideology. It thus provides a link between the views expressed by Aquinas in the first book of the *De regimine principum* and those expounded by Ptolemy of Lucca in the subsequent books about forty years later.

Ptolemy of Lucca also uses Aristotle to prove the superiority of republican over monarchical government, but he does so on the basis of the *Politics*, which he follows far more closely than did Aquinas. Government in the 'political regime' (*principatus politicus*) is elective, limited in time, and regulated by law; and law, for him, is not the 'higher law' of John of Salisbury, nor the natural and divine law of Aquinas, but statute law or, in Aquinas' words, human law. Unlike John of Salisbury and Aquinas, he takes it for granted that monarchs claim absolute power, according to the Roman maxim that 'they hold the laws in their breasts'[20] without at the same time mentioning their voluntary submission to them, and contrasts this with the *rectores politici*, who 'are restrained by laws'.[21] *Regimen politicum* derives from the Greek word *polis*, 'which is a plurality or a city'. Ptolemy thus saw 'political rule' as especially characteristic of cities.[22]

Unlike Aquinas, who used it as a synonym for state or *res publica*, Ptolemy related the Aristotelian term *politia* firmly to the city, and was thus able to interpret the *Politics* mainly in the context of the Italian city state: whereas in Aristotle's time, 'political rule' existed in Athens, it does so now 'especially in Italy'.[23] He explained this in terms of the Aristotelian principle of the suitability of different constitutions to different peoples:[24] those who are 'manly, courageous and fully confident of their intelligence',[25] can only be governed by a 'political regime', which includes aristocracies. Hence monarchy cannot exist in Italy without becoming tyranny: the islands, Sicily, Sardinia and Corsica accordingly have always had tyrants, while in Lombardy, with the exception of Venice, no perpetual rule could exist 'except through tyranny'.[26]

'Perpetual rule' was the rule exercised by the *signori*, whose constitutional position was in fact that of 'perpetual lords'.[27] By the time Ptolemy was writing, republican opposition to despotic rule had become widespread and articulate, and many citizens would have agreed with Francesco da Barberino that 'they are mad who live in the land of tyrants'.[28] Ptolemy placed this opposition in a conceptual framework derived from the *Politics*.

While the *Politics* provided Ptolemy with his most powerful arguments in favour of the political regime of Italian city republics, his Florentine contemporary Remigio de' Girolami saw in Aristotle's concept of the common good the answer to the factional strife which beset his city at the turn of the century and which he believed was threatening to destroy it. He subordinated the individual to the common welfare to an extent which went far beyond Aristotle's theory of the common good; his 'extreme corporationism' is indeed yet another example of the length to which Italian political thinkers could go in adapting Aristotelian doctrine to fit contemporary problems and conditions.[29] Aquinas had used the notion as yet another argument in favour of monarchy;[30] Remigio endows it with a decisive role in the civic community, as the force binding it together. In this civic formulation, the theory of the common good received its most powerful expression, towards 1340, in the allegory of Good Government in the Palazzo Pubblico of Siena, in which the citizens are shown to have elected 'a Common Good for their lord'[31] – the common good thus taking the place, in the peaceful and well-ordered society of a city republic, held together by harmony and regulated by justice, of the *signore* and his arbitrary rule.

Ptolemy's republicanism and Remigio's corporational patriotism are inseparable from their historical outlook. Their praise of the Roman republic and of the civic virtues of its citizens reflects a new sense of the Roman past, but also shows how, around 1300, Roman history could be used to support political ideas.[32] Brunetto had set up Cicero as a model of a republican statesman, Ptolemy condemned Caesar as a tyrant who had ruined the republic.[33] As Charles Davis has observed, in Italy 'the development of republican institutions and ideology naturally led to a patriotic reaffirmation of the Roman republic'.[34]

Ptolemy also saw, in a highly personal version of the hierocratic doctrine, the Roman republic as the predecessor of the Church, and the Papacy as its rightful heir as the fifth monarchy.[35] There could hardly have been a greater contrast to the views of Dante and Marsilius of Padua and yet Ptolemy has in common with Marsilius a theory of government under law, a definition of the latter in terms of statute, not natural, law, and opposition to arbitrary rule. Marsilius, on the other hand, shares with Dante an opposition to papalism which, despite differences in arguments and conclusions, has a common Italian basis in their lament over the division of Italy, for which they held papal usurpation of imperial authority responsible. Their attacks on the

[159]

hierocratic doctrine have their place in the European reaction to papalism; but while Dante delivers his criticisms from the base of an extreme imperialist theory, Marsilius integrates the clergy into the structure of the secular state and consequently subordinates it to the government elected by and dependent upon the consent of the people. Marsilius' and Dante's insistence on the autonomy of the state from interference by the Church has to be seen in its wider European context, but it also had its Italian connotations in the relations between Church and state in Italian city republics.[36]

Marsilius also drew more radical and unqualified conclusions from Aristotle's political doctrine for his theory of the secular state than any other political thinker of his time. His debt to contemporary scholasticism, and especially to Averroism, was no doubt great, and he wrote *The Defender of Peace* in Paris, but his political Aristotelianism cannot be fully understood outside the world of the Italian city republics. This new world had enabled Aquinas, notwithstanding his absolute preference for monarchy, to accept republican government as one of several constitutional alternatives; Marsilius showed relatively little interest in Aristotelian constitutional classifications and priorities and concentrated on a general theory of the state; but his analysis of its structure and problems, while based on the Aristotelian model, owes much to that of Italian city republics.

Marsilius' native Padua was one of the last great city republics of northern Italy to fall under despotic rule; after an abortive attempt in 1318, it was finally established there four years after the completion of *The Defender of Peace*. In his concluding chapter, Marsilius states that the 'subject multitude' may learn from his book how to prevent the ruler assuming arbitrary powers.[37] Like Ptolemy's idealization of the 'political regime' and Remigio de' Girolami's notion of the absolute supremacy of the common good, Marsilius' theory of the sovereignty of the human legislator, in a state ruled by the laws and governed with the consent of its citizens, was a manifestation of the profound and enduring crisis of communal government after the middle of the thirteenth century. If the emergence and growth of the Italian communes provided the ground for a breakthrough in political thought, the threat to their republican institutions added a new and rich dimension to it. Not until the time of Machiavelli did Italian political ideas undergo so great a change as in the late thirteenth and early fourteenth centuries; and when this happened, it was once more in response to an Italian crisis. It could be argued that the extraordinary flourishing of political thought during those decades left little trace on its subsequent development during the trecento, that Ptolemy and Remigio remained isolated figures, that Dante's *Monarchy* was condemned as heretical, as was *The Defender of Peace*, and that Marsilius' influence did not begin until the Great Schism, and then in the sphere of ecclesiastical policy. The scarcity of political literature in the later trecento makes an answer to this argument difficult, but it may be said that Ptolemy's section of the *De regimine principum* was generally believed to have been composed, like its first book, by Aquinas (and consequently enjoyed the authority of the *doctor eximius*), that the Aristotelian–Thomistic notion of the common good provided the inspiration, in the 1330s, for the Sienese allegory of good government, painted in the prestigious council chamber of the Nine, and that *The Defender of Peace* was translated into the Florentine vernacular in 1363.[38] But, whatever the direct influence of these men on later generations, they had asked questions about the relative value of republic and monarchy, about the place of the common good in civic society, about the role of the citizen in a republican state; these – like their civic patriotism and the admiration for the Roman republic – were to remain dominant themes in Italian political thought. They also left to later generations the legacy of political Aristotelianism. They laid the foundations of Renaissance political thought.

Their new and seminal ideas on politics were closely related to new attitudes to history, and especially to Roman history, which in their turn reflected political and social developments. From Ptolemy to Machiavelli, historical awareness formed a major facet of political thinking. This proved to be one of Renaissance Italy's principal contributions to the evolution of European political thought.

The knowledge which Italians had of ancient history in 1300 was far less extensive and critical than that of the humanists of the quattrocento and their interpretation of it was infinitely less sophisticated and profound than that of Machiavelli. Yet the translations into the vernacular of works of Roman historians, as well as such works as Benzo d'Alessandria's *Chronicon* and Riccobaldo of Ferrara's *Historia Romana*, testify both to the growing interest in, and the widening knowledge of, ancient Roman history.[39] Political thinkers considered that history was relevant to the political problems of their time and coloured it with their own political preoccupations and ideals. Thus their eulogies of civic virtues of Roman patriots, divorced from the reservations of St Augustine, reflect and reinforce the republicanism of Ptolemy and the corporationism of Remigio, and reflect a pervasive civic patriotism which saw in the Roman republic an ideal model. But Roman history could also offer lessons on the fragility of political structures and on their decline.

The pride of Italian citizens in the achievements, past and present, of their cities was compounded by the, usually exaggerated, picture they had formed of their origins; it also coloured their view of their more recent history. This is reflected in the interpretation urban chroniclers give of the development of their cities. 'It grew from small beginnings', writes Jacopo da Voragine of Genoa, 'and from small beginnings achieved greatness, and from greatness it became even greater.'[40] Giovanni Villani saw the history of Florence as one of continuous progress from the time of its 'refounding' by Charlemagne.[41] As early as c. 1130, the author of an historical poem celebrating Pisa's Balearic campaign, the *Liber Maiorichinus*, compared Pisa's victories with those of ancient Rome.[42] Conversely, from the mid-thirteenth century, we find Italians pointing to the decline of Rome as evidence for the results of internal division. That cities prosper through unity and are destroyed by discord had become, by the end of that century, a commonplace of political didactics, as is shown by model speeches for *podestà* as well as by historical works,[43] and Remigio de' Girolami argued, with relentless Thomistic logic, that discord and the neglect of the common good were destroying Italy in general and Florence in particular, and that 'once the city is destroyed, the citizen will remain a painted image or a form of stone, because he will lack the virtue and the activity which he once had'.[44] Ancient Rome provided a daunting historical example of the decline of cities.

Once again, St Thomas broke with tradition. Since the days of St Augustine and Orosius, the decline of the Roman empire had been seen as part of a divine plan and as punishment for sin, whereas Aquinas concentrated on Rome's constitutional developments, and thus saw her decline in the context of municipal history.[45] Writing at about the same time, Brunetto Latini took a knowledge of the crisis of the Roman republic so far for granted that he advised the *podestà* in their speeches to cite it as an example of how harmony 'enriches the townspeople and war destroys them, and remember Rome and the other good towns which have fallen and declined from internal strife';[46] and from about 1300, Italian citizens who did not know Latin could gather ample information on the decline of the Roman republic from Bartolomeo da San Concordio's translations of Sallust's works. But by the beginning of the fourteenth century, the decline of cities was also seen as part of a natural process: 'You will not think it strange or wonderful/To hear how families come to an end,/Since even cities have their term of life'.[47] Dante contrasts the decline of Rome with the rise of Florence, which in its turn will be followed by decline, and Villani, probably following Dante at this point, assumes the rise and decline of the two cities to be natural phenomena not requiring further explanation: 'considering that our city of Florence was in the ascendant . . . at the same time that Rome was declining'.[48]

Eugenio Garin has emphasized the importance of Arabic astrological speculations concerning conjunctions for 'questions of historical periodization and the crises of civilizations' in the late Middle Ages.[49] From the early fourteenth century onwards, astrological theories of the influence of conjunctions on major periodical changes in society, politics and religion also seemed to offer an explanation of the crises and political changes in Italian cities. Albertino Mussato combined an organic concept of urban development with the conviction that in his native Padua this development proceeded by way of a cyclic process, with periods of prosperity alternating with periods of decline. 'For the state of this city always changes with amazing regularity, since in cycles of about fifty years it enjoys periods of growth, during which everything that is good in nature springs up and burgeons.'[50] The Paduan astrologer, Peter of Abano, who probably influenced Mussato, distinguished conjunctions of Jupiter and Saturn (the most important every 960 years, the least important every 20) as determining human affairs; Alcabitius counts that of Saturn and Mars in the reign of Cancer, which occurred every 30 years, amongst those 'portending the destruction and changes which happen in this world'.[51] A contemporary of Mussato's, the Bolognese notary Armannino Giudice, records the opinion of 'the authorities' according to which by virtue of the 'course of the planets' 'earthly things change . . . about every thirty years, which is called the course of the age'.[52] Less learnedly than Mussato, and in contrast to his previous optimistic verdict on the rise of Florence, Villani draws, in the last book of his *Cronica*, on astrological calculations regarding the year 1345 to explain the causes of 'the changes in the city . . . which have happened almost every twenty years, or a little less'.[53]

While astrological theories of history were thus used, in Padua and Florence, to interpret their political development, they were so only in relation to the so-called 'minor' conjunctions, which could be taken to provide 'scientific' explanations of the frequent political crises and constitutional changes affecting Italian cities in the thirteenth and fourteenth centuries. Periodization, whether along astrological, organological or pragmatic lines, had by the mid-fourteenth century become a major element in Italian interpretations of urban history. Whether Italian citizens of the trecento also saw that history as part of a wider process of renewal after a period of darkness is another question. It would have seemed obvious for them to have viewed the history of their cities in these terms; but there is not sufficient evidence to suggest that this was in fact generally the case. The Venetians, whose city was founded during the Barbarian invasions, stressed the continuity in its development; the Milanese, while celebrating the last period of the western Roman empire as a climactic point of their city's power, as a 'second Rome', did not consider its subsequent history one of darkness followed by renewal.[54] In Florence, on the other hand, the early thirteenth-century *Chronica de origine civitatis* had already focused on the catastrophe which that city had allegedly suffered at the hands of the Barbarian invaders, and Villani completed this interpretation of Florence's 'medieval' history by postulating the renewal by the Romans (about 350 years after its alleged destruction) brought about by Charlemagne, who granted it liberty and a republican constitution on the model of Rome, thus antedating by more than 300 years the establishment of communal government in Florence. While the rebuilding of the city was thus a revival of its *romanitas*, Villani does not consider it as part of a general renewal of the Italian cities after the centuries of darkness following on the decline of the Roman empire; his concept of renewal is strictly confined to Florence, a Roman foundation rebuilt and repopulated by Romans under the guidance of the new Roman emperor. It was left to Leonardo Bruni to extend this concept to the Italian cities in general, and in particular to those of Tuscany.

It is instructive to compare Villani's interpretation of Florentine history with Cola di Rienzo's idea of Roman renewal. For Cola di Rienzo, the dark ages of Rome lasted until his own time, and it was under his leadership that the city was to be reborn; for Villani, the dark ages of his city had ended when it had been refounded by Charlemagne and the Romans. The Florentine's outlook was pragmatic and historical; Cola's ideological and programmatic. Despite the exaggerated claims made by Konrad Burdach,[55] Cola di Rienzo did not represent a broad stream of Italian thought and, outside Rome, his short-lived impact appears to have been most effective on Petrarch.

The Florentine trecento view of the political renewal of the city, as expounded by Giovanni Villani, was republican: when the city was rebuilt by the Romans, Charlemagne had laid the constitutional foundations of the commune by ordering that Florence 'should rule and govern itself as Rome had done, that is by means of two consuls and by a council of one hundred senators'.[56] By the end of the fourteenth century, the republican version of Florence's foundation legend had been extended back to include the original foundation of the city as well,[57] and Bruni gives this new version its definitive form when he states, in the *Laudatio Florentinae urbis*, that Florence was founded when 'the rule of the Roman people was very flourishing' and when 'that holy and untrampled liberty was still vigorous', though it was soon afterwards to be destroyed by the Emperors. This fact explains why the Florentines 'far more than others rejoice in their liberty and are utterly opposed to tyrants'.[58] Matteo Villani had already said that Florence, as well as Perugia and Siena, 'have maintained the freedom and the liberty inherited from the ancient Roman people'.[59] It was a liberty which could be defined both as independence from superior powers, and as republican freedom in contrast to tyranny.[60] It is in this latter sense that Matteo Villani could say that 'the Guelph Party is the foundation of the liberty of Italy and the enemy of all tyrannies', and 'tyrants . . . are natural enemies and oppressors of peoples which want to live in freedom'.[61] It is in the same sense, too, that Salutati could describe, in 1390, the war between Gian Galeazzo Visconti and Florence as a war 'between tyranny and liberty'.[62] Matteo Villani's views may be taken as representative of Florentine republicanism as strengthened after, and no doubt largely as a result of, the short-lived despotic rule of the Duke of Athens in 1342–3. But Florence did not play a prominent role in what proved to be one of the major innovations in Italian political thought during the fourteenth century.

The elaboration and exposition of a republican ideology of tyranny was left to such men as Ptolemy of Lucca, Mussato and Marsilius of Padua, at a time when, early in the century, despotic rule had triumphantly established its hold over northern Italy. For the medieval antithesis king–tyrant, they substituted that of republic–despotism. They examined, with extraordinary insight, the nature of despotism, the causes of its rise and the ways of preventing it. While much of this debate was based on contemporary experience, as is borne out by the role of historians in it, it also drew on ancient history and political theory.[63] While Ptolemy, in defining republican and despotic governments, took Aristotle as his guide and adapted his ideas to fit contemporary conditions, Mussato, who belonged to the pre-humanist group centred in Padua, turned to Sallust and Seneca to help explain the rise and success of despotic government. His invective against Marsiglio of Carrara, who (with the help of Cangrande della Scala) put an end to Paduan republican liberty, culminates in a quotation from Seneca's *Hercules furens*. Mussato's tragedy, the *Ecerinis*, concerned Ezzelino who had become to Italian republicans the prototype of the Italian tyrant, and while directed against Cangrande it was likewise modelled on Seneca.[64] Both Mussato and Marsilius warned Italian citizens to beware of arbitrary government, and Mussato voiced a widely held view of its origin, when he branded internal division as its principal cause: 'O dire feuding among nobles, o popular fury! the desired end of your conflict is at hand; the tyrant is here, the gift of your raging.'[65]

After the fall of the Paduan republic in 1328, eastern Lombardy ceased to be the intellectual centre of trecento republicanism. Instead we find in northern Italy, from the early fourteenth century, the emergence of a positive theory of despotic government. The *signore*–tyrant of the republicans is replaced by the benevolent ruler who brings peace and unity to the strife-torn cities, imposes justice, and cares for the common good. Arguments in model speeches can provide valuable evidence for contemporary public opinion; in one composed by Filippo Ceffi in 1325 or shortly afterwards, to be used 'when the city . . . wants to elect a new lord', the latter is described as a 'just lord', 'joined by love and by trust' to the citizens, whom he directs to 'perfect justice' and extricates from 'party strife and divisions', bringing 'victory without and concord within'.[66] Far from being a tyrant, others claim, he puts an end to the tyranny of the people; far from being an arbitrary autocrat, he rules his city 'with equal laws', his 'principal concern' being 'to obey the laws, statutes and legal judgments in a state of peace; and to treat everyone equally'.[67] Similar sentiments were expressed by Petrarch. We are not here concerned with the question of the evolution of his views on autocratic government; nor with the possible ambivalence of his attitude to despotism,[68] but only with points of contact between his views and those we have just illustrated. 'I think the tyranny of one man is easier to tolerate than the tyranny of a people', he wrote to Boccaccio in 1366; 'for where there are no tyrants, the people behaves as a tyrant';[69] the da Carrara lords of Padua, he insists, are rulers of the state, not tyrants, and, in 1373, he accordingly addressed to Francesco da Carrara a long letter on the ideal prince.[70] About thirty years later, at the moment when the last lord of Padua, Francesco Novello, was unsuccessfully fighting against superior odds for the survival of the da Carrara rule, his former chancellor, the humanist Giovanni Conversini, emphasized, in his *Dragmalogia*, the superiority of lordship over republican government, and concluded that 'the rule of one man – not only of the one best man but of a middling good man – is more desirable'.[71] The full title of his treatise is *Dragmalogia de eligibili vitae genere* (on what kind of life is to be chosen), and Conversini explains that this must be the contemplative life, and that only a political order established and protected by a prince can provide the freedom which makes it possible to pursue the *studia litterarum* in peace.[72] Baron has pointed out that by the time of his discovery in 1345 of the *Letters to Atticus* and his consequent condemnation of Cicero the statesman, Petrarch had moved away both from his earlier praise of the Roman republic and from his evaluation of the active life, and that 'the two changes were inseparable'.[73] This is not the place to discuss the chronology of Petrarch's intellectual biography, but what is evident is the connection between a preference for the solitary and contemplative life, and for autocratic government, and that Petrarch was the first humanist to make it.

One of the foremost achievements of Garin's and Baron's studies of Florentine humanism has been to show the central importance in it of the question of the active life and the contemplative life. By emphasizing the role this question played in Florence from the end of the fourteenth to the middle of the fifteenth century, they have also greatly contributed to our understanding of humanism elsewhere in Italy. Within the context of this essay, we must consider its significance for the development of Italian political thought.

If, as Garin writes, 'early humanism was devoted to the exaltation of civic life',[74] nowhere could this be seen more clearly than in the celebration of the active life by humanists such as Salutati and Bruni, and in their attempts to reconcile it with the ideals of the contemplative life. One should, at the same time, bear in mind the personal aspects of this question for men who, whatever their professional status, were also scholars and men of letters. Indeed, it could be argued that it was precisely the greater involvement of humanists in political life and government affairs which made the problem of how to combine the active life with the life of studies so important and pressing for them. Hesitations and inconsistencies in finding an answer to this problem testify to a very real and acutely felt tension – a tension which is now only too familiar to scholars involved in university administration and committee work. Salutati is a case in point: his 'greatest contribution to humanism from the layman's world' was, in the words of Baron, 'his part in the vindication of the *vita activa-civilis*', and his example illustrates, as it were, the archetypal predicament of humanist scholars who were also professional civil servants. Later in his life his youthful secularism gave way to 'tensions and frequent alternations between opposing attitudes', and to an insistence on the superiority of the contemplative over the active life.[75] But even Bruni, who more than any other Florentine humanist formulated the ideals of 'civic humanism', was not free from such tensions and alternations: in his *Vita di Dante* he praises Dante for having lived the life of a citizen, for having married and having held public office in his own city-republic; in the 'parallel' *Vita di Petrarca* he states that Petrarch was wiser in remaining detached from political life.[76]

For citizens who were not professional humanists the problem had a different complexion. The urge to participate actively in political life was so pervasive and powerful among the ruling class of Florence in the early fifteenth century, and was founded on so ancient a tradition, that it certainly did not need any encouragement from the humanists. Criticism of political involvement, as expressed in Leon Battista Alberti's *Della Famiglia*,[77] was motivated by economic, social and possibly political but not by intellectual considerations: voluntary withdrawal into the closed world of the family was a very different matter from withdrawal into that of study and contemplation as a result of enforced exclusion from political life, as in the case of Palla Strozzi. Niccolò Niccoli's detachment from that life and criticisms of Florentine policy, and Cino Rinuccini's bad-tempered diatribe against the young intellectuals who did not want to have anything to do with family life and politics, do not seem to me to warrant the assumption that social irresponsibility was anything but an exceptional phenomenon among citizens who had devoted themselves to classical studies.[78]

That the combination of the patrician's life of intense involvement in the government and administration of the republic with the *studia humanitatis* should have become both an ideal and a reality in fifteenth-century Florence, and to a lesser extent Venice, was no doubt primarily due to the influence of prominent humanists such as Salutati and Bruni, whose writings both promoted and celebrated a convergence between the active and the contemplative life;[79] but the importance of public life and the desirability of holding high office were too widely accepted in the Florentine and Venetian political class to create for its members the kind of problems that the dichotomy between a life of action and a life of contemplation posed for the humanists. It was only when participation in public life became progressively restricted as a result of Medicean ascendancy that withdrawal into contemplative life became a political problem as well. The major document of this development is Landino's *Disputationes Camaldulenses*. Landino's argument for the supremacy of the contemplative life has its counterpart in Alamanno Rinuccini's complaint, in his near-contemporaneous *De libertate*, that Medicean autocracy was forcing citizens to withdraw into the private life of study.[80] However, it should not be forgotten that Leon Battista Alberti, in Landino's dialogue, concludes (after having eloquently demonstrated the superiority of thought over action) by admitting that the true man is he 'who understands and combines both kinds of life': the man who follows Martha as well as Mary.[81]

Whereas Landino's ideal of the wise man guiding the state was influenced by Plato, Bruni's translation of Aristotle's *Politics* was, in Garin's incisive words, 'almost an ideal consummation of the vision of the republic to which he had completely dedicated himself'; and not only Bruni, but, according to Garin, 'the whole civic humanist movement in Florence in the early fifteenth century developed under the influence of the rediscovered moral philosophy of Aristotle'.[82] Bruni and his circle, in rediscovering Aristotle, 'theorist of the republic',[83] thus took up a thread which led back to the political Aristotelianism of the early trecento. But they did not ask the same questions, nor did they find in Aristotle the same answers.

Bruni's attitude to the problem of translating the *Politics* is a case in point. In his preface, he explains that he was primarily concerned with replacing the barbarous translation of William of Moerbeke with one which did justice to the 'golden stream' of Aristotle's eloquence.[84] As for the content of that work, it was meant, in this purified and liberated form, to speak for itself. In the same preface, Bruni states that the most eminent place among the moral disciplines is occupied by precepts 'concerning states, and how they should be governed and preserved'. He considers that there could be no discipline more useful to man than to know 'what is a city and what is a republic . . . and how civic society is preserved and how it perishes'.[85] These are, indeed, fundamental questions of classical political philosophy, but Bruni does not discuss them at any length. His only systematic attempt to make use of Aristotle's political theory is in his Greek treatise on the Florentine constitution, which, following Aristotle's concept of the mixed constitution, he considers a mixture of aristocracy and democracy, with the middle class holding the balance.[86]

Neither Bruni nor, for that matter, the other Florentine humanists of the early quattrocento who emphasized the 'primacy of civic life' were systematic political thinkers. Divorced from, and critical of, the scholastic approach to knowledge, Bruni no doubt felt that a truthful version of Aristotle's work was all that was required to make it possible to learn from it.[87] But however important humanist philology was in promoting a better understanding of the text, it did not necessarily also promote a discussion of the questions raised and the answers provided by it, nor their application to contemporary experience. Rather than stimulate such discussion, it provided humanists with materials with which to build their own model structures of a republican polity. Matteo Palmieri's *Della vita civile* is the fullest account we possess of such a model, and it draws heavily on Aristotle and Cicero as well as on ancient Roman history. His ideal republican state is based on civic union and supported by civic virtues; in it, the common good prevails over private interests, and political offices as well as fiscal burdens are distributed among the citizens equitably, following Aristotle's principles of distributive justice.[88]

Palmieri composed, for his 'beloved citizens', and in particular for

[169]

those who held high office and thus 'represented' the city, a guide to 'the best way of life for men who live in cities', which was to convey to those who were ignorant of Latin the teachings of the ancients.[89] In his *Laudatio* Bruni describes Florence as a perfect city: 'it is such that nothing more brilliant and resplendent can be found in the whole world.'[90] This is manifested in her physical appearance and is borne out by her Roman origins; it is also shown by her political order: 'this city is admirable both in her exploits abroad, and in her internal order and institutions'.[91] The Florentine constitution is based on the rule of law and the protection of liberty, and is designed to hold in check excessive power on the part of social groups as well as of the *Signoria*. Although Aristides' *Panathenaic oration* served Bruni as a model for the *Laudatio*, its idealized picture of Florentine government and institutions owes more to Florentine political traditions than to classical prototypes, and more to Cicero than to Aristotle. His lucid analysis of some of the basic principles underlying Florentine political institutions is a remarkable achievement, and constitutes a new point of departure in the descriptions of Italian cities. But it should be added that Bruni's insistence on such concepts as the supremacy of law over sectional or private interests had been, since the days of the Ordinances of Justice of 1293, deeply embedded in Florentine political ideology. It is difficult to see much more than a rhetorical device, to match his account of the geographical position of the city, in his contention that nowhere else can be found 'such careful arrangement . . . so much elegance . . . such symmetry' as in the 'internal order and institutions'[92] of Florence. About ten years later (but long before he had embarked on the translation of the *Politics*) he turned to Aristotle's constitutional theory for a definition of the Florentine constitution. In his 'letter to the Emperor', which has been dated 1413, he defined the Florentine form of government as a 'popular regime', that is 'the third legitimate type of government'.[93] But Aristotle called the third 'true' constitution πολιτεία, and its perverted counterpart δημοκρατία, which William of Moerbeke had, literally, translated as '*politia*' and '*democratia*'. However, Aquinas in his commentary equated democracy with popular regime, and Bruni evidently follows this equation.[94] The reason is obvious: according to traditional Florentine usage, the city's constitutional regime was a popular regime,[95] although perhaps Bruni was encouraged to define it as one of the 'legitimate types of government' by Aristides' eulogy of the Athenian δημοκρατία as the greatest of all Athenian constitutions.[96] It is only in his Greek treatise of c.1439 that Bruni described the Florentine constitution as a mixed form of government, that is, a fusion of aristocracy and democracy.[97] He had just completed his translation of the *Politics* and may have been writing under the fresh influence of Aristotle's praise of the mixed constitution as the best form of government in actual practice; or else his application of this concept to Florence may reflect the deeper and fuller knowledge of Florentine government which he had acquired as Florentine chancellor. Thus the mean, *mediocritas*, which he had previously singled out as one of the principal social ideals Florentine legislation was trying to achieve, was now seen, in correct Aristotelian terms, as the linchpin of the balance provided by the mixed constitution.[98]

Bruni may have also wished to offer a Florentine response to the view that the Venetian constitution was better than any other Italian state's because it was mixed. This view had been expounded by Bruni's friend Pier Paolo Vergerio in his *De republica Veneta*, recently dated between 1400 and 1403.[99] It was not for the first time that the Aristotelian model was applied to the Venetian constitution. At the beginning of the fourteenth century, the Dominican friar Henry of Rimini had stated that the best form of government, with the exception of monarchy, combined monarchy, aristocracy and polity, '*politia populi*', and had singled out Venice as being alone in possessing a constitution which 'seems to approximate to this mixed regime'; thus 'the Venetian people . . . enjoys peace and security'.[100] That the Venetian constitution was 'a realization of the classical idea of mixed government',[101] or of that of aristocracy, remained a major theme of eulogies of Venice from the fifteenth century onwards, and humanists were soon to see Plato as the second classical authority to support this new formulation of the 'myth of Venice'. George of Trebizond argued that Venice not only possessed the mixed constitution which Plato, in the *Laws*, had described as the best state, but also that she was the only state to have realized that model.[102] Contrary to Plato's and Aristotle's views on the realizability of ideal forms of government, George of Trebizond and others after him saw the mixed constitution realized in Venice, just as Cicero saw it realized in Rome.[103] It would be wrong to dismiss this approach as exclusively panegyrical since comparison of actual political structures with ideal models could also promote a better understanding of the former. Yet it was precisely the panegyrical element in such 'idealistic' analyses of existing constitutions that limited their usefulness – this is borne out by the repetitiveness and lack of originality in fifteenth-century comparisons between the Venetian republic and classical models of perfect constitutions. Not surprisingly Machiavelli, while considering that 'the Venetian republic . . . excels among the best modern republics', did not consider such ideal models acceptable instruments of political theory.[104]

What all such comparisons have in common is that they are descriptive and not normative, that they are designed to demonstrate that existing constitutions conform to ideal models, not to argue that they ought to conform to them. This applies whether Venice or Florence is being compared, and whether with Plato's ideal state of the *Laws*, or with Aristotle's constitution which is 'best relatively to actual circumstances'.[105] They also all concern republics and reflect traditional civic values such as, in Venice, peace, security, and liberty; in Florence, equality, the mean, and liberty; and in both the supremacy of law and of the common interest.[106] In so far as these comparisons assume that existing republics actually conform to these values, they differ from a didactic treatise such as Palmieri's *Della vita civile*, which postulates and discusses these values within the moral discipline of the *studia humanitatis*, 'civic life' being the 'perfection of the individual',[107] and which takes as its model not ideal constitutions, or 'the imaginary goodness of citizens never seen on this earth, such as Plato and other great intellects dreamed up, perfect in virtue and wisdom'. Instead, Palmieri wants to 'demonstrate the actual life of virtuous citizens with whom one has lived', such as Agnolo Pandolfini, 'that venerable and well-instructed citizen'.[108]

The distinction between eulogies based on classical ideal models of existing constitutions, and didacticism inspired by classical political philososphy, applies not only to republics but also to monarchies. Panegyrical descriptions of city republics have their counterpart in the eulogies of princes, the humanist teachings on civic life have theirs in the treatises on princely government composed by humanists, who were quite prepared to provide either. This was not only because this was their function as professional teachers of moral philosophy and as rhetoricians. There was a long tradition, going back to John of Salisbury and before, of drawing on ancient political precepts in *specula principum*;[109] and Aquinas had, by his reading of the newly discovered *Politics*, laid the foundations of an Aristotelian theory of monarchy. Thus Bruni could state, in the proem of his translation of the *Politics*, that there was no discipline more fitting to man than the one expounded by Aristotle which enquires 'what is a city and what a republic',[110] and then send his translation to King Alfonso of Aragon on the grounds that the *Politics* was 'a great and rich implement of royal government'.[111] Platina, on the other hand, could use different versions of the same text for his treatises *On the prince* and *On the ideal citizen*.[112]

That he could do so without much difficulty was due to the fact that he dedicated the *De optimo cive* to Lorenzo de' Medici, and in it represented Lorenzo's grandfather Cosimo as the *'optimus civis'*. In Medicean Florence, the gap between the prince and the 'ideal citizen', to whose care 'the Florentine republic . . . is about to come',[113] could well be seen to be closing, so that, apart from an additional book devoted chiefly to the military and other actions of the prince, much the same advice could serve either. Yet there remained a fundamental difference between the 'ideal citizen' and the 'ideal prince', which was clearly recognized by Platina. For the humanists, the Roman prototype of the former was Cicero, the defender of the republic,[114] but Platina explicitly describes Florence under Cosimo and Lorenzo as a 'popular state', and adds that it is the concern of the good citizen that no one obtains 'the rule of the city' on account of great wealth and then turns it into a tyranny; instead, the good citizen's duty is 'to preserve . . . the city in its prosperity' and 'repel disasters and dangers' when necessary.[115] Platina probably had Cosimo's posthumously bestowed title of *pater patriae* in mind, when he referred to the Roman senate's conferment of it to Augustus;[116] but Cicero was also called *pater patriae*.[117] Platina adds that, while 'the citizens preferred to delegate all powers to one man' in order to put an end to civil war, 'Roman sovereignty had not yet completely devolved on to one man'; and he makes Cosimo admonish Lorenzo to seek true fame by being 'a good citizen of great merit' 'in a free city'.[118] At the same time, the counsel of the many good and wise citizens was to be followed, and the high offices of the republic filled with men 'of true nobility'. Although Platina uses the conventional humanist definition of nobility – 'it is virtue which ennobles' – he explains that it is generally agreed that those who descend 'from better stock . . . will be better both at governing and at being governed'.[119] Platina quotes Plato's statement in the *Republic* on the rule of philosophers,[120] but his concept of the model citizen, who governs the state as *pater patriae*, is closer to the Ciceronian ideal of the *bonus civis*, *moderator rei publicae* and *conservator patriae*, who is *optimus* through virtue and intelligence, and not because he is one of the *optimates*.[121] His treatise fits the style of Medicean government, with its mixture of autocracy and oligarchy, remarkably well – at least before Lorenzo had succeeded in further concentrating power. The praise of Cosimo's good government of Florence may well have had political overtones, and may have been designed as a reminder to the young Lorenzo who, after his succession, declared, in connection with a projected electoral reform, that he intended to follow the example of his grandfather in acting in as constitutional a way as possible.[122]

Platina's *De optimo cive* stands half-way between Palmieri's republican treatise on the *vita civile* and works on princely government.

Quattrocento writings on princely government concentrated on the virtues and duties of princes, thus following the tradition of medieval *specula principum*, as represented by the enormously popular *De regimine principum* by Egidio Colonna.[123] Where they parted company with their medieval predecessors was in their emphasis on fame as a reward for princely virtue, and in their much greater use of classical authorities to support their ethical teachings.[124] Some of them were frankly eulogistic, in that a particular ruler was portrayed as a model prince, just as Cosimo was set up by Platina as a model citizen. Thus Giuniano Maio, in his *De maiestate*, singles out King Ferrante of Naples (to whom he dedicated the work) as the exemplar of an ideal prince.[125] Conversely, Antonio Beccadelli records Ferrante's father Alfonso as the wisest and greatest of all princes of his time.[126] But generally humanist writings on princely government, as distinct from eulogistic literature, deal with problems of rulership relevant to contemporary conditions and offer advice and guidance on matters ranging from moral virtues to courtly manners; and although they often do so along the traditional lines of medieval mirrors of princes, they could also raise questions of a more general political nature, such as whether it is better for a prince to be loved or feared.[127] Over and above this, they might also, similarly foreshadowing Machiavelli, affirm, as did Francesco Patrizi, that 'the virtues of a king are different from those of private individuals'.[128] What is striking is the scant attention paid in them to the institutional aspects of princely government. Thus Francesco Patrizi uses the traditional scholastic argument from Aristotle's classification of constitutions that the rule of one man is the best form of government, but does not feel called upon to discuss it, except in criticizing republics for their tendency to turn into the extremes of tyranny or mob rule.[129]

While Aristotle had been, from the thirteenth century onwards, the principal classical authority for the superiority of both monarchy and republican government, now Plato's *Republic* and *Laws* also came to be used in support of them. Uberto Decembrio, having translated the *Republic*, with Manuel Chrysoloras,[130] used it to expound the duties of the perfect prince in his own *De republica*, which he dedicated to Filippo Maria Visconti;[131] his son Pier Candido (who in his turn translated the *Republic* between 1437 and 1439) by a remarkable *tour de force* identified timocracy, which according to Plato was the one existing constitution which came closest to the ideal state, with monarchy. Pier Candido saw in Gian Galeazzo Visconti the perfect prince who, 'eager for honour and victory, assumed the leadership . . . so that by fighting nobly and by ruling the republic ably and well, he might win praise for himself and advantage for his country'.[132] The reference to

Plato's philosopher-king might have been more attractive, but even an accomplished panegyrist would have found it difficult to fit Gian Galeazzo into this role: perhaps this is why Decembrio described Plato's ideal constitution as aristocratic and omitted to consider it, since 'up to now it has never in fact existed'.[133] Matters stood differently with Cosimo and Lorenzo de' Medici, both of them students of philosophy as well as statesmen. Giovanni Argyropoulos likened Cosimo to Plato's philosopher-ruler;[134] Marsilio Ficino praised Lorenzo for combining 'philosophy with supreme authority in public affairs'; in this way, he said, Lorenzo was realizing what Plato 'above all, hopes for in great men';[135] but he exercised his 'supreme authority' within the framework of a republican constitution. As we have seen, this is what Platina had in mind when he quoted Plato's 'divine saying' that no state can be happy unless its rulers combine political power with philosophy: 'this combination . . . he thought could preserve states, if supreme power were held by a man dedicated to learning, virtue and prudence'.[136]

Platina cites Scipio Africanus, Laelius, Cato, Lycurgus and Solon as classical examples of this maxim: supreme examples of civic virtue, 'who thought of nothing else in life and did nothing else but what might redound to the honour and glory of the state and to the well-being of its citizens'.[137] Scipio could serve as prototype of the 'best citizen' governing the republic; he could also stand for republicanism against tyranny. The controversy between Poggio and Guarino, which Pietro del Monte joined on Poggio's side, over the respective merits of Scipio and Caesar, has been described as central to the issue of republic versus monarchy in quattrocento political thought;[138] yet by this time the theoretical question of the respective superiority of monarchy and republic had lost much of its earlier force. Comparisons between the two forms of government were incidental rather than systematic. In 1404 Giovanni Conversini affirmed the superiority of monarchy in the wider context of a critique of Venice;[139] in his reply to Antonio Loschi's invective against Florence, recently dated soon after 1406,[140] Cino Rinuccini rejected Loschi's alleged contention that the government of one was better than that of many, although Loschi had not said anything of the sort, and referred to the achievements of the Roman republic to demonstrate the superiority of republics.[141] In his belated reply to Bruni's *Laudatio*, Pier Candido Decembrio raised, once again, 'the frequently asked question' of 'whether it is better for the republic to be ruled by the counsel and authority of one man or by the will of the many', and answering in favour of the former immediately turned to an eulogy of Gian Galeazzo Visconti.[142]

By the early fifteenth century, possibly because of the relatively stable division of Italy into republican and monarchical states, the ideological positions seem to have crystallized to a point where the old question of the superiority of one of these forms of government was, for the time being, considered less in general terms than in relation to individual states, where it could serve to enhance eulogistic descriptions or to support invectives. To return to the controversy over Scipio and Caesar, it may also be asked whether Poggio, while simultaneously praising Scipio and denigrating Caesar, in so far as this had any contemporary political implications at all, had not Cosimo de' Medici rather than the Florentine republic in mind. His letter to Scipione Mainenti, which started the controversy, was written from Florence in April 1435, that is only a few months after Cosimo's return from exile, during which Poggio had compared him with Camillus, Scipio Africanus and other *patriae conservatores* who had suffered exile 'on account of envy and civil strife'.[143] It was also written at a time when Cosimo and his friends were busy exploiting their victory over the Albizi faction and consolidating the new Medicean regime.[144]

The controversy yields remarkably little as far as general political questions are concerned; those which are raised are almost drowned by learned references to historical examples. Guarino counters the accusation that Caesar had destroyed Roman liberty with the argument that that liberty was already extinct, and that in fact he had restored it. He says that 'when the state became so unsettled and disturbed that the rule of one man became necessary', Caesar established 'countless institutions pertaining to the best-ordered states', and that these were 'signs of a restored and expanded liberty'.[145] While Guarino's argument recalls the earlier defence of despotism on the grounds of restoration of law and order,[146] Pietro del Monte relates his condemnation of Caesar to his own Venetian origins: having Venice, that 'true and inviolate temple of liberty', as his fatherland, he wanted to preserve liberty; no wonder that he should detest the 'subverter of Roman liberty'.[147]

Pietro del Monte's outburst is typical of republican thinking in the quattrocento, which concentrated on basic political concepts rather than involving itself in the discussion of problems of political philosophy. Of these basic concepts, by far the most important was that of liberty. The fact that it formed an integral part of a republican tradition, which went back to the thirteenth century and before, and that it was abundantly used – and abused – in war and diplomacy, for propaganda,[148] does not by itself reduce its importance in the political thought of the early Renaissance. Indeed, it could be argued that political propaganda and invective helped to refine its definition and increase awareness of its complexity. The chancellor Salutati's reply to

Antonio Loschi's invective against Florence turns largely on the 'true' meaning of liberty; and by the unusual procedure of incorporating Loschi's entire text into his own treatise, Salutati shows the different meanings attached to the term in Florence and among her enemies. He also seeks to demonstrate, in this way, his success in refuting the contention that Florence was, in fact, suppressing the liberty of her subjects, and in expounding the Florentine claim that nowhere does a liberty exist 'which is freer or more untainted than Florentine liberty', in contrast to the 'Lombard race', which alone, 'whether by nature or whether by custom', does not appear to love and desire it.[149] Salutati was the first and foremost Florentine chancellor to make liberty a central theme of Florentine public letters; he also went beyond publicistic policies and Florentine traditions in extending that theme (in conformity with his own appreciation of monarchy) to monarchical states under the rule of law.[150]

It was Leonardo Bruni who, with the help of Cicero, related the republican concept of *libertas* to *aequalitas* and to *ius*. According to Bruni, these three concepts formed a triad of fundamental principles dominating Florentine political institutions, *ius* being defined in terms not only of the rule of law but also of equality before the law: 'in this way liberty flourishes and justice is religiously observed in the city'.[151] The connection between liberty and law is further elaborated in his *Historiae Florentini populi*, where Giano della Bella defines liberty as consisting 'in two things . . . that is, in laws and in legal judgements': when these wield more power than private citizens, liberty is preserved; when not, it is finished.[152] Equality also meant for Bruni equal opportunity of holding public office – a concept which was formulated as early as 1328 in a Florentine constitutional law, and which sharply contrasted with the limitations both legal and practical, to which it was subjected in fifteenth-century Florence. But he stopped short of extending it to fiscal equality.[153] That he omitted to discuss the existing contrasts between these ideas and the inequalities of Florentine public life may be explained by the panegyrical character of much of his writing on this subject, but also reflects the value of his statements as evidence of Florentine political thinking. The records of the debates in the advisory councils of the *Signoria*, the *pratiche*, although in their turn often influenced by humanist rhetoric, provide invaluable evidence of shared political assumptions and an awareness of political problems.[154] Later in the century, they show that republican constitution-alism was by no means extinct in Medicean Florence, but that – apart from a brief period of revival under Piero di Cosimo in 1465–6 – it had gone 'underground'. It was during this period that a speaker in a *pratica* could, once more, state the republican doctrine that *utilitas publica* consisted of *securitas civium, libertas sententiarum,* and *equalitas tributorum,* that is, civic liberty, freedom of speech, and equitable taxation; while another declared that civic concord was achieved 'through the observance of justice, the equal distribution of offices and relief from excessive taxation'.[155] But the most important document of republican opposition in Medicean Florence is Alamanno Rinuccini's *Dialogus de libertate,* written in 1479 during the war of the Pazzi conspiracy. In his *Dialogue* Rinuccini reiterates Bruni's thesis of liberty and equality as the twin foundations of the Florentine republic – 'who is there who does not know that equality is the principal foundation of civic liberty?'[156] – with the difference, however, that what Bruni had praised as existing in the present, Rinuccini describes, nostalgically, as a thing of the past. Then, he says, there was no other city in all of Italy 'which protected liberty so resolutely and for so long, or where liberty herself flourished so extensively and uncorrupted', and 'the city lived in obedience to its own laws',[157] so that Florence not only excelled over all other Tuscan towns, but was also 'an outstanding example of the good life'; now the laws are held in contempt. Then freedom of speech reigned in the Florentine councils, which may be compared 'with the silence there today'. Thus the city is deprived of what Aristotle attributes to 'free republics . . . which should be like a single body' with many members; for now 'a very few men . . . usurp for themselves alone what belongs to all the citizens'.[158] In accusing Medicean 'tyranny' of having robbed Florence of its most precious possessions and corrupted her free constitution, Rinuccini breaks with precedent. Humanist accounts of republican institutions had been basically descriptive and prevalently panegyrical; Rinuccini's discussion of liberty is critical and prescriptive. The fact that Florentine liberty had, in his view, been lost, gave him a sense of distance from the past which earlier eulogies had lacked, while his condemnation of the present regime has as its corollary the withdrawal into contemplative life, following Plato's warning against getting involved in politics: his study of letters taught him that 'happiness lies in freedom and tranquillity of mind'.[159]

Leonardo Bruni also affirmed the republican origins of Florence by antedating her foundation to the time of Sulla, when 'that sacred and untrampled liberty was flourishing'. This, he claimed, was the reason why 'the Florentines especially delight in freedom and why they are extremely hostile to tyrants'.[160] Baron has shown how much this 'new view of history' influenced Florentine historical thought in the early quattrocento, and has discussed its political implications. It may

be added that, like the chronicles of the trecento, humanist historiography of the quattrocento yields evidence of contemporary political
thought which one would seek in vain in political treatises.

Bruni's thesis of the republican origins of Florence, stated first in the
Laudatio, is definitively expounded in the first book of the *Historiae*;
another major theme of this work is the evolution of Florentine liberty.
Following Giovanni Villani, he mistakenly dates the establishment of
communal institutions to the time of Charlemagne, but, unlike Villani,
does not see the 'medieval' history of Florence as one of a free city, since
she was subject to the Empire until the death of Frederick II.[161] The
problem of dominion had been at the centre of the polemic between
Loschi and Salutati, since it had provided the Milanese secretary with
ammunition to reject the Florentines' claim that they were defending
liberty against oppression;[162] Bruni treats it as a major theme of
Florentine history. After being released from subjection to the Empire,
Florence was aiming first at hegemony in Tuscany, and then at
territorial expansion, which culminated in 1406 in the conquest of Pisa.
As a result, he says in his *Commentarius*, 'the fame of the Florentine
people grew far more than it had done in all the previous wars'.[163]
Although Bruni connects expansion with the desire for security he also
considers it desirable for its own sake and, as such, self-generating. This
is the gist of Pino della Tosa's speech in 1329, in favour of the
acquisition of Lucca, the formulation of which in Book VI of Bruni's
Historiae no doubt reflects Florentine concern with the same project a
hundred years later: to those citizens 'who advising you that you have
got enough, consider that you should protect it', Pino replies that
further expansion would serve 'to protect . . . what we already possess',
and advises them to imitate the Roman people, 'our parent' who 'would
never have obtained a world empire if they had contented themselves
with their own posssessions and shrunk from new enterprises and
expenses'.[164] Empire thus joins equality as another adjunct of liberty,
and Pino clinches his argument by pointing out that, in contrast to
private modesty and frugality, public 'magnificence consists in glory
and grandeur'.[165] Under the aristocratic regime established after the
Ciompi revolt, and in particular during the period following the death of
Gian Galeazzo Visconti, Florentine foreign policy 'fluctuated between
aggressiveness and accommodation', between 'concepts of honour and
considerations of utility'.[166] Bruni's *Historiae*, begun in 1415, reflect
these fluctuations. As a Florentine historian, Bruni treated the
problems of expansion and dominion in the context of the history of
Florence; Machiavelli and Guicciardini were to discuss them as
fundamental problems of politics.

[179]

Much the same applies to the problem of factionalism. Beginning with the division between Guelphs and Ghibellines, factional strife runs like a thread through the *Historiae*: 'that is how the love of faction arose, which was the beginning of great calamities'.[167] Once again there is the link, this time negative, with liberty: when the republican regime was restored in 1343 after the expulsion of the Duke of Athens, civic strife returned 'together with liberty'.[168] If faction must be avoided to preserve liberty, social upheaval must be prevented in order to protect the ruling class: the Ciompi revolt of 1378 should be a constant warning 'to the leading citizens that armed uprisings must not be allowed to come under the control of the masses'.[169]

The second humanist history of Florence, by Poggio, although making more extensive use of orations than Bruni's, is more jejune when it comes to fundamental problems of Florentine politics, beyond such traditional themes as the description of the war with the Visconti as one between liberty and tyranny.[170] References to general political concepts are, not surprisingly, scarce in the eulogistic works of humanist historians of princes; thus Giorgio Merula explains the success of the Visconti *signoria* at the beginning of the fourteenth century as a result of internal division, which necessitated the establishment of peace and order by a single ruler[171] – an explanation which takes us back to trecento arguments in favour of the *signoria*. Nor were Venetian historians of the quattrocento much given to an evaluation of the history of their city in such theoretical terms; Bernardo Giustinian's account of the original Venetian *libertas* refers to one of the corner-stones of the Venetian 'myth', that is, the city's independence from superior authority. Giustinian, like Bruni, connects liberty with empire but, in a more moralistic strain, relates them both to virtue, which alone can secure their survival; conscious of the ultimate inevitability of decline he sees the only remedy for it in the 'care and diligence of the rulers (*principum*)', the *principes* being the Venetian nobility.[172] In Florence, on the other hand, the historical dimension of political thought had a long tradition, and this tradition was enriched and refined by Bruni, who combined great classical learning with political experience. On a more modest level, the same dimension is also shown in the minutes of fifteenth-century *pratiche*, where historical precedents or examples are cited time and again in support of political arguments.

No other Italian city possesses so rich a source of political opinion as the minutes of these advisory meetings summoned by the Gonfalonier of Justice. Concerned as they were with concrete issues facing the government, the debates in the *pratiche* provide evidence of basic

[180]

political attitudes on such questions as the priority of honour and utility, and of the importance of civic unity for the proper functioning of the body politic, while during the brief period of reaction to the Medici ascendancy, republican values were, as we have seen, given a fresh and forceful expression.[173] Under Lorenzo de' Medici, the *pratiche* gradually lost importance and were, in 1480, for all practical purposes replaced by the new council of Seventy. But after the fall of the Medici regime they were revived, and under the republican regime from 1494 to 1512 played a central role in Florentine politics. A comparison between the debates in these later *pratiche* and those of the early fifteenth century shows much continuity in basic political assumptions, although the new problems resulting from Florence's isolation in Italy after the French expedition of 1494, and the subsequent vicissitudes of Italian politics and diplomacy, created new and daunting issues which could also be interpreted as part of the wider question of the relationship between reason and fortune. To quote from Felix Gilbert's seminal essay on Florentine political assumptions during that period, 'the concepts which were used to describe the true nature of the Florentine government were freedom, equality, republic'; 'in order to achieve equality or freedom . . . it was considered enough to have laws and justice', and thus concord.[174] We seem to be back in the days of Leonardo Bruni. It is often overlooked that the Medici regime, which produced its own political themes, did not wholly eliminate earlier republican ideas and values; they had been given a new and forceful expression early in the century, inspired by classical theories and models, and after briefly surfacing again in 1465 witnessed a dramatic revival after the fall of that regime.

The survival, and ultimate revival, of Florentine republican ideology after 1434 provides one of the clues to Machiavelli's political thought. Historians have moved away from the notion that Machiavelli represented a decisive break with the 'medieval' traditions of political thought, but this antithesis, so convenient for purposes of periodization, still serves historians of political ideas to explain the 'originality' of Machiavelli. They might postulate a medieval model characterized by such generalizations as 'medieval hierarchy' and ignore, or underrate, the specifically Italian manifestations of political thought from the thirteenth century onwards. In contrast to this approach, Baron has stressed the links which connect Machiavelli with Bruni, while Felix Gilbert has pointed to the literature on princely government during the second half of the century as preparing the ground for some of the ideas expressed in *The Prince*.[175] Rudolf von Albertini and Gilbert have also broken new ground in connecting

Machiavelli's ideas with contemporary developments in Florentine political thinking.[176] These studies, and others which have followed, have deepened and refined our understanding of Machiavelli's originality. They have also if anything confirmed the applicability of Machiavelli's own claim, made in a more restricted sense in the preface to the *Discourses*, to have 'decided to enter a way as yet untrodden by anyone else',[177] to the whole body of his political doctrine. The fundamental difference between Machiavelli and his humanist 'sources' has been defined by Gennaro Sasso as reflecting the 'extreme decadence' of Florence and Italy after 1500, so that, if Machiavelli had derived from the 'more mature and articulate thought of Florentine civic humanism some themes for his political questions . . . his formulations are nevertheless as remote from those of the humanists as were the political conditions of Florence in his day from theirs'.[178] In more general terms, it might be said that the events which followed the French invasion of 1494, and which profoundly affected not only Florence but Italy as a whole, had a traumatic effect on Florentine political thinking, and made possible new questions and unprecedented insights, and not only because these changes could appear to reflect decadence or corruption. An outstanding document of this traumatic experience is the dramatically succinct account given by Guicciardini in about 1508 in his *Storie fiorentine* of the crisis which had overtaken Italy in 1494, when 'like a sudden storm . . . the unity of Italy was broken and shattered', and when 'states began to be preserved and ruined, given and taken, not by plans drawn up in studies, as in the past, but in the field by force of arms'.[179] The events which took place four years after Guicciardini wrote these lines, and which led to the restoration of the Medici in Florence, added new and dramatic evidence to his analysis, which has its echo in the observation, in chapter 25 of *The Prince*, that Italy 'is the seat of these changes', and 'a country without embankments and without any defences'; where 'one sees a prince prosper today and be ruined tomorrow, without having seen him change his nature or any of his characteristics'.[180] Guicciardini limited himself to a statement of historical facts; Machiavelli tried to explain their causes; and, if the absence of *virtù* is the chief among them, it is not the only one.

A major aspect of the problem of Machiavelli's originality as a political thinker is his dependence on classical sources. Like Guicciardini after him, Machiavelli criticized abstract models such as those constructed by Plato, and this is sometimes taken to imply an over-all rejection of classical political doctrines. But Machiavelli, like Guicciardini, used such basic notions of Greek political theory as that of the mixed constitution, and was by no means averse to using Aristotle's *Politics* when it suited his argument.[181] In fact his detachment from classical political theories appears in the questions he asked and omitted to ask, and in the methods he used to answer his questions, rather than in his, rhetorically emphasized, rejection of a political philosophy based on absolute standards and ideal models. The distance which separates him from the political Aristotelians of the thirteenth and fourteenth centuries can be gauged by comparing his republican theory with Savonarola's attempt to prove that 'republican government is best in the city of Florence' by applying Aristotelian constitutional theory as adapted by Ptolemy of Lucca to Florence, with the result that the Florentine people is seen as being naturally suited to a republican regime. The *Trattato del reggimento di Firenze*[182] was written less than two decades before the *Discourses*, but the two works seem to belong to different worlds.

Machiavelli had no need to turn to Aquinas and Ptolemy for information on Aristotle's political doctrine; he ignored fundamental questions of Greek political philosophy – such as the question of the origin and *telos* of the state, the relationship between state and citizen, the nature of justice – because he considered them irrelevant to his purpose. He also ignored a question which occupied a central place in Thomist Aristotelianism, that of political obligation.[183] The nearest he came to adopting classical political doctrine was in his theory of *anakyklosis*. But after giving, in *Discourses* I, 2, an account, based on Polybius, of the theory of constitutional cycles, their causes and the remedies that must be used to counteract change, he turns from the notion of constitutional decline to the much wider one of social and political corruption. The concept of the common good, which was so central to political Aristotelianism, was used to underpin his republican theory and to justify amoral actions, not to provide, in the traditional manner, the criterion by which to distinguish true from perverted constitutions. He showed as little interest in this last distinction as he did for formal classifications of constitutions in general. The forms of government which mattered to him were monarchy and republic, and the mixed constitution, and if he followed humanist precedent in this, he did not formulate the comparison between the former primarily in terms of liberty and despotism.

Machiavelli asked questions which had not been asked before by political thinkers – or had not been asked since Antiquity – such as those of the role of force, of religion, of *virtù* in politics, of the place of the civic militia, of the methods of territorial expansion, of the function of founders and reformers of states, of the interaction of society and

[183]

institutions and its connection with corruption, of the relationship between will and necessity, between *virtù* and *fortuna*. In the *Discourses*, he considered his historical method to be his chief claim to originality, but he underrated the extent of the harvest he was to gather through his political reading of history. Guicciardini was the only one of his contemporaries to ask questions of comparable originality and relevance, and he did so, predominantly, within the confines of Florentine experience. Machiavelli too owed a great deal to that experience, but his generalizations were designed to have universal validity, and were on this account criticized by Guicciardini.[184] His empirical generalizations were also to provide statesmen in general, and princes in particular, with rules for effective political action and (in so far as he believed in the feasibility of arresting decline and reversing corruption) with an analysis of conditions in which reform might be possible. It is legitimate to surmise that he also considered this question in relation to Florence. There is an oblique reference to it in the *Discourses*, I, 55, but it was only two or three years after completing that work that he openly and systematically applied to his city his theory of the creative powers of reformers.[185] This was when he expounded to Pope Leo X and Cardinal Giulio de' Medici a scheme of reform which was to pave the way for the restoration of republican government in the form of a 'well-ordered republic' and thus, unlike its predecessors, 'stable'; a reform which would earn the Medici supreme glory, for 'no man is more exalted for any deed as much as those who have reformed republics and kingdoms with laws and institutions'.[186]

Machiavelli's is one of a number of schemes for constitutional reform which were drawn up in Florence after the death of Lorenzo de' Medici the younger in 1519, when a return to republican government seemed to some citizens to be practicable. But proposals for such reforms had not been lacking before the restoration of the Medici in 1512, in which year Guicciardini wrote the first, and in some ways the most lucid, of his treatises on constitutional problems, the *Discorso di Logrogno*.[187] Nor was Florence the only Italian republic in which constitutional reform was, then, the subject of systematic enquiry and discussion. Domenico Morosini's *De bene instituta re publica*, composed between 1497 and 1509, combines the traditional idealization of Venice with a critique of certain aspects of Venetian institutions and politics, and ideas on how to correct these defects.[188] Morosini's treatise is an early example of a political literature which, in the second and third decades of the sixteenth century, was centred in Florence, and which temporarily substituted for the descriptive, and largely eulogistic, accounts by humanists of existing constitutions, critical analyses of such constitutions and prescriptions for their reform. The primary cause of this change in approach and method has to be sought in the political developments of Italy after 1494. Morosini not only attacked the expansionist policy of Venice which, in the year of his death, was to lead to the disaster of Agnadello, but also related that policy to what he considered to be fundamental shortcomings in the structure and workings of Venetian politics in his time.[189] Guicciardini in his turn proceeded from a detailed and searching critique of the Florentine republic of 1494–1512 to proposals for reform and, in his *Dialogo del reggimento di Firenze*, composed between 1521 and 1526, to a comprehensive scheme of a perfect Florentine republic inspired by the idealized Venetian model.[190] Machiavelli too based his proposal for giving Florence a 'well-ordered government' on a critical analysis of Florentine constitutional developments, extended as far back as the establishment of the aristocratic regime at the end of the fourteenth century. His procedure was later adopted, in a more comprehensive and detailed fashion, by Donato Giannotti in his *Della repubblica fiorentina*.[191]

What all these treatises have in common is the social context into which they place constitutional reform. The interaction of society and institutions and its effects on political change is a dominant theme of Machiavelli's *Discourses*; another, closely related, is the antithetic role of social classes in the development of states. Together, these themes constitute a major breakthrough in political theory. Machiavelli, concentrating on the history of republican Rome, saw the tensions and conflicts between nobles and plebeians as the creative element in the formation of a perfect republic. His argument, rejected by Guicciardini,[192] is based on the general premise that 'in every republic there are the powerful and the commoners',[193] a premise which served him not only for his analysis of republican institutions, but also for his enquiry into the methods by which a new prince could secure his power.[194] While this generalization was primarily based on the history of the Roman republic, Machiavelli also saw it borne out by that of Florence. Class conflicts here were destructively divisive in contrast to ancient Rome; but in both cities they resulted from two different and conflicting currents, exemplifying the further generalization that 'there are in every republic two different temperaments, that of the people and that of the powerful'.[195]

Machiavelli upheld the twofold division of society into *popolo* and *grandi* in *The Prince* and the *Discourses*, as well as in the *History of Florence*. But in the *Discourse* on Florentine government, which he wrote in the intervening period, he used a threefold division: *primi*, *mezzani* and *ultimi*, top, middle and bottom, and stated that this division, though particularly applicable to Florence, existed 'in all cities'.[196] A similar threefold division was made in 1516 by Lodovico Alamanni in a discourse on how the restored Medici regime could best be preserved and strengthened, and there may be a connection between these two treatises.[197] Yet it should be pointed out that the threefold division of civic society was Aristotelian,[198] that Italian political thinkers had been familiar with it since the thirteenth century, and that Domenico Morosini had recently applied it to Venice.[199] Moreover, this kind of social analysis had a long tradition in Florence, which reflected actual developments in the social structure of politics, developments in which the legal distinction between *magnati*, or *grandi*, and *popolani*, commoners, adopted at the end of the thirteenth century, played a seminal role. During the trecento the threefold distinction between *grandi*, *popolani grassi* and *popolo minuto*, which might be translated as 'the most powerful', 'the rich commoners' and 'the lesser people', became common usage. It corresponded to a large extent, though not entirely, to the institutional division into *magnati*, *artigiani maggiori* and *artigiani minori* – magnates, greater guildsmen and lesser guildsmen. More complex and sophisticated distinctions were made in the quattrocento, no doubt partly owing to the radical reduction of the ranks of the magnates after 1434, and to the political and economic decline of the guilds. Bruni, in his treatise on the Florentine constitution of *c*.1439, divided Florentine society into four groups, of which the top and the bottom ones, the magnates and the plebeians, are excluded from government; about half a century later, Piero Guicciardini, the historian's father, divided the section of the population which was entitled to hold public office into five groups, the *nobili*, that is, the descendants of the old magnate nobility, the *popolani antichi nobili*, 'the long-established noble commoners', the *mezzo* or middle, composed of 'certain houses which are not yet noble and yet are not completely ignoble', *the artefici più nobili*, 'the more noble artisans', and those *ignobili*.[200] Piero Guicciardini's definitions occur in an account of the electoral scrutiny held in 1484, in which he participated. They are practical, not theoretical, and were used to explain the distribution of qualifications for office among different social groups, and the changing fortunes of single families, which might pass from one group to another.

The use of social categories for political analysis could be descriptive, but it could also be prescriptive. Machiavelli and Guicciardini, as well as Domenico Morosini, believed that it was essential to distribute public office among different social groups in such a way as to prevent any one of them acquiring excessive power, and thus to achieve political stability. A balanced and stable regime of this kind was provided by a constitution which merged different forms of government representing different social interests; and it was in the mixed constitution that those Florentine citizens who, after the Medici restoration in 1512 and again after 1519, were hoping for a return to republican government, saw the panacea for a stable and well-ordered republic. Although Guicciardini explicitly rejected classical political doctrine as irrelevant to the analysis of concrete political problems, the republican regime he proposed for his city was, in fact, a mixed constitution,[201] as was Machiavelli's scheme of constitutional reform.[202] When Machiavelli, in the *Discourses*, made Polybius' praise of the mixed constitution his own, he was looking back to the Roman republic which, 'remaining mixed, made a perfect republic'.[203] Guicciardini took as his model the 'Venetian government, which is . . . the finest and the best government not only in our own times, but which perhaps any city ever enjoyed even in ancient times, because all the different types of government go to make it up'.[204] After the fall of the Medici regime in 1494, the Florentines, following Savonarola's advice, imitated the Venetian constitution in setting up the Great Council, and the *ottimati* tried to create a senate at various times – at the turn of the century, briefly in 1512, and finally during the last republican regime of 1527–30.[205] Florentine admiration for Venice received its most comprehensive and perceptive expression in Donato Giannotti's *Della repubblica de' Veneziani*, written in that city and completed by 1527, described as the 'climax of Florentine political thinking on Venice during the Renaissance period'.[206] In his *Della repubblica fiorentina*, written after the Medicean restoration in 1530, Giannotti affirmed his city's suitability for 'a well-tempered government', for a '*stato misto*', a mixed constitution, which Aristotle had considered to be the best.[207] In classical political theory, the mixed government could be given a more democratic or a more oligarchical slant, and Giannotti, unlike Guicciardini who admired the aristocratic features of the Venetian constitution, wanted to give the *popolo* the decisive place in a judicious distribution of political power among the three classes of Florentine society, the *grandi*, the *mediocri* and the *moltitudine* – upper class, middle class and the masses; for it is the *grandi* who 'bring about changes of government', as had happened in Florence in 1494, 1512 and 1530.[208]

Giannotti's *Della repubblica fiorentina* was the last work on Florentine republican government written during the Renaissance, and it might be chosen as a fitting point to close this survey. Under the principate Florentine political thinking moved along different lines, relating to traditions which in fifteenth-century Italy were represented by the works on princely government, but which were now acquiring European dimensions in the theories of absolutism. Almost contemporaneously with Giannotti's treatise on Venice, Gasparo Contarini composed his *De magistratibus et republica Venetorum*; it too continues a tradition. His idealized picture of Venice[209] remained for a long time the most authoritative account of her institutions; first printed in 1543 and soon translated into French, English and Italian, it provided foreigners with a detailed account of what was still widely regarded as a perfect constitution. Giannotti's work on Venice was printed in 1540, and republished many times in the sixteenth and seventeenth centuries,[210] but his treatise on Florence was not published until 1721, Guicciardini's *Dialogue* not until 1858.

It is worth noting that during the last stage of Renaissance political thought, amid such a wealth of original and innovating ideas, early themes re-emerged, and that civic traditions and classical political theory continued to shape political thinking, at a time when political life and institutions had undergone such great and varied changes. One reason for this, no doubt, was that the city-state, which in the first place had created the conditions for the breakthrough in Italian political thought in the thirteenth century, survived so long. Indeed, it could be argued that some of its problems, which had been present all along, were only fully understood and analysed at the time when its very existence was threatened in that city in which, for over two centuries, awareness of political issues and problems, of their historical dimension and of their social implications, had been so much part of her civilization.

NOTES

1 Cf. e.g. W. Ullmann, *Medieval Foundations of Renaissance Humanism* (London, 1977), 89ff. On Italian political thought in the Renaissance, see also Q. Skinner, *The Foundations of Modern Political Thought*, I (Cambridge, 1978).

2 Cf. e.g. R.W. and A.J. Carlyle, *A History of Mediaeval Political Theory in the West*, III and IV (Edinburgh and London, 1915, 1922); W. Ullmann, *Principles of Government and Politics in the Middle Ages* (London, 1961).

3 *Policraticus*, IV, 2; VI, 20, C. Webb (ed.) (Oxford, 1909) I, 283; II, 58. Cf. H. Liebeschütz, *Mediaeval Humanism in the Life and Writings of John of Salisbury* (London, 1950), 45–7.

4 Cf. e.g. Giovanni da Viterbo, *Liber de regiminum civitatis*, ed. G. Salvemini, Bibliotheca iuridica Medii Aevi, III (Bologna, 1901), 215–80. The *podestà* is to be endowed, like a prince, with many virtues, including

the traditional 'political' ones, such as fortitude and magnanimity. At the same time, in keeping with his duties as a civic magistrate, he is to be also *'eloquentissimus'* (220).

5 Cf. J.E. Seigel, *Rhetoric and Philosophy in Renaissance Humanism* (Princeton, 1968), ch.7.

6 F.J. Carmody (ed.), *Li Livres dou Trésor*, II, 44 (Berkeley–Los Angeles, 1948), 211–15. Brunetto used the *Compendium Alexandrinum* of the *Ethics* (C. Marchesi, ed., *L'Etica Nicomachea nella tradizione latina medievale*, Messina, 1904, xli–lxxxvi; cf. lxiii–lxxiv).

7 R.M. Spiazzi (ed.), *In libros Politicorum Aristotelis expositio* (Turin–Rome, 1951), xxv.

8 Cf. J.P. Canning, 'The corporation in the political thought of the Italian jurists', *History of Political Thought*, I (1980), 9–31.

9 Ed. L.-F. Flutre and K. Sneyders de Vogel (Paris–Groningen, 1938), I, 28.

10 Ed. J. Mathis, 2nd edn (Turin and Milan, 1948), I, 1.

11 *'utilius . . . multitudinem hominum simul viventium regi per unum quam per plures'*; *'utilius . . . est regimen unius, quam plurium'*. ibid, I, 2.

12 *'omne . . . naturale regimen ab uno est'*; *'necesse est quod in humana multitudine optimum sit, quod per unum regatur'*. ibid.

13 *'Si quis praeterita facta et quae nunc fiunt diligenter consideret, pluries inveniet exercuisse tyrannidem in terris, quae per multos reguntur, quam in illis, quae gubernantur per unum'*; *'Exorta namque dissensione per regimen plurium, contingit saepe unum super alios superare et sibi soli multitudinis dominium usurpare.'* De regimine principum, I, 5.

14 *'exemplum cunctis, ut talium sit spernendum dominium . . . . Ecce nunc manifeste videmus quanta orribilia et nephanda tirapni tales operantur in civitatibus, quibus regnant.'* A. Bonardi (ed.), *Chronica in factis et circa facta Marchie Trivixane, Rerum Italicarum Scriptores*, VIII, 1, 109.

15 *'dum regimen regis desiderant, incidunt in saevitiam tyrannorum, rectoresque quamplures tyrannidem exercent sub praetextu regiae dignitatis'*. De regimine principum, I, 4.

16 *'incredibile est memoratu, quantum, adepta libertate, in brevi romana civitas creverit'*. ibid. Cf. *Bellum Catilinae*, VII.

17 *'si a communitate civium imponantur'*. ibid.

18 *Politics*, 1288a, 1288b; *Ethics*, 1160a.

19 *'principatus civiles tres sunt. . . . Et omnium optimus est regum principatus'*. *Compendium Alexandrimum*, lxxiii. *'la tierce est des communes, laquele est la trés millour entre ces autres'*. Trésor, 211.

20 *'in ipsorum pectore sunt leges reconditae'*. De regimine principum, IV, 1.

21 *'legibus astringuntur rectores politici'*. De regimine principum, IV, 1; cf. John of Salisbury, *Policraticus*, IV, 1; I, 237; St Thomas, *Summa theologica*, Ia IIae, qu. 96, art.5, ad 3.

22 *'proprie ad civitates pertinet'*. De regimine principum, op. cit., IV, 1.

23 ibid., IV, 1, 8. Cf. my essay 'Marsilius of Padua and Italian political thought of his time', in J.R. Hale, J.R.L. Highfield and B. Smalley (eds), *Europe in the Late Middle Ages* (London, 1965), 52ff., and Ch. T. Davies, 'Ptolemy of Lucca and the Roman Republic', *Proceedings of the American Philosophical Society*, CXVII (1974), 47.

24 *Politics*, 1296b, 1327b.

25 *'virilis animi et in audacia cordis, et in confidentia suae intelligentiae'. De regimine principum*, IV, 8.

26 *'nisi per viam tyrannicam'*. ibid.

27 Rubinstein, *'Marsilius of Padua'*, 63. Cf. E. Salzer, *Über die Anfänge der Signorie in Oberitalien* (Berlin, 1900), 49, n. 89; F. Ercole, *Dal comune al principato* (Florence,1929), 66–7.

28 *'nela terra del tiranno/Folli son quey che vi stanno'*. F. Egidi (ed.), *Documenti d'amore* (Rome, 1912), II, 219. The work was published in 1314. Cf. also 'Marsilius of Padua', 61ff.

29 Cf. Ch.T. Davis, 'An early Florentine political theorist: Fra Remigio de' Girolami', *Proceedings of the American Philosophical Society*, CIV (1960), 668ff.

30 *De regimine principum*, I, 2.

31 Cf. my article, 'Political ideas in Sienese art: the frescoes by Ambrogio Lorenzetti and Taddeo di Bartolo in the Palazzo Pubblico', *Journal of the Warburg and Courtauld Institutes*, XXI (1958), 181ff.

32 Davis, op. cit., 41ff.

33 Ch.T. Davis, 'Roman patriotism and republican propaganda: Ptolemy of Lucca and Pope Nicholas III', *Speculum*, L (1975), 415–16.

34 Davis, 'Ptolemy of Lucca', 32.

35 Davis, 'Roman patriotism', 415–17.

36 Rubinstein, 'Marsilius of Padua', 47–8.

37 *'ne principans . . . sibi sumat arbitrium'*. R. Scholz (ed.), *Defensor Pacis*, III, 3 (Hanover, 1932–3), 612.

38 Ed. C. Pincin (Turin, 1966).

39 F. Maggini, *I primi volgarizzamenti dai classici latini* (Florence, 1952); J. Berrigan, 'Benzo d'Alessandria and the cities of Northern Italy', *Studies in Medieval and Renaissance History,'* IV (1967), 127–92. On Riccobaldo's *Historia Romana* cf. T. Hankey, 'Riccobaldo of Ferrara, Boccaccio and Domenico Bandini', *Journal of the Warburg and Courtauld Institutes*, XXI (1958), 211ff.

40 *'a parvis incepit et de parvis ad magna profecit et de magnis ad maxima pervenit'*. G. Monleone (ed.), *Cronaca di Genova*, (Rome, 1941) II, 78ff.

41 *Cronica* (Milan, 1848), III, 1; VIII, 36.

42 C.B. Fisher, 'The Pisan clergy and an awakening of historical interest in a medieval commune', *Studies in Medieval and Renaissance History*, III (1966), 202. The author remarks that 'the poet's perspective was dominated by the comparison with ancient Rome'.

43 Cf. Rubinstein, 'Marsilius of Padua', 57–8.

44 *'destructa civitate remanet civis lapideus et depictus, quia scilicet caret virtute et operatione quam prius habebat'*. Cf. L. Minio-Paluello, 'Remigio Girolami's "De bono communi": Florence at the time of Dante's banishment and the philosopher's answer to the crisis', *Italian Studies*, XI (1956), 59–60.

45 Cf. Orosius, *Historiarum adversus paganos libri VII* ,VI, 14, 17; W. Rehm, *Der Untergang Roms im abendländischen Denken* (Leipzig, 1930), 25–6.

46 *'essauce les viles et enrichist les borgois, et guerre les destruit, et ramentevoir Romme et les autres bones viles, ki por la guerre dedens sont*

decheues et mal alees'. Trésor, III, 82, 404. The *Oculus pastoralis*, on which this passage is based, does not contain the reference to Rome (L. Muratori, *Antiquitates italicae medii aevi*, IV, Milan, 1741, cols 97–8).

47 *'Udir come le schiatte si disfanno, /Non ti parrà nuova cosa né forte, /Poscia che le cittadi termine hanno'.* Dante, *Paradiso*, XVI, 76–9, trans. by K. Mackenzie (London, 1979), 379.

48 *'considerando che la nostra città di Firenze . . . era nel suo montare . . . siccome Roma nel suo calare'. Cronica*, VIII, 36. Cf. G. Aquilecchia, 'Dante and the Florentine chroniclers', *Bulletin of the John Rylands Library*, XLVIII (1965), 30–55.

49 'Età buie e Rinascita. Un problema di confini', in *Rinascite e rivoluzioni. Movimenti culturali dal XIV al XVIII secolo*, 2nd edn (Naples, 1976), 3–38 (cf. 12–13).

50 *'Variatur siquidem civitatis semper huius status alteratione mirabili, quia annorum circiter .L. curiculis cunctis nature, que sub celo sunt bonis, pullulat et augescit.'*

51 *'significantes destructiones seu mutationes, quae fiunt in hoc seculo'.* Quoted in my essay, 'Some ideas on municipal progress and decline in the Italy of the Communes', in D.J. Gordon (ed.), *Fritz Saxl. 1890-1948. A Volume of Memorial Essays . . .* (Edinburgh, 1957), 169, 179.

52 *'che lle mondane cose mutamento ricevino . . . in capo di XXX anni, il quale si chiama il corso dell' evo'.* ibid., 181.

53 *'le novità state nella nostra città . . . che sono state quasi di venti anni in venti anni poco meno'. Cronica*, XII, 41.

54 Cf. on this and the following my essay, 'Il medio evo nella storiografia italiana del Rinascimento (Firenze, Milano, Venezia)', in V. Branca (ed.), *Concetto, storia, miti e immagini del medio evo* (Florence, 1973), 429–48.

55 *Vom Mittelalter zur Reformation*, II, 1 (Berlin 1913-28), 528ff.

56 *'si reggesse e governasse al modo di Roma, cioè per due consoli e per lo consiglio di cento sanatori'. Cronica*, III, 3.

57 Cf. R. Witt, 'Coluccio Salutati and the origins of Florence', *Il Pensiero Politico*, II (1969), 161–72, who pre-dates the beginnings of the republican theory of the city's foundation to the early years of Salutati's chancellorship, that is after 1375.

58 *'eo maxime tempore deducta est quo populi Romani imperium maxime florebat . . . vigebat sancta et inconcussa libertas'; 'maxime omnium libertate gaudeant et tyrannorum valde sint inimici'.* H. Baron (ed.), in *From Petrarch to Leonardo Bruni. Studies in Humanistic and Political Literature* (Chicago and London, 1968), 245; cf. his *The Crisis of the Early Italian Renaissance*, rev. edn (Princeton, 1966), 61ff.

59 *'hanno mantenuto la franchigia e la libertà discesa in loro dall'antico popolo romano'. Cronica* (Milan, 1848), III, 1.

60 Cf. my paper, 'Florence and the despots. Some aspects of Florentine diplomacy in the fourteenth century', *Transactions of the Royal Historical Society*, 5th ser., II (1952), 30ff., and R. Witt, 'The rebirth of the concept of republican liberty in Italy', in A. Molho and J.A. Tedeschi (eds),

Renaissance Studies in Honor of Hans Baron (Florence, 1971), 173–99. Witt points to a third aspect of Salutati's concept of liberty, that is government under law (194ff.).

61 *'la parte guelfa è fondamento . . . della libertà d'Italia, e contraria a tutte le tirannie'*; *'i tiranni . . . per natura sogliono essere nemici e oppressatori de' popoli che vogliono vivere in libertà'*. *Cronica*, VIII, 24; IX, 20.

62 *'inter tirannidem et libertatem'*. Cf. 'Florence and the despots', 30, n. 6. On Salutati's defence of Florentine liberty, cf. E. Garin, 'I cancellieri umanistici della Repubblica fiorentina da Coluccio Salutati a Bartolomeo Scala', in *La cultura filosofica del Rinascimento italiano* (Florence, 1961), 6ff., and P. Herde, 'Politik und Rhetorik in Florenz am Vorabend der Renaissance', *Archiv für Kulturgeschichte*, XLVII (1965), 212ff., who emphasizes 'die Zweideutigkeit der Florentiner Freiheitspropaganda' in Salutati's public letters.

63 Rubinstein, 'Marsilius of Padua', 60ff.

64 *De gestis Italicorum post Henricum VII*, Muratori, *Rerum Italicarum Scriptores*, X, cols 766–8; L. Padrin (ed.), *Ecerinide* (Bologna, 1900), 33–7.

65 *'O dira nobilium odia, o populi furor:/Finis petitus litibus vestris adest;/Adest tyrannus, vestra quem rabies dedit'*. ibid., 33.

66 L. Biondi (ed.), *Le Dicerie* (Turin, 1825), 2–3.

67 Pietro de' Faitinelli, in A. Massèra (ed.), *Sonetti burleschi e realistici dei primi due secoli*, I (Bari, 1920), 191: he is happy that Castruccio has 'tutte spente queste tirannie'; Ferreto de' Ferreti, *Carmen de Scaligerorum origine*, in C. Cipolla (ed.), *Opere*, III (Rome, 1920), 29–31: *'Cura fuit, leges et plebiscita forumque/Pacifico servare statu, remque omnibus equam/Dividere . . . .'*

68 Cf. R. De Mattei, *Il Sentimento politico del Petrarca* (Florence, 1944), 73ff.; Baron, *From Petrarch to Leonardo Bruni*, 34ff.

69 *'Pati hominem credo facilius quam tyrannum populum . . . ubi enim tyranni desunt, tyrannizant populi'*.

70 *Sen.*, VI, 2; XIV, 1.

71 *'unius non modo optimi . . . sed rel mediocriter boni eligibilius esse regimen'*. H.L. Eaker and B.G. Kohl (eds), Lewisburg, Pa., 1980, 106. Quoted by Baron, *The Crisis*, II, 1st edn (Princeton, 1955), 490. On Giovanni Conversini's treatise cf. *The Crisis*, rev. edn, 134–45, and I.C. Duff, *Giovanni Conversino da Ravenna's Dragmalogia de eligibili vitae genere*, M. Phil. thesis (London, 1971). On Giovanni Conversini, cf. R. Sabbadini, *Giovanni da Ravenna . . .* (Como, 1924), and Kohl, ed. cit., introduction.

72 Cf. Baron, op. cit., 139–40.

73 'Petrarch: his inner struggles and the humanistic discovery of man's nature', in J.G. Rowe and W.H. Stockdale (eds), *Florilegium historiale. Essays presented to Wallace K. Ferguson* (Toronto, 1971), 37–8; cf. also *The Crisis*, 123.

74 *L'umanesimo italiano* (Bari, 1952), 103.

75 *The Crisis*, 106–12.

76 Cf. A. Solerti (ed.), *Le vite di Dante, Petrarca e Boccaccio scritte fino al sec.*

XVI (Milan, 1904), 293: 'si può rispondere al primo argomento della vita attiva e civile, che il Petrarca più fu saggio e prudente in elegger vita quieta ed oziosa che travagliarsi nella repubblica . . . .' Cf. also Baron, op. cit., 531, n. 82.

77 *I primi tre libri della famiglia*, ed. F.C. Pellegrini and R. Spongano (Florence, 1946), 273ff. In the version which went under the name of Agnolo Pandolfini, Alberti's theme is made part of the advice Giovanni Rucellai gave his sons at a time when he himself was 'sospetto allo stato': 'Non vi consiglio . . . che voi cerchiate o disideriate ufici e stato' (A. Perosa, ed., *Giovanni Rucellai ed il suo Zibaldone*, I: '*Il Zibaldone quaresimale*', London, 1960, 39–43, 122; cf. 146, n. 1). Cf. also Giovanni di Paolo Morelli, *Ricordi*, ed. V. Branca (Florence, 1956), 274ff.

78 *Invettiva contro a cierti calunniatori di Dante e di messer Fιancesco Petrarca e di messer Giovanni Boccaccio*, in A. Wesselofski (ed.), *Il Paradiso degli Alberti* (Bologna, 1867), II, 2, 314–15; on the *Invettiva*, see G. Tanturli, 'Cino Rinuccini e la scuola di Santa Maria in Campo', *Studi Medievali*, ser. 3, XVII (1976), 644ff. Cf. Baron, *The Crisis*, 315ff.; L. Martines, *The Social World of the Florentine Humanists* (London, 1963), 154–63.

79 Garin's essay, 'Donato Acciaiuoli cittadino fiorentino', in *Medioevo e Rinascimento* (Bari, 1954), 211–87, is the fundamental biography of a citizen who conformed to this ideal.

80 Ed. F. Adorno, in *Atti e Memorie dell'Accademia Toscana di scienze e lettere 'La Colombaria'*, XXII (1957), 297–8. See also below, 178.

81 'qui utriusque vitae rectam rationem habens, utramque coniungat'. E. Garin (ed.), *Prosatori latini del Quattrocento* (Milan–Naples, 1952), 788.

82 Garin, *L'umanesimo italiano*, 110–16.

83 *La cultura filosofica*, 60ff, 66.

84 Leonardo Bruni Aretino, *Humanistisch-Philosophische Schriften*, ed. H. Baron (Leipzig, 1928), 73–4.

85 'quid sit civitas, et quid res publica . . . et per quae conservetur intereatque civilis societas'.

86 Ed. C.F. Neumann (Frankfurt, 1822), 68.

87 See G. Holmes, *The Florentine Enlightenment, 1400–50* (London, 1969), 27ff.

88 Ed. F. Battaglia (Bologna, 1944), 109ff.

89 ibid., 3ff., 109. Palmieri's concept of 'representation' is derived from Cicero, *De off.*, I, 34.

90 'eiusmodi est ut nichil neque luculentius neque splendidius in toto orbe terrarum inveniri possit'. *Laudatio Florentinae urbis*, ed. Baron, in *From Petrarch to Leonardo Bruni*, 232.

91 'cum foris hec civitas admirabilis est, tum vero disciplina institutisque domesticis'. ibid., 258.

92 'tantus ordo rerum . . . tanta elegantia . . . tanta concinnitas'. ibid. Cf. Baron, *The Crisis*, 206–7; *From Petrarch to Leonardo Bruni*, 168–71.

93 'tertia speties gubernandi legitima'. Ed. H. Baron, in Humanistic and Political Literature in Florence and Venice (Cambridge, Mass., 1955), 182; for the date, cf. 173ff. For this and the following, cf. my essay, 'Florentine constitutionalism and Medici ascendancy in the fifteenth century', in N. Rubinstein (ed.), Florentine Studies (London, 1968), 444ff.

94 In libros Politicorum expositio, 138, 139; 'Letter to the Emperor', in Baron, op. cit., 182.

95 Cf. e.g. Giovanni Villani, Cronica, VIII, 2.

96 Aristides, Panathenaic Oration, 384 (314D).

97 Quoted above, n. 86.

98 'Letter to the Emperor', in op. cit., 183. On the Florentine Constitution, 68.

99 D. Robey and J. Law, 'The Venetian myth and the "De republica Veneta" of Pier Paolo Vergerio', Rinascimento, XV (1975), 38–9; for the date, 29.

100 'ad hoc regimen mixtum videtur appropinquare'; 'Venetorum gens . . . pace et securitate fruitur'. The passage is from Book II (on justice) of his work on the cardinal virtues, ibid., 54–5 (cf. 52–3). The authors point out that while Henry's notion of the mixed constitution is derived chiefly from St Thomas, Summa theologica, Ia IIae, qu. 105, the latter applies it exclusively to monarchy. In fact, Henry's use of Aristotelian constitutional theory is yet another instance of bypassing Aquinas in the application of it to contemporary conditions.

101 F. Gilbert, 'The Venetian constitution in Florentine political thought', in Florentine Studies, 468ff.

102 Cf. the dedication of his translation of the Laws to Francesco Barbaro, ed. F. Adorno in Studi in onore di Antonio Corsano (Manduria, 1970), 14–17: 'Si quis eas leges Platonis, quas ille sancit . . . diligentius penitus inspiciat, is . . . negare non poterit primos venetae libertatis fundatores sintillas rivolosque constituende civitatis sic a Platone accepisse, ut maiores inde fluvii emanarint'; accordingly, 'si quis omni ex parte optimam rempublicam mente confingat, non aliam fingere possit quam venetam'. Cf. F. Gaeta, 'Giorgio di Trebisonda, le Leggi di Platone e la costituzione veneziana', Bullettino dell'Istituto Storico Italiano per il Medio Evo, LXXXII (1970), 481ff.

103 Cf. Gilbert, op. cit., 468ff.

104 'la Republica viniziana . . . intra le moderne republiche è eccellente'. Discorsi, I, 34; Il Principe, xv.

105 Politics, 1288b.

106 Cf. Henry of Rimini, in op. cit., 55, n. 89; on Bruni, 'Florentine constitutionalism', 448–9.

107 Garin, L'umanesimo italiano, 57.

108 'l'imaginata bontà de' non mai veduti in terra cittadini, i quali da Platone e più altri nobilissimi ingegni considerati e finti, di virtù e sapienza perfetti'; 'mostrare la provata vita de' civili virtuosi co' quali più volte s'è vivuto'; 'antico e bene amaestrato cittadino'. Op. cit., 5.

109 Cf. Liebeschütz, op. cit., chs 5 and 6.

110 Ed. in Bruni, *Humanistisch-Philosophische Schriften*, 73-4.

111 *'magnum ac dives instrumentum regiae gubernationis'*. L. Mehus (ed.), *Epistolarum libri VIII* (Florence, 1741), II, 130-4. Cf. E. Garin, 'Le traduzioni umanistiche di Aristotele nel sec. XV', *Atti e memorie dell' Accademia fiorentina 'La Colombaria'* , XVI (1947-50), 67.

112 *De principe*, ed. G. Ferrau' (Palermo, 1979); *De optimo cive*, ed. F. Battaglia (Bologna, 1944). Platina sent the *De optimo cive* to Lorenzo in April 1474: cf. A. della Torre, *Storia dell'Accademia Platonica di Firenze* (Florence, 1902), 534, and *I Protocolli del carteggio di Lorenzo il Magnifico*, ed. M. Del Piazzo (Florence, 1956), 512 (23 April 1474).

113 *De optimo cive*, 184.

114 Cf. e.g. Pietro del Monte's letter to Poggio (see n. 147), 628: 'Cicero optimus civis.'

115 *'domesticos tyrannos eos appello, qui propter ingentes divitias . . . in civitate sua . . . principatum obtinent'*; *'florentem . . . civitatem conservare . . . eiusdem calamitates atque pericula propulsare'*. Op. cit., 192, 204.

116 ibid., 205.

117 Cf. A. Alföldi, *Der Vater des Vaterlandes im römischen Denken* (Darmstadt, 1971), 80ff.

118 *'Maluere . . . cives ad unum deferri omnia'*; *'Nondum . . . ad unum omnino imperium Romanum venerat'*; *'bonus civis . . . de pluribus benemeritus'*. *De optimo cive*, 205, 206.

119 *'virtus est quae nobiles facit'*; *'ex melioribus ortos, meliores futuros, tum ad imperandum, tum ad parendum'*. ibid., 198-9, 220.

120 ibid., 212.

121 E. Lepore, *Il principe ciceroniano e gli ideali politici della tarda repubblica* (Naples, 1954), 76, 106, 217, 286. Cicero, *Pro Sestio*, 97, 143; *De re publica*, VI, 13 (*Somnium Scipionis*).

122 *'seguire li modi del avolo suo, che era di far tal cose cum più civilità si potesse'*. Sacramoro to Galeazzo Maria Sforza, 3 July 1470, quoted in my *The Government of Florence under the Medici, 1434-1494* (London, 1968), 178, n. 5.

123 Cf. W. Berges, *Die Fürstenspiegel des hohen und späten Mittelalters* (Stuttgart, 1938), 211-28 ('der am weitesten verbreitete abendländische Fürstenspiegel'; cf. 320-8).

124 For this and for the following, see F. Gilbert, 'The humanist concept of the prince and *The Prince* of Machiavelli', *Journal of Modern History* XI (1939), 449-83, reprinted in *History, Choice and Commitment* (Cambridge, Mass.-London, 1977), 91-114.

125 Ed. F. Gaeta (Bologna, 1956).

126 *De dictis and factis Alphonsi regis Aragonum libri quatuor* (Basle, 1568), 271: 'tamquam speculum quoddam virtutum.'

127 Cf. Giovanni Pontano, *De princip principe*, ed. Garin, *Prosatori latini*, 1038ff. He dedicated the work to Duke Alfonso of Calabria.

128 *'aliae sunt regis virtutes, aliae privatorum'*. *De regno et regis institutione libri IX*, III, 1 (Strasbourg, 1594), 148-52. Cf. Gilbert, op. cit., 100.

129 Op. cit., I, 3, 16-17: *'Popularis autem status cum ab aequalitate . . . discedit, . . . quumque aut nimis uni viro defert, aut multitudini nimis*

indulget, in alterutrum ut incidat opus est, aut in tyrannidem . . . aut in plebeium dominatum'. He adds that. '*monendi sunt nonnulli, qui falso opinantur popularem statum et plebeium unum et eundem esse.'*

130 Cf. E. Garin, 'Ricerche sulle traduzioni di Platone nella prima metà del secolo XV', in *Medioevo e Rinascimento. Studi in onore di Bruno Nardi* (Florence, 1955), 342–4.

131 Cf. Baron, *The Crisis*, 425–7.

132 *'honoris victorieque avidus principatum capit . . . ut ingenue belligerando rem publicam diligenter et egregie tuendo, sibi laudem, patrie vero utilitatem pariat'*. *De laudibus Mediolanensis urbis panegyricus*, in F. Fossati (ed.), *Opuscula historica, Rerum Italicarum Scriptores*, XX, 1, 1017. On his translation of the *Republic*, cf. Garin, op. cit., 347–57, and V. Zaccaria, 'Pier Candido Decembrio traduttore della "Repubblica" di Platone', *Italia Medievale e Umanistica*, II (1959), 179–206. His letter to Humphrey of Gloucester is ed. in M. Borsa, 'Correspondence of Humphrey Duke of Gloucester and Pier Candido Decembrio', *English Historical Review*, XIX (1904), 512–13, and Garin, op. cit., 352–3.

133 On this passage, see also the observations of Tanturli, 'Cino Rinuccini', 637–8.

134 Cf. A.M. Brown, 'The humanist portrait of Cosimo de' Medici. Pater Patriae', *Journal of the Warburg and Courtauld Institutes*, XXIV (1961), 196.

135 *'philiosophiam una cum summa in publicis auctoritate'*; *'in magnis quondam viris potissimum exoptat'*. In his dedication to Lorenzo of the *Theologia platonica*, in *Opera* (Basle, 1576), I, 78. According to E. Wind, 'Platonic tyranny and the Renaissance Fortuna. On Ficino's reading of *Laws*, IV, 709A–712A', in M. Meiss (ed.), *Essays in Honor of Erwin Panofsky* (New York, 1961) I, 491–6, Ficino was setting up the tyrant-legislator of Plato's *Laws* as a secret model for Italian despots; but Ficino's letter to Giovanni Rucellai, which he quotes in support of his thesis (ed. P.O. Kristeller, *Supplementum Ficinianum*, Florence, 1937, II, 169–73), hardly seems to warrant such an interpretation, nor does the author supply any evidence for his interesting suggestion that Plato's image of the tyrant guided by philosophy helps to explain the fascination he exercised for Italian despots.

136 *'hanc coniunctionem . . . saluti censuit civitatibus esse posse, si is summam potestatem haberet, qui in doctrina, virtute, prudentia studium omne suum collocasset'*. Op. cit., 212–13.

137 *'qui nihil aliud cogitarunt in vita, nihil egerunt, nisi quod praeclarum et laudabile pro salute omnium et dignitate patriae videretur'*. ibid., 206–7.

138 *The Crisis*, 66–9. Cf. F.v. Bezold, 'Republik und Monarchie in der italienischen Literatur des 15. Jahrhunderts', *Historische Zeitschrift*, LXXXI (1898), 433ff., and E. Walser, *Poggius Florentinus. Leben und Werke* (Leipzig–Berlin, 1914), 164ff.

139 See p. 166. Baron, *The Crisis*, considers the 'comparison between Renaissance Tyranny and Renaissance Republic . . . the core of the book'; but cf. Cooper, op. cit., (see n. 71), 18ff., who argues that 'the full scope of the dialogue is much too large for such a characterization'.

140 Cf. Tanturli, op. cit., 644.

141 Ed. D. Moreni in appendix to the *Invectiva Lini Colucii Salutati* in *Antonium Luschum*. . . (Florence, 1826), 219–20. R. Witt, 'Cino Rinuccini's *Risponsiva alla Invettiva di Messer Antonio Lusco*', *Renaissance Quarterly*, XXIII (1970), 145–8, suggests that the passage is an interpolation of the translator of the original Latin text, added after, and in reply to, Decembrio's panegyric; but cf. Tanturli, op. cit., 637–9.

142 '*utrum* . . . *res publica unius consilio atque auctoritate, an plurium arbitrio aptius regatur*'. *De laudibus*, 1017.

143 *Epistolae*, ed. T. de' Tonelli, II (Florence, 1859), 44–5. Cf. Brown, op. cit., 188–9.

144 See Rubinstein, *The Government of Florence*, 10ff.

145 '*cum status tanta perturbatione fluctuaret ut rebus unius dumtaxat gubernationem exposceret*'; '*innumerabilia optime formatae civitatis instituta . . . restitutae et amplificatae libertatis signa sunt*'. Letter to Poggio of June 1435. Garin (ed.), *Prosatori latini*, 314–77 (368, 372).

146 See above, 166.

147 '*verum est et inviolatum libertatis templum*'; '*Caesarem* . . . *eversorem romanae libertatis*'. Letter to Poggio of 31 January 1440, ed. R. Fubini, in Poggio Bracciolini, *Opera omnia*, IV (Turin, 1969), 617–39 (632).

148 See, in particular, Herde, op. cit.

149 '*quae sit Florentinorum libertate liberior aut integrior*'; '*quam solum Lombardorum genus, sive natura, sive consuetudine, nec videntur diligere nec optare*'. *Invectiva*, 21–2. He was thus also demonstrating his competence as a professional rhetorician, as he did, for instance, in his two discourses in favour of and against hereditary monarchy, ed. B.L. Ullman, 'Coluccio Salutati on monarchy', in *Mélanges Eugène Tisserant*, V (Vatican City, 1964), 401–11, dated by Garin around 1381 and by Ullman probably between 1383 and 1390: cf. E. Garin, 'A proposito di Coluccio Salutati', *Rivista critica di storia della filosofia*, XV (1960), 75–6, with extracts from the short treatise, and Ullman, *The Humanism of Coluccio Salutati* (Padua, 1963), 34.

150 R. Witt, 'The *De tyranno* and Coluccio Salutati's view of politics and Roman history', *Nuova Rivista Storica*, LIII (1969), 458ff. Cf. Salutati's *De tyranno*, ed. F. Ercole (Bologna, 1942), 32.

151 '*hoc modo et libertas viget et iustitia sanctissime in civitate servatur.*' *Laudatio*, 260. For this and the following, see Rubinstein, 'Florentine constitutionalism,' 442ff.

152 '*duabus rebus contineri: legibus scilicet atque iudiciis*'. E. Santini (ed.), *Rerum Italicarum Scriptores*, XIX, 3, 82.

153 Such equality was later claimed for the Catasto introduced in 1427; cf. 'Florentine constitutionalism', 452.

154 Cf. G. Brucker, *The Civic World of Early Renaissance Florence* (Princeton, 1977), 284ff., and 'Humanism, politics and the social order in early Renaissance Florence', in *Florence and Venice: Comparisons and Relations* (Acts of two Conferences at Villa I Tatti in 1976–7), I: *Quattrocento* (Florence, 1979), 3–11.

155 *'iustitie observantia et honorum distributione equali et tributorum exoneratione'*. The minutes of the *pratiche* of this period have been edited by G. Pampaloni, 'Fermenti di riforme democratiche nelle consulte della Repubblica Fiorentina', *Archivio Storico Italiano*, CXIX (1961), 241–81; CXX (1962), 521–81. The passages quoted in the text are in CXIX, 252 and 258.

156 *'quis ignorat aequalitatem civium libertatis precipuum esse fundamentum'*. Op. cit. (n. 80), 283.

157 *'quae tam obnixe, tam diu libertatem tutata sit, aut ubi tam ampla, tam pura viguerit ipsa libertas'*; *'suis legibus parens civitas vixit'*. ibid. 272–3, 283.

158 *'cum hodierna taciturnitate'*; *'ut sint quasi corpus unum'*; *'Nunc . . . paucissimi . . . homines id quod est omnium civium commune sibi solis usurpant'*. ibid. 283, 284.

159 *'in animi tranquillitate libertateque positam esse . . . foelicitatem.'* ibid., 297–8.

160 *'vigebat sancta et inconcussa libertas'*; *'ut Florentini homines maxime omnium libertate gaudeant et tyrannorum valde sint inimici'*. *Laudatio*, 245.

161 Cf Rubinstein, 'Il medio evo nella storiografia italiana', 431–4.

162 *Invectiva in Antonium Luschum*, 18ff.

163 *'tantum crevit florentini populi nomen, quantum non omnibus bellis superioribus creverat'*. *Rerum suo tempore gestarum Commentarius*, ed. C. di Pierro, *Rerum Italicarum Scriptores*, XIX, 3, 437.

164 *'qui satis vos habere monentes, id quod est tuendum censeant'*; *'Populus romanus parens noster nunquam orbis imperium nactus esset, si suis rebus contentus nova coepta impensasque refugisset.'* *Historiae*, 139–41. Cf. the Ph.D. thesis by Diana Webb, *Tuscan Historiography c. 1400 – c. 1450 and the Problem of Florentine Hegemony in Tuscany* (University of London, 1977), chs 3 and 6.

165 *'magnificentia in gloria amplitudineque consistit'*.

166 Brucker, op. cit., 185, 347.

167 *'hinc studia partium coorta, magnarum calamitatum initia fuere'*. Op. cit., 25. Cf. D.J. Wilcox, *The Development of Florentine Humanist Historiography in the Fifteenth Century* (Cambridge, Mass., 1969), 74ff.

168 Op. cit., 168.

169 *'praestantibus in civitate viris, ne motum et arma in arbitrio multitudinis devenire patiantur'*. ibid., 224.

170 G.B. Recanati (ed.), *Historia florentina* (Venice, 1715); cf. 48–52.

171 *Antiquitatis Vicecomitum libri X* (Milan, 1629), 82–3.

172 Cf. P.H. Labalme, *Bernardo Giustiniani. A Venetian of the Quattrocento* (Rome, 1969), 279ff.

173 See above, 177–8.

174 F. Gilbert, 'Florentine political assumptions in the period of Savonarola and Soderini', *Journal of the Warburg and Courtauld Institutes*, XX (1957), 187–214 (212).

175 Gilbert, 'The humanist concept of the prince', cit. n. 124.

176 R. von Albertini, *Das florentinische Staatsbewusstsein im Übergang von*

der Republik zum Prinzipat (Berne, 1955); F. Gilbert, *Machiavelli and Guicciardini. Politics and History in Sixteenth-Century Florence* (Princeton, 1965). See also the survey of literature on Machiavelli by E. Cochrane, 'Machiavelli: 1940–1960', *Journal of Modern History*, XXXIII (1961), 113–36.

177 *'deliberato entrare per una via . . . suta ancora da alcuno trita'.*

178 *Niccolò Machiavelli. Storia del suo pensiero politico* (Naples, 1958), 317–18.

179 *'come per una subita tempesta . . . si roppe e squarciò la unione di Italia . . . gli stati si cominciorono a conservare, a rovinare, a dare ed a torre non co' disegni e nello scrittoio come pel passato, ma alla campagna e colle arme in mano'.* R. Palmarocchi (ed.), *Storie fiorentine* (Bari, 1931), 92–3.

180 *'la Italia, che è la sedia di queste variazioni . . . una campagna sanza argini e sanza alcuno riparo'; 'si vede oggi questo principe felicitare e domani ruinare, sanza averli veduto mutare natura o qualità alcuna.'* Cf. also *Discorsi*, II, 30.

181 When in August 1513, Francesco Vettori in a letter to Machiavelli expressed his belief that the Swiss, however admirable, 'non possano diventare altri romani', and referred him to 'la *Politica*' in support of his argument that 'una repubblica, come quella divulsa, [non] possa fare progresso', he clearly took it for granted that Machiavelli was familiar with that work; and Machiavelli's reply, 'non so quello che si dica Aristotile delle republiche divulse', does not indicate that this was not the case (cf. P. Villari, *Niccolò Machiavelli e i suoi tempi*, 2nd edn, Florence, 1895–7, II, 284), but rather that he could not recall any such statement in the *Politics*, which in fact does not occur in that work: Machiavelli, *Lettere*, ed. F. Gaeta (Milan, 1961), 289, 294. On Machiavelli's use of the *Politics*, cf. L.J. Walker, *The Discourses of Niccolò Machiavelli*, (London, 1950) II, 273–7; B. Guillemain, 'Machiavel lecteur d'Aristote', in *Platon et Aristote à la Renaissance*, XVIe Colloque International de Tours (Paris, 1976), 163–73.

182 Ed. A. de Rians (Florence, 1847), I, 3.

183 See I. Berlin, 'The originality of Machiavelli', in M.P. Gilmore (ed.), *Studies on Machiavelli* (Florence, 1972), 160: 'there is . . . something extraordinary in the fact that he completely ignores the concepts and categories . . . in terms of which the best-known thinkers and scholars of his day were accustomed to express themselves.'

184 Cf. e.g. his *Considerazioni intorno ai Discorsi del Machiavelli*, in *Scritti politici e Ricordi*, ed. R. Palmarocchi (Bari, 1933), 33 (on *Discorsi* I, 26).

185 *Discorsi*, I, 10, 11, 55.

186 *'non è esaltato alcuno uomo tanto in alcuna azione, quanto sono quegli che hanno con leggi e con istituti reformato le repubbliche e i regni'.* Discursus *florentinarum rerum post mortem iunioris Laurentii Medices*, in S. Bertelli (ed.), *Arte della guerra e scritti politici minori* (Milan, 1961), 261–77 (275). Cf. *Discorsi*, I, 10, 11.

187 In R. Palmarocchi (ed.), *Dialogo e discorsi del reggimento di Firenze* (Bari, 1932), 218–59. Cf. Gilbert, *Machiavelli and Guicciardini*, 81ff.

188 Ed. C. Finzi (Milan, 1969). Cf. the fundamental article by G. Cozzi, 'Domenico Morosini e il "De bene instituta re publica"', *Studi Veneziani*, XII (1970), 405–58.
189 ibid., 415ff.
190 Ed. in *Dialogo e Discorsi*, 3–172.
191 See above, 187.
192 *Dialogo*, 148–52; *Considerazioni*, 10–11 (on *Discorsi*, I, 4).
193 '*in ogni republica sono uomini grandi e popolari*'.
194 *Discorsi*, I, 5; *Il Principe*, ix.
195 '*e' sono in ogni republica due umori diversi, quello del popolo e quello de' grandi*'. *Discorsi*, I, 4; cf. P. Carli (ed.), *Storie fiorentine*, II, 12, III, 1 (Florence, 1927); *Il Principe*, ix.
196 Op. cit., 268.
197 Ed. in von Albertini, op. cit., 362–77. Cf. G. Guidi, 'La teoria delle "tre ambizioni" nel pensiero politico fiorentino del primo Cinquecento', *Il Pensiero Politico*, V (1972), 243ff.
198 Cf. *Politics*, 1295b.
199 Op. cit., 73: '*cum autem in unaquaque civitate tria sint hominum genera, scilicet civium mediocrium, potentiorum et multitudinis relique*'.
200 Ed. in Rubinstein, *The Government of Florence*, 322–3. Cf. Bruni's treatise cited above, n. 86, 68ff.
201 Cf. *Dialogo*, 11–12, 138–9.
202 Cf. *Discursus*, 268–72, 274–5.
203 *Discorsi*, I, 2.
204 '*governo viniziano, el quale . . . è el più bello ed el migliore governo non solo de' tempi nostri, ma ancora che forse avessi mai a' tempi antichi alcuna città, perché partecipa di tutte le spezie de' governi*'. *Dialogo*, 138–9.
205 Cf. Gilbert, 'The Venetian constitution', 477ff.
206 ibid., 490.
207 *Opere*, ed. F.-L. Polidori (Florence, 1850), I, 70–7, 98. Cf. G. Bisaccia, *La 'Repubblica fiorentina' di Donato Giannotti* (Florence, 1978). The first version of this treatise was completed in 1532: ibid., 28.
208 Op. cit., 136; cf. 29. Cf. von Albertini, op. cit., 155ff.
209 *Opera* (Paris, 1571), 267–8: '*[maiores nostri] eam vero in hac republica moderationem ac temperamentum adhibuere . . . ut haec una Respublica et regium principatum et optimatium gubernationem et civile item regimen referat, adeo ut omnium formas pari quodam libramento commiscuisse videantur . . . .*' Cf. F. Gilbert, 'The date of the composition of Contarini's and Giannotti's books on Venice', *Studies in the Renaissance*, XIV (1967), 172–84.
210 Cf. *Opere*, I, xlii–xliv.

6

THE RENAISSANCE AND THE HISTORY OF LITERATURE

CECIL GRAYSON

 N 1952 AT a congress in Florence on the subject of 'The Renaissance: its meaning and extent', Umberto Bosco dealt with the theme of Italian literature and sketched the underlying motives which characterize Italian prose and verse from Petrarch to Tasso. He laid special emphasis on the 'classicism' of this literature in the sense that, whilst drawing inspiration from ancient writers and reflecting varied contemporary experience, it aimed, as did the figurative arts, at a serene representation of life, transcending particular passions and events, and giving them an ideal, universal form. Man, conscious of the limitations placed on him by Fortune, did not, however, as in preceding ages, give up the possibility of action, but attempted to resolve personal and historical problems arising from the conflict of *Fortuna* and *Virtù* within strictly human limits. Hence the varied solutions of Alberti, Machiavelli and Guicciardini. Or alternatively, in spite of these adverse forces, man took refuge in an idyllic, imaginative, chivalric or pastoral literature, free from didacticism and satisfied with its own enclosed world; and here the supreme example would be Ariosto. At the height of the Renaissance, therefore, we would have a literature mainly characterized by escapism, fantasy and purity of form, detached from the mêlée of real life, which the poet viewed from a distance with a knowing smile. There are other important observations in Bosco's paper (on imitation and vernacular humanism) as well as reservations (particularly concerning Dante), but in its main lines it attempted to define the 'sense' of the age we call the Renaissance as distinct from that which followed and from the preceding Middle Ages.

At the congress this paper aroused discussion, but it was nothing compared to the controversy provoked by other speakers on art, philosophy and science, and on economic, political and religious questions. It was a time of continuing debate on the relations between

Middle Ages and Renaissance, with scholars sharply divided on the issue of continuity or clean break, and the discussions threw into relief the difficulties of reconciling within the concept of Renaissance, and within mutually acceptable geographical and chronological limits, the evidence and ideas related to such diverse fields of activity. Apart from this major question of defining the Renaissance in European or even in Italian terms, there also appeared serious differences within each discipline. To those who objected that the poets and thinkers of the age were not all of a piece, Bosco acknowledged the fact, but concluded: 'I felt it my duty to trace between the differences the substratum common to all writers. This seems to me the only possible way in which we can respond to our need to reconstruct the history of the past.' The fact that in the years since 1952 Italian literary studies have not evolved along these lines does not invalidate Bosco's approach; but, if I am not mistaken, it would be difficult today to imagine calling a conference to define the motives and basic attitudes of an entire era. In saying this I offer an historical observation, not a judgement; and I have taken the 1952 congress as my starting-point, not only because I was present and there met Eugenio Garin for the first time, but because it gives me the opportunity to stress an important point, viz. that Italian Renaissance studies in the past thirty-odd years have proceeded without excessive concern for the kind of broad issues which then preoccupied scholars. This is not to say that such debates were of no use, nor that the questions are not still alive, if in more restricted form. Nor was it a matter of a sudden change of direction, as if scholars in the 1950s became aware of the impossibility of solving such questions with the means and methods at their disposal, and so turned to more tractable issues and tasks. The change had been prepared for with the emergence in post-war years of the so-called 'new philology' against a critical background dominated for several decades by Croce and his aesthetic. Scepticism about broad generalizations and rigid historical periodization certainly played some part, but the real difference was a fundamental change in the way of looking at literary history and in the methods and means of studying it.

Croce's criticism undoubtedly taught some positive lessons, emphasizing the uniqueness of the individual literary work and its essentially poetic qualities; but it also had negative effects, discouraged historical and philological studies, and fostered, as well as subjective dilettantism, a pseudo-historicism conceived in spiritual terms. Fortunately, something of the old historical tradition continued to flourish, especially but not only in Dante studies (I refer to the work of Parodi, Rossi, Barbi and their disciples); and it was from this tradition, or more precisely from Barbi's, *La nuova filologia e la edizione dei nostri classici da Dante a Manzoni*, in 1938, that post-war studies took their start, and in the field of Renaissance literature moved decisively in the direction of historical and philological research. I say decisively because it is possible as early as 1938 to find a few such contributions (some by Garin himself) in *La Rinascita*, the periodical of the National Centre for Renaissance Studies founded in Florence in that year. But you only have to read the speech in the Senate by Vittorio Cian and some of the articles in the early numbers to see how studies then were dominated by discussion on Middle Ages, Renaissance and modern times, and marked by strong nationalistic feelings in the defence of the Italian tradition from Dante to Tasso against medievalists on the one hand and critics of the moral and political corruption of Italy in the Renaissance on the other. There lay the origins, though in a very different political climate, of the continuing debate on the content and chronology of the Renaissance which was still there in post-war years at the 1952 congress.

Meantime, perhaps through weariness of such debates, but more through a realization of the need to change direction and fill significant gaps in knowledge, Renaissance scholars had already begun to prepare new editions of major and minor authors and to research into aspects of literary history long neglected or even unexplored. It is no exaggeration to speak of a revolution in literary studies, which has changed our knowledge and our whole perspective. The basis of this revolution is the exhaustive study of the literary text in all its aspects – composition, sources, tradition, transmission, fortune, etc.: in other words a method of as complete a recovery as possible of the literary work, both in itself and in the historical context of its creation. This was not a revival of a literary science of the positivist type, but a more comprehensive inquiry into the manifestations of literary history in their true physical and human dimensions, free from ideological structures and aesthetic prejudices – which does not mean a renunciation of aesthetic values or of broad questions of historical periodization, but a recognition that aesthetic values cannot be judged outside their relevant context (except, in the Crocean sense, as 'pure act'), and that questions of periodization can be resolved, if at all, only from within history itself, not by superimposing on it schemes of convenience (or even, in effect, of extreme inconvenience). This methodological distinction seems to me fundamental. The old way of trying to look at the Renaissance globally from the outside is giving way to a rigorous examination of its individual phenomena from the inside. I shall try to clarify this important point in the course of this chapter.

In attempting to explain in general terms how and why what was

[203]

once the burning question has, if not altogether disappeared, become far less urgent, I am aware of having cast an aura of myth around post-war developments. I hasten to correct this impression and to discuss in concrete terms how one might now view the relationship between Renaissance and literary history. Thanks in particular to Simone and Ferguson we are considerably better informed now about the origins and history of the concept of the Renaissance, i.e. of that myth of wide-ranging renewal which was created and developed during the nineteenth century on the basis of the expression of awareness, in the fourteenth and fifteenth centuries, of the rebirth of eloquence and humane studies, and of the figurative arts. Knowledge of this history has made it possible to exorcise the spirit which has lain like an incubus on Renaissance studies and often made them fight with mere shadows. One is free to accept or reject the testimony of men of the fourteenth and fifteenth centuries: at least they were there and could be expected to know what they were talking about. The greatest caution is needed, however, before accepting the concept of Renaissance in far wider terms handed down to us by nineteenth-century historians. I shall not go further into this historiographical question (dealt with in other chapters of this volume) except to make one point. Writers of the fourteenth and fifteenth centuries repeatedly spoke of the *rebirth* at a specific time of Latin (and later Greek) language, literature and thought, and only marginally or by implication of the *birth* of a vernacular literature. In the concept of the Renaissance developed from the nineteenth century we are faced with the story of a whole age, in which humanistic Latin and Greek play a relatively minor or even retrograde role, while the new modern vernacular literature shines progressively more brilliantly against a social background of political and moral corruption. In this broad Romantic concept of a great cultural upsurge after the 'sleep' of the Middle Ages, some historians saw a certain conflict between the new vernacular and the reborn classics, eventually resolved with the triumph of the modern idiom in the sixteenth century. They arrived, that is, at the paradoxical conclusion of opposing humanism and Renaissance, of opposing what was the true renaissance, conscious of its existence, the Renaissance par excellence, to what was in effect a part historical, part ideological construct of their own. I am not denying value to this historiographic concept of Renaissance: I am merely pointing out the absurdity of a distinction which for a long time tended to keep apart two traditions which were strictly bound up together. The literary history of the fourteenth to the sixteenth centuries is inevitably a bilingual history, and humanism and Renaissance are in a sense the same thing.

Thanks to Campana and others we are also better informed as to the origin and history of the term 'humanist' (first used in the early sixteenth century), and of the concept of 'humanism', which again was born in the nineteenth century on the basis of the testimony and activities of fourteenth and fifteenth century students of 'studia humanitatis', but extended to embrace the entire cult of Antiquity and to mean, not precise intellectual pursuits, but a sort of spiritual animus dedicated to the perfection of human capacities in contrast with the supposed outlook of a preceding age characterized by renunciation of this world. A great deal of what passed and still passes under this catch-all label concerns the history of thought rather than of literature, but I shall speak briefly of it here for various reasons. Firstly because Garin himself has illuminated, perhaps better than any other scholar, the substance and significance of fifteenth-century humanism, largely by making the texts speak for themselves. By studying, besides well-known works, others little known and less read, and many unknown and unpublished, he has made possible a deeper knowledge of the thought and literature of the fifteenth century. I am referring, of course, to his numerous essays collected in well-known volumes, and to editions of texts such as those in Prosatori latini del Quattrocento, which are essential reading for anyone concerned with the literary history of the period, and not only that written in Latin. This method of bringing discussion back to the solid ground of contemporary texts and documents seems to me typical of the post-war direction of Renaissance studies. As a proof of this, and as an indication of how the old ideological (rather than historical) debate about Middle Ages and Renaissance has declined, one could cite the case of the review Italia medievale e umanistica, which has appeared since 1958 under the editorship of Billanovich, Campana, Dionisotti and Sambin, who saw no need to outline a programme in their first issue, nor to explain the marriage between Middle Ages and Renaissance, which twenty years earlier would hardly have been thinkable. You only have to scan its pages to see that there is no shadow of the old debates, and to appreciate the fact that, whatever the nature of a particular contribution, the relevant textual and philological groundwork is always there. So, by studying what has been done and written in precise contexts and in relation to past traditions and to new ideas and discoveries, the vital problems emerge from the facts and texts, and history is reconstructed, not in blocks or compartments, but in its complex and fluid evolution. In this process the major currents are not lost sight of; indeed, they become all the clearer through this more detailed analysis. What does go by the board (and rightly so) is the old emotive content of the terms Middle Ages, humanism and Renaissance.

I referred above to the considerable activity in the last thirty years in the preparation of critical editions of major and minor authors. At the same time, the taste has come back for the unknown and the unpublished; not the former antiquarian taste for the justly forgotten, but the genuine desire to find known but lost works, to fill gaps in knowledge, to repopulate, as it were, neglected or unoccupied tracts of literary history. The history of literature for a long time in Italy (and indeed elsewhere) was, and by some still is considered to be, the history of those works which were judged aesthetically successful. I do not think such criteria hold good any more either on philosophical or historical grounds. Those works which to later ages have seemed mediocre and excludable from consideration may well have been quite important in their time. Concentrating on the big trees in the wood and admiring their size, usually means ignoring what looks like undergrowth and hence the true ecology of the very area from which those same large trees arise. Symptomatic of such closer study of this 'ecology' is Spongano's initiative in taking up again, after an interval of more than fifty years, the two series of texts published by the Commissione per i Testi di Lingua in Bologna, in which a number of new or little-known works of the Renaissance have already appeared. These are of particular importance for the period which Croce christened the 'secolo senza poesia' – a century none the less full of verse of all kinds, and whatever its quality it cannot be excluded from literary history, which ought to reckon with and explain the low as well as the high points of literary production. It is certainly a remarkable fact that there is no real poet between Boccaccio and Poliziano, although there is no lack of verse, much of it full of passion and enthusiasm, which could hardly be said of any Latin poetry of that time. The humanists who judged the Certame Coronario of 1441 in Florence, criticized the rather poor entries, but they could not have done better themselves in any language. Nor was the position better at the time in Latin or vernacular prose, except for Alberti, who stands out against this background as a poet and prose-writer of great vigour and novelty. In fact, we may say that Italian literature, given a flying start by Dante, Petrarch and Boccaccio, then entered a period of arrest, and was revived in mid-fifteenth century at the moment when the conscious symbiosis begins of humanist and vernacular culture which up to then had evolved on separate, parallel lines. The how and why of this process seem to me to constitute the real inner problem of what we call the Renaissance as seen from a literary point of view.

I shall attempt to explain and illustrate this 'problem' later in this chapter. For the moment I am concerned to stress those developments in recent studies which serve to throw new light on the literary

[206]

landscape and on the network of major and minor roads which traverse it. An excellent illustration of the kind of thing I mean is Dionisotti's *Gli umanisti e il volgare fra Quattro e Cinquecento*: largely based on research into little-known or forgotten texts, it provides a wholly new understanding of the emergence of vernacular humanism. Or again, for an aspect of the Italian literature of this same period, no less neglected but highly relevant to the composition of *Orlando Furioso*, one should read the same scholar's work on the numerous mediocre chivalric poems published in those years. It is true that Ariosto's extraordinary poetry cannot be explained through such minor writers, but only against such a background can one understand Ariosto's decision to take up this particular genre with so different a spirit and art. The tall tree is more clearly seen from the undergrowth which grows from the same soil. But I will not pursue this point further, as I do not wish to give the impression that minor and mediocre authors are more worthy of attention, or that Dionisotti and other scholars give them more importance: their main objective is to understand and explain the major currents and authors. Let us now turn our attention to these.

It has long been debated whether Dante should or should not be included within the Renaissance. Much of the argument has rested in the past on the supposition that there exist qualifications for entrance possessed by the majority of those living in a certain period of time. I shall not attempt to define such qualifications either on literary or other grounds, because that would imply pre-empting the issue; and in any case it is an anti-historical way of posing the problem. It is better to approach from another angle, and to study (along the lines of two excellent studies by Garin and Dionisotti) the varied fortunes of Dante and his works in the centuries after his death. Here we find that his fame as a poet reached its apogee (with reference to the *Comedy*, *Rime* and *Convivio*) in the age of Lorenzo de' Medici, only to go into progressive decline and be overtaken by Petrarch by the turn of the century. It is not so material, therefore, to establish when a hypothetical Renaissance begins, and whether with Dante or not: there is absolutely no doubt that the great Italian literary tradition begins with him. It is more important to know how and why Dante's works survive up to a certain point, and then fail to pass the barrier of a literary criticism nurtured on the Latin Ciceronianism of the late fifteenth century. If we follow the same exercise for Petrarch, we find the fame of his vernacular and of some of his Latin works unbroken throughout; which would seem to prove what is commonly believed, that the Renaissance begins and continues with him. But I prefer not to play with such general terms. There is no doubt about the novelty of Petrarch's philological activity, from which humanism in the true and strict sense starts (and here Dante has no part). There is also no doubt about Petrarch's different poetic sensibility, even though it is expressed through traditional forms and language. Yet there are other aspects of Petrarch's work which no longer corresponded by the end of the fourteenth century to the interests of his successors, who were quite differently involved in affairs and teaching. His unfinished Latin epic *Africa* had virtually no following; the religious sensitivity which at times dictated renunciation of this world, the dissatisfaction with himself and his age which made him look back to the past or upwards towards heaven, seems to find no echo in humanist circles. There are no imitations of the *Segretum* or *De remediis* (though this work enjoyed wide circulation for a long time). This is not the Petrarch who continues at this cultural level into the fifteenth century, even though some of the questions he raised, such as that of the active and contemplative lives, continued to be debated and differently resolved. On the literary plane too, that inner conflict which was the moving force of his poetry has no true imitators before the sixteenth century: fifteenth-century Petrarchism is superficial and external. Bembo was the first to appreciate and recreate the spirit as well as the form of Petrarch's poetry. This brief sketch of the fortune of Petrarch, like that for Dante, reveals assimilations, rejections, imitation and disagreement throughout the fourteenth and fifteenth centuries according to the knowledge, tastes and understanding of readers. Yet the presence of both Dante and Petrarch, however incomplete or reinterpreted, dominates the literature of the following centuries, so that any history of Renaissance literature has no alternative but to start from Dante. The question whether he is or is not a Renaissance writer (in some broad sense) seems an idle one. It is obvious that Dante is different from Petrarch; not so obvious perhaps, but no less true that the so-called Renaissance is crammed full of differences and contrasts.

It used to be fashionable in the wake of De Sanctis's criticism to contrast the *Divine Comedy* with Boccaccio's 'human comedy' in his *Decameron* , and to interpret it as the clearest indication of the passage from Middle Ages to Renaissance: the *Comedy* severe, menacing, based on faith and aimed at salvation; the *Decameron* light, pleasurable, based on human nature and aimed at entertainment, especially of women. One can certainly make such a contrast, and it tells us a lot about the differences between the two writers. Whether it demonstrates a transition to a new age is another matter. Twenty years ago Vittore Branca published some of his essays under the title *Boccaccio medievale* with the intention of stressing not so much the novelty of Boccaccio's works as those elements in them which relate to past traditions of a cultural level totally different from those frequented by Dante and Petrarch. So, without losing any of its stylistic or human originality, the *Decameron* can be seen as the apotheosis of a long popular narrative tradition in which Boccaccio celebrates the actions of merchants, the middle class and court society of the early fourteenth century – an epic, therefore, in content and structure no less 'medieval' than the *Comedy*, despite its different sense of values. Furthermore, whatever his antecedents in translation and adaptation of medieval French romances and in the works of *cantastorie*, Boccaccio certainly gave, through his minor works, tremendous impulse to the chivalric tradition which, in a verse form possibly invented by him (*ottava rima*), runs right through the following centuries. The debt to Boccaccio of the *novella* from Sacchetti onwards is plain to see: less evident but equally significant is the debt to him of the romance in prose and verse, of pastoral and mythological poetry. In these sectors the relatively minor works of Boccaccio (*Filocolo, Filostrato, Teseida, Ameto, Ninfale*) are all in some ways linked to traditions which were alive in Dante's time or before and unconnected either with the new humanism or with most of the Italian literature which precedes them. The question arises as to how and why works with such distant medieval origins could exercise so much influence and determine for so long the form and spirit of what we call Renaissance literature.

Of the three major fourteenth-century writers Boccaccio is the one most changed by modern studies. In all three the autobiographical element constitutes a problem, but in Boccaccio's case it had for a long time led critics on a false trail. Shorn of the legends of exotic birth and aristocratic loves, Boccaccio's biography and biographical myths now appear (thanks largely to Billanovich and Branca) in their true light. His origins and formation now look even more different from those of Dante and Petrarch. But they had something in common; all were exiles of a kind: Dante, resentful of his expulsion but attached for ever to Florence and her language, while he roamed in spirit over and under the world; Petrarch, born in Arezzo, but a citizen of the republic of letters and of no city in particular; Boccaccio, reared in Naples on the margins of the court society, but compelled to return to Tuscany and thereafter ever nostalgic for his golden youth. Each of them was destined, because of these varied backgrounds, to be the mouthpiece of a different literary tradition. While Petrarch alone opened up the possibilities of a new or at least renewed Latin eloquence, all three in their different ways offered examples of a new literature in the vernacular potentially valid, like Latin, for the whole of Italy. The choice between the two roads, Latin and vernacular, and the resolution of the problems as models implicit in the very different works of these three writers, constitute the central issues to be faced by later literature. In this sense Dante, Petrarch and Boccaccio are the key to understanding the literature of the fifteenth and sixteenth centuries. This is evident not only from the frequent and varied imitation of their works, but from the central position they occupy in the discussions of both humanist and vernacular writers from the early fifteenth century onwards. This, therefore, will be our starting-point for considering what I have termed the inner problem of the Renaissance.

In the last twenty-five years one particular discussion of these three authors has received a great deal of attention, viz. that represented by the *Dialogi ad Petrum Histrum* of Bruni, which is undoubtedly a very important text for understanding the outlook of a group of Florentine humanists at the beginning of the fifteenth century. We must be careful, however, not to attribute to it motives and significance of a political-cultural character which it may not possess. One of the many merits of the historian Hans Baron has been to draw attention to the dating and interpretation of the *Dialogues* in the context of the attempt by Gian Galeazzo Visconti to extend his rule, not only over Lombardy and Emilia, but over Tuscany as well. Whilst one can fairly readily agree with Baron's demonstration of separate composition of the two dialogues with the *Laudatio Florentinae urbis* in between, there seem less grounds for accepting his explanation of the contrasting judgements in them, one negative, the other positive, of the achievements of Dante, Petrarch and Boccaccio, in terms of a radical revaluation of fourteenth century culture provoked in Bruni by the political situation. According to this view the Visconti crisis caused a volte-face in Florentine humanist circles, particularly in relation to fourteenth-century verna-cular traditions, constituting a new attitude on the part of this élite more sympathetic to the city's contemporary interests and her recent and past traditions; and this would mark the beginnings of that Florentine civic humanism typical of the first half of the fifteenth century. It seems unlikely, however, that the pessimistic judgement of the first dialogue was meant by the author to be final: it must surely be seen (as in some rhetorical works of Antiquity) as the point of departure for a positive celebration in the second. The interval of time between them may well have a practical, political explanation, but not necessarily an ideological one. None of which detracts from the important fact that precisely at that moment Bruni and his colleagues chose to review the cultural balance sheet in relation to both ancients and moderns, evidently in order the better to determine their own direction; and this historical-cultural awareness of the *Dialogues*

[210]

seems far more significant than any possible political or ideological implications.

At the same time these *Dialogues*, together with the *Laudatio*, may be seen as an affirmation of Florentine traditions and their past and present superiority over the rest of Italy. Baron was right, therefore to stress those opening years of the fifteenth century as a turning-point in Florentine humanism, which from then on asserts itself in the vanguard of Italian culture, and in contrast with the old imperial tradition, forges a new link between ancient republican Rome and republican Florence in terms of culture and civic institutions. But if such an attitude inspired the Florentine humanists at that time, it was a local phenomenon without special impact on other centres, which were influenced by Florentine historical, philological and philosophical activities, not by her civic example. It is right to take account of the republican element in Florentine humanism at that time, but wrong to exaggerate that civic factor in relation to the development of humanist studies elsewhere. Hans Baron's works have stimulated many other useful studies in Florentine history of the period; to the neglect, in consequence, of other centres, where without the benefit of the political stimuli experienced by Florence, important contributions were made to humanism and the development of education. I am referring particularly to the Veneto, to Padua and Mantua, and to Guarino, Barzizza, and Vittorino; and whereas much has been done for Padua and its university in recent years, other cities and people have been less studied because they seem off-centre in relation to Florence, and because they were less or not at all involved in political conflicts of the same kind. For these the Florentine yardstick is not applicable: it will not explain, for example, Valla or Flavio Biondo. In any comprehensive view of the Renaissance we need to reduce this Florentine angle of vision, and especially not to exaggerate, in relation to the culture of the age, the apparent contrast between republican and princely rule. I shall return to this point in my conclusion.

In the past much emphasis has been placed on humanist opposition to the vernacular on the evidence of a few invectives and defences. Baron has rightly stressed the more positive evaluation of the vernacular by Bruni in the works already quoted and in his later *Lives* of Dante and Petrarch; but that did not justify for Bruni or others the use for serious purposes of a language considered to be different and distinct from Latin and of inferior capabilities. It was not a case, then, so much of hostility to the vernacular, as of a quite understandable belief at that time that the future lay with the renewed and stable Latin, not with the multiform, unstable vernacular. Against the large and growing corpus of classical texts, the relatively recent tradition of the modern vernacular could hardly compete as guide and model, especially since it was either serious or amorous in verse (and as we saw, Bruni's generation was not much for poetry), or lightweight or amorous in prose. At that time, too, and against that background, the Latin of the trecento did not impose itself: Dante's Latin works were mostly forgotten, Petrarch's only partially influential, and Boccaccio's even less so. This is why – and Bruni's *Dialogues* seem to prove it – we have the impression that humanists at the beginning of the fifteenth century felt themselves to be starting almost *ex novo*. It should not surprise us, therefore, to find Alberti in the 1430s, when attempting to write a serious, learned vernacular prose, starting virtually from scratch and without reference to the fourteenth-century writers. It is true that in his amorous prose and verse there are echoes of Dante, Petrarch and Boccaccio, and that in these genres (though not among humanists) these writers functioned as masters and models; but for the expression of higher thought which preoccupied humanists, they offered little or no help or precedent. The only way in which the vernacular could compete with Latin was through a writer like Alberti who deliberately set out to use it for learned subjects, and to defend it, not on the basis of its past achievements, but on its intrinsic merits and by a demonstration that it possessed grammatical regularity similar to the Latin from which it descended. Hence the character of his prose, which owes so much to Latin in its vocabulary and syntax. The absence of Dante, Petrarch and Boccaccio from Alberti's use and defence of the vernacular in the 1430s and 1440s shows how little the fourteenth-century tradition then counted at that level of culture. At lower levels – in amorous, moral and political verse, and in narrative prose – that tradition had remained uninterrupted. Such literary stratification is typical of the cultural situation of the first part of the fifteenth century.

The situation in Florence changed completely in the last thirty years or so of the century in the age of Lorenzo de' Medici, when times were ripe for the renewal of interest in the Tuscan tradition, especially in Tuscan poetry. It began with Alberti's young friend and admirer Cristoforo Landino, and was promoted by the neo-Platonic revival of Ficino and his circle, which gave new dignity to poetic expression and brought Dante, Petrarch and other Florentine poets to the forefront of learned attention. At this point, when the political circumstances had also changed, taking the form of a kind of *Signoria* not very different from the rest of Italy (and certainly different from the Florentine situation at the opening of the century), the cult of Florentine writers became almost a deliberate programme; there then came to the surface not only the great writers of the past but also the tradition of popular verse, which had hitherto remained more or less in the shadows. In Lorenzo's time we see a democratization of culture, and simultaneously a mixing of the vernacular and classical traditions which had so far largely remained apart. The result is that eclecticism typical of the late fifteenth century, with conspicuous contrasts not only between writers but within writers themselves – a clear indication that Dante, Petrarch and Boccaccio had not yet become established as the dominant guides and models, but were confused with the rest of the vernacular tradition. Some signs of historical perspective and critical awareness of the relative merits of Tuscan poets are evident in the *Epistola a Federigo d'Aragona* and the *Commento* of Lorenzo to some of his *rime*; but perhaps more significant, because it transcends the limits of local traditions, is the criticism of Landino (most recently studied by Cardini), which poses the problem basic to understanding certain aspects and debates of late fifteenth-century literature, of the relationship between nature and art, between free expression and tradition – the problem, that is, of imitation, which Landino resolves in general terms, stressing the need for the discipline of art learned from the classical as well as vernacular traditions. In his well-known formula: 'è necessario essere latino chi vuole essere buono toscano' ('you have to know Latin to write well in Tuscan'), which has literary as well as linguistic implications, he gives explicit expression to the concept, exemplified in Alberti's practice, of deliberate fusion of the two traditions. This concept was to produce very varied results in Florence and elsewhere, from the *Stanze* and *Orfeo* of Poliziano to the *Arcadia* of Sannazzaro, and even the *Hypnerotomachia Polyphili*. These works take us to the linguistic crisis of the late fifteenth century (studied by Folena and Dionisotti), which involves both Latin and the vernacular, and concerns not simply languages but literature and style.

The last decades of the fifteenth century from a literary point of view are a time of infinite possibilities and uncertain standards. Ever since Petrarch and Boccaccio there had been much discussion of poetry and imitation, but it had little effect on literary practice outside the field of Ciceronian Latin prose. While Italian and Latin remained two distinct media and levels of culture, the question seems to have had little actuality and substance, but the more they came together, the more urgent became the need to resolve the problem for both. They had been brought closer for one thing by the important recognition in the 1430s that Latin had also had a vernacular existence, and was not, as had hitherto been thought, an artificial medium divorced from speech: furthermore, Latin had given rise to the modern language by a process of corruption. As the century advanced, the patrimony of Latin literature had been enriched by new discoveries, and there developed, especially with Valla, a new historical sense of the language even more evident in the wider knowledge of texts and keener linguistic sensitivity of Poliziano (cf. the important publication by Branca and Pastore Stocchi of his 'lost' *Seconda Miscellanea*, 1960). But this new philology and the new texts do not altogether explain that widening of interest and change of taste, towards the end of the century, for late Latin, so different in its vocabulary and style from the Ciceronian. This tendency, followed but kept under control by Poliziano, reached extravagant proportions in some lesser writers. Against this background are to be seen the discussions about imitation between Poliziano and Cortese, Bembo and G-F. Pico, and other lesser-known documents of the time studied by Dionisotti. As for the vernacular, the literary tradition of the fourteenth and fifteenth centuries offered a variety of choice almost as rich as that of Latin, and more accessible to all for being in the live, modern idiom. The literary works of Lorenzo and his circle illustrate this point in their amazing diversity from the lowest to the highest level in content, form and language. Here there was novelty and freshness as well as continuity with the earlier traditions, and a kind of experimentalism which inspired writers to try out, often with remarkable felicity, every sort of poetry from rustic, bucolic verse to sacred drama, from the mythological poem to the chivalric romance, from the carnival song to amorous lyrics in *stilnovo* fashion. It was an experimentalism not only of a technical and thematic nature (without prejudices as to the relative legitimacy of this or that genre), but also of intellectual origin in a generation of men of restless temperament, in whose works it is difficult to pinpoint the central core of their thought or to follow some definite line of development (Lorenzo himself was perhaps the best example). The contrasts to which I have referred are not explicable, therefore, solely in the historical and literary terms so far indicated; they correspond also to a certain social and cultural situation which was both happy and flourishing and at the same time complex and full of uncertainties. Poliziano was, of course, a case apart. In exquisite Latin and Italian verse he celebrated fleeting feminine beauty in settings of classical myths and reminiscences; even in his popular poetry he had an elegance all his own. All this he produced on the margins, or, in his *sylvae*, in the midst of humanistic, philological activities of great consequence for European scholarship. If in his *Giostra* he seems to meet Pulci on common ground, it is only to depart in a totally different direction. Only in Lorenzo's Florence can the coexistence of the *Stanze* and *Morgante* be appreciated and explained. Pulci took up the tradition of the Carolingian tales, and continued it in a completely different spirit and style, using it as basic material for his own extravagant comic imagination and linguistic exuberance, in which there is something of everything from Dante to the neo-Platonists, from Florentine slang to Petrarchan phrases: not a trace of nostalgia for the age of chivalry, but a hilarious take-off of events and figures seen not as history, but as stories for entertainment. It is a curious fact that in this Florentine context no one took up the prose tradition of Boccaccio, preference going to his verse, to the *ottava rima* and themes of the *Ninfale* and *Teseida*, and the *terza rima* of *Ameto* and the *Caccia*. All these works enjoyed great popularity also outside Tuscany; but only there do we find imitation of Boccaccio's prose works, especially the *Decameron*.

So far I have tried to characterize the literary production of the area which dominates the Italian cultural scene for a great part of the fourteenth and fifteenth centuries. It is time to transfer attention to those regions which appear to produce little of note before the mid-fifteenth century, and from then on prepare to supplant the Tuscan hegemony and take over its language and literature, calling it Italian. Speaking generally, one might say that up to the end of the fifteenth century humanist culture evolved on a national plane, and that the vernacular developed more on a regional one while pursuing in different ways the leads given by the works of Dante, Petrarch and Boccaccio. From the early sixteenth century on, coinciding with the political crisis of the French wars, vernacular literature began to shed its local characteristics and moved in a national direction. It is certainly possible to identify some local characteristics in some humanist groups – Florentine civic humanism, Paduan educational ideas, Roman antiquarianism – but for the most part humanistic activity developed on a supra- or inter-regional level, dealing with general moral historical and philological matters, not simply ones of local interest. This inter-regionalism was fostered by the disposition of scholars to travel from one city to another, from one teaching-post to another, from one patron to another; and these movements increased as patronage grew and humanistic studies penetrated the universities. Latin was their universal language, valid everywhere within and outside the boundaries of Italy. On the other hand, by saying that vernacular literature was regional in the fifteenth century I am not meaning to underrate the influence from the fourteenth century onwards of Tuscan language and literature on the rest of Italy both through the diffusion of written works and the presence of Tuscans in many parts of the peninsula. In consequence a rich tradition of amorous and moral verse arose, especially in northern Italy, which imitated the themes, style and language of the great (and the lesser) Tuscan poets. But not all these versifiers succeeded like Francesco di Vannozzo (nor perhaps even strove to do so) in shedding all their regional features: whilst following the content and metrical form of the Tuscans, they stopped, as it were, half-way linguistically and wrote in a kind of northern *koine*. A similar phenomenon occurred elsewhere: if the origins of the Roman Giusto de' Conti are not apparent in his poetry, one cannot say the same about Giustinian, even though he did not write in pure Venetian; or about Boiardo, whose fine Petrarchan verse is full of Emilianisms. In lyric poetry, therefore, whether or not in Tuscan metrical forms, there was a strong Tuscan influence; but this did not preclude a certain linguistic hybridism, which persisted and grew throughout the fifteenth century down to the courtly lyric of Tebaldeo and Serafino Aquilano, around whom the key questions of imitation, of nature and art, of free expression and discipline based on tradition, were to arise. The position outside lyric poetry was no different, in other poetic genres (e.g. the chivalric poems of Boiardo and others) and in prose, where hybridism is more marked and complicated by a large dose of Latinisms, as in the *novelle* of two imitators of Boccaccio, Sabbadino degli Arienti and Masuccio Salernitano. The regional character of vernacular literature can, therefore, be said to be largely linguistic, with strong tendencies towards a mixed literary idiom, combining local, Tuscan and Latin elements. It is this development, particularly evident in the last decades of the quattrocento, which was to constitute the practical background to the defence in the early sixteenth century of the concept of a courtly language in opposition to Tuscan. The phenomenon is well documented from early in the fifteenth century in northern Italy and Emilia; it appears later, but is certainly present in the south, in Naples in the circles of Pontano's 'academy' – the first redaction of Sannazzaro's *Arcadia* reflects very clearly the literary-linguistic situation of the turn of the century.

Greater or lesser linguistic hybridism does not of course constitute the measure of the literary value of the works referred to (and others like them), any more than loyalty to their particular local tradition and language guarantees the merit of works written by Tuscans. This problem was inherent in the situation, but no criteria for its solution had begun to emerge at that time. Certain developments had occurred, however, outside Tuscany, destined to have great influence in later literature, which had little or no dependence on Tuscan traditions: first, the *Orlando Innamorato* of Boiardo, who took up the Carolingian epic at the same time as, but with a quite different spirit from Pulci, and, mingling it with Breton legends, created the new chivalric poem;

second, the *Arcadia* of Sannazzaro, who from classical sources, from Boccaccio's *Ameto* and from the poetry of Dante and Petrarch created the pastoral romance, from which European pastoral was to evolve in all its forms. Beside these I would put Poliziano's *Orfeo*, a mythological-pastoral drama written in Mantua, where it fitted well in the context of a court society already accustomed to theatrical representations, and destined together with Ferrara to be the centre of important future developments in the theatre. I give these examples from areas outside Florence and Tuscany to illustrate the fact that by Lorenzo's time other regions had developed or were developing a vernacular literature dependent in part but not wholly on the old Tuscan traditions. In such centres, not in Florence, there arose the 'courtly lyric' which was to be all the rage in the last decade of the fifteenth and the first two decades of the sixteenth century. Valid from Rome to Milan, mainly frivolous, social, often improvised, this poetic fashion had its origins in the Petrarchan imitation of the earlier fifteenth century, and owed its particular character to the flourishing of court societies in which women played a conspicuous part. By this time printing was already well under way in Italy, and proved a two-edged weapon. On the one hand it promoted the wide diffusion of good works in Latin, Greek and the vernacular; on the other it showed up all too well the defects of ephemeral vernacular compositions, which might impress the hearer on recitation, but revealed their poverty of invention on the printed page. So, whilst the 'courtly' poets of Italy (and some from outside) joined in lamenting the premature demise of the 'divine' Serafino in what is probably the first poetic *Festschrift* in European literature (1504), other voices were raised in criticism of the lack of seriousness and substance in this fashionable lyric. Some indirect evidence of such criticism can be found in Colocci's defence of Serafino in the preface to the 1502 edition of the latter's verse, but the most explicit and forth-right statements are in Calmeta's writings of the early years of the century. Some of the chapter headings give a good idea of his approach: 'Whether it is right to criticize living writers'; 'Whether it is possible to be a good vernacular poet without knowing Latin'; 'What style should one imitate among vernacular poets?' Calmeta also reviewed Tebaldeo's collected poetry, and here and elsewhere did not spare his colleagues and friends. He also hit the mark in other chapters, extending his criticism to the social behaviour of the courts, and underlining the connection between a society and its literature, which had lost all sense of decorum, discipline and cultural values. Others were to formulate more stringent criteria for remedying this situation, but Calmeta's criticisms constitute the clearest contemporary evidence of awareness

[217]

that literature was in a state of decay, and in need of reform by recourse to the example of good writers in Latin as well as in the vernacular.

By this time Italy had been involved in war for several years and the most flourishing branch of modern poetry had been broken with the deaths of Lorenzo and Poliziano. After 1494 Florence's position in literature as in politics changed dramatically. The cultural scene came to be dominated instead by the northern courts, Rome and Naples. Italian literature was all courtly lyric, eclogues, mythological poems and chivalric romances (though, as Dionisotti has shown, there were some indications of a sense of disquiet at the contrast between this literature of fantasy and the often bloody reality of war). Two major factors, therefore, helped to throw into relief the critical situation of vernacular literature: the awareness of the distance between contemporary poetry and the great poetry of the past both vernacular and classical, and a sense of the widening abyss between literature and life. In these circumstances the problem arose acutely of how to create a serious and disciplined vernacular literature comparable with that of the ancients. The problem was not altogether new. Dante had posed and resolved it in his own way; Alberti consciously faced it for vernacular prose. But with very few exceptions fifteenth-century literature offers no examples of like determination. In consequence the writer who was to attempt to solve it in the early sixteenth century, and look back in search of models, virtually ignored the entire quattrocento. Before solving it in theory with his *Prose della volgar lingua* (1525), Bembo faced it in practice with *Gli Asolani* (1505), showing how, on the subject of the nature of love, it was possible to achieve gravity and gracefulness of expression in prose and verse by following the language and style of Dante, Petrarch, Boccaccio and *stilnovo* poets. As Bembo himself later declared in a letter to G.-F. Pico, this practical demonstration arose from the problem of imitation: he had been distracted from the pursuit of perfection in Latin through the imitation of Cicero and Virgil by the need to attend to the contemporary condition of the vernacular:

> Because many depraved and distorted things had been composed by many in that language, no longer mindful of its correct and proper usage in writing, it seemed, therefore, that in a short time, unless someone came to its aid, it would so far decline as to remain for ages without honour, without splendour, without any reverence or dignity.

The *Prose* are too well known to require further exposition here. I would simply stress the way in which, both in that work and in his letter to Pico, he applied the same humanistic criteria of imitation to resolve the problems of the dual crisis of Latin and vernacular. At the same time, because it was historically bound up with the literary problem, Bembo resolved the linguistic problem of hybridism; by taking poetry and prose back to imitation of the great Tuscan models of the trecento, he also cut the ties and dispelled the confusion between literary language and Latin and modern Florentine.

Between 1494 and 1530 the political future of Italy was decided largely by foreign powers. During those same years Italy also passed through a cultural crisis, and emerged with a clearer, quasi-national linguistic and literary identity. During those years Trissino (and others, but not Bembo) began to talk of an Italian language, and the debate known as the 'questione della lingua' was launched. Whatever the precise stages of evolution of this debate between 1502 and 1530 (a subject much to the fore in recent studies), we know enough to appreciate its fundamental importance for understanding the literature of the time. While the writers and supporters of an Italian 'courtly' language offered some resistance to Bembo's theories, others began to accept them and to conform more and more to the older Tuscan norm. Even Castiglione turned out to be more of a Tuscan writer in this sense than his own declarations and the discussions of *Il Cortegiano* suggest. Other authors, who had no direct part in the debate, like Sannazzaro and Ariosto, corrected their works, removing Latinisms and regionalisms. Grammar and orthography, hardly considered in the fifteenth century, became the subject of discussions and publications. Florentines and other Tuscans reacted strongly against what seemed to them the robbery of their language and their literary patrimony, and the disputes continued throughout the century, culminating in the writings and Dictionary of the Florentine Academy and the Crusca. But this is another story, or rather another chapter of the same story, written in different historical circumstances from those of the earlier sixteenth century, with which we are at present concerned. It is true that the great literary works of this period are not explicable only in the terms of the problems outlined above. But the *Arcadia* would not be the pastiche it is without the prevailing eclecticism and Tuscan linguistic influence of those years, nor would *Il Cortegiano* have dealt with questions of society, language and love, if these had not been related themes in the forefront of everyone's minds at that time (there is a good dose of neo-Platonism in Bembo's aesthetic-linguistic theory as well as in the *Asolani*). It is perhaps more difficult to explain why Ariosto should take up, at a time when the genre was in decline, the threads of Boiardo's *Innamorato* which had been broken off at the first clash of real arms in 1494. As Dionisotti has shown, Ariosto must have made his decision in full awareness of the situation and of his purpose to create something quite new. The fact that he used the chivalric legends as fable rather than as history, enriching them with classical elements, does not mean that he was taking refuge in a dream-world purely for artistic satisfaction. It cannot be called escapist literature, unless one is prepared to ignore the very serious human and moral substance within and behind the tales of the paladins. The intricate, interwoven adventures, brilliantly handled and elegantly expressed, illustrate the constant mutability of fortune and emotions, the joys and tragedies of human life. Classical in its spirit and equilibrium of form, *Orlando Furioso* is the finest expression of the new vernacular humanism.

The basic principle of this vernacular humanism was imitation, understood by Bembo as a means not an end: 'that we may actually surpass what we followed' (' . . . *ut quem assequuti fuerimus, etiam pretereamus*'). Ariosto's poem is a good example of this in a purely Romance genre. But, as the vernacular gained acceptance, another possibility presented itself, that of imitating ancient genres in the modern language. Bucolic verse, for instance, had already been attempted in the fifteenth century; yet only in the sixteenth century did writers think of filling certain obvious gaps in drama and epic poetry – obvious, that is, to a generation which now felt able to compete with the ancients, not as before in their language, but in vernacular. Ariosto was in the vanguard with the first comedy (*I Suppositi*, 1508). Before him there had been a long tradition of humanist Latin comedies (texts and studies in recent years by Perosa and Stäuble); after him followed a spate of more or less free imitations of Plautus and Terence, on which the European comic theatre built. Trissino led with the first epic (*L'Italia liberata dai Goti*, 1548) and the first tragedy (*Sofonisba*, 1524) – the epic had little following (except for its metrical form), whereas the tragedy began a tradition even richer than that of comedy. One should also mention in this context the various attempts to reproduce the structures of Latin verse in Italian, as they are an example of the tendency to carry the imitation of Antiquity even to extremes. In the early days of these important innovations no theories or rules were known for the genres concerned apart from some scattered observations in Donatus and other commentators; so the texts of Plautus, Terence, Seneca, Homer and Virgil provided the models. Aristotle's *Poetics* came out in translation and with commentaries from 1536 onwards; after that date the *Poetics* and the *Rhetoric* weigh more or less heavily on literary composition and most particularly on the numerous treatises on the Art of Poetry which proliferated in the later sixteenth century – a sign of the increasing literary conformity.

[220]

THE RENAISSANCE AND THE HISTORY OF LITERATURE

In the first thirty years of the sixteenth century the main cultural focus is in northern Italy, and literature and language, from local and provincial, move towards becoming national and Italian. Florence was not wholly outside or indifferent to these developments, though more out of defensive reaction than positive initiative. Machiavelli was certainly an exception in his own field of history and political thought. But as a writer he was clearly tied to the habits of the late fifteenth century, expressing himself vigorously in modern Florentine larded with Latinisms of vocabulary and syntax. He stood, at least in practice, outside the contemporary question of an Italian language. In his *The Prince* and *Discourses*, however, he went beyond any local limits to embrace the problems of Italy, basing his reflections on continual comparison of ancient and modern times: he was a humanist, therefore, in spirit if not in form. Among his literary works his comedies, partly but not entirely explicable in terms of the new genre begun shortly before by Ariosto, stand out well above the rest, especially the incomparable *Mandragola*. In comparison his poems seem to belong more to the history of his political thought than to the history of literature. As a literary figure Machiavelli appears an exception even in relation to his immediate Florentine background, being more provincial in a certain sense than some of his friends of the *Orti*, who aspired like Trissino to a more Italian literature. They were difficult years in every respect for Florence. In those who remained there, like Machiavelli, it is not surprising to find oscillations between optimism and pessimism as the city's fortunes changed. When the Republic fell in 1530, it marked the beginning of an entirely different era in politics and culture. Guicciardini, who had lived through it all on both the Florentine and Italian levels, had no optimism, no faith either in men or the lessons of history. His great *Storia d'Italia* might be said to represent the consciousness and the epitaph of a national reality which did not materialize.

In the circumstances Italy had to be content with her cultural pre-eminence in a Europe of which war had made her too well aware. In the field of scholarship this pre-eminence rested on the achievements of distinguished humanists of the late quattrocento – Poliziano, Pico, Barbaro, Pontano – and on the editorial activities of men like Aldo Manuzio (as well as, of course, the entire Italian tradition of published texts and commentaries of Latin and Greek authors); but it began to decline around the mid-sixteenth century as that older generation was not replaced, and eminent thinkers and philologists emerged in other countries. The great tradition of Italian humanists came to an end with Vettori. In literature it had given its best with the Latin poetry of

Poliziano, Sannazzaro, Pontano, Mantovano (and finally Vida). After them, despite attempts at revival, Latin came to be regarded more and more as a dead language, for the schoolroom not for real life. From the fourth decade of the sixteenth century on, and outside the classroom, another activity of great importance began – the divulgation of ancient and also modern works through Italian translations in prose and verse, significant for the general enrichment of culture and the education of the vernacular in broader fields of expression. The object and the effect of Bembo's *Asolani* and *Prose* had been to direct Italians towards the making of a serious vernacular literature based on the best writers of the trecento (which in practice meant Petrarch for poetry and Boccaccio for prose). Generally speaking, this lesson was accepted. But it was particularly valid for certain kinds of composition, outside which writers managed as best they would and could by following the examples of modern Tuscan or Tuscanizing authors. It is not true, therefore, to say that Bembo put the Italian language into a fourteenth-century straitjacket; nor is it correct to believe, as critics did until not long ago, that his imitation of Petrarch dictated to the cinquecento a single type of slavish Petrarchism which can be dismissed en bloc for its servility and insincerity. In its best exponents the sixteenth-century lyric shows how rich and flexible such imitation could be. On the other hand, Bembo had ruled Dante out of court because he had tried to be more than a poet (with consequent grave damage to his language and style); and since no one in the cinquecento seemed to have had similar ambitions, Dante withdrew among his fellow Florentines who zealously defended him and illustrated his work in their academy speeches. Echoes and explicit imitation of Dante can be found in Michelangelo, Ariosto and others, but they became rarer as the century advanced. Alongside Petrarch, modern poets were favoured as models – Bembo, Sannazzaro, Della Casa. In prose Boccaccio was the major model for writers of love treatises, and naturally for the newly flourishing genre of the *novella* (Lasca, Firenzuola, Bandello, Giraldi); but in general Boccaccio cannot be said to dominate as model of language and style (as Petrarch did for poetry) the far wider, more varied and less disciplined field of prose. In their *Vocabolario* the Crusca academicians, guardians of the language of the trecento (the 'buon secolo') and defenders of good modern Tuscan, arrived at the compromise of reinforcing the former with the latter, and thereby ratified a process which was in effect well under way – to the great satisfaction of the Tuscans, for whom the dictionary was the culmination of a long granducal campaign to affirm the linguistic predominance of Tuscany. But by that time the door was already wide open. Writers of every part of Italy no longer thought of composing in a regional or hybrid language, or they did so on purpose, and conscious dialect literature was born.

While Italy had been engaged in war in the first thirty years of the sixteenth century, the Reformation had begun in Germany and elsewhere. The measures taken by the Church to suppress its manifestations in Italy were at first moderate, but became more severe after 1540. After the Council of Trent the Counter-Reformation made itself felt through censorship and the prohibition of books. The intellectual climate changed and moved towards religious and moral conformity. The confidence in man and nature which had characterized and inspired writers and men of action in the fifteenth and early sixteenth centuries dwindled away. Those who felt oppressed or persecuted fled to Venice or abroad. Doubts and suspicions invaded individuals and society at large. While the abbé Bandello could still decline responsibility for the moral content of his *novelle* (ed. 1554), only a few years later Giraldi presented his collection of stories, *Hecatommithi* (1565), with the precise intention of 'condemning vice, teaching morals and good conduct, honouring the papal authority and the dignity of the Roman Church'. In 1573 Boccaccio's *Decameron* was published in the version corrected by a Florentine committee, purged in its content and language, and partly rewritten to satisfy the ecclesiastical authorities. This change in climate had already begun to produce a rich tradition of sacred verse, in which everyone joined – even the author of the scurrilous *Ragionamenti*, Pietro Aretino, in whom one can observe in extreme form the typical contrasts of the mid-sixteenth century between aspirations to liberty (or even to licence) and the desire to submit or conform to the dictates of religious conscience and authority.

The last great poet of the sixteenth century, Torquato Tasso, responded to these developments in his own particular way, but not at the outset of his literary career. His early romance *Rinaldo* and his pastoral fable *Aminta* seem far from being preoccupied with great moral or spiritual concerns. In the chorus to *Aminta* he could celebrate Nature and Love according to the formula: 's'ei piace, ei lice' ('if it gives pleasure, it is permissible'), while many of his early amorous and occasional lyrics are free from any spiritual anxiety. In his *Gerusalemme Liberata*, on the other hand, we can observe a more conscious sensuality and a characteristic, often sombre awareness of the limitations imposed on human desires and ambitions by external and internal forces, which make life mysterious, unpredictable and tragic. When it appeared without his consent, Tasso's personal crisis

[223]

had already begun, and from this there followed his religious preoccupations, the defence of his poem against the critics and its eventual
rewriting under the new title, *Gerusalemme Conquistata*, which
changed its character and tone in so many ways. Even his earlier lyrics
were then submitted to revision, in general for the worse. As an
exquisite poet who used Italian with great freedom and boldness, and at
the same time a tormented, unhappy soul, he ended up as a victim of his
own conscience and of the times in which he lived. Their spirit was
summed up by the reverse of Tasso's formula in *Aminta*, as it appears in
Guarino's pastoral drama *Il pastor fido*: 's'ei lice, ei piace' ('if it is
permissible, it gives pleasure'). The parabola of Tasso's life and literary
production seems to reflect exactly the cultural development of the
sixteenth century.

What conclusions can we draw from this rapid sketch? – that the
Renaissance ends with Tasso, or at least the main problem of the
Renaissance? It can, I think, be said that from Dante to Tasso there
extends an era of Italian literature coherent in many respects. Dante was
heir to two traditions, the Latin and the vernacular – the first classico-
medieval, substantial and long-standing, the second recently born,
slight, and limited in its range. Poised between the two, he eventually
chose the vernacular, extending its range and capacities, and infusing
into it whatever Latin culture he possessed. In his *Comedy* and in his
theoretical writings (especially *De vulgari eloquentia*) he was the
prophet of the future of Italian language and literature, the first example
of deliberate symbiosis of ancient and modern. Petrarch made a
different choice, keeping the two traditions apart but opting mainly for
Latin: even so, his Italian poetry shows signs of classical culture, more
in its polished form than its content. Boccaccio's works also present the
two traditions with an almost clear chronological division due to choice
made late in life under the influence of Petrarch: none the less, his
vernacular works written in the early part of his career owe something
of their material to classical sources. As I have tried to show, Italian
literature between the fourteenth and sixteenth centuries evolves in
great part on these lines and under the aegis of these three great writers,
finally favouring the modern language and assimilating into it the
virtues and forms of the revived language and culture of antiquity. It is
true that the classical patrimony inherited by Dante and his way of
looking at it were different from those of Petrarch, true that in this
respect later ages had more affinity with Petrarch than with Dante, but
this does not disqualify him in my view as the forerunner on the literary
plane of the basic underlying problems of the age. We must in any case
take care not to suppose that the differences which we are accustomed

to make between Dante and Petrarch were necessarily in the minds of immediately succeeding generations. The fortunes of their works would recommend caution on this point. At the same time, in reducing the dialectic of the Renaissance period to the interplay between two languages and two cultures, I am aware of over-simplifying a complex picture, and of omitting aspects which others might consider equally or more important. I have, however, deliberately confined myself to indicating main developments after 1530, not simply for reasons of space, but because by this date the major problem of the Renaissance, as I see it in linguistic and literary terms, had largely been resolved.

Why then carry the story on down to Tasso, and see in him the end of the age which opens with Dante? Because what characterizes and indeed permits the cultural developments of the three centuries between them is intellectual freedom, which is already in decline at the middle of the sixteenth century and in crisis around and within Tasso himself. In his Life of Petrarch Bruni outlined the history of Latin letters from Cicero to Petrarch, laying emphasis on the intimate connection between culture and freedom. His thesis was aimed primarily at stressing the similarity between the Roman Republic and the Republic of Florence, but it was valid also outside those particular political institutions wherever civic conditions placed no restrictions on the free cultivation of study and literature. In general one could say that such activities developed in Italy from Dante onwards without meeting such restraint; indeed, for the most part they were favoured and patronized by kings, princes, popes, local rulers and republics alike. It is true that Dante had to fight for his particular liberty, and there were occasions when wars and local rivalries directly impinged on cultural developments, arresting them, e.g. in Rimini, or favouring them, e.g. in Naples. None the less, down to the time of the foreign invasions, the ensuing bloody battles, the sack of Rome and the fall of the Florentine Republic, this cultural progress neither encountered serious external obstacles nor was beset by doubts and dissensions from within. But after that period those favourable conditions declined both because of external political and ecclesiastical causes (formation of new states, Counter-Reformation), and because of internal problems (disillusionment, spiritual anxiety, religious and moral conformity). To these we might add an increasing literary conformity dictated by Aristotelian rules. The consequences of these changes in the intellectual climate are already evident in the writers of the mid-sixteenth century, but Tasso represents the best and most extreme expression of the tensions within the religious and cultural make-up of the times. We may say, therefore, that Tasso marks the end of an era,

[225]

provided we do not think of it as a full-stop. Naturally Italian literature goes on to develop the same genres, themes and styles of the late sixteenth century, but with certain notable preferences, for the elaborate lyric, often set to music, for the tragic and pastoral theatre, and for sacred verse – literature on the one hand light and entertaining, on the other grave, moral and religious. Only in the areas of religious and scientific thought can we still thereafter sense the tensions typical of the end of the century – in Bruno, Campanella and Galileo.

In conclusion, the problem of the Renaissance on the plane of literary history consists in the meeting and interaction of two cultural and linguistic traditions, which works itself out between Dante and about 1530; but in a second phase, while from this process there emerges a more serious and varied and more Italian literature, fresh problems of a different nature arise to limit and undermine its further free development. Tasso was heir to the resolution of the first problem, and succumbed to the increasing pressures of that second phase. This is the guide-line I have tried to illustrate in this chapter. I have given little attention, except in passing references, to literary criticism (or its history), and concentrated instead on attempting to identify, among so many other aspects of the history of that period, what seems to me to be the linguistic-literary nucleus. It should be obvious that this nucleus does not stand on its own, and cannot be studied outside the evolution of other currents and problems which are the subjects of other chapters in this volume. So, whilst I took it to be my task to indicate and describe a particular basic theme, I am far from believing that the study of literary history ends there: it must always consist in thorough examination of individual authors and their works in their historical context and in relation to the cultural traditions from which they arise, be they philosophical, scientific, artistic, philological or literary. Only by such study is it possible to understand and evaluate each contribution and to recognize the stages and turning-points of the continuous and complex evolution of history.

7

THE ARTS DURING
THE RENAISSANCE

ANDRÉ CHASTEL

T APPEARS essential today to remedy the distortions and fill the gaps wrought in the fabric of history by the very ideas which have themselves made the Italian Renaissance an object of such intense and fascinated study.

No one would have the effrontery to suggest that Michelet, or Burchkhardt, can be dismissed, that the 'discovery of man and the world' is no longer of any importance, or that the 'classic art' of Wölfflin has passed into oblivion; but it may be legitimate to suggest that the powerful and meaningful formulas which were so important for the definition of the Renaissance have now become problems in themselves. The appearance of Michelangelo or Leonardo was not written in the stars; the widespread demand for 'representation', the rapid multiplication of artifices was, in fact, inherent in the structure of the ever-expanding societies of the time, large and small. These large perspectives have themselves become so many problems, and these problems continually bring us back to the genesis of modern civilization, as Voltaire, Goethe and Nietzsche in their various ways appreciated. They glitter, so to speak, amid the real conditions which nowadays are being with some success reconstructed. Since they reflect the changes taking place in the western world, riven by the sudden and swift expansion of the limits of space and time (both in a geographic expansion and in a greater awareness of history), they become, once they are interconnected, of distinct anthropological interest. This point of view leads to a tendency to consider attitudes, practices, even the significance of the works themselves, only as part of the particular facet of the moment. We have entered – or so it would appear – a phase where, instead of the universal qualities which formerly were the sole consideration, it is now the individuality of cultural phenomena which is of major concern.

[227]

For art, this orientation may be more easily justified, after a half-century of changes in taste which have pushed the works of the Renaissance so far back in time that they now risk being misunderstood and forgotten. Yet it is not quite as simple as all that: the 'desacralization' of art, which has been – or seems to have been – achieved, leaves behind a kind of emptiness, a chasm, between the splendid sequences of the forces of civilization which were the concern of yesterday, and the fuller analyses which are today's concern. This gap can, and must, be filled by the examination of actual circumstances. No matter the viewpoint from which one considers the fifteenth and the sixteenth centuries, full account must be taken of the impact of the development of the media through books, through the appearance of new forms of representation such as engraving and through the long association with the arts of scientific disciplines – anatomy, perspective or archaeology. In this there are many kinds of links which were usually loosened later, but which at the time stimulated many important developments in the 'workshops'. And since from these workshops there issued great men who dominated all around them, and involved also the potentates of the age, it is difficult to avoid coming to the conclusion that art appears to have become of crucial importance, perhaps even played too great a role in the rhythms and movements of social life. However distant the event may now be, the knowledge of such historic episodes cannot be unimportant in an age such as our own, which has witnessed so enormous an evolution of the media, and has seen the intricacies of technical research gain thereby in complexity. Nevertheless, in thus summing up what appears to be one set of facts, we cannot be certain that we are not once again projecting a totally modern idea, that of the 'Fine Arts', on to an historical reality of which it never formed part. Even this basic statement evokes multiple questions, extremely revealing in themselves.[1]

We are therefore always forced into a reappraisal of the terms in which the major preoccupations of the period were formulated by its actors and its audience. In innumerable texts an acute awareness of the present is accompanied by a kind of chafing, by sharp criticisms, by peremptory judgements condemning laggards in style and by the encouragement of innovators. Over the last twenty years, the body of these references has been considerably enlarged, opening the way for unlooked-for shades of meaning and precise judgements in areas which had never been adequately explored before, such as Mantua and Ferrara in the middle of the fifteenth century.[2] If we can now better understand how a revulsion against certain traits of style which had been as

[228]

traditional in painting and architecture as they were in literature, finally led to the polemical ideas of the 'Middle Ages', this retrospective fiction concerning the past (which is only important because of the passion with which it is believed in) naturally has as its antithesis an equally anticipatory fiction, or – as it has sometimes been described – a 'myth' of the future in which were based all the meanings of the longed-for *renovatio*.[3]

The historian's task is perhaps to redefine these passionate movements, where necessity, or desire – to use twentieth-century language – appeared naked and alive. This is where art is rather privileged, through what it offers us, and through what it teaches us. It has been possible, in the formidable mass of surviving works, to reconstitute certain artistic upheavals, solely through the changes caused by the arrival on the scene of a master, or even of an outstanding picture. One can even guess at the nature of the arguments which continually followed upon each other's heels in Italy. To recall the best known, it is very revealing that the quattrocento opens with a competition in Florence for the second doors for the Baptistery, and with a discussion in Milan over the continuation of the work on the cathedral.[4] In Milan the scholastic arguments came to a dead-end; in Tuscany, there was a decisive advance, for there the will to innovate was patent. An exquisite art was then current all over Europe – in Paris, Prague, Verona and Siena. In Tuscany, a severe art was to emerge, the fruit of an intellectual drive which would permit Brunelleschi, Donatello, Masaccio – despite their differences in age – to profit from the experience of the critical acuity, the ambition, the stern ardour of the Florentines. Soon, Florence came to consider herself unique; wrongly, as we now know. But, with the benefit of an aptitude for theory, a parallel literary movement, a gift for anecdote which was to provide an unrivalled framework for the first history of art, founded by Vasari in 1550 on the slogan 'from Giotto to Michelangelo', the idea of the 'Florentine miracle' has been indelibly inscribed at the heart of our thinking.[5]

This very intelligence which guaranteed their premier position to the Florentines, and for a time put them in the forefront of operations, has, in a sense, falsified the whole picture. Moreover, not only did chroniclers and historians develop a tendency towards a 'pan-tuscanism', provoking often clumsy defensive reactions in the past[6] and requiring long and patient revision by modern historians,[7] but a double exaggeration, common to Tuscans, weighed on the artistic history of the Renaissance. They demanded, in effect, that art should be entirely subject to knowledge through the double primacy of theory over practice, and the model of the antique over modern forms. These notions, illusory and dangerous for the historian who holds them, were precisely those which, emanating from the Tuscan power-house, provided the driving force for development, as a stimulant to artists and an incitement to clients. These notions also played a part in an all-embracing inner conviction which tends to blur continuity in order to extol change, and above all to attribute outstanding success to intellectual capacity. These ideas can be seen to emanate from the elaboration of two doctrines which all through the Renaissance were used to render modern developments intelligible – the two new keys of cultural history. Firstly, there was the inevitable and obsessive idea of a 'revival', of a return to the antique – to the foolishly lost rightful heritage of the Mediterranean world, an idea which gained rapid currency as a *restitutio antiquitatis*, which even Dürer in 1523 calls *Wiedererwachung*, and which was eventually crystallized in the sixteenth century under the term *rinascità*; and secondly, the complementary idea of a natural parallelism in literature and art, expressed from the middle of the quattrocento onwards in Aeneas Silvius' famous formula: 'Learning saw the light after Petrarch; the hands of painters gained strength after Giotto' *(Post Petrarchem emerserunt literae; post Jotum surrexerunt pictorum manus)*. If one wants to get inside the mental processes of the Italian Renaissance, one has to get to know these well-trodden paths, and test their validity. A new evaluation of the facts will then probably emerge virtually on its own.

THE ANTIQUE

The highest praise for an artist was, as Landino said of Donatello, 'to be numbered among the artists of Antiquity' (1480). What Filarete remembered of his passage through Florence was that, about 1460, 'they built according to these antique styles' (Book IX). When, in the Third Book of his treatise, Serlio deals with 'the antique buildings which may be seen in Rome' he describes a certain number of prototypes: the Pantheon, the most marvellous of all; the temple of Bacchus; the basilica of Constantine which he calls, according to custom, the Temple of Peace. To these he adds Bramante's project for the new St Peter's of which 'it may be said that he revived good architecture, which from antique times until then had been buried' (f° 64 V°). By placing Roman models and their modern counterpart on the same level, Serlio formulates what was a general conviction, and was to become a doctrine. It was through architecture and sculpture that, in a sense, it all began: the transformation of the appearance of the building, the square, and the street. Structures or figures, the most striking novelties were derived from three-dimensional forms, and it was for them that the authority of 'the antique' seemed to be indispensable.

The development of drawing – and its subsequent extension into the print – was indispensable to this new cultural balance. It was no longer a matter of monuments – symbols, of which every city had a local example, but of 'models' which were intended to circulate. In fact, one can even follow their propagation through copies, and in the progressive enrichment of the repertory as a result of archaeological discoveries (frequently recorded)[8] or in the collections heaped up in palace court-yards and often competed for by amateurs.[9] From many standpoints, this is the best studied aspect of Renaissance culture, and the most directly in touch with what one may call the 'ideology' of the Renaissance.

So marked a change of direction presupposes new principles. One frequently has the impression, when reading the statements of the texts, that all through the fifteenth century and even beyond it, it was a fairly generally held conviction that what they should be doing was to restore an order which should have been established long since, or, and it comes to the same thing, which had been established by the Ancients, before it suffered an inexplicable eclipse. How does Dürer excuse his ambition of writing a treatise on proportion in painting? – 'If we still had before our eyes the book which the Ancients wrote on the art of painting, one could with reason object to my project.'[10] Did Dürer know that we would never see 'those books by Apelles, Phidias, Protogenes . . . which were without doubt the most valuable texts'? To write a treatise, to define a doctrine in the domain of the arts, was at the same time to rationalize a practice and to rediscover a missing work.

The mention of lost treatises troubled men's minds and acted as an intellectual stimulus; in the same way, the obsession born of the summary evocation of vanished masterpieces provoked a kind of incitement to recreate them. The lists of empty names, found in Pliny, were recited as if they had an incantatory value not without imaginable errors. Even the mere names of works evoked a desire to re-create them.[11] In many ways, the art of the fifteenth and sixteenth centuries reflected the desire – sometimes admitted – to repair the misfortunes of history, and to produce for an astonished world the equivalent of works which should never have disappeared. It is the strange doctrine of the 'absent model', intensified by the conviction that, since it concerned the half-discovered treasure of the Mediterranean world,

[231]

they were there in the midst of it, as if living in the same area could abolish time.

The first Italian author to mention Flemish painting, Bartolomeo Fazio (c. 1454/5), can only explain the technical innovation of 'Joannes Gallicus' – i.e. Jan van Eyck – by supposing it to have been gained from 'reading the ancients, Pliny and others'.[12] It was the only way to explain away a discovery being made in the North. Vasari avoids mentioning any such thing, being already preoccupied by having to explain how a northern process could have fertilized Italian art. But the reaction of Antonio Manetti in his Life of Brunelleschi was not very different: the architect was the great practitioner of perspective, 'which, it was said, he invented or rediscovered' ('ritrovatore o inventore').[13] There again the hesitation was to be short-lived. But the suspicion remained that, even if in a particular case a Greek or Roman precedent were unknown, there had been nothing of any importance in the theory of the arts which was not known in Antiquity. One was always a follower; Antiquity was assumed to be cognizant of all the complexities of modern knowledge.

In the rhetoric of praise two formulas were competing. The first was to declare that never before had such a thing been seen in the world – this is what the Dominican Domenico di Giovanni wrote c. 1470 about the Baptistery doors;[14] the second was to declare that one was in the presence of a reappearance of classic art, of true art, of a resurrection or an *anamnesis*; this was the attitude in the case of the works of Donatello and Brunelleschi. It often becomes no more than two ways of saying the same thing, and it would not be particularly useful to seek to list the innumerable epigrams, where the names of Daedalus, Phidias or Apelles are invoked in a generic fashion; it is in vain that we might puzzle ourselves to discover a precise analogy, which would postulate a special critical appreciation. The art of the *encomium* only rarely demanded such discernment.[15]

Modern historians have concentrated, far more than the contemporary connoisseurs or chroniclers, on finding a precise source for the 'quotations' from antique motives in Renaissance works. These borrowings reveal quite clearly the state of antiquarianizing intoxication to be found in each circle, but if the obvious quotations, such as the *Spinario* in the Brunelleschi relief of 1401, are a kind of manifesto, they should not be allowed to conceal the more subtle though not less significant trends. It is well known, for example, that the half-figure of the young Isaac, and several others in Ghiberti's competition piece, were also derived from antique models. Ghiberti, like his competitors, claimed to be a connoisseur, even an expert, on the subject of Roman remains.[16] The conflict which thus appears, from the beginning of the fifteenth century, between two ways of relating to antique art, deserves some attention.

Take for example the relief by Michelozzo which forms part of the tomb of Bartolommeo Aragazzi at Montepulciano (finished in 1437), which Leonardo Bruni mentions in a letter to Poggio of 1430/1;[17] in one of the lower courses, the pontifical secretary can be seen bidding his family farewell on his deathbed.[18] The Roman content, if one may refer to it in this way, is imposed quite perceptibly, yet in a very discreet manner, in a frieze composition, consonant with the tradition of funerary monuments, but which at the same time echoes the equally traditional use of the *deploratio* and the farewell to one's family. The drapery cutting across the nude torso gives an 'antique' look to two of the figures, and the three *putti* make their emotions explicit by their gestures. Less than a half-century later, in the Arcosolium tomb of Francesco Sassetti in Sta Trinità in Florence, where the Christian symbols are oddly missing, the scene of the separation appears on the framework with a funerary couch, weepers, nudes, draperies, of a purely pagan character which have been, as has been firmly established, transposed from an identifiable model in the Meleager sarcophagus at Ostia.[19] Moreover, the left part of the relief includes a bacchanal of *putti* inspired by some other Roman relief, which may also have been part of a tomb. The whole composition is thus forcibly associated with the antique; it is a clear instance of the classical, Roman, handling of a familiar theme. We have therefore to underline the will to a deliberate 'revival', which is stressed in the decoration of bucrania, carved in the hard and costly material of porphyry. But did the sculptor, perhaps Giuliano da Sangallo himself, have in mind to emphasize the antique origins of the tradition itself? In the same way, Poliziano, Sassetti's friend, was careful to stress in his verse the etymological value of words, and to demonstrate the Latin under the vernacular.

To develop this banal but always useful comparison, the poets of the early cinquecento may well have been faced with a difficult decision, when they were writing in Italian: to enrich the language through the study of classical literature while remaining within the innate 'genius' (still to be defined) of the language, or to go the way which was to be that of the Dream of Polyphilo and the 'macaronic'. An analogy with sculpture immediately becomes clear: the sculptor of the Sassetti tomb is working in Latin – with a few Italianisms. But the sculptor of the curious relief, difficult both of identification and attribution, a fragment of the possibly dismantled tomb of Francesca Tornabuoni, which is contemporary with the Sassetti tomb, is an example of a determinedly vernacular style, composed in a language which draws both from earlier solutions and also from antique models.[20] A quarter of a century later, Riccio displays in the della Torre tomb an antiquarian purism, a *sermo latinus*, which goes so far as to add a panel with pagan funeral rites – including a complete model of the tomb – near the deathbed scene where everything – bed, gestures, draperies, torches – was clearly taken over from the antique.[21] But in the accompanying panels of the Elysian Fields, clearly less inspired, and the allegory of *Virtus*, *Mors* and *Gloria*, the amalgam is ill-managed, the modern elements supervene, and here one is faced with a complete artistic 'macaronic'.[22]

What has to be accepted, in our opinion, from these easily multiplied instances, is that the balancing act between discreet assimilation and obvious imitation became continuous, and virtually congenital to the Renaissance.[23] It would be unwise to say that either one or the other direction was truer or more significant. It depends on the commission, on the workshop, on the moment of time, whether one mode or the other was adopted. There were certainly centres in which it was more or less customary to emphasize the antique content; Rome compared with Florence, Padua compared with Venice. In each of these more favoured centres, however, one should also take into account the alternative movement which meant that every spectacular new development was absorbed during the following period and became part of the common repertory.

The fame of Michelangelo is the outcome of the success of this vast enterprise. It would probably be enough to grasp all its aspects in order to realize the problems of 'imitation' during the Renaissance. This at least appears to be the impression made on the innumerable historians who have studied Michelangelo's extraordinary abilities. Their importance and standing make any further discussion unnecessary.[24] Two comments, however, suggest themselves: Michelangelo only very rarely uses direct quotation,[25] even in works of his early youth which are hardly more than exercises, such as the *Battle of the Centaurs* (Casa Buonarroti), where he reworked an antique form in his own fashion, yet without seeking to harmonize it with contemporary formulas; he refines, in fact, the antique repertory in his own way. The programmes are clearly modern, but somehow treated as they would have been by a Roman sculptor of the Imperial age.[26] This is what puts Michelangelo beyond all comparison, and it is, unfortunately, what has also made his works so subject to imitation. The powerful delineation of his figures, their plastic quality, has been particularly useful to painters, and, in the always risky operation involved in the transpostion of a sculptural form into a painted one by the intermediary of drawing, Michelangelo made things much easier for his contemporaries, including Raphael.[27] He may well have complained at being invited by Julius II to paint instead of carve: but the immense undertaking of the Sistine ceiling forced him to reveal in all its seductiveness the classical principle of his draughtsmansip, which came to weigh so heavily on Italian art, and still astonishes us.

Known, studied, divined, dreamed, antique art, taken as a whole (with a few local or historical variations) has been closely linked, paradoxically, by the Italians with the 'freeing' of styles. It became the passport for the modernity which European art was often to associate with the works of modern artists which it considers classic, with a periodic tendency to dissociate them from it by a concern for purism. But the huge labour of manipulation which almost all the studios undertook for a century (and the pictures one has of the *'officine'* prove this) also affected the production of decorative objects for everyday use. Trinkets, plaquettes, medals, frames, armour, caparisons, but also tables and inkwells, lavabos and beds,[28] were decorated with a verve, sometimes even with a comical exuberance, derived from a repertory which justified its fantasies by appealing to the authority of the ancient pagans. One of the most typical manifestations is the new treatment of inscriptions, monumental or of other kinds, which marks the emergence of a more noble form of lettering, and is associated with the reform of handwriting.[29] At St Maria Novella, at the Tempio Malatestiana, or in a still more private monument, in the Sepulchre in San Pancrazio, Alberti sets an example and creates new models of remarkable elegance.[30]

A simple and precise example illustrates how the antique, closely examined, became the pretext for new developments. In the fifteenth century a sculptural frieze from a Roman temple was in S. Lorenzo-fuori-le-mura. As Wittkower acutely observed, this work, which consisted of a straightforward row of liturgical objects, played a definite role in the formation of the theory of 'hieroglyphs'.[31] Mantegna used it to ornament his *Triumph of Caesar* with, it seems, a tendency to treat each of its motives in a simple and direct manner; patens, vases, cornucopiae, and so forth, all endowed with a simple emblematic meaning, appeared in the works of Sebastiano del Piombo and Giulio Romano. Everyone knew the frieze. At the beginning of the *Hypnerotomachia* Francesco Colonna described an inscription inspired by the same models – perhaps even by the same frieze – suggesting a kind of rebus. In the mingling of the two levels, there is a revealing innovation: a graphic oddity mixed with a bookish erudition ends up, as is quite usual, half-way between a learned amusement and the arcane. The *Hieroglyphica* of Horos Apollo was in circulation for two

[235]

generations among humanists before the *editio princeps* by Aldus Manutius in 1505. This pictographic writing, of which only the principles were grasped, appeared fantastically useful; by means of drawing it overcame linguistic barriers (according to Alberti), and responded to 'synthesis' in thought (as set out by Ficino): a universal vehicle in fact for intuitive intellectual processes. From Rome the next step backwards was Egypt, in the elaboration of a philosophical interpretation, which was at the same time both confident and wrongheaded, but which nothing could shake for the next three centuries.[32] Confidence in the religious values of hieroglyphs even resulted in their sometimes being used on tombs.[33]

If the justification for emblems is to be discerned in this kind of idea, then it is rather more a deviation than a derivation. It is one of the charming creations of the period, born from the satisfaction provided by these attractively hermetic veilings of learning – a condensed form, to which a laconic motto gave a personal motivation. Learned culture sustained this fashion in which could be discovered the charm of an ambiguous and recondite statement. When Alberti, affected by the heady quality of hieroglyphs, set out in his *Anuli* the rather simple symbol of his emblem, 'a winged eye inside a wreath' (laurel/joy, open eye/vigilance, wings/omnipresence), he gives no explanation of the arcane value of either the motive or the motto, *'quid tum'*.[34] The obscure image only acquired prestige when it was linked to the antique through a rediscovered esoteric learning. Among other surprising developments worth noting was the huge and absurd agglomeration of emblems in the Ehrenpforte commissioned in 1515 by the Emperor Maximillian from his engravers.[35] It displays quite clearly the consequences of the strict conjunction of image and symbol which fascinated various Italian centres.[36]

Recent research has enabled us to trace the sudden and rapid diffusion of the light and fantastic decorative schemes found about 1480–90 in the Golden House of Nero on the Esquiline and called, for want of a better name, grotesques.[37] These infinitely adaptable decorative devices appeared at exactly the right moment for the decoration of frames friezes, ceilings and such like, all *all'antica*, replacing less thoroughgoing forms such as candelabra and rinceaux. Their early use by Pinturicchio in Rome and Umbria, their brilliant use by Signorelli at Orvieto, show very clearly that it was not originally thought of as a mere decorative device; by endowing what had been derived from the antique with a learned and mysterious background (which might well have been encouraged by the exploration of the buried rooms on the Esquiline), the creators of the cloister of Sta Giustina in Padua (of which only the borders of the scenes survive), the Camera di S. Paolo in Parma, and the Loggie of the Vatican, were able to furnish their new decorations with motives of an emblematic character, with droll inventions like those of small Paduan bronzes, and thus to give the imagination a free rein into the marvellous, the irrational, the bizarre.

For a long time the range of a kind of ornament which enabled artists in the South to create a successful rejoinder to Gothic monsters in the ornamental repertory in the North was not properly recognized. Cellini specifically called them *monstra*; this is the domain of *aegri somnia*, where some kind of intellectual disquiet gets mixed up in the exuberant decoration. It is, after all, the very finest representation of the unintelligible. But, at another moment, of which Raphael's Loggie are an excellent example, the fantastic yields place to the fascinating, which Giovanni da Udine enriched with a vast number of naturalistic details.[38] On a quite different plane, this is exactly what happens with attempts to describe Michelangelo's assimilation of the repertory of antique sculpture. Raphael and his team took over, so to speak, the decorative resources of the antique, by an easy occupation of the very heart of the territory, so that they appeared as its privileged interpreters.

From then on, the distinction between the 'real' antique and its modern reinterpretation was no longer even possible. Was the study of Greek and Roman works which accumulated in gardens and palace courtyards ever disinterested? Certainly, archaeology and epigraphy were born and went their own quiet way. But the antique world – and it has often been said – would only slowly be discerned through the perspective of history. This complete takeover in the domain of art at the beginning of the sixteenth century, of which Michelangelo and Raphael were the first to give a striking example, resolved all the problems at a stroke. And, as we well know, there was almost no antique piece which was not restored or adapted as by right.[39] Modern ideas of authenticity never came into it.

In architecture, things only appeared to be clearer. According to Vasari, Bramante's strength came from his having rediscovered the formula for Roman concrete, just as Giovanni da Udine had for stucco.[40] Vitruvius was available. There, at least, theoretical principles and practical recipes were laid down. Alberti bravely tackled this mediocre text, only to conclude that it would be better to write an entirely new treatise for modern architects. There was a text, but it had to be rewritten. The learned who insisted on acquiring one in a corrected edition (1485), with a commentary (1521), with illustrations (1511), demonstrated a mixture of confidence and obstinacy which lasted until the creation of a Vitruvian Academy, charged to produce a vocabulary of architecture, which was never done.[41] But the Roman author's confused statements only made the analysis of the apparatus, the orders, the structures, even more necessary. The obsessive quality of his descriptions led sometimes to unclassical solutions, as for instance in the interpretation of *atrium* at the Farnese Palace.[42] But everyone knew that palaces and churches belonged to a programme which had never been written. One extreme case: the Palladian reconquest of the Roman lesson was the most striking demonstration of the results of familiarity with the antique; it exalted the modern which replaced it.[43]

The same observation could be made about the planning of the house and, more generally, of its interior; the appearance of the rooms with their mural decorations, their coffered ceilings and their stucco ornamentation acquired, as a result of progressively 'archaeological' accretions, an 'antique' flavour, provided one is willing to recognize Roman decor in its metamorphosis.[44] The *soffitto* transformed into a compartmented ceiling soon to be filled with illusionistic paintings, is one of the creations so quickly assimilated to classical taste that the circumstances which led to its invention would be forgotten.

If these observations are correct, it is always the same initial impulse and the same final distortion which have to be recognized as typical. In its relations with the antique, the Renaissance can be held to be a gigantic enterprise of cultural 'pseudo-morphosis'. This is perhaps its best definition. In its efforts to rediscover Antiquity it creates something quite different. And there were even moments when the participants could flatter themselves that they had succeeded: '. . . rather may Your Holiness, always keeping alive the imitation of the antique, equal it and surpass it, as you in fact do with great buildings . . .' wrote Raphael and Castiglione to Leo X in 1519.[45]

THE GODS

Everyone knew it: the statues, the reliefs on sarcophagi, the vase paintings, all represented pagan gods and heroes; the buildings which one tried to restore through drawings and which one sometimes imitated, had been those of a civilization whose idols Christianity had had to banish. In the energetic repudiation of the manifestations of Byzantine tradition, in designating Gothic aberrations as the origin of all ills in the world of art, there still remained the knowledge that both were the product of a Christian culture. This was so true that a large number of duecento and trecento works – usually miraculous Madonnas – were incorporated into modern compositions during the fifteenth and the sixteenth centuries.[46] Thus, the models which most conformed to Christian faith were unacceptable for aesthetic reasons; the models which one desired to follow did not belong to the Christian faith.[47]

This situation can be defined as a characteristic situation without outlet for the art of the Renaissance. It only became grave – dramatic even – to theologians worried about innovations, and then to the Reformation. It tended to establish a distinction, which was destined to become very important, between *form*, which ensured nobility and quality in style, and *significance*. But the increasing importance given to the formal point of view, in composition and style, never resulted in a lack of understanding of the themes or programmes. Also, one has to ask what was the attitude of artists and patrons to the representation of purely mythological subjects – scenes from classical myth, for instance? As may easily be seen, a considerable part of the fabulous tales from Antiquity were, like events in its history, treated as part of the history of the world. Secular art profited from this, as did families and cities, which claimed to have originated in legendary times. A very considerable change of fortune was, however, to take place in this domain; a most powerful cultural movement worked on style, through the 'revival' whose strength has already been discussed, as well as upon themes, through the learned work of humanists to achieve a proper *reconstitution* of classical mythology and its poetic exaltation.

First it was necessary to overcome the obsession with the baleful idol. So far as concerns folklore, in modern and romantic tales, it has never stopped being that. But, when the cultivated circles of the readers of Dante and Petrarch, Poggio and Niccolò Niccoli, became interested in pieces of sculpture which represented pagan divinities, they broke with their inhibitions and converted execration into a kind of cult. Nude figures could always arouse theological censors to condemnation; they were none the less an object of considerable – and understandable – interest to artists from the trecento onwards. They were always used as idols in biblical scenes, or whenever it was necessary to illustrate the conflict between the pagan world and Christian truth.[48] There had to be a certain change of intellectual climate for a statue of such provocative nudity as Donatello's bronze *David* to become possible. It had to become, as has recently been shown, a civic symbol, Goliath's huge winged helmet recalling the emblem of the Visconti, with whom Florence was at war, probably at the exact time of the execution of the work (1425–7).[49] At least, it represented a biblical hero, but the antique echoes of the work are so strong that a modern scholar has proposed a rather unlikely fusion between David and Mercury. The sculptor's only truly pagan work is the little one where he has chosen to represent a strange and lewd divinity, difficult to identify, but quite clearly demonic, the so-called *Atys-Amorino*. The pointer is a valuable one; the personages of antique mythology, once they appeared in works of art, overwhelmed the normal parts of the representation by their nudity, and their actions. The advocates of humanism were fully aware of the difficulty. Boccaccio explained it as best he could in the fourteenth and last book of his *Genealogia deorum*. As antique philosophy had been 'saved' by invoking reason, so one must 'save' mythology for the sake of poetry. But one cannot be satisfied with the arbitrary glosses of an *Ovide moralisé*. The idea is that through the histories of the gods is manifested a knowledge of the relations between man and the world, which one could not arrive at any other way: *magnalia naturae et hominis*. The fact that antique mythology was deeply and permanently linked with this aspiration to the 'poetic' – a mixture of sacred and profane feeling – was a very important cultural event. The most common way in which these poetical seams could be mined was – unfortunately – through allegorical interpretation, and the humanists were not loth to exploit it.[50]

As has often been shown, the structure of the universe, the articulation of its visible elements, that which was the concern of cosmology, physics, physiology and so forth, made during the Middle Ages a splendid composition – what C.S. Lewis has called 'the Model', whose authority lasted for centuries.[51] However, this grand schema was made up entirely of 'scientific' elements of antique origin, rooted in a vocabulary which constantly married them to the gods of myth. This Model, which is perfectly expressed in Dante, was not violently modified during the Renaissance, as people often seem to think. The analysis of the evolution of scientific thought is none of our business here. It is enough to recall that if scientific thought necessarily modified the nature of the Model, it could not prevent the Model's survival in the imagination, where it could acquire an existence which was ghostly, fictive, poetic all at the same time, because it was in accord with 'appearances'. Antique myth, which had already undergone this metamorphosis, certainly helped to maintain the sense of the necessary 'fiction'. It has the power of a religion when 'it is no longer an object of faith'.[52]

Mythology had, in fact, one support which rooted its representations in the everyday, and gave to its figures an almost familiar appearance. It can be seen in full force when one realizes how seriously Marsilio

Ficino, for example, set out the course of his life and his works in terms of the transits of Saturn through Aquarius.[53] Through the network of astrology, the gods of Antiquity rendered western culture the immense service of linking together the various elements of the real and of rendering intelligible many obscure aspects of existence. Astrology supported the idea of the occult, while at the same time it endeavoured to decipher it.[54] It has taken us quite a long time to realize the degree to which astrology controlled the greater number of the major figurative cycles of secular art – and even sometimes certain religious ones. It was normal to paint the vault of a chapel or apse as a *caelum*; but at S. Lorenzo, it is a real horoscope which had been painted on the little dome of the sacristy. The cycle of the months was not new in a decoration, but at the Palazzo Schifanoia the register of the Decani – technical figures in some way astrological analyses – adds a specific reference between the triumph of the gods and the scenes of everyday life.[55] Whence came numerous series, in particular in engraving, in calendars and the like, where all is organized round the typical occupations of the children of the planets. These repesentations were everywhere, in villages as in palaces; a science which made *objective* groups and classifications of temperaments, social groups, occupations . . .; the profane, the playful, the sacred, constituted in fact the common anthropology of the Renaissance, an anthropology which tended obstinately to express itself in images.

The operation which only painters and sculptors could perform was to end the long divorce between types and figures, and to restore to the gods of mythology their true identity. This has been admirably explained by Aby Warburg, and is among the lasting achievements of his school.[56] The 'exact' representation of the gods and heroes required an intellectual premise: the full range of humanist discourse, capable of extracting the essential particulars from the best-known text. It required an archaeological premise; the accumulation of models made possible through collections of works and archaeological information. It required an artistic premise: a deployment of 'naturalistic' means adequate to allow of a correspondence between text and model. For over a half-century now the study of the connections between these three terms has shown ever more clearly how slow was the adjustment. In fact, it was at Rome, and late at that, that finally, after innumerable fantasies, representations were achieved which were sufficiently coherent. The loggia of Psyche at the Farnesina marks without any doubt the moment of achievement, where a calm and controlled style gives the myth a firm place in the imagination, that is, in secular decoration. It has permanently entered the house, as in the stuccoes of

[241]

the Villa Madama or the Palazzo Massimo . . ., but also, and chiefly, in those places which were to be devoted to *otium* and voluptuousness, like the Palazzo del Tè at Mantua. The phenomenon would soon spread all over Europe.

So long as no illustrated manuals existed, the decorators created their own documentation. But from the moment that treatises of any breadth were published, the balance disappeared. This is not the only singularity of the history of the antique gods; since no one actually believed in them, they could be modified and rearranged according to taste. Erudition exploited late and oriental sources, where divinities were given attributes, forms, strange properties which bore no relation to the classical divinities. The illustrations in the *Imagini degli dei degli antichi* by V. Cartari (lst edn, Venice, 1566) offered unheard-of creatures, where Syrian and Egyptian divinities, Serapis, the Juno of Hierapolis, Mars in the form of a stone, a Diana with three heads, were introduced at the expense of the Olympians.[57] Fantastic forms created an effect of the unusual, and the interest evoked by the bizarre quality of these figures, which were the darlings of mannerist artists who were prepared to introduce them into complicated and arcane decorations, extended also to the learned commentaries, often esoteric in orientation, which accompanied them.[58]

It was quite normal for these fictional characters, spectacular and full of meanings, to enter, like a troop of masquers, in the service of fêtes, games, divertissements, since they had become an irrepressible political and social fashion. The antique divinities allowed the programme of 'entries', carnivals and the like, to be enriched by learned traditions and made apposite by recondite analogies. The phenomenon is now well understood; but the description is incomplete if one forgets the other domain, less ephemeral but just as amusing and fanciful, where myth played so great a role: in gardens, where the statues matched each other in arbors and fountains, from grottoes to clearings. Under the sign of *otium*, made explicit by the figures of *hilaritas* and *voluptas*, and their train of fantasy, all the resources of mythology went to organize the decoration of a hundred famous villas – that of Cardinal Giulio at the Villa Madama, from 1520–1 onwards, the Villa d'Este at Tivoli and so on.

The gods and the heroes of mythology had thus found a refuge, which would assure them centuries of survival. Fiction, which can be adapted to all needs, was now recognized as indispensable in western society, for its own enjoyment and self-description. Obviously, this left plenty of room for all kinds of 'moralizations' and allegorical combinations. It is

[242]

enough to recall, among a hundred similar examples, Sansovino's Loggetta in Venice with its four statues.

Through a foreseeable conjunction momentous in its consequences, at the very moment when the mythological repertory spread by poems and comedies was complete and familiar, sculpture, and after it painting, had also achieved the means of producing for the eyes, with a sort of reasonableness (that is, in a style *all'antica*), the corresponding scenes of the parade of the gods and heroes. Astrological superstition might well be a sufficient support for the ceiling of the Farnesina; it had nothing to do with Raphael's *Triumph of Galatea* or Correggio's *Camera di San Paolo*. These places were now planned to receive this type of decoration. Signorelli's panel of *Pan* painted for Lorenzo de' Medici, and Botticelli's *Primavera* painted for his cousin, were great novelties in their day; we can guess – and even then it is not too clear – what they meant to the patrons who commissioned them for their rooms. After a few beginnings of this kind it became possible, and then general, to display this type of pagan decoration – which alone was con-sidered suitable and poetic – in the interior of wealthy houses. Around a few great fables, destined by calculated allusions to ennoble, to exalt, the masters of the house, a whole army of fauns, nymphs, *amorini*, took their places in the ornamental repertory of western culture. It would be well worthwhile knowing more about the '*stufette*' of which, fortunately, some good examples still exist. The decoration of the Palazzo del Tè, a princely villa, shows clearly what themes could be called upon; from the grand banqueting hall to the grottoes for the promenade, every part of the building had its appropriate decoration, which one could exercise one's wits to elaborate.

It is not difficult to imagine how pleasant was the research and the execution of a programme of this kind. Turn and turn about, at once both declaimed and illustrated, subject to the variations of poets and the decorations of painters, the myth imposed itself on all, because through it – and only through it – could the infinite nuances of feeling be expressed: it was fully descriptive of human diversity. The disguising of experience also enriched it, as if every situation and, in any case, all those which were of interest – love with its confused impulses, the aspiration to culture, the conflicts, the desolations, found there the equivalents which ennobled them. In bringing in Daphne, Diana or Saturn, one enlarged expression so greatly that a notable dose of irony and buffoonery became possible. The frescoes of Silenus, and the comic Feast of the Gods, like the caricatural figurines of Paduan knick-knacks, introduced through humour a new breath of air. Mythology also opened

[243]

the way to an unexpected permissiveness; the engraved series of the 'Loves of the Gods' by Rosso and Parmigianino are an example of the use that could be made of it.

Antique mythology only responded to all these needs because it was totally adaptable. Several of its 'pseudomorphoses' changed the course of art; for example the 'Reclining Venus' which appeared about 1509/10 in Venice, via Giorgione, by a phenomenon still ill-explained. As Saxl has pointed out, this is a case of a creation after the antique, for which no prototype exists or was ever suggested.[59] The presence of Eros (later blotted out) on the right of the bed, indicates that it was indeed the goddess and not a nymph, as is sometimes seen in Roman reliefs, a prey to the concupiscent gaze of satyrs. The gesture of the *Venus pudica* has been transferred to this beauty dreaming in a landscape, giving the authority of nature to the nobility of nudity – something rare and pure, noble in the passionate cult of beauty, and without precedent.

The success of the theme is less mysterious than its first appearance. There was no Venetian painter who did not exploit it. Its vogue was such that Michelangelo, who could not resist, did not hesitate to compose a *Venus and Cupid* (*c.* 1532) and the *Leda* originally destined for Alfonso d'Este, the energy of which is seen even in Cornelis Bos's engraving. Thus Titian, when he came to Rome, replied with his *Danaë* (1545) for the Farnese. In effect, the theme of the 'Reclining Venus' gave rise to a second growth in the *Venus of Urbino* (1538), where the fusion of a mythological marvel with the familiar was achieved with a charming ambiguity. It becomes in fact a kind of 'marriage picture'.[60] As if he realized that he had gone too far towards the everyday world, Titian then developed the theme of 'Venus with a musician', in a deliberately unreal setting, and himself furnished the reply to the problem of the identity of these figures by calling *poesie* all those pictures of Diana and Venus which he supplied to princes. Mythology was susceptible, as was seen several years earlier with Correggio,[61] of marvellous melodic variations for the erotic imagination.

The European fame of Titian's mythologies suggests that the answers had been found in Venice, the symbolism having become a sort of latent content that commentators risk over-elaborating. What confirms this is that Titian deliberately avoided all learned and archaeological settings in his bacchanals as in the Diana series. One even has the impression that he was quite satisfied with the starting-point supplied by the illustrated editions of Ovid. Venice had gained a head-start through the production of illustrated books. The vignettes in the 1497 Ovid, for example, brought within the reach of all an abridged mythology which, thanks to the new media, allowed the varied and amusing characters of myth to enter into the common culture. There was, after these popular little woodcuts, a veritable flowering of little decorations painted '*à l'Ovide*' for cassoni, bedheads and the like, which even Giorgione did not despise (according to Ridolfi). The arts worked the antique repertory so hard, and with such brilliant and ingenious results, that Hercules, Apollo, Mercury, Ganymede, etc., ended by occupying an over-important place in the decorations, and for some spectators, one difficult to understand. By a kind of osmosis which could easily be foreseen, the pagan models tended to reappear in the midst of Christian art.[62] Around 1525, it was possible to observe, except in the repetitions of types difficult to avoid, an inflection which immediately appears ambiguous in religious compositions. Correggio, and above all Parmigianino, went as far as they could, and the *Madonna with the Rose* in Dresden could be taken for a Venus. For a long time past, the great events in the Bible and the Gospels – in the series of tapestries of the *Acts of the Apostles* for example – had assumed, thanks to the noble and easy style of Raphael, the appearance of episodes from Roman history. It was in the same spirit that Leo X had encouraged Latin poets to write Christian epics. But in the *Ciceronianus*, Erasmus, vigorously attacking Sannazzaro and Vida, makes Nosoponus say: 'I don't know if it is more reprehensible that a Christian discusses profane matters in a profane manner, without revealing he is a Christian, or that he discusses in a pagan manner Christian matters.'[63] This rigorist warning made no difference.

Heemskerck, in about 1545 after his return from Rome, presented in his *St Luke painting the Virgin* the Madonna and Child as if He were a little Hercules held by an Alcmene in a *cortile* filled with antiques. But a breaking-point had been reached and the optimism of humanist culture was now in question.

NATURE AND REASON

The taste for festive display has often been cited since Burckhardt as a revealing characteristic of Italian society in the fifteenth and sixteenth centuries. This phenomenon, which involves such collective forms of spectacle as theatre and decoration, has had all sorts of interesting consequences for the arts.[64] But festivities make the particular point that, from top to bottom of society, everyone sings and dances. In different ways, it is true, but it is helpful to introduce right away this

[245]

idea of *modus* – that is, the manner of expression in the domain of entertainment.

The *ballata*, a dancing song with a sprightly rhythm and a lively tune, was particularly suited to the carnival. Since continuity was as natural as it is obscure in this area, an old Mediterranean origin probably lies behind it. In the fifteenth century, the enrichment of music resulted in the introduction of a greater variety of forms in these songs and we know, through an interesting conjunction between the aristocratic and the popular, that Lorenzo de' Medici and his friend Poliziano amused themselves by composing *Canzoni a ballo*, the words of which were often pretty improper.

The deliberate insertion of mythology into folklore was one of these little novelties. In Florence about 1480, when the group of Bacchus and Ariadne surrounded by nymphs was presented beside masked figures leaping about and singing ribald songs, or village maidens singing the praises of the market produce of Arcetri, it was impossible to avoid the incongruity of having characters from myth singing what were obviously playful modern couplets. For historians *'Quant'è bella giovinezza . . .'* has become a symbol or a familiar bench-mark; Lorenzo's song is a warning that one should not forget to restore to the period, along with music and dance, the institutional practices of festivities.[65] It was not only that this afforded regular work to decorators and costumiers, which should never be dismissed as unimportant when it may possibly be the work of Botticelli or Leonardo;[66] it was also an opportunity to inject into the gaiety of carnival or the ceremonial entry all sorts of representations, allusions or contemporary events, just as happened in the music hall revues of the twentieth century. One may well be astonished by the incredible load of learning displayed in some of the scenarios written during the middle of the sixteenth century; it was imposed on what was an originally popular framework, and there is no doubt that, together with the strangeness of the decorations and accoutrements, this made it acceptable. The crowd could appreciate without understanding, participate without having to work it all out (and this included the guests, even the ambassadors who were often mystified). There was a certain tone to the manifestation, a general disposition, which was far more important than the 'iconological' structure, even when this was essential to the whole.

During the fifteenth century notable novelties were introduced into dancing. This was an occupation considered to be essentially profane, regarded with suspicion by the religious authorities, the occasion for love-games but also for a luxurious display of an imaginative

[246]

inventiveness; it was associated with a joyfulness, a state of exaltation bordering on the marvellous, as may be readily realized in observing the 'choirs' of angels. The illustration of the *Primum mobile* (the motive force of the world, no less) in the famous Ferrarese cycle of the tarot cards, is of a light and dancing nymph.[67] The dance included figures and steps which were beginning to be described with precision in treatises towards the middle of the fifteenth century.[68] The slow dance, *bassa danza*, strictly measured, with well-defined figures and between the movements set poses of the tableau vivant type, might reproduce scenes from secular painting. Since the 'arguments' of the ballets often derived from myth, it is probable that the groupings and poses of the mythological figures had been tried out in court balls before appearing in frescoes. The fashion for the 'mythological portrait', which would later have such a vogue, must have been reinforced by this development, which, however, set it half-way to fantasy. The phenomena which have previously been described could now appear in a very different way. The conventions of Florentine art, which from about 1460 onwards seem with Botticelli to be haunted by a whole corps de ballet of nymphs, can by these means be seen in a truer light.

It must however be stressed that for elegance in court festivities and their costumes north Italy possessed resources which were unknown to the Florentines. Here it is necessary to digress for a moment. The recent discovery of the extraordinary epic cycle in the Reggia at Mantua has made clear the extent to which the 'precious' art of Pisanello could be enlarged through the influence of courtly and imaginative taste.[69] The artistic culture of this region to the south of Padua was obviously an extension of late international Gothic. But it was revitalized and brought up to date in two ways: by a spare and precise naturalism, which in the famous collections of drawings of plants and animals reveals a constant freshness and curiosity; and on the other hand by a methodical study of antique reliefs, medals and the like, which, though it was pursued quite differently from the Florentine way, was none the less significant and full of promise for the future.[70] The idea that a spontaneous and brilliant Renaissance, full of fantasy, emerged in the cities of north Italy during the first half of the fifteenth century becomes ever more obvious in that it too benefited from the contribution of humanists and of an appropriate literary development. Such expressions as '*mesura*' and '*prospectiva*' associated with '*disegno*' and '*naturale*' could without difficulty be applied to Pisanello in 1442.[71] Not only were the Tuscans not alone, but their contribution, when the northern centres were brought in, was as much influenced by the 'marvellous' as by the '*naturale*'. This line of evolution can no longer be ignored: it modifies very considerably the physiognomy of the quattrocento. It can help to explain, for example, two generations later, the extraordinary independence of an artist such as Correggio, at the time of the apogee of Roman art.

If we come back to dancing, it should be noted that towards 1450/60, another amusement in a quite different style began to become popular, one which was for long considered part of the realm of the jester – the *morisca*, a wild and energetic dance with a great display of thrashing arms and legs – a sort of 'rock and roll'. It even affected courtly circles. Warburg drew attention a long time ago to the letter of April 1465 which described the *brigata amorosa* in which Lorenzo de' Medici's favourite led this dance with a young man described as extravagantly got up.[72] These silhouettes can be seen in the centre of the plate devoted to Venus in the series of the 'planetary children'. But – and it is a striking thing – the same violent gestures, the same wild movements are to be found at the very same time in the frescoes in the Villa Gallina at Arcetri. It is generally agreed that Pollaiuolo made use of some antique model or other, probably a vase on which a Dionysiac group was depicted. Stranger still, the famous statues of acrobatic dancers by Erasmus Grasser at Ulm are of the same period; nothing illustrates better the international vogue of this highly successful type of dance.[73] But the important thing is also that, where certain original forms of expression, of *modi* that governed daily life, deportment and attitudes are concerned, it is impossible to limit oneself purely to Italian instances, in order to interpret certain outstanding phenomena in Italian art.

The place occupied by music requires a major rectification of the view we have of western culture, since we tend to forget the point to which it affected both feelings and models. Despite a few major composers, and of the popular type of *laudi*, or *ballate*, the fifteenth century 'is characterized in Italy by strong influences coming from France and above all from the Netherlands'.[74] Italy played no part in the supreme invention of polyphony, which rapidly swept the board, and profoundly transformed the art of composing. It is only necessary to run through the names of the *maestri di cappella* and organists in Florence and Rome, to be convinced that despite its links with, and its roots in, popular tradition, music depended very largely on what was imported. The *ars nova* which transformed singing and the feeling for harmony in the West was a gift from the North.

We must therefore accept the idea of a situation in the most active centres in Europe which is unequal in the functioning of its various disciplines, as brilliantly suggested by a great and honoured historian. The regions of Flanders and northern France were full of new ideas in painting, where with a more flexible medium, it was possible to develop rapidly towards the conquest of new formal values and an art of great expressiveness, whereas the architectural framework of late Gothic was never even questioned. One therefore has to sum up these relationships, inverted in their response to change by a kind of chiastic diagram, valid in its general formulation despite inevitable exceptions.[75]

It is obvious that it is through the monumental arts, architecture and sculpture, closely associated in their programmes, that we have to place the meridian of maximum change during the fifteenth century in Italy. It is usual, and in one sense quite normal, to parallel the sober and taut style of Masaccio with that of Donatello and Brunelleschi. However strong, however grave they may have been, the reforms introduced by Masaccio appeared incidental to an art which had already changed so greatly with Giotto, in its transition from the *maniera greca* to the Latin, to use Cennino Cennini's term clearly familiar to all. But, as has been pointed out, north Italian art was pursuing a different path. Nowhere was the evolution 'linear' – straightforward. The severe teaching of Masaccio was, if one may so express it, enlarged by the contributions of a new feeling for colour, by the luminous palette traditionally associated with the emergence of Domenico Veneziano, and, a little later on, by knowledge of Flemish technical procedures and the beautiful 'textures' necessary to a modern picture. Personalities as different and as powerful, both in Florence and outside Tuscany, as Piero della Francesca and Giovanni Bellini were involved in this development. If we have to sum up in broad terms a particularly rich half-century of activity we are forced to admit that at the moment when the new repertory of ornament coming from the South finally became current all over Europe, oil painting and the naturalistic qualities which it encouraged travelled down into Italy.[76] The development in the South is caught up in an international movement of expansion, to the point that at certain moments the northern world, with its fashions, its music and its famous pictures, weighed in the scales of development as heavily as did the rediscovered Mediterranean heritage. The history of the art of the Renaissance should, if it is to be properly done, both take into account national differences and transcend purely national boundaries.

In order to arrive one fine day at the longed-for synoptic history, two forces may be underlined – the two dominants of the North and the South in painting – by repeating the terms of the admirable analyses which have been made of the works themselves.[77] The inevitable parallelism between the Eyckian reform and Masaccio's is perhaps only valid as a generalization; but we are always forced back on the contrast between the coherence of the space represented – through submission to what Alberti called 'the central view-point construction' – and nature recreated with all the precision of landscape seen in a light transformed by atmosphere. There is a polarity which develops towards 1420–40, which cannot be minimized, and which controls even more strongly all that follows; the professional concentration on the richness of effects dominates the studios in the North as it does those in the South.

The original position taken up by the Venetians allowed them to assimilate more rapidly than any other Italian centre the landscape tradition of Flanders. The Antwerp 'Romanists' adapted and transposed Mediterranean architectural models and forms '*all'antica*'. This symmetry was so well known, so familiar that historians availed themselves of it in presenting the modern age, the conclusive maxim expressed in the epigraph under the portrait of Amstel being: '*Propria Belgarum laus est bene pingere rura/Ausoniorum homines fingere sive deos*' ('The Belgians are especially famous for painting the countryside, And the Italians for representing men and Gods'). (From Lampsonius' epigraph on van Amstel, quoted by Carel van Mander, *Het Schilder Boek*, Haarlem, 1604.)

Myth and human stories were the privilege of the South, nature and its singularities, that of the North. Hence, therefore, it is easier to understand the disdain expressed by Michelangelo and his friends for the fashion for 'landscapings'. There was in Italy an instinctive resistance to an art which appeared to be a matter of pure practice, of pure empiricism, since it disregarded that splendid fiction, the intellectual domination of form.[78]

Contrary to the hyper-speculative interpretation which has been given to it by certain modern writers, it may be affirmed that perspective – that is, the mathematical structure of the space represented – emanated from the desire to create a satisfactory setting for a composition. For more than a half-century, the painters of important works had struggled (particularly since Pietro Lorenzetti) with the treatment of architectural backgrounds, and these provided another opportunity for the predominance of the monumental, which was evident all over Florence. The *costruzione legittima* engendered successes which demonstrated its soundness, and its usefulness to other workshops. The grouping of forms round a central axis and their

[250]

proportional diminution was a constraint which, on the other hand, gave a clarity and a new authority to the composition. By a kind of trick of perception, the convergence of orthogonals 'created' depth, and gave the picture a truthfulness which must have seemed incredible to those who looked at the works of Angelico, Castagno and Filippo Lippi.

In the learned language of the trecento, *prospettiva* meant optics; with *prospettiva pingendi* the term subsumed the meaning of the mathematical construction of space. But the common usage of the word in the second half of the quattrocento raises the question of the architectural views in intarsia work. If one takes into account the enormous success which the recipes of perspective artists had in the art of intarsia, one can speak of an intimate association between the analytical setting out of the mathematical construction which reduces all forms to a geometric contour, and the puzzle of pieces of wood arranged by the makers of inlays. An interesting technical link is not the only thing to enter into it; it reveals, like all phenomena connected with ornament, a general taste for 'cubism' and geometricization, which would be looked for in vain outside Italy. Nothing indicates more certainly the strength of a movement which insists, by means of art, that nature and its diversity must submit to a positive order.[79]

The insistence that the field of the representation should be structured in a clearly visible manner by means of the geometric grille did not convince everybody, and was not followed everywhere. It certainly responded to the idea that the mind can and should govern space – that is, the world of nature, where man evolves, although among so many judgements and observations on the arts this viewpoint was never formulated. That which was proclaimed was the will to construct a setting for the painted composition which would be rational and true at the same time. What we see is groups arranged in echelon in a space set out with temples, porticoes, triumphal arches – in other words, with architectural models in the new style. The *St Sebastian* by Antonello gives us a fair idea in its rather strained feeling of something of the satisfaction which comes more from 'the marvels of geometry' than from reality. The development of architectural settings often has a quality of anticipation about it which historians have remarked on, but all its consequences have not yet been fully appreciated.

Often the surrounding architectural setting is part and parcel of the theme; for instance, in scenes of the Nativity the Arch of Constantine introduces an interesting 'historical time-shift'. In narrative panels such as the *Miracles of St Zenobius*, porticoes and loggie define an important central space, a place of honour which is, by definition,

[251]

proper as a site for an edifying event. It seems legitimate to consider together panels in painting or in marquetry, destined for the decoration of walls or the backs of choir-stalls, which show squares surrounded by buildings, isolating in the heart a city one can guess at in the receding 'wings', a place designed for ceremonies or festivities.[80]

This device, which became a commonplace in Italy, not only concealed nature, but tended to give to scenes from the Old or New Testament the appearance of urban events. Landscape only appeared in the margins, the predellas, rarely in the panels themselves, and even then always in a conventional guise. Even the Umbrians, so bent on describing a soft and tender landscape, never created more than *loci amoeni*. The initiator of the change of attitude which made landscape important was Leonardo, together with Piero di Cosimo and the Emilian and Venetian painters. Nothing could be more surprising, at first sight. As witness and judge, Leonardo was intent upon formulating and establishing the principle which subordinates the perception of space not to the direction of lines, but to the changes in the colours of objects, and even, more subtly, by their changing appearance.[81]

Yet, it is around Leonardo that have accumulated, concentrated and deepened to a speculative degree sometimes approaching the enigmatic, all the problems of art-scienza. All the drives towards naturalism, all the preoccupations of artists in the creation of animated and 'speaking' figures, converge on him. The high doctrine which was never explicit in its definition of perspective was to be elaborated so that it might be destroyed. Leonardo called in question landscape elements and all other natural forms; he was led to embark upon what one might call the revision of the traditional cosmological and anthropological Model, inherited from Antiquity and well organized by western thought. The genius of Leonardo lay in understanding that it was necessary to give a new impetus in all areas of critical analysis, whence his striking approach to the 'enveloping forces' present in nature and in the definition of living things. To this was joined an incapacity to systematize the incredible treasures of his accumulated observation, and the impossibility of bringing to a conclusion a universal enquiry with unlimited ramifications.

His contemporaries, anxious and bemused with astonishment, reproached Leonardo with having gone outside art and then of re-entering it in a disconcerting way. Not unreasonably, the artist obviously hoped to limit himself to *decisive* achievements, in whatever field he worked in – mural painting, altarpieces, monumental sculpture, and so on, and every time, whether he succeeded or not, he in effect provoked serious repercussions in the development of style. Some vital points still have to be raised so that he may take his rightful place in the general picture which is here being adumbrated. On the one hand, the attitude of Leonardo towards the antique, as a repertory of forms, is more complex; it obviously represents the highest point of the tendency towards 'assimilation', which is more Florentine than Roman. It is with him that we sense most fully how an awareness of the unrenewable originality of the present gives a more intense drive to modern aspirations. The *Horse* commissioned by Lodovico il Moro would have been an equestrian statue superior to all those known from Antiquity. As heir to Florentine rationalism and universalism, Leonardo revealed the idea of an exploration of the world of which there was no previous example; he thus, consciously or not, gave new life to certain mythical figures. When Leonardo pronounced the word *'scientia'*, he meant knowledge, or more exactly, theory, as has been accurately observed by J. Ackerman.[82] When he spoke of mathematics, he meant a rational process, and this is why he insisted that painting had to be subjugated to the 'mathematical sciences'. But when he spoke of painting, what exactly did he mean? A system of representation which proceeded from a new perception, and which would be able ultimately to dominate and encompass the whole world of appearances. What else does he say in the famous passage, '. . .the science of the painter has a divinity which is such that the mind of the painter is transmuted into a similitude to the divine mind', where he is concerned only with inexhaustible phenomena of nature?[83] No one has studied the incredible 'programme' formulated and largely worked out by Leonardo without experiencing a sort of unease when considering what, in effect, Leonardo's painted oeuvre was, with its few themes and the great number of unfinished works. Between the total power of painting grasped as an intellectual principle and its effective realization, there was a gaping divide which presents us with an insoluble problem and which left his contemporaries bemused. How could he have proposed the necessity of refounding the whole of knowledge in order to establish painting, the supreme art, on a satisfactory basis? By whom would he have been understood? Nevertheless, all the world has grasped that he gave himself up to this intellectual quest, by bringing his art to such an amazing level of dignity that wonders were expected of it. All these propositions lend themselves to an evaluation of the extraordinary evolution which took place during the second half of the fifteenth century, and above all in the first ten or twenty years of the following century.

But there was in Leonardo's art a vast quantity of discoveries which could be assimilated, leaving aside the banality of 'a certain smile': the all-conquering pyramidal composition, the hazy and 'lunar' morphology of landscape, and, above all, the *sfumato* handling, the third great technical innovation of the fifteenth century. The responsibility for all this is Leonardo's, whose subtleties of handling all contributed, according to Vasari, to 'give greater relief' to his figures. The quest for smooth and blended handling is no longer concerned with the search for explicit form, which was the great lesson of the quattrocento. His *sfumato* handling may have been suggested to Leonardo by his obsession with the *Paragone* – that is, the desire to create a sense of sculptural form by enveloping form in a soft penumbra which would reduce it in some way to painting, and which would thus demonstrate the superiority and the excellence of painting. The *sfumato* technique, moreover, allowed the artist to achieve a 'merging of tone' by breaking the tones down. There, at least, it seems we are faced with a truly modern discovery, and yet we have always had to ask if the explanation given by Pliny, and translated by Landino in 1476, of the process which Apelles practised, of using glazes (*atramentum*) in order to subdue the colours, did not encourage and even justify the technique.[84] In any case, one can observe a sudden vogue for 'dark painting' around 1515–20, beginning with Raphael's *Transfiguration*.[85]

The result of so much knowledge and subtlety was, paradoxically, to favour the affectation of ultra-refinement at the expense of intellectual content. Nothing is more difficult than to assess the dose of 'Leonardism' which was necessary to Andrea del Sarto, that penetrating master, from whom proceeded the hyper-sensitive and unstable temperaments of the 'mannerists' Rosso and Pontormo. The phase of Italian art which begins about 1520 has taken a long time to be interpreted as it deserves. The term 'mannerism' which first gave it prominence, has probably compromised it by leading to a confusion between the aestheticism of 'art for art's sake' – which is proper to it – with the artificialities of court art. These complex movements, which ought to be more fully interpreted, cannot but be brought into relationship with the crisis in intellectual painting, provoked by the example of Leonardo, fascinating in itself and impossible to follow. Two movements then appeared in the artistic centres of the peninsula, both with important consequences: simultaneously, Correggio in Parma and Titian in Venice prevented painting from becoming just another intellectual game. The former exploited the charms of *sfumato*; the latter the robust solidity of the antique, and together they established and extolled painting for a very long time outside Florentine norms, enshrining its successes in the fullness of a hedonistic and learned culture.

MEN OF LETTERS AND ARTIFICES

Contrary to what historians of Christian art would so frequently have us believe, the extraordinary development of religious art in the Latin world was accompanied regularly, not with laudatory comment or even with marks of agreement, but with warnings about doctrine, and complaints about the excesses to which artists were only too often inclined. From Gerson, who was worried about the too great *imaginum et picturarum varietas* in 1410, to St Antoninus and Savonarola, and finally to the theologian Gilio who published a treatise with the significant title *Degli errori de' pittori* in 1564, the chain of suspicion and reproach was fairly continuous, so that – without having recourse to the bitter sarcasms of such critics as Erasmus or the German Reformers – it is possible to see that in the West art proceeded along a path which the Church did not really control. Practice swamped doctrine, by general consent, at least until the crisis of the sixteenth century.

The emancipation of art during the Renaissance did not arise from any kind of revolt. There was only an acknowledgement, in certain artistic circles, of a professional independence already firmly established, and a greater impatience with critics. On the first page of a drawing book of one of Benozzo Gozzoli's pupils – or perhaps of a collaborator – may be read the phrase 'Painters and poets have always had, and will always have, equal licence'.[86] This is, somewhat altered, a quotation from Horace, a *dictum Horatii*, which had been current for a good two centuries, and the vicissitudes it had undergone express fairly well what might have been a debate on the limits of art during the thirteenth and fourteenth centuries.

At the same moment when the Dominican Catarino was writing, 'In religious matters the old proverb "painters and poets have always had equal licence to attempt anything" is not approved of' (1542),[87] Michelangelo, in the conversations recorded somewhat later by Francisco de Hollanda, corrected the interpretation 'displeasing to painters' that was being given to Horace's verses. He affirmed, 'they mean that painters and poets may dare all, according to my view. They may dare what they please.' This claim to total liberty, in the style and treatment of religious themes, illumines Michelangelo's art. But it is

[255]

not a question of a late struggle between a particularly intransigent artist and censors worried about his new ideas. These ideas can also be found in the famous introduction where Cennino Cennini lays it down that '*si come gli piace*', 'as it shall please him', is to be considered as the status essential to the painter. It had become necessary to affirm, against critics who were not lacking at the time when Giovanni Dominici was attacking the 'abuses' of poets[88] in the same way, a certain independence of movement. The artist, in fact, was not willing to lose the benefit of innovations introduced by Giotto and his successors: he is to be autonomous in the creation of his work of art. Leonardo, so jealous of the liberty of the painter, was to say the same thing a century later.[89]

Approximately at the time when Cennini was writing, Filippo Villani, in his book on Florence (in 1381/2), introduced among the great men 'if mockers will permit, those excellent painters who brought back to life a bloodless and quite dead art' ('*irridentium pace egregios pictores qui artem exanguem et pure extinctam suscitaverunt*'). Despite a few mocking voices, the chronicler relied on the example of historians of Antiquity; he says so, and it is even possible to show that he was inspired by the manner in which Pliny (*H.N.XXXV*, 60-1) describes the accounts of Apollodorus and Zeuxis to arrange those of Cimabue and Giotto.[90] Artists are, however, introduced after the astrologers and the musicians, before the jesters and the captains, which should grieve no one since Villani was conforming to the common usage in the grouping of craftsmen. St Antoninus was to proceed in exactly the same way, in classing the painters with the joiners and barbers (*Summa Theologica*, III, Tit. 12, ch.10). But Villani is very informative about the beginnings of the evolution when dealing with Giotto, for, according to him, there were amongst the public clerics unfavourable to art and for whom artists' claims were laughable, while there were others, of whom Villani was clearly prepared to approve, who proposed the elevation of artists to the level of the 'liberal arts'.[91] This was what Cennino Cennini was reckoning on, and it was to become, increasingly, an obsession with progressive artists. The confirmation of intellectual dignity was not to be derived from knowing rules, but from talent and from the powers of observation on which the rules were founded. The surprising thing is that all these comments were made before 1400, before the competition for the Baptistery doors, and before the appearance of Brunelleschi and Donatello.

In his treatise *De ingenuis moribus et liberalibus adolescentiae studiis* of 1400/2, Pier Paolo Vergerio, in his efforts to establish an educational system based on the liberal arts which alone make men free, mentioned in passing four disciplines which were taught in

Greece: *litterae luctativa musica designativa*, adding concerning this last one, 'this is not now in very common use'.[92] It would be easy to add many other comments of this kind. But what conclusions would come from it? That the intellectual dignity of the art of design, admitted without question by certain groups in certain cities, was far from being unanimously accepted. Behind the remarks and sometimes even the initiatives made by the greatest artists – Leonardo, Michelangelo and such lesser figures as Gozzoli – there was what amounted to a continuous claim for consideration. Many patrons could call upon artists, without granting them the high status of the *letterati*.

The stages of the journey may be measured, when one finds in the first book of the *Cortegiano*, written more than a century later, the quiet statement that a man of quality must 'have a knowledge of painting' as much as of letters. Clearly, there was no question, in Castiglione's worldly dialogue, of a promotion to a university level, where the plastic arts could be assimilated to the fundamental disciplines. But if painting and sculpture are mentioned among the kinds of knowledge essential for a man of a certain rank, then this must be on the one hand because their assimilation to the liberal arts is implicitly considered as having been achieved, and because on the other hand one can then pick and choose among the activities of the mind those which most suit people of taste. It then rather becomes a double promotion, and the evolution is striking if one is willing at least to take seriously proposals emanating from a Roman circle.

The familiarity of 'enlightened' princes with artists, with Francis I of France and the Emperor Charles V imitating Roman pontiffs or the dukes of Mantua in this, is quite certainly a new and remarkable fact. It would be wrong, however, to conclude from this that there was a purely 'élitist' quality to the art of the Renaissance. The commissions came, naturally, from centres of power, but these, whether ecclesiastical or political, were held to certain rules, and had duties in matters of art, and even 'sumptuary' obligations. In public works, the participation of the people is a fact frequently attested more or less everywhere. In Florence, where we are particularly well informed, not only at the time of the 1401 competition, but all through the fifteenth century and even in the sixteenth at the time of Cosimo I (in contradiction to what is sometimes said),[93] a free and sometimes very sharp criticism was exercised concerning works of art, like those of the terrible Lasca, for example, against Zuccari in 1579. Can these facts be made into generalizations? In Rome, in Venice, and in other cities, there were popular reactions, sometimes interesting ones, about buildings, statues, new decorations. The people lived in much closer contact with these works than is generally imagined, and the more so in that grand entries, ceremonies and festivities were frequently created specially for them. Therefore, one can say that art, as a dramatic event as much as a creation of forms, became at the same time part of both aristocratic and popular culture with an authority which was not to be confused with that of clerics, and could even rival theirs.

The remarks and the praises of intellectuals and humanists accompanied an evolution which owed them nothing. In a passage in the *Oratio in principio sui studii* (1455), previously neglected, Lorenzo Valla clearly put it that the flowering of the arts as part of the achievement of a city presupposes the contribution of many men, of practitioners of the arts, of their capacity to communicate and their active competition, rivals striving for the prize. Valla seems to anticipate here the letter of Lorenzo to Federigo d'Aragona (1476) on the role of festivities and rewards in Antiquity, which it would be splendid to imitate. But what interested the humanist was the fact that without the Latin language Rome would not have left anything which authorized this meaning. With the intention always of strengthening praise of the Latin tongue, the same humanist proposed a *topos* which was one of the most firmly established in Italian humanism: the parallel destiny of the arts and letters.[94] Though the arts were thus so close to letters that they had the same fate, decline and regeneration, the idea was not pushed any further.

This formula of 'parallelism' became a stereotype which needs no further illustration, not only until the age of Vasari, but even up to that of Voltaire and the ideologues of the Enlightenment. With the Renaissance the formula was reinforced by the certainty that the same antique culture could revive, and had to be revived, by evoking the same development from the same principles. We have already asked ourselves earlier what to think about this illusion. This universal presentation of recent history suited the humanists, since they were also the dispensers of praises and the major keepers of chronicles, so that the result was a certain number of incidents, essential to the record of artistic life.

The theme of the 'cultural' couplings can be found as early as Quintilian, who saw in it an excellent *topos* (*Inst. Orat.* XII, X, 11); Lorenzo Valla exactly repeated it, in order to give a certain intelligibility to recent history. The idea of resting an artistic reputation on literary fame played a powerful role in the 'twinning': Dante–Giotto appeared from the trecento onwards. The equation even served, it seems, as a framework on which Vasari could later construct his Life of Giotto.[95] A remarkable and fortunate association linked, in Venice, Ariosto and

Titian. In contrast to such ready-mades as references to Apelles or Zeuxis, which could be applied to many kinds of artist, the Venetian parallel was not a vague label. There are other examples too.

There was, however, a precise meeting-point between the craft of the writer and that of the artist. Literature, and above all the new literature, that which took over for its own purposes the themes and aims of Greek and Roman texts, came closest to artistic activity in the description of imaginary works – the supreme classic procedure with the epic – or the evocation of real works, which is also covered by the classical Greek term ἔκφρασις (ekphrasis). It is a very large question of which we are only beginning to realize the profound implications.[96] Its importance obviously derives from the fact that the memory of so many antique works has been transmitted by texts of this kind (Lucian), or by elliptical mentions in Pliny which constitute that many ἐκφράσεις in nuce. Moreover, this literary form was used by Byzantine pedagogy as a fundamental exercise, which; through the intermediary of Guarino of Verona, was enthusiastically adopted by humanists. It was to become, in the emerging literature of art, an almost obligatory element in treatises and histories; Vasari was to dedicate some of his more memorable pages to it.

But the Renaissance utilization of ἔκφρασις is subject, for internal reasons, to serious limitations; its documentary value has to be treated with care. The *descriptio* tends, in effect, to free the *idea* underlying the work of art; in order to do this, it is forced to make use of explanatory devices which may involve introducing details essential to the explanation which had no part in the composition, as they might have done – perhaps even as they should have done. In the epigrams or the epistles where it is to be found, ἔκφρασις is not the direct expression of a reaction to the work, but primarily an interpretation of its meaning. This paradox is sufficient to explain why the Renaissance hardly ever tried to find a 'poetic equivalent', even if by chance some analogies to a statue or a picture strike us today. The divide between the two states is stressed in a way by the abundant literature of epigrams, references and catalogues. When they are analysed, one sees that the contribution made by the works constantly exceeds what is said in the texts, which have, at least, the merit of recording their existence and their creators.

It would be a very great advance indeed to be able to know and interpret the relationship between learned men and artists. This would be something original – a novelty for the period. But nothing is more difficult to reconstitute; important information is either lacking or is contradictory. The programme for the third Baptistery doors was drawn up by Leonardo Bruni in 1424, at a moment when it was not certain that the execution was going to be confided to Ghiberti. The Chancellor also defined the style, and for him, as is well known, the sculptor was merely an executant.[97] Ghiberti's flexible personality enabled him to get the upper hand; but the appearance of amateurs and of collectors, like Niccolò Niccoli, and of artists of great ability could, on the other hand, work in a manner more favourable to the creators of works of art. To the extent of involving them in the decisions about the programmes? No one knows.

Contracts reveal a certain reserve, often a mistrust, with regard to the conduct of artists, which often must have been fairly cavalier.[98] The *quidlibet audendi potestas* is much clearer in this context; the *artifex* was considered as a craftsman; this role was quite suitable, but he intended to exercise fully his right of composing, illustrating, developing the programme 'as best it pleased him'. Only the personality of the artist could claim the right to modify this relationship. Michelangelo was able to require a modification of the project planned for the Sistine ceiling. It could also happen that a strong personality surprised the commissioner, as happened with Titian and the *Assunta* of 1519. It was certainly a far too commonly held naive opinion among the historians of the last century to believe the artist was responsible, or even shared the responsibility for the learned, theological or humanist programme of his works. All that can be said is that, whether by intellectual affinity or not, he assumed this responsibility, though Perugino and Sodoma, for instance, were incredibly casual in this respect.

As we only rarely know the author of some of the particularly important programmes, it has seemed sensible to try to discover, whenever possible, the presence of an intellectual either in the circle of the artist or the patron who might be thought to have been responsible for the learned arrangement of the work. For example, the moral allegories of Bartolomeo Scala served as a framework for the panels of the frieze which the Chancellor commissioned from Bertoldo for his palace;[99] Botticelli's allegories have been connected with Ficino's epistles on *Venus Humanitas*;[100] and more recently the Hermetic views of Aegidius of Viterbo have been associated with the cycle in the Stanza della Segnatura.[101] These identifications, even if they assign intellectual responsibilities, are only indications; one artist could be replaced by another; and during the course of execution, the artist might well have taken liberties with the guidelines which he had been given. The difficulties which Isabella d'Este had with her painters throw an unfavourable light on the relations between artists and the literary 'arguments' which were given to them.[102]

It is, therefore, not without interest to note the spread in the use of signatures, a phenomenon which from being exceptional became current, and which is paralleled by another novelty of the age, the self-portrait.[103] Poliziano had noted the custom of using in signatures placed on vases or statues: εποιε (epoie) meaning *faciebat*, instead of εποιησε (epoiese), *fecit* (*Miscellanea*, ch. XLVII). The writers repeated after him, that this was a mark of modesty, a sort of artisan's scruple.[104] But with its commercial purpose, a signature operated as a means of achieving immortality. Nevertheless, the practice remained a very uneven one. Leonardo and his disciples never signed, the practice was not a constant one in Tuscany, and it is especially in north Italy and particularly in Venice that the *cartellino* developed. It became almost a habit with the Bellini, and with Carpaccio, for instance, it brings out interesting variations from *finxit* instead of *pinxit*, and even *fingebat*, to types of lettering which sometimes clearly imitate the epigraphy of inscriptions;[105] in fact, a whole humanist – even erudite – parade which serves to gain for the artist the prestige of an *auctor*.

The critical examination of titles – even of nicknames – given to works deserves to be studied. Certain names – *lo Zuccone, la Porta del Paradiso* – reveal the charms or spites of folklore, but the majority of specific titles are late-comers, and are due to the evolution of catalogues or to the vogue for prints of a completely fantasy type – Carpaccio's *Courtesans*, for example; or even totally falsifying – *la Derelitta* by Botticelli (which is neither a woman, nor a Botticelli). They have often led commentators astray.

We find, therefore – by hunting for them a bit – fairly explicit testimonies of the authority or the growing self-confidence of artists of a certain rank in a society which had a great need for works of art, images and artistic manifestations. But only rarely do we find written statements able to give an account – other than indirectly – of corresponding experiences. From this we may conclude that the artistic language, with the great figures that animate it, was finally, in certain respects, richer, more elaborate, susceptible of a greater number of shades of meaning, than the literary or philosophical language. Sometimes we are left with this impression, which is the same as to say that in their proper degrees the arts of space and figuration, treated then with an undeniable mastery, were able in some way to register a host of shades of meaning and new discoveries which are still a never-ending source of new perceptions and interpretations. But one must never fail to recognize the continuous semantic effort made in Italy, from Petrarch to Galileo, to create a critical language endowed with suitable means. The Latin term *disegnatio* and its Italian derivative *disegno* meet in the humanist vocabulary the Greek term *graphice*. From it,

Poliziano developed, with an entirely Tuscan quality of penetration, anticipating Michelangelo and Vasari, the universal principle of the arts.[106] He isolated the strict and abstract function of drawing. The attempt was favoured by the two values attached to *graphikè* and by the analogy writing–drawing, literature–painting, which all the authors delighted to harp on.[107] But caught thus in the sterility of humanist formulas the attempt failed, and it was *disegno* with its host of ambiguities which won, and came to define the principle of principles.

In other instances, the reading of the authors of Antiquity could suggest interesting turns of language. His knowledge of Pliny enabled Paolo Giovio to introduce the notion of *parerga* for the details which enrich the composition, as in Dosso Dossi, and this very valuable term had a certain currency[108] but not that of *obliquitates* to indicate the surprising viewpoints of a Titian, for example.[109] Even more interesting is the appearance of terms expressing appreciation where the derivation and the origin are not perfectly clear: words such as *vago*, *vaghezza*, which are found in Dante and Boccaccio, reappear with Leonardo, and with a nuance of charm, coquetry and an indefinable preciosity, infuse the works of Correggio and Parmigianino.[110] In the same way, *pellegrino*, *bizzaro* and the like, make their way from letters into critical literature, thanks to Vasari and his colleagues who made great use of the terms, evidently typical of mannerism.[111] Meanwhile, the didactic language of treatises and the technical vocabulary for perspective, colour and so forth, achieved for the plastic arts the equivalent of what was being organized for music; the professional vocabulary remained Italian for a long time.

It may be noted that around the 'great figures' yet another type of artistic literature was born. The preoccupation with the treatise, the complete manual of theory, treating the forms and the laws of art by principles and their consequences, had in a manner of speaking been taken over by Leonardo. By a kind of unwritten rule (derived perhaps from a naive continuation of Antiquity) only dead artists were included in the *uomini famosi*. It is striking that the first biography published during the lifetime of the artist was that of Michelangelo, and even more so that the first history of art placed him at the culminating point of evolution. It remained for Venice, however, to witness the foundation by Aretino, in the circle around Titian, of that *aura* of intimidation, news and gossip which defines journalistic criticism.

It has seemed reasonable to place one or two outstanding personalities of the Renaissance in a central position in each of the directions discussed: the antique, myth and nature. This procedure does not appear to be in conformity with the search for a highly diversified basis and the conviction that the 'Renaissance' is the sum of innumerable small components. But it is difficult to proceed otherwise, once one believes that it is necessary *also* to show that at a certain moment a stage had been reached where the idea arose that the final achievement had been reached with and through these outstanding figures. Everything seemed to start from the feeling that a deficiency had to be made good, an order had to be rediscovered; and by a sequence of happy accidents, there was suddenly a moment of resolution, a feeling that one could confront the antique and history from a position of equality. The next generation could have the feeling, always because of the now sacred 'heroes', that the Ideal, the 'Golden Age' was now behind them. To the coming period was now opposed as a counterpart a phase of fixity, of history and of the exploitation of the storehouse it provided. The analysis of these incredible vicissitudes are part of the study of the Renaissance; it is far from being exhausted.

The extravagant cult of these artists, who were suddenly treated almost fanatically as divinities, was in this sense essential. The mediation of the 'geniuses', pivots of a new history, formed an introduction to a convincing modern organization. Just as one had leaned on the antique, so now one leaned on these masters who were rivals between themselves and watched one another closely, but who were supported by a kind of marvelling consensus: Leonardo, Bramante, Michelangelo, Raphael, Giorgione. Each one of them would later be identified in another artist who extended his role while shifting his balance: Correggio, Parmigianino, Pontormo, Titian.

What unites all these figures, all these forces so solidly embodied, is something which seems simple and which it may also seem naive to formulate, given the degeneration in the meaning of words: this is the aspiration towards beauty. During the Renaissance the word was on every lip, with meanings which are always confused and difficult to make out. But, at least, it never appears as one of the rewards, as one of the fruits of labour, or the prize for success; beauty is felt as a universal motive force, as the principle of an activity which informs all nature – *natura artifex* – and is concentrated in man and raises him, or can raise him, above himself. If the philosophy of Marsilio Ficino, with its interminable literary rehashings, has drawn so many historians to study it for a half century now, it is doubtless because of its odd mixture of themes of theological speculation with all sorts of aesthetic overtones. It tackles themes in which this aspiration, this craving – to use twentieth-century language – appears to be present as a fact which it seems essential to restore to so many initiatives without considering either needs or utility, profane or religious.

The Renaissance was, in fact, the period when the aesthetic plea invaded the fully awakened philosophical and moral conscience, both individual and social. This conclusion would be of utter banalitiy, if we did not add that, contrary to Platonic hopes, it did not demonstrate any human aptitude for combining in one achievement the Beautiful, the True and the Good.

Translated from the French by Linda Murray.

NOTES

1 P.O. Kristeller, 'The modern system of the arts' (1951), republished in *Renaissance Thought, II: Papers on Humanism and the Arts* (New York, 1965), ch. IX.

2 The best synthesis still seems to be that by E. Panofsky, 'Renaissance – self-definition or self-deception?', in *Renaissance and Renascences in Western Art* (Stockholm, 1960), ch. I.

3 See A. Chastel, *Le mythe de la Renaissance* (Geneva, 1969), and M. Baxandall, *Giotto and the Orators. Humanist Observers of Painting in Italy and the Discovery of Pictorial Composition, 1350–1450* (Oxford, 1971).

4 R. Krautheimer, *Lorenzo Ghiberti* (Princeton, 1956); J.S. Ackerman, ' "Ars sine scientia nihil' ': Gothic theory of architecture at the Cathedral of Milan' in *Art Bulletin*, XXVI (1949), 84ff.

5 With a whole range of 'explanations' which run from the specific virtue of the 'air' (Vasari) to the emergence of the 'bourgeois' mentality (F. Antal).

6 G. Previtali, *La Fortuna dei primitivi, dal Vasari ai neo-classici* (Turin, 1964), on the arguments concerning Tuscan primacy and anti-Vasarianism in the seventeenth and eighteenth centuries.

7 Bernard Berenson can reasonably be called the heir of the Vasarian tradition, which was opposed by Longhi and Cesare Brandi, among others.

8 The discovery of the Laocoön (1506), the Belvedere Apollo (1510), the Farnese Bull, etc. See R. Lanciani, *Storia degli scavi di Roma*, 2 vols (Rome, 1902 and 1912, re-ed. Rome, 1975).

9 The Palazzo Valle Capranica, the Palazzo Sassi, etc., described in U. Aldrovandi, *Le antichità di Roma* (Rome, 1558); drawn by Marten Heemskerck, see C. Hülsen and H. Egger, *Die römischen Skizzenbücher von Marten van Heemskerck*, 2 vols (Berlin 1913–16, re-ed. 1975).

10 H. Rupprich, *Dürers schriftlicher Nachlass*, vol. 2 (Berlin, 1966). Also W.M. Conway, *The writings of Albrecht Dürer* (London, 1958). Dürer, *Lettres et écrits théoriques*, ed. P. Vaisse (Paris, 1964).

11 For example the two pictures by Apelles, *Venus Anadyomene* (in Pliny) and the *Calumny* of Apelles (in Lucian) which Botticelli tried to recreate. On the *Calumny* of Apelles, see. R. Förster, 'Die Verleumdung des Apelles in

der Renaissance', in *Jahrbuch der königlich Preussischen Kunstsamm-lungen*, VIII (1887), 29–56, and 89–113; G.A. Giglioli, 'La Calunnia di Apelle' in *Rassegna d'Arte*, VII (1920), 173ff.

12 B. Fazio, *De viris illustribus* (*c.* 1456; ed. Florence, 1745).

13 A. Manetti, *Vita de Filippo di Ser Brunellesco* (*c.* 1485; ed. E. Toesca, Florence, 1927); critical edn by Domenico de Robertis (Milan, 1976); English edn by Howard Saalman (London–Pennsylvania, 1970).

14 Krautheimer, op. cit., 16.

15 The example of Titian. See R.W. Kennedy, '*Apelles redivivus*' in *Essays in Memory of Karl Lehmann* (New York, 1964), 160ff.

16 Krautheimer, op. cit., 72.

17 H. Baron, *Leonardo Bruni Aretino. Humanistisch-philosophische Schriften* (Leipzig, 1928), 210.

18 J. Pope-Hennessy, *Italian Renaissance Sculpture* (London, 1958), 41, pl. XL.

19 F. Schottmüller, 'Zwei Grabmäler der Renaissance und ihre antiken Vorbilder', *Repertorium für Kunstwissenschaft*, XXVI (1902), 401–3.

20 H. Egger, 'Francesca Tornabuoni und ihre Grabstätte' in *Sta Maria sopra Minerva* (Vienna, 1934).

21 Pope-Hennessy, *Italian Renaissance Sculpture*, 345ff.

22 Which might also be said of the style of Fracastoro, for which see F. Saxl, 'Pagan sacrifice in the Italian Renaissance', *Journal of the Warburg Institute*, II (1939), 345, who recalls that he was a friend of the della Torre.

23 The point of view developed here does not agree with the demonstration by E.H. Gombrich, 'The style "*all'antica*": imitation and assimilation' (1961), republished in *Norm and Form* (London, 1966), which argues that the style of Giulio Romano shows a new inventive force in the use of the antique model. This analysis is perfectly justified, but it remains that Giulio intended to develop a style '*all'antica*'; others, who used the same repertory, pushed it less far.

24 J. Wilde, 'Eine Studie Michelangelos nach der Antike', *Mitteilungen des kunsthistorischen Instituts in Florenz*, IV (1932), 41–64.

25 One of the most surprising is that of the Hermaphrodite in the sky of the *Conversion of St Paul* in the Cappella Paolina, difficult to explain, except as an example of the insertion at all costs of the beautiful in sacred art.

26 According to the still-valid definition in H. Wölfflin, *Die classische Kunst* (Munich, 1898) (English edn as *Classic Art*, London, 1952 and later). See also A. Hekler, 'Michelangelo und die Antike', *Wiener Jahrbuch für Kunstgeschichte*, VII (1930), 201ff.

27 This was at least Vasari's theory, which is made clear in an addition to the 1568 edition (Milanesi, IV, 373). This opinion provoked a protest from G.B. Bellori, *Descrizione delle imagini dipinte da Rafaelle d' Urbino* (Rome, 1695, reprinted 1968), 86. See also J. Pope-Hennessy, *Raphael* (London, 1970), 31.

28 J. Evans, *Pattern: a Study of Ornament in Western Europe from 1180 to 1900*, 2 vols (Oxford, 1931).

29 M. Meiss, 'Towards a more comprehensive Renaissance paleography', *Art Bulletin*, XLII (1960), republished in *The Painter's Choice* (New York,

[265]

1976); J. Sparrow, *Visible Words* (Cambridge, 1969).

30 G. Mardersteig, 'Leon-Battista Alberti e la rinascita del carattere lapidario romano nel Quattrocento', *Italia medioevale e umanistica*, II (1959), 285ff.

31 R. Wittkower, 'Hieroglyphics in the early Renaissance' (1972), republished in *Allegory and the Migration of Symbols* (London, 1977), ch.8.

32 The work by E. Iversen, *The Myth of Egypt and its Hieroglyphs in European Tradition* (Copenhagen, 1961), remains a classic. The astonishing vicissitudes of the Egyptian 'myth' have been studied by J. Baltrusaitis, *La Quête d'Isis* (Paris, 1967).

33 The tomb of Canon Hubert Millemans (d. 1558) in Ste-Croix in Liège, illus. in E. Panofsky, *Tomb Sculpture* (London, 1964), no. 312 a/b.

34 R. Watkins, 'Leon-Battista Alberti's emblem, the Winged-Eye and his name Leo', *Mitteilungen des kunsthistorischen Instituts in Florenz*, IX (1959–60), 256ff.

35 Thanks to the Latin commentary of Pirckheimer, which contains all the references to Horus Apollo and to the contemporary events. See E. Panofsky, *Albrecht Dürer* (Princeton, 1943), 170, and on Pirckheimer, W.P. Eckert and Ch. von Imhoff, *Willibald Pirckheimer Dürers Freund* (Cologne, 1971).

36 E.H. Gombrich, '*Icones simbolicae*', reprinted in *Symbolic Images* (London, 1972), and E. Garin, in particular 'Le favole antiche' (1953), republished in *Medioevo e Rinascimento* (Bari, 1954).

37 N. Dacos, *La découverte de la Domus Aurea et la formation des grotesques à la Renaissance* (London, 1969).

38 N. Dacos, *Le Logge di Raffaello. Maestro e bottega di fronte all'antico* (Rome, 1977).

39 There is an excellent example in the Marsyas by Verrocchio. See W.R. Valentiner, 'Der rote Marsyas des Verrocchio', *Pantheon*, XX (1937), 329.

40 Vasari, *Vita di Bramante da Urbino*, ed. Milanesi, IV, 162.

41 J. Schlosser-Magnino, *La letteratura artistica*, 3rd edn brought up to date by O. Kurz (Florence, 1964).

42 P.G. Hamberg, 'G.B. da Sangallo detto il Gobbo e Vitruvio . . .', *Palladio*, VIII (1958), 15–21.

43 On Palladio and the antique, see L. Polacco, 'La posizione di Andrea Palladio di fronte all'antichità', *Bollettino del CISA*, VII (1965), and R. Wittkower, *Palladio and Palladianism* (London, 1974).

44 For Venice, see J. Schulz, *Venetian Painted Ceilings of the Renaissance* (Berkeley, 1968).

45 In V. Golzio, *Raffaello nei documenti, nelle testimonianze dei contemporanei e nella letteratura del suo secolo* (Vatican City, 1936; republished 1972). An English translation of the letter is in E.G. Holt, *A Documentary History of Art*, I (New York, 1957).

46 M. Warnke, 'Italienische Bildtabernakel bis zum Frühbarock', *Münchner Jahrbuch der bildenden Kunst*, XIX (1968), 61–102.

47 This state of doubt is well illustrated by the legend of St Gregory as a destroyer of idols which, during the fifteenth century, was an embarrassment to modernists. See T. Buddensieg, 'Gregory the Great, the

destroyer of pagan idols. The history of a medieval legend concerning the decline of ancient art and literature', *Journal of the Warburg and Courtauld Institutes*, XXVIII (1965), 44–65.

48 W.S. Hecksher, under 'Dornenzieher', in *Reallexikon zur deutschen Kunstgeschichte*, ed. O. Schmidt, IV, col. 290.

49 H.W. Janson, 'La signification politique du David en bronze de Donatello', *Revue de l'art*, 39 (1978), which leads the author to redate the work before 1430, as given in his *The Sculpture of Donatello*, 2 (Princeton, 1955), 77.

50 J. Seznec, *The Survival of the Pagan Gods* (New York, 1953). E. Garin, 'Le favole antiche', *La Rassegna della letteratura Italiana* (Oct.–Dec. 1953), 12.

51 C.S. Lewis, *The Discarded Image, an Introduction to Medieval and Renaissance Literature* (Cambridge, 1964).

52 C.S. Lewis, *The Allegory of Love* (Oxford, 1936), 83: 'No religion so long as it is believed, can have that kind of beauty which we find in the gods of Titian and Botticelli, or of our own romantic poets.'

53 Letter to Francesco Valori, 8 November 1482, Ep. XII, *Opera omnia* (Basle, 1576), 948.

54 E. Garin, *Les polémiques contre l'astrologie à la Renaissance*, lectures given in the College de France 1976; Italian edn *Le zodiaco della vita* (Rome, 1976).

55 In the sacristy of S. Lorenzo: the sky of 9 July 1422. See Seznec, *Pagan Gods*, 77. A. Warburg, 'Italienische Kunst und internationale Astrologie im Palazzo Schifanoia in Ferrara' (1922), reprinted in *Gesammelte Schriften*, I (Leipzig, 1932), remains the fundamental work on the Palazzo Schifanoia frescoes.

56 One should always consult E. Panofsky and F. Saxl, 'Classical mythology in medieval art', *Metropolitan Museum Studies*, IV (1933), 2, which should be supplemented by E. Panofsky, *Studies in Iconology* (New York, 1939), 18ff, and Seznec, op. cit.

57 Seznec, *Pagan Gods*, 236ff.

58 This syncretism of mythology easily permits the incorporation, though with considerable latitude, into set schemes, of the gods of Asia and America. See L. Pignoria, *Discorso intorno le deità delle Indie Orientali et Occidentali* . . . (Padua, 1615). J. Seznec, 'Un essai de mythologie comparée . . .', in *Mélanges d'Archéologie et d'Histoire* (Rome, 1931).

59 F. Saxl, 'Titian and Pietro Aretino' (1935), reprinted in *Lectures* (London, 1957), 162ff.

60 Th. Reff, 'The meaning of Titian's *Venus of Urbino*', *Pantheon*, XXI (1963), 159ff.

61 E. Verheyen, 'Correggio's *Amori di Giove*', *Journal of the Warburg and Courtauld Institutes*, XXIX (1966), 160ff.

62 A good example is the *Bacchus* by Jacopo Sansovino, a life-sized nude inspired by the antique. See J. Pope-Hennessy, *Italian High Renaissance and Baroque Sculpture*, 2 (London, 1972), 351–2. Fra Bartolommeo often used it as a model, notably in the *St Sebastian* destined for the convent of S. Marco (1515–16). According to Vasari, the artist, irritated by criticisms 'that he didn't know how to do nudes', was so successful that less than ten years

later the work was removed as lascivious and pagan (ed. Club del Libro, III, 489). See also J. Cox-Rearick, 'Fra Bartolommeo's St Mark Evangelist and St Sebastian with an angel', *Mitteilungen des kunsthistorischen Instituts in Florenz*, XVIII (1974), 3, 339ff.

63 '*Haud scio utrum sit magis reprehendum, si christianis prophana tractet prophane, christianum se est dissimulans, an si materias christianas tractet paganice.*' In A. Renaudet, *Erasme et l'Italie* (Geneva, 1954), 202.

64 The present state of the work done on this theme since the volumes published by J. Jacquot from 1956 onwards in *CNRS*, may be found in A.M. Lecoq, 'La *Città festeggiante*', *Revue de l'art*, 33 (1976).

65 W. Rubsamen, 'The music for *Quant' è bella giovinezza* and other carnival songs by Lorenzo de' Medici', in Ch. Singleton (ed.), *Art, Science, and History in the Renaissance* (Baltimore, 1967), 163ff.

66 See for example E. Bertaux, 'Botticelli costumier' in *Etudes d'Histoire et d'Art* (Paris, 1911).

67 J. Seznec, *Pagan Gods*.

68 A. Michel, 'The earliest dance-manuals', *Medievalia et Humanistica*, III (1945), 119–24. M. Baxandall, *Painting and Experience in Fifteenth-Century Italy* (Oxford, 1972), 77ff., cites the *De arte saltandi et choreas ducendi* by Domenico da Piacenza (*c.* 1440 *et seq.*), in the B.N. Paris, and the *Trattato dell'arte del ballo* by Guglielmo Ebreo (*c.* 1470), in the B.N. Paris. The treatise by Domenico da Piacenza underlines under the heading of '*maniera*' the sense of a movement which must be 'neither too much nor too little, so gentle the person seems like a double-oared gondola crossing the ripples of a calm sea'.

69 G. Paccagnini, *Pisanello e il ciclo cavalleresco di Mantova* (Milan, 1972). See also W. Juren, 'Pisanello', *Revue de l'art*, 27 (1975).

70 B. Degenhart and A. Schmitt, 'Gentile da Fabriano in Rom und die Anfänge des Antikenstudiums', *Münchner Jahrbuch der bildenden Kunst* (1960).

71 The sonnet written by Angelo Galli of Urbino in honour of Pisanello (1442) is often quoted:

> *Arte, mesura, aere et disegno*
> *Manera, prospectiva et naturale,*
> *Gli ha dato il celo per mirabil dono.*

See Baxandall, *Painting and Experience*, 77. One may enlarge at will the brief mention in Panofsky, *Renaissance and Renascences*, 27, n. 3.

72 A. Warburg, 'Delle imprese amorose . . . ' (1905), reprinted in *Gesammelte Schriften*, I (Leipzig, 1932), 85.

73 We would be inclined to believe that the sixteen paintings of *moresca* mentioned in the inventory of Poggio a Cajano (see E. Tietze-Conrat, *Dwarfs and Jesters in Art*, London, 1957) may find a parallel in the sixteen statuettes by Grasser placed about 1480 in the Rathaus in Innsbruck.

74 P.O. Kristeller, 'Music and learning in the early Italian Renaissance' (1947), republished in *Studies in Renaissance Thought and Letters* (Rome, 1956), 451ff, and in *Renaissance Thought, II: Papers on Humanism and the Arts* (New York, 1965), ch. VIII.

We are now able to define the personality of the great 'universal' composer – one, that is, as admired, sung and imitated both north and south of the Alps, at once Flemish by the tradition of counterpoint, and active in Milan and Ferrara. This was the composer most fully published by the early musical editions, which were, as we know, those of Venice from 1502 onwards. 'We can give to Josquin, the pupil of Ockeghem, in music the same place as we give to our Michelangelo in architecture, painting and sculpture,' wrote Cosimo Bartoli in 1567 in his *Ragionamenti Accademici*. See H. Oustoff, *Josquin Desprez*, 2 vols (Tusing, 1962 and 1965); E.E. Lowinsky (ed.), *Josquin des Prez* (Oxford, 1977).

75 According to the formula of Panofsky, *Renaissance and Renascences*, 168, which still appears valid.

76 '*Non è casa di ciavatini che paesi tedeschi non siano*' (letter from Vasari to Varchi, 12 February 1547).

77 E. Panofsky, *Early Netherlandish Painting. Its Origin and Character* (Cambridge, Mass., 1953).

78 Francesco d'Ollanda records Michelangelo's anti-landscape attitude in *Da pintura antigua. Dialogos em Roma* (c. 1550), Italian edn by E. Spina-Berelli (Milan, 1964).

79 A. Chastel, *The Golden Age of the Renaissance: Italy 1460–1500* (London, 1965), 245ff.

80 A. Chastel, 'Les apories de la perspective au quattrocento' in *Actes du colloque* (Milan, 1977): *La perspettiva rinascimentale* (Florence, 1980).

81 Ms. B. 2038 of the Institut de France, 18/1, on the three kinds of perspective.

82 J. Ackerman, 'Science and art in the work of Leonardo', in *Leonardo's Legacy* (Berkeley, 1969), 205ff.

83 Cod. Urb. 36/36 v°; ed. McMahon, no. 280, 113.

84 On Leonardo and the antique: Sir Kenneth Clark, 'Leonardo and the antique', in *Leonardo's Legacy*, cited above, 1ff. The words of Leonardo, '*L'imitazione delle cose antiche é più laudabile che le moderne*' (Cod. Atl. 147 r° (b)) are only applicable to the problem of the equestrian statue.

85 For all these points see K. Weil Garris Posner, *Leonardo and Central Italian Art, 1515–1550* (New York, 1974).

86 '*Pictoribus atque poetis semper fuit et erit aequa potestas.*' Cf. B. Degenhart and A. Schmitt, *Corpus der italienischen Zeichnungen, 1300–1450*, 4 vols (Berlin, 1968), cat. no. 44, fol? 31. Studied on 478ff.

87 '*Non in causa religionis probatur quod quidam dixit: pictoribus atque poetis quidlibet audendi semper fuit aequa potestas.*' Similarly in G. Gilio (1564), '*il detto d'Orazio che al pittore e al poeta ogni cosa lecita sia*'. All these texts are brought together in A. Chastel, 'Le *dictum Horatii* "*quidlibet audendi potestas*" et les artistes (XIIIe–XVIe siècles)' in the *Comptes-rendus de l'Académie des Inscriptions et Belles-Lettres* (1977), 30ff., now in *Fables, Formes, Figures*, I (Paris, 1978), no. 7.

88 E. Garin, *Il pensiero pedagogico dell'Umanismo* (Florence, 1958), 1ff, has shown the importance for the future of the polemic between Dominici and Salutati.

89 The reaction against the hypocrites who claimed to forbid painters to draw on a Sunday (Cod. Urb. 38v/39r) is typical.

90 Baxandall, *Giotto and the Orators*, 66ff.

91 'Many people think – and not without reason – that painters are not inferior in intellect to those who are masters of the liberal arts, since these derive the principles of art, locked up in writing, from study and learning, while painters obtain their skill in art solely from depth of intellect and power of memory' (*'existimantibus multis nec stulte quidem pictores non inferioris ingenii his quos liberales artes fecere magistros cum illi artium precepta scripturis demandata studio atque doctrina percipiant, hii solum ab alto ingenio tenacique memoria, que in arte sentiant, exigant'*), quoted ibid., 147.

92 *'Nunc in usu non est pro liberali.'* Cf. Garin, *Il pensiero pedagogico*, 132.

93 Z. Wazbinski, 'Artisti e pubblico nella Firenze del Cinquecento', *Paragone*, 327 (May 1977), 3ff. There are many anecdotes of this type in Vasari's Lives. Savonarola was worried about the kind of aberration evoked by certain works (1492), etc. See also M. Wackernagel, *Der Lebensraum des Künstlers in der florentinischen Renaissance* (Leipzig, 1938), 292ff.

94 M. Baxandall, *Giotto and the Orators*, 117–20, texts on 171 and 176.

95 We have analysed this in 'Giotto coetaneo di Dante' in the *Festschrift H. Heydenreich* (Munich, 1964), which is to be complemented by E.H. Gombrich, 'Giotto's portrait of Dante', *Burlington Magazine* (August 1979).

96 H. Maguire, 'Truth and convention in Byzantine descriptions of works of art', *Dumbarton Oaks Papers*, 28 (1974); S.L. Alpers, *'Ekphrasis* and aesthetic attitudes in Vasari's Lives', *Journal of the Warburg and Courtauld Institutes*, XXIII (1960). On the role of Guarino, disciple of the Greeks, and his 'descriptions', see M. Baxandall, 'Guarino, Pisanello, and Manuel Chrysoloras' in the same journal, XXVIII (1965), as a complement to the pages on Guarino in E. Garin, *L'educazione dell'uomo moderno* (Florence, 1966).

97 Krautheimer, op. cit., 302.

98 The example of Filippo Lippi and his trial: see D.S. Chambers, *Patrons and Artists in the Italian Renaissance* (London, 1970), 201.

99 A. Parronchi, 'The language of humanism and the language of sculpture', *Journal of the Warburg and Courtauld Institutes*, XXVII (1964), 108–36.

100 E.H. Gombrich, 'Botticelli's mythologies' (1945), reprinted in *Symbolic Images: Studies in the Art of the Renaissance* (London, 1972).

101 H. Pfeiffer, *Zur Ikonographie von Raffaels Disputa: Egidio da Viterbo und die christliche-platonische Konzeption der Stanza della Segnatura*, Miscellanea Historiae Pontificiae, no. 37 (Rome, 1975).

102 It is not possible to accept the daring conclusions – criticized so energetically by C. Dionisotti in *Art Bulletin* (September 1950) – of E. Wind in *Bellini's Feast of the Gods* (Cambridge, Mass., 1948), but in it may be found the amusing history of Isabella and 'her' painters.

103 The self-portrait still remains to be studied.

104 In particular, P. Pino, *Dialogo di Pittura* (Venice, 1548), ed. P. Barocchi (Bari, 1960). On the *cartellino*, see Z. Wazbinski, 'Le *cartellino*', *Pantheon*

(1963), 278–83. On the general problem of signatures, see *Revue de l'art*, 26 (1974).

105 M. Meiss, 'Towards a more comprehensive Renaissance paleography' (1960).

106 *Panepistemon* (ed. Basle, 1553), 469.

107 Example: P. Gauricus, *De sculptura* (1504), ed. Chastel-Klein (Geneva, 1969).

108 Pliny, *Nat. Hist.*, XXXV, 101. See also E.H. Gombrich, 'The Renaissance theory of art and the rise of landscape' (1953), reprinted in *Norm and Form* (London, 1966), 113.

109 Pliny, ibid., 56 and 90. See also P. Giovio, *Fragmentum trium dialogorum* (*c.* 1525), in P. Barocchi (ed.), *Scritti d'arte del Cinquecento*, I (Milan–Naples, 1971), 22.

110 A. Castellano, 'Storia d'una parola letteraria, "vago" ', *Archivio glottologico italiano*, XLVIII (1963), 126ff.

111 See C. Ossola, *Autunno del Rinascimento* (Florence, 1971).

8

PROBLEMS OF THE
SCIENTIFIC RENAISSANCE

MARIE BOAS HALL

E WHO SETS out to honour a Cicero would do well to take him as a guide. Our Cicero produced a guide-book to this very problem in the now well-known and highly influential collection of lectures and essays entitled *Scienze e vita civile nel Rinascimento.*[1] The problems raised in it (and largely solved) are so very much the most necessary to consider in relation to Renaissance science that a paraphrase would almost suffice to give a fair picture of the state of such studies at the present time, a dozen years later. But Eugenio Garin would never be content merely to receive his own words back again, nor would this do him sufficient honour. He deserves to have set before him some indication of his influence, as well as of the ways in which scholarship since the publication of his book has both accepted and extended his views of the nature of the pursuit of science during the Renaissance. This is most striking when one examines a wider scene than he attempted, in extending his method to Europe as a whole, considering, that is to say, not the Italian scene alone (viable historical unit though it is) but the scientific, intellectual and social scene on a European-wide scale. For in this period intellectual activity north of the Alps was in no less a thriving state than was the case south of the Alps, and influences spread relatively rapidly from north to south and back again as books, correspondence and men journeyed to and fro.

Consideration of the scientific and social scene north of the Alps immediately produces our first problem: that of historical periodization. Like most writers focusing upon the Italian scene, Garin saw no need to inquire whether the term 'Renaissance' represented a viable and enduring historical concept. The thriving state of fifteenth-century Italian life and culture makes it seem quite natural to those who look first and foremost at Italy that something dramatic should be happening to society as a whole – and hence presumably to science – which merits a new appellation. This has never been the case with historians of science who look first at society north of the Alps; here, as far as the intellectual scene is concerned, the 'Middle Ages' have seemed to many to melt more imperceptibly into the 'modern' period – or to put it another way, there appeared to be less of a gap between the Middle Ages and the scientific revolution of the seventeenth century – than was the case in Italy. This has always been especially true for those who saw medieval science in terms of a 'Renaissance of the twelfth century' (to use Charles Homer Hoskins' phrase). Just because there was more of a 'Dark Age' in the North, perhaps, the 'High Middle Ages' were intellectually most startling and productive north of the Alps; hence, in turn, the changes of the fifteenth century seemed less novel and notable and so the term Renaissance less applicable. The extreme case was that of Lynn Thorndike who, deeply impressed by the range and scope of thirteenth-century thought, saw the fifteenth century as a period of decline in scientific activity, a new dark age.[2] No writer in the past twenty years has been as myopic as that; but those who are concerned with the achievements of the later Middle Ages – whether the fourteenth-century physics of Paris and Oxford or the philosophical developments of Paris, Padua or Salamanca – have inevitably seen the fifteenth and sixteenth centuries as far from glowingly novel. This view has naturally been reinforced by the study of the history of technology, where the numerous inventions of the medieval period seem more truly innovative, more transforming of society, than the ingenious but often impractical spate of inventions which characterized the fifteenth and sixteenth centuries. Indeed, an historian cannot fail to notice that the great 'triumphs of our new age' which were acclaimed by numerous sixteenth-century writers were preponderantly medieval. Gunpowder, the compass, windmills, the stirrup, distillation and silk – these were all medieval inventions or importations. True, there remain exploration, navigation, cartography and the printing press, not to mention the technology of chemistry and mining described in sixteenth-century books and mainly developed in the previous century, but it is easy to regard most of these as in some sense a continuation of medieval developments. Besides, exploration and navigation belong to the Mediterranean world in the first instance, and so are ambiguously related to the problem of a northern Renaissance. The printing press remains indubitably a northern and a fifteenth-century invention, and one highly explosive in its long-term effects upon science; no doubt in part the catchy alliteration of the title *The Gutenberg Galaxy* accounts for the acclaim given to Marshall McLuhan's book[3] (itself largely a patchwork compilation of other men's

[274]

opinions upon all sorts of topics), whose theme is the relatively simple one, that the spread of the printed book altered men's attitude to many aspects of life. (Whether the historian should accept the practice of guilt by enumeration, the *post haec ergo propter haec* form of argument, where the fallacy of *post hoc, ergo propter hoc* is lost when '*haec*' has a sufficient number of examples, may be questioned here.) But however great its psychological and aesthetic impact, it must be admitted that the printing press *initially* had little impact upon the development of science. As everyone is aware, and as historians of ideas are almost too fond of pointing out with surprise, fifteenth-century printers differed not at all from twentieth-century publishers: they chose to print what was both available and saleable. Thus they printed tried and true medieval texts rather than doubtfully popular contemporary ones, bestiaries rather than zoology, calendars and simple basic astronomical texts (for astrological use) rather than Ptolemy. This should occasion us no surprise; surely only the most naive among us would expect the situation to be otherwise. On the other hand the bibliographer's metaphor of 'incunabula' and the bookseller's magic phrase 'printed before 1500' should not blind us to the fact that there is no special significance in a centurial date, nor did men suddenly find themselves differently inclined in 1501 from what they had been in 1499. And soon *after* 1500 the Aldine Press in Venice (and others soon joined them) had totally transformed the context and even the shape of printing by producing a flood of cheap texts for university students, printed in a novel 'Italic' type, and in Greek as well as in Latin fount. This was certainly a triumph.

Just as there is a problem as to when (or whether) the Renaissance begins, so there is the question of when it comes to an end. Here again the magic of a change of century is often employed; and here, too, North and South have looked at things in very different ways. Francis Bacon is usually regarded as belonging to the seventeenth-century intellectual scene, and fairly so, since he had published nothing of relevance to the history of scientific and philosophical ideas when *The Advancement of Learning* appeared in 1605. Though he was born in 1561, so that his intellectual milieu should have been Elizabethan, only his essays belong to the Renaissance period (of literature); his most influential philosophical works were published (in Latin) as late as the 1620s. Similarly Galileo, born in 1564, was educated in the Renaissance society of sixteenth-century Italy, and with Bacon was a contemporary of the indubitably Renaissance William Shakespeare. Almost uniquely among physical, mathematical scientists Galileo completed his first great achievement in science (the discovery of the law of free fall) in middle age (c. 1605); almost equally unusually his first widely known book (describing original work begun and accomplished in the preceding year) was published when he was forty-six. The case is not dissimilar from that of Bacon; both were regarded later in the seventeenth century as belonging to that rather than an earlier age; yet historians of Italy have always found it easier to include Galileo within the Renaissance than historians of northern Europe have to include Bacon within the Elizabethan period. A similar ambiguity has attached itself to such figures as Tycho Brahe (1546–1601) and William Gilbert (1540–1603), even though they were both born almost a generation before Galileo; or Johann Kepler (1571–1630), born only seven years after Galileo. Should we not conclude that there is something more than mere tradition in all this? Perhaps there is truly some significant difference between intellectual life north and south of the Alps even though, as we are increasingly aware, the greatest of northern Renaissance scientific figures all drew much inspiration from the warm intellectual sunshine of the south.

However, recent work suggests that the problem has become of less importance in the past dozen years, when historians have tended to ignore precise periodization and to look more towards continuity, less towards demarcation. The medievalist has extended his range into the fifteenth and even the sixteenth centuries, tracing filiation and influence; equally the historian of the seventeenth century has often chosen to begin with the sixteenth century. And this is perhaps as it should be, showing that we have outgrown the excessive positivism of older historians of science, so that we look less for anticipations of modernity, and more for connections with the past. Is this perhaps because we ourselves, feeling rootless, look for stability in our own roots? In any case it is surely historically more justifiable to treat Copernicus for example as the last of the medieval astronomers rather than the first of the modern ones, always provided that in so doing we do not thereby deny to him all originality – for that is to abolish him. But however little the question of precise periodization may arouse excitement nowadays, it is fair to say that few historians of science think it possible to do without some name to cover the period of, say, 1450–1630, since it so manifestly is required for an understanding of the way in which science developed: no one could now suppose that the fourteenth century led directly to the triumphs of the seventeenth century. On the contrary, we are now almost too conscious of the stresses and strains of the period of transition.

In all this, consideration of the social scene is vital. Whether we reflect upon the differences between North and South or between the

thirteenth century and the sixteenth, we shall achieve full comprehension generally only if we have regard to differences in intellectual
outlook. These are certainly reflected in the social scene, whether in the
'civic life' of Florence or in the technological and commercial
background of Nuremberg and Augsburg, or the political life of
northeastern Europe. Here Garin has pointed the way: *Scienze e vita
civile nel Rinascimento* was notable for attempting for science what
had, I think, been attempted previously only for art, literature and
politics: the consideration of the development of a human activity in
conjunction with, and against the background of, the social community
in which the notable practitioners of the age lived and flourished,
without at the same time lessening the importance of their ideas. And
here scientists of the Renaissance differ markedly from their
predecessors. Medieval scientists, on the whole, are known to us almost
exclusively by their intellectual achievements; what we know of them
is what those they influenced knew of them, their ideas and their
doctrines. (But even so more probably could be done than has been to
relate, say, the ecclesiastical preoccupations of an Albertus Magnus or
of a Grosseteste to the writings available for study.) But the fifteenth
and sixteenth centuries constitute, as Burckhardt long ago proclaimed,
an age of individualism, at least in comparison with preceding
centuries. We know these men not only because we can read their
philosophical and scientific writings but because their lives are well
documented, and (often) they have left us autobiographical fragments,
or even complete autobiographies. These can be and have often been
ignored, 'or else treated as mere narrative biography, unrelated to the
subject's intellectual activity. (This can produce such travesties as
picturing Copernicus as an isolated, dry-as-dust ecclesiastical recluse,
fearful of sharing his astronomical interests, whereas biographical
research has shown that, on the contrary, he was an active and
successful administrator, with many friends who shared and even
encouraged his astronomical preoccupations.) And it has also become
apparent that when dealing with Renaissance figures we should not
merely *say* that they tended towards universality, but realize how this
width of horizon affected the development of their thought. Often what
a man does in other fields casts illumination upon what he does in one
particular field – often, but not of course invariably, for many men do
have compartmentalized minds and keep their activities relatively
separate. Here again, however, we cannot perceive how an artist's non-
artistic preoccupations, or a scientist's non-scientific preoccupations
should be dealt with unless we are thoroughly familiar with the
intellectual and social background of the age, so that we can appreciate

[277]

how contemporaries – and the man himself – regarded these activities. As an example, we know now that great interest in the Hermetic sciences was normal in the sixteenth century; equally we know that the Hermetic sciences never received full social and ecclesiastical acceptance, but were always only quasi-licit. Hence we should not be surprised that that excellent mathematician Cardan was an avid astrologer, but neither should we be surprised to discover that he was somewhat ashamed of his devotion to this mystical science, which he knew to be unlawful, although popular and attractive.

Until relatively recently sophistication in the study of science and society was lacking. Science, even the science of the Renaissance, had most often been studied in relative isolation from the everyday life of the age, with the exception of those who sought to find in contemporary technology the sole causative factor of the development of scientific thought. This notably naive form of 'external' history of science stemmed almost entirely from Marxist-oriented economic history, trying to correlate a flourishing science with technological needs in the same spirit as that in which Weber had correlated capitalism with the Protestant ethic. In a truly eclectic spirit historians and sociologists tried to substitute 'science' for 'capitalism' and relate the emergence of seventeenth-century science to war, capitalism, religion, even coal and iron. This began in the 1930s, with dramatic but patently naive studies.[4] In the 1940s, less naively, the sixteenth century was studied in respect to the 'interface' (to use a now fashionable word) between the world of the artisan and that of the learned academic.[5] This was stimulating, but inconclusive, and in the 1950s, largely under the benign influence of Alexandre Koyré, the emphasis turned more to the detailed study of what has come to be called 'internal' history of science, that is the filiation of ideas and their diffusion, a form of investigation which proved immediately and satisfactorily successful. It was, further, a very necessary development if the relations of science and society were to be fully understood, for much of the naiveté of earlier attempts at this correlation had suffered grievously from an incomplete understanding of what scientific development in the period under consideration actually was and in what precise ways it differed from that of earlier periods. This blunted the point of the attempt to relate the society of the age to the development of scientific thought; for without a clear understanding of that development it is impossible fruitfully to discuss causative influences. This historiographical trend has been so successful and is so patently necessary that it needs no further discussion here. It is merely worth remarking, perhaps, that there is in the late 1970s some small danger that younger scholars may feel that it has all been done, that the last word on Galileo (say) has been said, and that novelty is only possible with minor figures. Certainly it is less easy to find new things to say about a Galileo than about his obscurer contemporaries, but it is by no means impossible, though more difficult than it was twenty-five years ago.

A second difficulty in the development of a socio-economic study of sixteenth-century science arises in connection with the work of the artisans. Here, in the history of technology, tremendous strides have been made in the past twenty years, and our understanding of the 'internal' history, if I may call it so, of technology – how and when advances were made, how diffused, and how developed one from another – has only recently become an established discipline. So recently indeed has it become so that it is all too apt to slide back into mere chronology and collecting, and no one could possibly think that the last word had been said upon any particular aspect of this form of human endeavour. Yet it now has become more reasonable to talk about the interrelations of science and technology than it was a quarter of a century ago, although the problem has not as yet been sufficiently clarified for a consensus of opinion to be possible. Among the most suggestive attempts has been Paolo Rossi's *I filosofi e le macchine (1400–1700)* which, published in Italy in 1962, has influenced a wider audience since its translation into English in 1970 under the title *Philosophy, Technology and the Arts in the Early Modern Era*.

But more of this in its proper place. Here it may suffice to say that although a number of works have appeared in the past dozen years which by their titles appear to attempt for the wider scene what Garin's book so notably did for the Italian, few have done more than assemble chapters on the development of science, followed by, or intermingled with, chapters on technology or society. The only notable exception is that excellent work by W.P.D. Wightman, *Science in a Renaissance Society* (1972), avowedly profoundly influenced by Garin (among others). Interestingly, this is far more successful for the Italian complex of science and society than it is for the northern one, and the fifteenth century rather than the sixteenth. Like Garin's book it is lucid, short, suggestive and allusive rather than detailed and definitive. Can it be that it is both easier and more valid to suggest certain relations between science and society than to document them extensively, to touch on such relations rather than to probe them? Certainly it has proved always more exciting to speculate about such topics than to explore them deeply. Social relations are never, of course, sufficient to explain or permit us to understand the development of truly influential figures like Galileo or Copernicus, though they may be so for minor figures who, by definition, do not possess powerful original minds. So studies of the relation of instrument-makers to astronomers and exponents of magnetism have always been successful, or practical arithmeticians and pure mathematicians. Too often, however, it is easier to speculate than to establish facts. Thus we may know that John Dee spoke in praise of practical mathematics, that Petrus Ramus believed in the practice of useful techniques, that Francis Bacon spoke of the usefulness of science 'for the relief of man's estate' – but what we have not been able to establish is how far the idea became reality. More often the will to be useful was an encouragement and justification to research rather than a cause, and certainly more often stimulated pure science than created useful, practical results. For learned men recorded the practical knowledge they acquired from artisans for other learned men, but seldom for other artisans. Mathematicians of the sixteenth century not infrequently complained that sailors refused to try to utilize methods of navigation that were perfectly practicable – practicable, that is, when employed by learned men ashore, but not so practicable for an unlearned man on a tossing ship. And as late as 1671 Robert Boyle was to note (in *Some Considerations Touching the Usefulnesse of Natural Philosophy*, vol. II) that artisans were often not at all pleased to have learned men prying into the secrets of their crafts, and perhaps giving away these secrets in print.

The one area where we can surely document good relations between practitioner and mathematician is when the practitioner was an artist. It is no accident that both Garin and Wightman have had much to say about Alberti,[6] nor that Leonardo should figure as Garin's ideal universal Renaissance man. The fifteenth- and sixteenth-century Italian artist was no mere craftsman but always and by necessity a deeply learned man, even though himself often conscious of not being academically learned. (It is hardly necessary to note that Leonardo could not have performed academic exercises that the youngest Bachelor of Arts could perform with ease, but that this did not preclude his having had a large library of learned books, mainly in Latin, which he had patently read and absorbed.) The Renaissance artist, whether an Italian or a German, a Verrocchio, a Dürer or a Holbein, was necessarily well grounded in the *mathematical* art of perspective, as well as the *medical* art of anatomy. Leonardo is a special case because, more brilliant even than the generality of his near-contemporary fellow artists, he dazzles by the range as well as the quality of his achievement. Besides, he went further than they in each of the fields he undertook to explore and, supreme artist as he was, always carried his artistic sensibility and creativity into every sphere of endeavour. Thus his anatomical drawings captivate even the most highly skilled modern anatomist by their artistic ability to relate the various organs to the body as a whole, so that the fact that they are less than anatomically exact in every case becomes less important than the fact that they represent the body as an organic whole.[7] Similarly Leonardo's work in optics relates the physical science to both human anatomy and perception in a way never attempted until relatively recent times.[8] So too it is difficult to view Leonardo's drawings of machines without being so carried away as to see them in a modern light. Three-quarters of a century ago Duhem was so dazzled by Leonardo's achievements in mechanics that only his ideological presuppositions allowed him to move backwards in historical time to appreciate the medieval predecessors upon whom Leonardo drew. This latter is a theme explicitly argued by Zubov in his highly perceptive, interpretive biographical study of Leonardo: as he puts it, Leonardo saw the potentialities of man to lie in the creativity that comes from first understanding and then transcending nature, so that the scientist, the artist and the engineer are all one, because it was Leonardo's artistic perception which dominated his work, whether in anatomy, mathematics, science or art.[9] And this is a Renaissance view, not a modern one.

This is true of Leonardo's work in practical mechanics or engineering as well, and has in part led to the supreme fascination which his brief descriptions and superbly suggestive drawings have exercised upon historians of technology, who have found an almost obsessive tendency to interpret sketches as finished, 'modern' designs. Regrettably, the close bond which existed in the Renaissance between art and technology no longer obtains, so that to find detailed studies of the artist as civil engineer, architect or inventor one must, in general, consult first a work by an art historian on the artist, architect or painter, and then a work by an historian of technology on the mathematician's development of perspective, or the civil engineer's conception of structures or hydraulics. The latter have recently contributed greatly, and as historians rather than as modern scientists or engineers looking admiringly at a great predecessor. One thinks of Bertrand Gille's admirable *Leonardo e gli ingegneri del Rinascimento*,[10] or the many careful, scholarly, perceptive studies of the late Ladislao Reti, culminating in his superb edition of the technological manuscripts preserved in Madrid.[11]

One must not forget Gille's warning, 'une étude sur les ingénieurs de la Renaissance est fatalement dominée, et quelque peu faussée, par la grande figure de Leonard da Vinci', a warning ironically ignored by his translator. Something has lately been done in this regard, not least by

[281]

Gille himself in the work to which this warning was a preface. It is much to be regretted that Reti's plans for an edition of Juanello Turiano, notable for his hydraulic work in Spain, were interrupted by the excitement of the rediscovery of the Madrid codices, but this may yet bear fruit.[12] There have been editions of the manuscript works of various fifteenth-century Italian engineers in recent years, usually in facsimile with transcription and (often) translation into English: Francesco di Giorgi Martini's *Trattati di architettura ingegneria e arte militare*;[13] Filarete's *Trattati di architettura*;[14] Mariano Taccola's *De machinis* and *De ingeniis*;[15] excerpts of the writings of these and other fifteenth- and sixteenth-century authors in *La città ideale nel Rinascimento*;[16] there has been a recent English study of the technology of Brunelleschi,[17] while in 1977 tremendous work was undertaken on both his theory and practice in architecture (appropriately by discussion, analysis and in practice). The trend towards publishing facsimiles and/or translations into modern languages, begun in the late 1930s, has continued to give us good modern editions of very many sixteenth-century machine books and technical treatises.[18]

All this work has markedly helped us to understand better both Italian urban society of the fifteenth and sixteenth centuries and the place of Leonardo himself in a developing tradition. A different, but very stimulating kind of study is that which Carlo Cipolla has made peculiarly his own: the study of the history of technology in its relation to economic history. Here the technological story and its intricacies has not been slighted, but the developing technology is set in the social and (above all) the economic setting of its times, and facts and figures are organized and employed in the manner characteristic of modern economic historians.[19] This is also a useful, as well as a stimulating new approach.

So much for technology proper, that practical series of techniques which man has employed throughout the ages to control and exploit nature, consciously or unconsciously. But as Rossi long ago pointed out, there was another method widely employed during the Renaissance to control nature, the method of magic. Magic was in that period an operative art like any other; it differed notably from technology in being based upon a theoretical substructure and in being at least quasi-illicit.[20] The Middle Ages, of course, had known Ptolemy's *Tetrabiblos*, that useful, advanced treatise on 'applied astronomy'; it had also known a few texts belonging to what is known as the Hermetic Corpus. How this later came into European – initially Italian – consciousness through translation of neo-Platonic texts by Ficino, among others, was first influentially pointed out by P.O. Kristeller in the 1930s.[21] However it must not be forgotten that it came well within the competence of the Warburg Institute, founded to study the Platonic tradition, and indeed notable studies of Italian neo-Platonism have emerged from that institution. Textual evidence for future studies was provided first by the edition of the *Corpus Hermeticum* published between 1945 and 1954[22] and of then by Garin's *Testi umanistici sull'ermetismo*[23] and Rossi's influential study *Francesco Bacone: Della Magia alla Scienza*.[24] It is not surprising that Frances Yates of the Warburg Institute, turning to the study of Bruno, saw the chief roots of his ideas as lying in Hermeticism. Her *Giordano Bruno and the Hermetic Tradition*[25] was immediately and immensely successful in the English-speaking world, and led her and others to devote much thought and ink upon the possible influence of Hermeticism upon science. This has been most successful for the sixteenth century, and (naturally) for those sciences and those practitioners who were, as historians had always known, most mystically inclined. Paracelsus, for example, had always been known to have mystical elements in his chemistry and philosophy, and Walter Pagel did not need the new studies in Hermeticism to be aware of this.[26] Allen Debus, however, has used these studies to deepen his own interest in the mystic force of the later followers of Paracelsus.[27] Similarly we all knew that Fludd was a great mystic; the question explored in recent years is how far his mysticism was acceptable to, and influential upon, thinkers hitherto regarded as 'rational'. Opinions here have varied, but the latest scholarship shows a decided swing away from whole-hearted acceptance of the Yates thesis, especially when applied to the seventeenth rather than to the sixteenth century. At the symposium[28] on 'Reason, Experiment and Mysticism in the Scientific Revolution' the weight of exposition was against mysticism as a dominant force in the evolution of science; not that the historians concerned wished in any way to minimize the existence of mystic, even Hermetic thought, but they were inclined to reject it as a principal, or even very strong causative factor. This was most strikingly the case with the paper of Paolo Rossi, who seems to stand a little aghast at what his earlier, tentative suggestions had wrought – not surprisingly, for had he not entitled his work on Bacon *from* magic *to* science? An even stronger rejection has recently come from a younger historian of science, originally a great proponent of the importance of mysticism in, particularly, the thought and achievement of Johann Kepler: Robert Westman, in 'Magical reform and astronomical reform: the Yates thesis reconsidered' sets out the newer thesis that although many sixteenth- and early seventeenth-century natural philosophers were Hermeticists and mystics, their Hermetic beliefs had little or no

[283]

positive influence upon the development of their scientific ideas, and indeed these may be seen as having developed in spite of, rather than because of their Hermeticism.[29]

A curious paradox in this regard is the state of studies on mathematics in the Renaissance. We are all now well aware that in the fifteenth and sixteenth centuries 'mathematics' was equated as much with astrology as anything else, which is presumably why cautious fathers (like those of Fernel and Galileo) warned their sons against its profound study. Hence the high degree of correlation between mysticism and success in mathematics – as with Cardano, equally skilled in casting horoscopes and solving cubic equations, or (in England) John Dee, who encouraged work in navigational mathematics, lectured on geometry and taught young mathematicians like Thomas Digges, cast horoscopes for Queen Elizabeth, and lost his fortune and his wife in the deep waters of crystal-gazing. Yet not all mathematicians in the fifteenth and sixteenth centuries concerned themselves with the mystic aspects. Much work, for example, has been done on Rafael Bombelli, that distinguished sixteenth-century algebraist, who did good work in hydraulic engineering.[30] Similarly, the more distinguished French mathematician François Viète seems to have had little interest in any form of mathematics outside its purest forms.[31] A more 'Renaissance' figure was the Englishman Thomas Harriot, whose work in pure mathematics (little of which was published) paralleled that of Viète. Harriot was interested in mathematical navigation, of which he had practical experience on his voyage to the New World, wrote much on optics, and was one of the first to make telescopic observations, especially of sunspots. But he belonged to the intimate world of Renaissance patronage, and his work was long virtually unknown outside of the curious free-thinking entourage of the 'Wizard Earl' of Northumberland, except for what his associates described. (In spite of this association, Harriot seems curiously untouched by mysticism.) He has recently attracted much attention for his anticipations of seventeenth-century discoveries; but plans for publication of his manuscripts have not so far been brought to fruition.[32]

One important non-mystical aspect of mathematics was the study of perspective, already mentioned among Leonardo studies. This has been more considered by art historians than by historians of mathematics, for the simple geometric optics employed does not go much beyond Euclid, although the artistic effects could be so intricate. Attention has, however, recently been drawn to the connection between mathematics and humanism.[33] Here both Hermeticism and pure mathematics benefited from the new enthusiasm for what was primarily a literary movement, for both subjects were given new texts, and new translations. To many, humanism has seemed primarily anti-scientific, for whereas art and science have for long been accepted as natural companions, influencing one another in countless ways, science and literature have for long seemed to belong to different worlds. Indeed, this view has often been elevated into the status of a thesis, arguing that the essentially literary movement of humanism, which absorbed the creative force of so many eager spirits in the fifteenth century, was alien, perhaps even deleterious, to the growth of science, which was checked, only to move forward as it escaped the baneful influence of a movement which looked back to a golden age of Antiquity, not forward to a developing world. Further, it froze Latin into a classical mould, and killed it dead; and it concentrated on words and literature rather than things and nature. True; but, perhaps paradoxically, humanism began as a lively, constructive, liberating movement, which embraced scientific texts as well as literary ones. And although by the later sixteenth century many forward-looking spirits criticized and rejected humanism as reactionary and old-fashioned for science, others still found it relevant, and even included it among 'the triumphs of our New Age'. Besides, the fact that it was criticized in the later sixteenth century does not mean that it was totally unimportant, nor that even if it was outmoded then, it had not been novel and even innovative in an earlier age. As Garin has tried to show, largely successfully, the humanism which began by imitating Antiquity came to find a new solution first to literary problems, then to problems in philosophy; and here, having begun with political and ethical philosophy, humanists applied their methods to metaphysical and natural philosophy as well. Certainly the humanists, elevating Plato above Aristotle, emphasized the role of physics, and made geometry a part of a gentleman's education. But above all, humanists tried to revive what they took to be the characteristic which most differentiated classical from medieval society – its concern with man and his activities measured in purely human terms, not divine ones – and, more simply, to first revive and then emulate classical achievements in art, literature and science.

This latter activity, although it led to the stultifications of philological scholarship and the standardization and ultimate decay of Latin, was new and exciting in the fifteenth century, and still thriving in the sixteenth century. What was its relevance for science? Without arguing the (irresolvable) question of the effect of humanist scholarship on the development of a critical approach to learning generally, we can yet say surely that the rediscovery and translation of ancient texts was a notable contribution to science. Even the medievalist who would deplore the interruption to the steady progress of medieval effort will grant that the increased study of Greek texts had *some* effect, while most Renaissance scholars would argue that it had a profound, possibly critical effect. It is difficult not to agree with Alexandre Koyré that the Archimedean spirit is more characteristic of the late sixteenth century than of the late fourteenth century, and that the effect of it was beneficent. Even those like Marshall Clagett who have pursued Archimedean texts painstakingly through the Middle Ages (and two large volumes) would agree that, translations and references not-withstanding, there is no comparison between the influence which the Archimedean method exerted in the earlier and the later periods, and truly one might argue that the very difference betweeen the use made of Archimedes in the thirteenth century and that made in the sixteenth arises from the difference of approach between the two epochs, which this difference makes plain. Even more dramatic, of course, is the example of those texts virtually or entirely unknown to the whole of the medieval period (although some were then potentially easily recoverable) and avidly discovered, published, translated and read in the fifteenth and sixteenth centuries. One thinks of Ptolemy's *Geography*, triumphantly brought back from Constantinople with an already prepared translation in 1410, or, shortly after, the finding of Lucretius by Poggio Bracciolini, or Celsus, by Guarino (in 1426), or Galen's *Natural Faculties* translated by the Englishman Thomas Linacre only in the sixteenth century, and his *Anatomical Procedures* translated shortly after by the Rhinelander Johannes Guinther of Andernach, or Apollonios and Diophantos, translated after 1550, or the works of Hero of Alexandria, translated by Italian humanists and engineers. Or the case of the two young German humanists, Georg Peurbach and Johannes Müller (Regiomontanus), scheming about 1460 to get from far-away Vienna to Rome, to find a reliable Greek text of Ptolemy's *Almagest*.

Certainly the influence of this kind of humanism was very great upon young university scholars of this period, whether literary, medical or philosophical in their interests, and certainly again sixteenth-century science would have been very different without it. We perhaps have not yet studied the effects deeply enough, nor has there been wide enough consideration of the problem to correct the old errors about the place of Greek texts in university life. We should know that Galen's influence in the medieval university was necessarily very different from his influence in the sixteenth century, because 'Galen' represented a totally different tradition, set of books and method in the two periods. More attention has recently been paid to the role of humanism in science, but the results so far have tended towards the obvious, and the deeper issues have not been probed.[34]

A curious parallel to Renaissance interest is that recently shown by the revival of fifteenth- and sixteenth-century texts, either in facsimile or in translation, which has made many more texts available to the modern scholar, including the less learned of these who possess no Latin. Other parallels include the study of archives (particularly, as it happens, such relatively restricted archives as those of the Vatican – as in the Renaissance, one goes to Rome for manuscripts). This has produced, of course, some relatively unknown treatises, but these are of minor importance compared with the discovery of manuscript copies of books with restricted circulation. Thus, for example, the discovery of a manuscript copy of the radical *Christianismi Restitutio* has suggested that this may have been more widely diffused than had been previously supposed.[35] This is interesting, though one may still wonder whether it was physiologists and anatomists who read these copies, or those concerned with radical Christianity. Obviously other similar cases may be discovered. An interesting parallel is the search in libraries for copies of individual books, or of books with annotations. The most fruitful of these searches is that instituted for copies of the great work of Copernicus, an international search which has produced interesting results. Thus for example it has been found that no fewer than thirty copies of the first edition of *De Revolutionibus* survived in France in 1974, and five further copies were known to have been recently lost, while twenty-nine copies of the second edition survived, three further having been lost.[36] In a surprising number of cases sixteenth- and seventeenth-century owners were even identified. Such a survey has not yet been attempted for other important works, but would surely be desirable; it allows us not only to compute the size of the original edition, but to study diffusion. A supplementary study of the work of Copernicus is that instituted by Owen Gingerich – the search for *annotated* copies.[37] This has resulted in the discovery of a number of copies of invaluable importance, but not those belonging to Tycho Brahe, whose annotations have materially added to our knowledge of the history of sixteenth-century astronomy. Clearly much remains to be done in a field of scholarship whose pains are considerable, but whose rewards may be great.

The happy coincidence of the 400th anniversary of the birth of Kepler (in 1971) followed by the 500th anniversary of the birth of Copernicus (in 1973) had an effect on the study of the work of these men, and meant a tremendous burst of activity in the history of Renaissance astronomy. The Copernicus celebrations were so widespread, and so prolonged, that a far deeper range of scholarship than is usual on these celebratory occasions emerged in a series of collaborative articles and commemorative conferences and volumes.[38] Naturally Polish scholars led, especially in biographic details, but the Germans east and west were not behind; a convenient summary of new biographical research, by Marian Biskup, appeared in *Revue d'histoire des sciences* in 1974.[39] Much useful material has emerged, pertaining to both the personal and the intellectual life of the great astronomer. Among other interesting details, the case of Copernicus suggests how strongly influential was Italian culture north of the Alps: for the academic environment of the University of Cracow was strongly affected by Italian thought and methods when Copernicus was a student there, and his years in Italy gave him friends also accustomed to Italian aims and methods, as well as a residue of Italian-based astronomy. There have been new translations of his *Commentariolus* and of *De Revolutionibus* itself.[40] There have been, of course, technical studies of his achievement. A new departure, and significant for our understanding of sixteenth-century science, was a series of studies on the reception of Copernican astronomy, especially by Robert Westman;[41] this has shown the existence of a whole school of German astronomers who treated the *De Revolutionibus* as a valuable source-book for parameters and a guide to predictive mathematics without worrying about the Copernican *system*, and at the same time has shown how much more widespread and familiar Copernicus' work was than had previously been believed by most historians. Kepler did not receive so extensive a treatment by any means, but there were several international symposia, and a large output of learned articles, conveniently assessed in 1976 by E.J. Aiton.[42]

No other scientist has received comparable treatment in recent years, mainly perhaps because few have been so fortunate in their commemorative dates. One might have expected that Vesalius would have been extensively studied in 1964, since he was born in 1514 and died fifty years later, but this as it turned out was not especially the case,[43] perhaps not surprisingly since the 400th anniversary of Galileo's birth was also only modestly celebrated. The history of medicine has indeed been only moderately investigated in the past dozen years. Among useful work one may cite the production of facsimiles (as of Vesalius' *Fabrica* and Realdus Columbus' textbook) and many collections of anatomical studies. More significant for our understanding of medical science has been the study of methods of (and method in) medical teaching in sixteenth-century Italy and elsewhere. Here a philosophic approach has revealed much more about the age's understanding of the proper content of medical teaching than had been

[288]

appreciated hitherto.[44] Moreover, since medical teaching was often bestowed on other than a purely medical audience[45] – Galileo attended medical lectures in Pisa in 1581 – the method of resolution and composition was taken over into the consideration of subjects within natural philosophy. This kind of investigation has led to a clearer understanding of the teaching and discussion of scientific method in the sixteenth century than had been the case earlier.

Another new approach to the history of medicine has been the study of public health. For the Renaissance, Carlo Cipolla has contributed greatly by his studies combining economic history and the control of epidemics.[46] In an age when medical practice could do little to cure disease, and even less to stem an epidemic, public health officials were all important. In trying to contain an epidemic they were compelled to fall back upon late medieval practice (derived from the Arabs); recognizing the disease as contagious they were driven to organize society to limit the spread of the contagion. How they coped illuminates both medical practice and social and economic conditions of the period.

From any point of view, medicine was powerfully influenced by the intellectual as well as the social currents of Renaissance society. Here Italy was influenced by the North, although she was to return the compliment in due course. The Paduan school of anatomy, so influential throughout the sixteenth century in both Italy and the North, was instituted by a northerner, Andreas Vesalius, born and given a humanist education in Louvain, who studied medicine in Paris under a humanist steeped in the new Galenism, Guinter of Andernach, and who edited Galen before – following his methods – he was able to correct him. Without doubt the Paduan school reached its culmination with its influence upon another northerner, the Englishman William Harvey, educated in Galenism at Caius College, Cambridge and introduced to the new Italian anatomy at Padua by Fabricius of Aquapendente. Curiously little attention has been paid in Italy in recent years to the successors of Vesalius at Padua, Realdo Colombo, Fallopio, Fabricius, although more has been given to Cesalpino, regrettably rather as a forerunner of Harvey than as an original plant physiologist.[47] The most original, fruitful and stimulating study of Harvey himself has been that of Walter Pagel, *Le idee biologiche di Harvey* (1967),[48] with its examination of textual and intellectual sources and its careful appraisal of conceptual influences upon Harvey's discovery of circulation and of his relation to his contemporaries. As an intellectual study it can hardly be bettered; it is also a useful corrective to the tendency to seize upon all new methodological approaches to the history of science as not only applicable but essential to the study of particular figures, for Pagel has abundantly shown that 'Hermeticism' played no essential role in the development of Harvey's ideas, however tempting it may have been to try to demonstrate that it did so. On the other hand the essential Aristotelianism of many of Harvey's ideas has remained clear, and even been reinforced by recent study.[49] There has also been a series of translations of his minor works, as well as numerous studies relating him to Francis Bacon and the intellectual milieu of the English seventeenth century (though it is perhaps a little embarrassing that Harvey was a staunch royalist, though his followers were to become more or less revolutionary Parliamentarians). Although no doubt there will always be room for studies of Harvey's achievement and of his methodology, it cannot be said that his work requires a great new appraisal in the immediate future.

What can one say of the greatest of all transitional figures, Galileo Galilei? Once it was thought that the last word had been said with Favaro's magnificent effort, coupled with Duhem's monumental study of his predecessors in physics, and Wohlwill's of his share in the scientific and ideological challenge of the Copernican system.[50] Then Alexandre Koyré showed how *explication de texte* and a strictly intellectual approach opened up the whole question of his originality and achievement once again,[51] while the challenge to intellectual freedom in the United States of America in the 1950s led the Italo-American Giorgio di Santillana to explore in dramatic fashion the trial and condemnation of Galileo by the Church,[52] a study which led in turn to further archival research. In the last twenty years the leading Galileo scholar has undoubtedly been the American Stillman Drake, who has produced valuable new translations for student and scholar, a range of studies on Galileo's life and work, and a stimulating series of studies and possible reconstructions of many of Galileo's discoveries by detailed examination of manuscripts, many of them fragmentary.[53] There have been many attempts to resolve the question raised by Koyré of what the experiments cited by Galileo in the *Dialogues* and *Discourses* meant to him, and whether he felt it necessary to perform them. A number of historians of science have examined the experiments, finding that they are perfectly satisfactory experiments in themselves, as described by Galileo – that is, one can reconstruct them without difficulty, and they do indeed give the results he claims for them – or even that they had been described by others, from whom Galileo could have drawn them.[54] But the debate over Galileo's use of and reliance upon experiments continues, and there is a very large literature on Galileo's methodology from the philosophical point of view.

A point raised by Garin originally and reiterated by Drake was the need to study in more detail both the transmission of the medieval sources which might have been known to Galileo and the works of the sixteenth-century writers and teachers who certainly were known to Galileo. A recent investigation of sixteenth-century Italian university textbook writers[55] (especially of Buonamici) has shown that although these universally refer to medieval writers on physics by name, this is more commonly in reference to their method than to their practice, and there is remarkably little about details of the latitude of forms, impetus theory or the Merton rule. We thus still do not know the precise origin of Galileo's recorded knowledge of medieval results. The lead given by Garin towards consideration of the published work of Jacopo Mazzoni has not been neglected.[56] But this is a field where there is room for further study.

Relatively less emphasis in recent years has been placed upon Galileo the astronomer. This reflects current research interests rather than lack of scope. After all, Galileo won his first public acclaim for his astronomical observations, which moreover provided him with his first public acclamation of the Copernican system, to which he had previously only subscribed privately. The debate upon his use of experiment could well have been extended to include his use of astronomical observation. Recently important work has been undertaken by Albert Van Helden, who has reopened the whole question of the invention of the telescope and the diffusion of knowledge of its existence.[57] He has in so doing revealed how enormously better were the telescopes made by Galileo than those made by his predecessors and contemporaries, and has in particular examined Galileo's work on Saturn and its subsequent history.[58] Almost certainly any further work on seventeenth-century observational astronomy will throw more light upon Galileo the astronomer, for, as is obvious, Galileo's work in that field (whatever may be true of physics) looks entirely forward to the new world of the scientific revolution, and not at all back to the new world of the Renaissance.

Anyone who has read so far must see that I have deliberately ignored, as far as possible, a major area of Renaissance historical scholarship of great importance for the growth of science, namely the role of universities, and in particular Italian universities in the fifteenth and sixteenth centuries. This is fully dealt with in the chapter by Charles ·Schmitt. It is obvious that such diverse scientific figures as Copernicus, Galileo and Harvey owed much to their education in such universities. Above all, a great deal has been made in recent years of the development by philosophers of new ideas on scientific method: Randall long ago wrote on 'Scientific method in the School of Padua' while more recently much work has been done on Zabarella;[59] there is the study of Italian medical method mentioned above; and for France and England an interest in the work of Petrus Ramus.[60] And much more. It is encouraging to find a whole field of study here which is helping to reshape our view of the place and content of science in Renaissance society.

In his *Advancement of Learning* Francis Bacon, analysing the defects of learning, scholarship, philosophy and science of the first forty years of his life, tried to appraise each field critically in the light of what was possible. Of only a few (and these few in general did not rate highly in his hierarchy of knowledge) could he bring himself to say 'This I may report as not deficient'. By contrast, as I have tried to show here, modern scholarship in the history of science has left few areas truly deficient. In almost all there has been made what Bacon would have called 'a good beginning'. The scientific Renaissance is no longer the problem it was twenty years ago; rather it is a viable and important aspect of historical study presenting many rewards to the contemporary scholar.

NOTES

1 Bari, 1965; enlarged English translation, 1969.
2 *Science and Thought in the Fifteenth Century* (New York, 1929).
3 London and Toronto, 1962. More useful, scholarly and straightforwardly factual is L. Febvre and H.-J. Martin, L'*Apparition du Livre* (Paris, 1958).
4 B. Hessen in *Science at the Crossroads* (London, 1932); reprinted as *The Social and Economic Roots of Newton's 'Principia'* (New York, 1971); R.K. Merton, *Science, Technology and Society in Seventeenth-Century England* (*Osiris*, 1938; 2nd edn, New York, 1970); J.U. Nef, *The Rise of the British Coal Industry* (London, 1932) and 'An early energy crisis and its consequences', *Scientific American*, 237 (1977), 140–51. On all this see A.R. Hall, 'Merton Revisited', *History of Science*, 2 (1963), 1–15.
5 A leader here was Leonardo Olschki, *Geschichte der neusprachliche wissenschaftliche Literatur*, 3 vols (Vaduz, 1965), a reprint of the original edn (1919–23). Also E. Zilsel in P.P. Wiener and A. Noland, *Le radici del pensiero scientifico* (Milan, 1970), translation of *Roots of Scientific Thought* (New York, 1957). A recent discussion bringing together Alberti's theory of colour, Renaissance optics and the relations of Ptolemaic cartography is S.Y. Edgerton, *The Renaissance Rediscovery of Linear Perspective* (New York, 1975). The problem of linear perspective in the Renaissance was examined at a symposium held in Milan in 1977. Yet another sort of example is to be found in S. Drake, 'Renaissance music and experimental science', *Journal of the History of Ideas*, 31 (1970), 483–500.

6 There is a wealth of literature on Alberti which is relevant here; suffice it to cite a few examples. Joan Gadol, *Leon Battista Alberti, Universal Man of the Early Renaissance* (Chicago, 1969); E. Garin, 'Il pensiero di Leon Battista Alberti e la cultura del quattrocento', *Belfragor*, 27 (1972), 501-22; G. Arrighi, 'Il "modo optimo" dell' Alberti per la costruzione prospettiva', *Physis*, 14 (1972), 295-8.

7 New edition edited by K.D. Keele and C. Pedretti (London, 1980).

8 This has been studied by K.H. Veltman in *Optics and Perspective* (University of London thesis, 1975); he and Keele are at work at a study of Leonardo and vision. See also A. Borsellino and C. Maltese, *Physis*, 18 (1976), 221.

9 The original Russian text was published in 1962; English translation (Cambridge, Mass.), 1968.

10 Milan, 1972; published as *Lés ingénieurs de la Renaissance* (Paris, 1964); English translation 1966.

11 *The Madrid Codices*, 4 vols (New York, 1974). Among other recent studies suffice it to cite Margaret Cooper, *Inventions of Leonardo da Vinci* (New York, 1965), a typically laudatory description of 'Leonardo the modern man' and the much more balanced and well informed, although equally eulogistic volume edited by L. Reti, *The Unknown Leonardo* (London and New York, 1974).

12 There is some account of his work in Norman Smith, *Man and Water* (London, 1976). Further work is under way by A.G. Keller.

13 Ed. C. and L. Maltese (Milan, 1967).

14 J.R. Spenser (ed.), *Filarete's Treatise on Architecture* (New Haven-London, 1965).

15 Ed. Gustina Scaglia (Wiesbaden, 1971) and J.H. Beck (Milan, 1970), respectively. There is also F.D. Prager and G. Scaglia, *Mariano Taccola and his book* De Ingeneis (Cambridge, Mass., 1972).

16 Ed. G.C. Sciolla (Turin, 1975).

17 Ed. F.D. Prager and Gustina Scaglia (Cambridge, Mass., 1970).

18 Most notably those edited by Cyril Stanley Smith. But machine books like those of Zonca and Ramelli have appeared in facsimile.

19 Carlo Cipolla, *Guns and Sails in the Early Phase of the European Expansion, 1400-1700* (London, 1965); *Clocks and Culture 1300-1700* (London, 1967).

20 The title of a recent work reminds us, however, that architecture at least had some connection with theoretical mysticism: *Pythagorean Palaces: Magic and Architecture in the Italian Renaissance* by G.L. Hersey (Ithaca, NY-London, 1976).

21 He edited an edition of Ficino's writings in 1937; in 1953 appeared *Il Pensiero filosofo di Marsilio Ficino* (Florence) which had appeared in English ten years earlier.

22 At Paris, edited by A. Festugière and Arthur Darby Nock in 4 vols. There had been an earlier edition translated into English and edited by Walter Scott under the title *Hermetica* (Oxford, 1924).

23 Rome, 1955.

24 Bari, 1957; English translation, London, 1968.

25 London and Chicago, 1964. Compare the more explicit statement as regards science proper in her article, 'The Hermetic tradition in Renaissance science' in *Art, Science and History in the Renaissance* (Baltimore, 1967).

26 For a full bibliography up to *c.* 1972, including the most important of Pagel's own works, see his article 'Paracelsus' in the C.C. Gillispie (ed.), *Dictionary of Scientific Biography*, X (New York, 1974). For more on the same theme, see S. Domandl (ed.), *Paracelsus, Werk und Wirkung* (Vienna, 1975).

27 In e.g. *The English Paracelsians* (London, 1965). See also in general A.G. Debus (ed.), *Science, Medicine and Society in the Renaissance: Essays to Honor Walter Pagel*, 2 vols (New York, 1972).

28 Held under the auspices of the Ronchi Foundation, and published in New York and London, 1975, ed. by M.L. Righini Bonelli and W.R. Shea.

29 R.S. Westman and J.E. McGuire, *Hermeticism and the Scientific Revolution* (Los Angeles, 1977). McGuire devoted himself to showing that one need not look to any Hermetic influences to explain Newton's neo-Platonic bent.

30 See *Dictionary of Scientific Biography*, II, for an excellent article by S.A. Jaywardene, including bibliography to *c.* 1965.

31 His early scientific work was a cosmology and elementary (Ptolemaic) astronomy, out of which his trigonometric work arose: see *Dictionary of Scientific Biography*, XIV.

32 Cf. for example J.W. Shirley (ed.), *Thomas Harriot, Renaissance Scientist* (Oxford, 1974). Also J.A. Lohne, 'Dokumente zur Revalidierung von Thomas Harriot als Algebraiker', *Archive for the History of Exact Sciences*, 3 (1966), 185–205.

33 See here P.L. Rose, *The Italian Renaissance of Mathematics* (Geneva, 1975), which has much about mathematics, humanism and manuscript transmission. It fails, however, to draw these threads together very effectively.

34 See e.g. Antonia MacLean, *Humanism and the Rise of Science in Tudor England* (London, 1972).

35 Giuseppe Ongaro, 'La scoperta della circolazione polmonare e la diffusione della *Christianismi Restitutio di Michele Serveto* nel XVI secolo, in Italia e nel Veneto', *Episteme*, V (1971), 3–44.

36 René Taton and Maylis Cazenave, 'Contribution à l'étude de la diffusion du *De Revolutionibus* de Copernic', *Revue d'Histoire des Sciences*, XXVII (1974), 307–28.

37 See Owen Gingerich, 'Copernicus and Tycho', *Scientific American* (December 1973), 87–101. Both Gingerich and Robert Westman have been successful in finding copies with important annotations and provenance.

38 It is impossible to mention all the symposia and their resultant volumes here. The Poles naturally led, with volumes of their *Studia Copernicana*, a whole series of separate volumes, much in *Studia Warmińskie* and elsewhere. The French produced a volume *Avant, Avec, Après Copernic* (Paris, 1975), ed. H. Huguennard-Roche *et al.*; the Italians, *Convegno internazionale sul tema: Copernico e la cosmologia moderna* (Rome, 1975); the Germans, *Nicolaus Copernicus zum 500. Geburtstag* (Cologne, 1973), ed. F. Kaulbach, U.W. Bargenda and J. Blühdoorn, and *Nicolaus Copernicus, 1473–1973* (Berlin, 1973); the Russians, *K 500-letiu so dniia rozhdeniaa Nikolaiia Kopernika* (1972); there is in English A.K. Beer and

K.A. Strand (eds), *Copernicus Yesterday and Today* (Oxford, 1975); *Vistas in Astronomy*; O. Gingerich (ed.), *The Nature of Scientific Discovery* (Washington, 1975); R.S. Westman (ed.), *The Copernican Achievement* (Los Angeles, 1975). And many more.

39 XXVII, 289–306.

40 There is a new partial translation of *De Revolutionibus* into Italian by Corrado Vivanti (Turin, 1975); a complete new version into English by A.M. Duncan (London and New York, 1976) and one published by E. Rosen. There is a new English translation of his *Commentariolus* by N. Swerdlow, in *Proceedings of the American Philosophical Society*, 117, 6 (1973), 413–50 (along with papers given at a symposium sponsored by the Society), and a French translation in *Avant, Avec, Après Copernic* (see n. 38).

41 See, for example, 'The Melanchthon circle, Rheticus, and the Wittenberg interpretation of the Copernican system', *Isis*, 66 (1975), 165–93, and further in *The Nature of Scientific Discovery* (see n. 38) and in J. Dobrzycki, *The Reception of Copernicus' Heliocentric Theory* (Dordrecht, 1973).

42 *History of Science*, XIV (1976), 77–100. There is an extensive bibliography here.

43 The most important work was the biography by C.D. O'Malley (Berkeley–Los Angeles, 1964).

44 See e.g. W.P.D. Wightman, '*Quid sit Methodus?* Method in sixteenth-century teaching and discovery', *Journal of the History of Medicine*, XIX (1964), 360–76 and A.W. Wear, 'Logic and Contingency in Renaissance Anatomy' (University of London thesis, 1973), as well as the chapter on universities by C. Schmitt (below).

45 Cf. R.K French (ed.), *Anatomical Education in a Scottish University, 1620* (Aberdeen, 1975).

46 *Cristofano and the Plague* (London 1973); *Public Health and the Medical Profession in the Renaissance* (Cambridge, 1975).

47 On all these, see the bibliographies attached to the articles on Cesalpino, Fallopio and Fabricius in the *Dictionary of Scientific Biography* (curiously, the article on Fabricius does not mention the English translation by K.J. Franklin of his *De Venarum ostiolis*, published with facsimile at Springfield, Ill., in 1933).

48 Published as *William Harvey's Biological Ideas* (Basle and New York, 1967); Italian translation (Milan, 1972). See also 'Harvey revisited', *History of Science*, 8 (1969), 1–31, and 9 (1970), 1–41, expanded as *New Light on William Harvey* (Basle, 1976).

49 See Erna Leskey, 'Harvey und Aristoteles', *Sudhoffs Archiv für Geschichte der Medizin*, 41 (1957), 289–316, 349–78, and C. Webster, 'Harvey's *De generatione*: its origins and relevance to the theory of circulation', *British Journal for the History of Science*, 3 (1967), 262–74.

50 P. Duhem, *Etudes sur Léonard da Vinci: Ce qu'il a lu et ce qui l'a lu* (Paris, 1906–13), and E. Wohlwill, *Galileo und sein Kampf für die Copernische Lehre* (Hamburg–Leipzig, 1909, 1926).

51 *Etudes Galiléenes* (Paris, 1939).

52 *The Crime of Galileo* (Chicago, 1955), translated into Italian as *Processo a Galileo* (Milan, 1960).

53 See especially *Galileo Studies* (Ann Arbor, 1970), and his *Galilean Gleanings* (in various journals).
54 See e.g. T.B. Settle, 'An experiment in the history of science', *Science*, 133 (1961), 19–23, and 'Galileo's use of experiment as a tool of investigation', in E. McMullin, *Galileo: Man of Science* (New York–London, 1967), 314–37, and, more recently, J. Maclachlan, 'Galileo's experiments with pendulums: real and imaginary', *Annals of Science* (1976), 173–85, and R. Naylor, 'Galileo: real experiment and didactic demonstration', *Isis*, 67 (1976), 398–419.
55 C.J.T. Lewis, 'The Merton Tradition and Kinematics' (thesis, 1975 published Padua, 1980), and 'The fortunes of Richard Swineshead in the time of Galileo, *Annals of Science*, 33 (1976), 561–84.
56 F. Purnell, 'Jacopo Mazzoni and Galileo', *Physis*, 14 (1972), 273.
57 *The Discovery of the Telescope* (Philadelphia, 1977).
58 'The Study of Saturn's Rings' (University of London thesis, 1970).
59 J.H. Randall, Jr, 'The discovery of scientific method in the School of Padua' in *Le radici del pensiero scientifico* and in *The School of Padua and the Emergence of Modern Science* (Saggi e Testi 1), Università di Padova Centro per la storia della tradizione Aristotelica nel Veneto (Padua, 1961). More recently, C.B. Schmitt, 'Experience and experiment: a comparison of Zabarella's view with Galileo's in *De Motu*', *Studies in the Renaissance*, 16 (1969), 80–138, and 'Towards a reassessment of Renaissance Aristotelianism', *History of Science*, 11 (1973), 159–93 (with very full bibliography). Also A. Poppi, 'La dottrina della scienza in Giacomo Zabarelli' (Saggi e Testi 12), Centro per la storia della tradizione Aristotelica nel Veneto (Padua, 1972).
60 W.J. Ong, *Ramus, Method and the Decay of Dialogue* (Cambridge, Mass., 1958) is an important study. For a study of Ramus' influence on Bacon see L. Jardine, *Francis Bacon: Discovery and the Art of Discourse* (Cambridge, 1974), which also places Bacon in his Renaissance setting.

9

PHILOSOPHY AND SCIENCE IN SIXTEENTH-CENTURY ITALIAN UNIVERSITIES

CHARLES B. SCHMITT

INTRODUCTION

INCE serious historical studies of Renaissance intellectual history have begun, it has remained a commonplace – either stated explicitly or implicitly understood – that the university philosophy and science of the period was of little positive value for the future development of modern science and philosophy. This viewpoint still persists in the writings of most students of the Renaissance, though it is becoming increasingly clear that – within certain limits – philosophy and science were of more importance than has previously been recognized. On the whole, however, there has been little systematic attempt to study philosophical and scientific thought as it developed in the universities of the Renaissance. As a consequence we are not yet in a position to put forward anything but the most cautious of hypotheses, based upon a very selective, even accidental, fraction of the available evidence. Bibliographical and doctrinal studies are lacking on all but a few of the most important figures and, to make matters worse, the study of individual universities during the Renaissance period is still in a very rudimentary state. Recent studies serve to show,[1] more than anything else, how much we have still to learn about this subject.

The topic stated in the title of this paper must eventually be seen in a European-wide context. Though specific monographic studies are useful and, indeed, indispensable, the cultural and linguistic unity of Europe (and its dependencies in the sixteenth-century New World) make it absolutely necessary at a certain stage to view the situation as a whole. Several years ago I tried to give a brief, synthetic statement to this effect.[2] In my present paper my aim is a bit more restrictive, though once again far too broad to give anything but a superficial impression based on the present state of my knowledge and on current research. Here I shall deal only with philosophy and science in the universities of sixteenth-century Italy. I hope to be able to show that the subject is perhaps more important and interesting than has previously been thought and that it is worthy of further study. After sketching in some of the main points about my subject, I should like to conclude by raising several important problems about how the study of the universities relates to the whole so-called 'problem of the Renaissance'.

There were significant noticeable differences between universities in the various parts of Europe during the sixteenth century – and I think that this fact is undeniable – but when we begin to consider regional differences within Italy the situation is more problematic. The Italy of the sixteenth century was broken up into very diverse regions with many different intellectual and cultural traditions. The country did not have the same political unity as did France or England. On the other hand, at least as far as universities are concerned, there was a degree of similarity that cannot be discounted. For one thing the traditional structure of Italian universities differentiated them from most northern European universities, founded as they were on the Paris model as corporations of the masters. Moreover, a tradition of professional study in law and medicine going back to the origins of the *studio* of Bologna also distinguished them from the universities of northern Europe. Therefore, in at least these two ways the Italian universities of the Middle Ages and Renaissance were quite different from those of most of the remainder of Europe. Throughout the period there is clear documentary evidence to show that northern Europeans came to Italy to study law and medicine (e.g. Copernicus, Linacre and Harvey) while Italians went north to study theology (e.g. Thomas Aquinas, Paul of Venice and Giovanni Pico). This pattern changed only when the Counter-Reformation took hold and began to provide theological education in Italian universities in conformity with post-Tridentine norms. Even then, however, northern students of law and medicine continued to come to the great Italian centres until at least the middle of the seventeenth century.

REGIONAL VARIATIONS

In my view the *differences* between Italian universities and those of the remainder of Europe are to be emphasized, while the *similarities* of universities within Italy are to be equally stressed. Consequently, I do not feel that the historiographical tradition which emphasizes the uniqueness of a particular Italian university, e.g. Padua, has given adequate consideration to the very real similarities between different universities or to the question of professorial mobility. What is more, far too much stress has been laid on the distinction between 'Paduan Aristotelianism' and 'Florentine Platonism'.[3]

One of the major arguments which militates against the development of strong regional traditions in universities lies in the fact that, particularly at the senior levels, there was a great deal of professorial mobility in sixteenth-century Italian universities. It was a period not only of the wandering scholar, but also of the wandering professor. When an adequate prosopographical analysis of sixteenth-century Italian professors has been undertaken, I am convinced that the results will show that there was an unusually high degree of mobility throughout the century. While a Zabarella can be uniquely connected with Padua or an Aldrovandi with Bologna, these are the rather rare exceptions. Competition for important chairs was keen and men considered to be near the top of their fields were consistently tempted away from one comfortable teaching position to another through enticements of higher salary and a variety of added perquisites.

Agostino Nifo (1469/70–1538) illustrates perhaps as well as anyone the mobility of sixteenth-century university professors, as well as the dangers involved in placing too much confidence in a label such as 'Aristotelian'.[4] He was born south of Naples, but came to Padua to study. As soon as he had taken his degree he began teaching at Padua (1492–9), but then lectured successively at Naples, Salerno, Rome and Pisa, before moving back for a further stint at Salerno and Naples. Between times he held a succession of non-academic posts, among other things taking an active role in the *Accademia Pontaniania*, one of the leading cultural institutes of southern Italy. Late in his life he was offered the possibility of returning to both Pisa and Rome, but refused, being content to remain in the vicinity of Naples. This is not the stuff from which strong indigenous local traditions are made. Even less does Nifo conform to the conventional picture of an 'Aristotelian'.[5] While it is true that he commented on and expounded perhaps a wider spectrum of Aristotelian writings than any of his contemporaries, he was a man of very wide-ranging interests and does not at all coincide with the rather narrow and rigid scholastic, which the term 'Aristotelian' conjures up in the minds of most people. Besides making a point of learning Greek as a mature man, he assimilated a good deal of neo-Platonic, astrological and occult materials into his writings and even wrote specific treatises on several topics which go far beyond the traditonal Aristotelian university curriculum. Part of this is, of course, due to Nifo's unusual

[299]

personality, which made of him a *cortigiano* and trimmer the equal of nearly any of the Renaissance, but there is also a general lesson to be learned from his case.[6] In short, he cannot be said to represent any specific local tradition of Aristotelianism.[7]

The same can be said for any number of other university teachers. Luca Ghini, who founded a school of botanical studies at Bologna, was enticed to Pisa for several years, where Cesalpino was among his students, before he returned to Bologna to spend his final few years.[8] Girolamo Borro, one of the lecturers on natural philosophy heard by the young Galileo, taught at Perugia as well as Sienna, Rome and Paris besides filling a number of non-university jobs, in addition to his two teaching stints at Pisa.[9] Girolamo Mercuriale, one of the century's most sought-after professors of medicine, divided his teaching career among Padua, Vienna, Bologna and Pisa.[10] Thus was the pattern for the sixteenth century; men of eminence moved from chair to chair with great frequency. While this path was not open to all university teachers, the fact that it was followed by the more eminent – and one would think that among these are to be numbered the more original and more decisive thinkers – precludes any rigid formulation of locally different traditions within universities.

Having made this point, however, I should like to modify the conclusions to some extent. Within certain limits, local traditions were possible.

Some universities had more resources and prestige at their disposal than did others. Pisa could induce a Ghini, Porzio or Fallopio to come at a time when there was a great infusion of Medici wealth, influence and enthusiasm, but they were not successful in attempts to bring Alciati there.[11] Rome, enjoying papal power, could bring Cesalpino, Patrizi and Mazzoni there within the period of a few years. Padua or Bologna could depend upon long-standing traditions of prestige to entice a succession of outstanding teachers into their precincts, for example, Robertello.[12]

As far as the subjects which formed the core of instruction in the sixteenth-century universities are concerned (natural philosophy and medicine), I must confess that I have been unable to find specific regional traditions which would distinguish Padua from Pisa say, or Naples from Pavia, at least for more than a generation or two. Certain teachers, of course, put a definite stamp upon their work and, as in the case of Zabarella, occasionally dominated at a particular university for some years.[13] Cases are much rarer – or even non-existent – of such an intellectual tradition lasting for more than a generation. Padua, for example, largely I think because of its proximity to the great

[300]

printing centre of Venice, was heir to a number of different traditions of sixteenth-century Aristotelianism. These include (1) the tradition laying emphasis on Averroes and the medieval Latin interpretations of Aristotle,[14] (2) the tradition which goes back to the Greek interpreters for inspiration,[15] and (3) the philological, humanistic tradition.[16] All of these were well represented within the university throughout the sixteenth century, sometimes two or more blending together in a striking fashion in a single individual. While one can with some justification speak of Paduan Averroism, one can with equal justification speak of Paduan Thomism,[17] Scotism,[18] or humanistic Aristotelianism.[19] All strands were represented throughout most of the sixteenth century. The same is true of other major universities, which had enough resources to gain a portion of the best teachers and which were large enough to have several representatives of each of the major disciplines teaching at all times.[20]

When we come to more 'marginal subjects' – and here I shall consider botany and mathematics – the situation is somewhat different. There are several reasons for this. Firstly, in these cases the teaching was usually wholly in the hands of one man and the stamp of an individual personality becomes more evident.[21] While the staff of teachers of natural philosophy or practical medicine at a major university such as Bologna or Padua would be of the order of a half a dozen at any one time, there was seldom more than a single botanist or mathematician teaching his special subject.[22] Therefore, the personal stamp of the individual could be much more marked and specific local traditions could be established. This, I think, was the state of affairs with regard to botany at Bologna, a subject which enjoyed a great development and prestige after it was established by Ghini and was then later expanded into something even more important by Aldrovandi. Given such a situation it was possible for the one energetic young teacher – or a prestigious older one – to get various concessions and special privileges through which he could develop his subject in a particular way. We know that both Ghini and Aldrovandi were particularly favoured by the university officials, which made it possible for them to expand and develop botany teaching at Bologna into something of European-wide significance.[23] With only a single teacher in a given subject, a specific idiosyncratic tradition could be easily formed, and a dynasty, passing the tradition on from master to favoured student, could easily be established. A sympathetic university administration with at least some spare financial resources was also necessary, however. This explains in part at least how the teaching of Platonic philosophy came to develop at Pisa and Ferrara, but not at Padua and Bologna.[24]

[301]

The case of mathematics requires further investigation and it must be looked at in a comparative way which includes several of the major universities of Italy. It is my contention that here local traditions meant more. At Padua there was a strong tradition of practical and theoretical mathematics, relatively little tainted by occultism, throughout the sixteenth century until Galileo came there in 1592.[25] At Pisa, on the other hand, the teaching of mathematics was largely in the hands of undistinguished clerics, whose interests lay more in casting horoscopes than in publishing commentaries on Euclid or discussing the relationship of mathematics to logic.[26] At Bologna, where Cardano, Ferrari and Bombelli were all active for a time, there seems to have been a mixture of the two traditions.[27] I must emphasize that this is merely a general impression of mine and an exhaustive study of extant evidence is now called for.

To conclude this discussion on regional differences within universities let me say that we must be cautious in generalizing that the arts teaching at one university was significantly different from what we find at others; and we must be especially wary of exaggerating the differences which lasted more than one generation, except perhaps in what I have called 'marginal subjects'. The impact of a given teacher – even the most distinguished one – seldom lasted more than a few years after retirement. Consequently, I can see no good reasons to support the traditional distinction between 'Paduan Aristotelianism [or Averroism]' and 'Florentine Platonism'. This over-bold distinction is questionable even for the fifteenth century taken as a whole[28] and for the sixteenth century holds no water whatever.[29] Not only was the Florentine university (i.e. Pisa) predominantly Aristotelian, but there was also a strong Aristotelian strand in Florentine academic life as found in Varchi or Vettori.[30] Even Verino Secondo (Francesco di' Vieri, the younger) was as much an Aristotelian as a Platonist.[31] While at Padua the move to introduce the teaching of Plato officially into the university curriculum was unsuccessful, at least the mathematical sections of the *Republic* were taught by Francesco Barozzi,[32] and the non-university academic life of both Padua and Venice had its share of Platonism.[33] Even so militant a Platonist as Francesco Patrizi was converted to that direction of thought while a student at Padua, where his first introduction to Neo-Platonism was through hearing a Franciscan friar defend certain conclusions of Plato.[34] There can be no doubt. There was both a good amount of Platonism at Padua and much more Aristotelianism in Medicean Tuscany than is generally admitted.

RENAISSANCE PHILOSOPHY AND SCIENCE

NEW INFUSIONS OF ENERGY DURING THE RENAISSANCE

Let us now look at the situation in another way. To what degree was university practice of the period a mere continuation of medieval usage and to what degree did universities change? The standard text-book interpretation is of course that universities were stagnant and regressive, while the truly novel and progressive elements of Renaissance culture came from elsewhere.[35] In my view this is an exaggeration. As I interpret the situation, the Renaissance universities were a mixture of old and new, of conservative and progressive. Being established institutions, modification and progress were sometimes difficult to insert into the structure, but a surprising amount found its way there none the less. I should like briefly to illustrate this by several examples.

There can be little doubt that one of the most characteristic aspects of the Renaissance was the humanistic movement, which gradually transformed intellectual life in all its aspirations. By 1500 humanistic methods were having a distinct impact upon universities in Italy, as well as elsewhere in Europe. The progress of this has been partially charted, from the cautious beginnings in fourteenth- and early fifteenth-century Italy to the more far-reaching effects noticeable from the late fifteenth century onward, at first in Italy, but eventually reaching to the universities throughout Europe and the European dominions in the New World. At first, the humanistic impact with its strong emphasis on new philogical, rhetorical and historical methods was evident primarily in fields such as rhetoric and Greek and Latin language and literature, but eventually many medical and philosophical subjects were transformed as well. This was true even for a traditional university study such as Aristotelian philosophy, which had formed the basis of arts instruction from the beginning of the universities in the twelfth century. The earliest study of Aristotle was based on the rather scrappy Latin translations coming through Arabic, but the situation later improved with the introduction of better translations based directly on Greek. The Latin *Corpus* of Aristotle's writings was finally codified in the thirteenth century with a group of excellent translations by William of Moerbeke and others. With the coming of humanism, however, the approach to Aristotle, as to other classical authors, was transformed by new philological methods and by a far deeper understanding of the Greek language. This resulted in a new group of more self-conscious translations of Aristotle during the fifteenth century.

The beginnings of the transformation of the study of Aristotle within universities can be localized at the end of the fifteenth century, when we find the *editio princeps* published at Venice. At roughly the same time we find the first introduction of the new humanistic translations into university-oriented editions,[36] Poliziano's application of his new method to the study of Aristotelian texts,[37] the first attempt to teach Aristotle from the Greek text,[38] and the utilization of certain of the humanistic methods by Nifo[39] and others including Lefèvre d'Etaples in France.[40] In the sixteenth century this impetus continued with notable effect. After the first Greek edition of Aristotle, an increasing number of editions of the original text of separate works appeared, the first issue of the Greek *Organon* appearing at Florence in 1521.[41] Increasingly – and not only for the works of moral philosophy – the versions of humanist translators supplanted the medieval versions. Translations of Bruni, Trapezuntius, Argyropoulos, Filelfo, Gaza and Bessarion became standard along with a very large number of new sixteenth-century translations, again for the most part following the humanist directives for translating and interpreting classical texts.[42] Even in the few cases where the medieval versions continued to have some currency, e.g. the *Organon*, the earlier translations were revised repeatedly and new interpretative material drawn from more recent writers, among them Poliziano and Raphael of Volterra, was included to provide a degree of *aggiornamento* even for the most ancient translations.[43] What is more, humanistic method was inserted even in those places where we might least expect it. The great Giunta edition of Aristotle–Averroes, which first appeared at Venice in 1550-2, represents in many ways a return to medieval tradition and a turning aside from the new emphasis on studying Aristotle in Greek.[44] On the other hand, however, a closer look discloses the absorption of many humanist techniques in preparing the truly monumental edition. Not only were the Hebrew scholars and their Italian colleagues aware of the revived philological demands when they prepared new Latin versions of the commentaries themselves, but the treatment of the Latin translations of the Aristotelian texts shows a clear recognition of the validity of the new humanist versions. The great Venetian Aristotle–Averroes editions of the sixteenth century indicate very clearly a refusal to go to the extremes of some humanist translators, but the editors certainly benefited greatly from the philological revolution in preparing the texts which were to be standard in the universities for several generations.

In some ways, however, the most important infusion of new blood into the teaching of Aristotle was through the partial recovery and re-evaluation of the Greek commentaors. To a degree, known already in the Middle Ages, the writings of Alexander, Themistius, Ammonius Hermeae, Simplicius, Philoponus and several others played an immense role in reshaping many aspects of Aristotelian teaching, but especially in logic and natural philosophy. The role of Alexander, Simplicius and Themistius in psychological discussions have been charted and the importance of Philoponus' commentary on the *Physica* is now realized if not fully documented.[45] The reading of sixteenth-century writings on Aristotle – Nifo, Boccadiferro, Balduino or Zabarella offer excellent examples, as do Gianfrancesco Pico, Francesco Patrizi or Galileo Galilei from another perspective – shows most clearly the deep penetration of the Greek commentators into the fabric of thought.[46] Providing a Platonic element, which is not often allowed for by modern interpreters, these writings give another dimension to the variety of Renaissance 'Aristotelianisms' and provide yet another element in the tradition of a Platonized Aristotle linking up with the participation metaphysics of Thomas Aquinas and the Platonizing tendencies of a wide variety of pseudonymous works including *De mundo, Oeconomica, De causis, Theologia,*[47] and several others. Most of the very numerous sixteenth-century editions of the Greek commentaries, both in the original language and in several different Latin versions, came from the Venetian presses which provided the basic texts not only for the University of Padua, but for the universities of the remainder of Italy and the rest of Europe as well.[48]

As far as Aristotle is concerned, we can find, even at the very end of the sixteenth century, some university teachers whose courses differed very little from enlightened medieval fare. We can also find other contemporaries who knew and read Greek well, were versed in both the Greek and the medieval commentators, and who used humanist philological method alongside an increasingly well-informed philosophical method. There were also many teachers who fell between the two extremes, which I think can be usefully instanced by Borro and Zabarella. In summary we can say that the Aristotle of the sixteenth-century universities was quite diverse from time to time and place to place, though it is difficult to generalize at a local level. Alongside a Borro at Pisa was a Flaminio Nobili and a Mainetto Mainetti, both of whom did new translations of Aristotelian works, displaying a good knowledge of humanist methodology and translation technique.[49]

In addition to new approaches to traditional subjects the Renaissance, of course, brought new sources not known to the Middle Ages. During two or three decades at the very end of the fourteenth and beginning of the fifteenth century a rather spectacular amount of previously unknown Greek material came into Italy largely through the efforts of a handful of humanists. Besides the Greek commentaries on Aristotle a wide range of literary, scientific, medical and philosophical texts were recovered. Among the scientific and philosophical works were the Greek mathematicians, including Archimedes and Pappus, Theophrastus, Hero, Ptolemy, Plato, Plotinus, Proclus, Sextus Empiricus, Diogenes Laertius and a number of others. The assimilation of the knowledge contained in these works furnished one of the bases for the transformation of western culture. This is not to say that the transformation was immediate and one cannot help being struck at how long it took for certain ancient writings to be properly appreciated.[50] Even the full assimilation of Plato, perhaps the Greek author most quickly accepted, took nearly a century from the time of the Chrysaloras–Decembrio translation of the *Republic*, around 1400, until Ficino had completed his translation of all of the works in the 1480s.[51] Plato, however, along with Plotinus, Iamblichus, Proclus, Pseudo-Hermes, enjoyed a great revival during the quattrocento, so that by 1500 most of the extant Platonic and neo-Platonic texts were available to learned circles in Italy and the influence had begun to spread to the remainder of Europe. Other texts newly recovered by the humanists had a delayed impact. Eventually a good deal of this found its way into university courses in one form or another. Ptolemy's *Geography* was widely taught in the sixteenth century, often supplemented by new information based on the Renaissance geographical discoveries.[52] Theophrastus' botanical works were used by at least Aldrovandi in teaching the subject at Bologna towards the end of the sixteenth century.[53] Some of the new mathematical learning found its way into universities, but it did not really supplant the dominance of the traditional texts – Euclid, Ptolemy and Sacrobosco – as the core of university lecture courses any more than did the recovered text of the Aristotelian *Mechanics*.[54] A part of the new material could be rather easily integrated into the existing curriculum, while other newly recovered Greek texts, e.g. Sextus Empiricus or some Platonic writings, could scarcely be adapted for direct use into an Aristotelian-based programme of studies.[55]

The case of Plato requires particular comment.[56] Though there were scattered instances of the teaching of one or another Platonic dialogue in several universities during the early sixteenth century, it was not at all common and only during the last quarter of the century were specific chairs established – at Ferrara, Pisa, and at Rome – for the teaching of Platonic philosophy. Even then it remained an optional subject for students who were educated as before primarily through the study of the standard Aristotelian texts. Nevertheless, it is important to keep in mind that at least some headway was made in breaking down the Aristotelian domination of the curriculum. Holders of the chairs include two of the more important representatives of late sixteenth-century Platonism in Italy, Francesco Patrizi, whose views on space link up with Newton, and Jacopo Mazzoni, who can definitely be tied to Galileo.[57]

Besides the impact of the humanism and the accompanying revival of newly recovered texts, sixteenth-century Italian universities were open to the winds of change from other directions. It seems quite evident that the century saw a significant expansion in the number of different scientific subjects with which it was possible for a student to gain an acquaintance while at university. Most of this expansion came from developments which were at least partially internal to the universities; and those which came from outside, i.e. the Copernican system, never seem to have gained much of a foothold, at least in Italy.[58] I think that the failure of Copernicanism to be accepted by the universities of the sixteenth century has led historians to overemphasize resistance to change within the universities. In medical and mathematical subjects there were a good number of new and significant developments, which can be localized to university contexts.

Within medical faculties there are many instances of innovation and improvement. Anatomy was completely transformed during the sixteenth century, the work of Vesalius merely being the high point of a more than century-long development at Padua, starting with at least the first anatomical theatres in the 1490s and continuing through the work of Fabricius of Aquapendente in the early seventeenth century.[59] In this development we see clearly the interaction of theory and practice,[60] the refinement of many techniques, and a vast improvement of the textbook tradition, both in terms of anatomical description and in terms of illustration.

Sixteenth-century Italian medical faculties saw the beginnings of an age of increasing specialization. The traditional separation of medicine into practical and theoretical gave way to a more specialized approach with the creation of chairs in individual subjects including surgery, anatomy and botany.[61] Publications disclose an even greater number of sub-specialities with the first books appearing on such topics as paediatrics, geriatrics and plastic surgery.[62] The age of printing brought with it the possibility of the proliferation of specialized monographic treatises on a wide range of medical subjects. It also made possible, as Vesalius' great work shows so well, the broad communication of illustrative material.[63] The revolution in painting technique during the Renaissance had repercussions for science both within and outside the universities. The importance of this seems little appreciated by historians of science and even less so by historians of art. Jacopo

Ligozzi's position as a collaborator with Aldrovandi has not been studied as much as it should have been, but such technique made it possible to record and preserve many facts of natural history otherwise lost forever.[64] Such preservation of information could only have the effect of improving the accuracy of teaching, in the same way as the drawings brought back from the great explorations by naturalists of later centuries did.[65]

Botany in particular developed during the sixteenth century into an independent and flourishing science. As much as any subject it illustrates how information from different sources – writings recovered from Antiquity, new empirical investigation, communication of information from one centre to another, geographical explorations – contributed to the definition of a new science, or at least to the refounding of an old one.[66] It developed particularly quickly in Italian universities during the last two-thirds of the sixteenth century.[67] After the first establishment of chairs of botany within the medical faculties of several different universities it became well established and rapidly grew to encompass a wide range of subjects. It was a growth-point for the development of several different fields of natural history including zoology, minerology and various branches of biological science. The botanical garden, which almost immediately came to be a concomitant to the university teaching of botany, gave scope not only for an empirical and practical approach to its study, but also the possibility for experimentation.[68] Ghini[69] was the initiator of much of this, and it was through his students Aldrovandi, Anguillara, Cesalpino and Maranta, in addition to several others such as Mattioli[70] and Alpini,[71] that botany came to be an important university subject by the end of the sixteenth century. With Aldrovandi at Bologna the subject came to represent a general university-based teaching of natural history replete with botanical garden and museum devoted to the natural world in general and encompassing specimens from many geographical localities.[72] In few subjects did the old and new interact so usefully. The writings of Theophrastus, Dioscorides, Galen and Pliny were consistently updated by reference to new specimens, and there was a constant attempt to relate known plants to those described by the ancients. Much of this was in a university context, indeed in the same medical faculties where the study of anatomy was developing apace.

The mathematical sciences had a parallel growth during the sixteenth century. As mathematics was then understood it encompassed not only what we understand by the term, but also a wide range of other subjects, including astronomy, optics, astrology and other fields of enquiry making use of computational techniques in one way or another.[73] This

[308]

does not mean that the astrological matters were central interests of a Copernicus, a Commandino or a Benedetti, but for many mathematicians casting horoscopes went side by side with computing the position of planets and proving geometrical theorems. The spectrum of interests of a Girolamo Cardano, a Giovanni Antonio Magini or a John Dee characterizes the many-sided careers of numerous sixteenth-century 'mathematicians'. While it would be rash to claim that most of the best mathematics of the sixteenth century was university mathematics, by the same token it should not pass unnoticed that some of the more important developments in the subject were not totally absent from the universities. Indeed, in a way similar to botany, mathematics came to be a sort of general catch-all subject in the physical sciences. Such an approach was already inherent in the make-up of *mathematica* as transmitted from the Middle Ages;[74] the sixteenth century, however, saw a further expansion of material included under its general umbrella. Thus, such diverse – and, perhaps to our way of thinking, 'unmathematical' – topics as geography, fortification and certain aspects of meteorology were sometimes included. Indeed, a glance at John Dee's *Mathematical Preface* shows us how wide a range of topics fell under the general title of 'mathematics'.[75]

It may well be true, as Bortolotti contended,[76] that Bologna was the most distinguished of the university centres for mathematical studies in Renaissance Italy. During the sixteenth century the key names associated with the development of algebra and the solution to cubic equations were associated with that university. These include Pacioli, Del Ferro and Ferrari. Cardano also taught at the same university but as a medical man, while of the other two important names in the story, Bombelli also had close ties with Bologna, but neither studied nor taught there.[77] Tartaglia alone of the great names of the Italian school of algebraists did not spend important years of his life in Bologna. The interests of these men all went beyond what we conventionally consider mathematics. Pacioli is famous above all for his work on so mundane a subject as bookkeeping, but also wrote on architecture and perspective. Bombelli spent most of his life as an engineer and was responsible for several important engineering projects in various parts of Italy. Cardano, as is well known, had interests and competence in nearly *omne scibile*. This was generally the pattern for mathematicians of the sixteenth century. They were seldom narrow specialists or pure theoreticians. This can be said not only of Bombelli, who drained marshes,[78] and Cardano and Tartaglia, who wrote treatises on practical mechanics,[79] but also of Galileo, who left behind several treatises on fortification.[80]

[309]

Mathematics, like botany, was what we have called a 'marginal subject'. It was not so closely governed by tradition and by curricular requirements as were philosophy or medicine. It gave the instructor more scope for innovation and, perhaps, originality in teaching practice. The usual teaching texts were Euclid's *Elements*, the *Sphaera* of Sacrobosco, and various writings of Ptolemy, including the *Geography* and astrological works as well as the *Almagest*.[81]

As is now well known – to a large degree through the efforts of Professor Garin and several of his pupils[82] – mathematics, as it developed in the Renaissance, encompassed two quite different traditions of thought. Besides the tradition of technical mathematics, which resulted in the development of algebra, Copernican astronomy and Galileo's utilization of Archimedean methods, there was also something quite different. This occult and mystical side of mathematics allied with Ficinian neo-Platonism, attended more to horoscopes and *genethliaka* than to geometrical proofs and beam balances. While a Galileo is largely in the former tradition and a Giuntini in the latter, there are many, such as Cardano, who made use of both traditions. While these two strands seem quite separate to the modern, in the sixteenth century they were both part of what was called indifferently *mathematica*. Consequently, it is often difficult to see where the two traditions are joined together in any given sixteenth-century thinker. Even more difficult is any sort of objective evaluation of the merits of mathematical and astronomical works in which the two aspects are so intimately – and often skilfully – interwoven.[83]

The mystical and pseudo-scientific side of Renaissance mathematical arts was not merely the predilection of the private scholar or wandering *magus* unfettered by a contractual responsiblity to prepare students as qualified professional men: it was also most evident in mathematics teaching within the university. Even a cursory glance at what was taught in various Italian universities of the Renaissance reveals that the twofold tendency can be discerned there. Which gained ascendancy at any particular time or place may have had something to do with local conditions and traditions, but it is not easy to determine to what extent this was so. I feel safe in saying, however, that the mathematical tradition which Galileo inherited at Pisa when he took up his lectureship in 1589 was rooted more in the mystical and astrological tradition than in that of algebraic analysis and geometrical proof.[84] At Padua, on the other hand, where Galileo moved in 1592 to a better job, there was not only a richer and more distinguished tradition of mathematics, but also one more closely allied to the conception of mathematics as we generally understand the term.[85]

We have already noted the rather restricted nature of the curricular requirements in mathematics in Italian Renaissance universities; in actual practice it was somewhat broader. Optics, mechanics, geography, cosmography (a combination of astronomy and geography), anemography and hydrography were all sometimes taught.[86] While it is unlikely that many students of the sixteenth century could have heard lectures on all of these subjects during their university years, it would not have been unusual to gain contact with several of them. Geography and cosmography were quite widely taught, principally from the Ptolemaic basis which conformed to the letter of the statutes.[87] Nevertheless, often a substantial amount of additional material was added, including some new information derived from recent geographical explorations. One new type of work which emerged were *compendia* of geographical and astronomical knowledge. For example, Galileo's predecessors in the Pisa mathematics lectureship, Giuliano Ristori and Filippo Fantoni, had a hand in the composition of such a work.[88] Morever, we find the term *cosmographia* in the official title of the lectureship in mathematical studies at Ferrara about the middle of the sixteenth century, thus indicating that the subject had by then become an integral part of the mathematical arts.[89]

The pseudo-Aristotelian *Mechanics* also entered university teaching after its recovery and assimilation at the beginning of the sixteenth century.[90] The text was lectured on frequently at Padua from the 1560s until 1610 by Catena, Moleto and Galileo. It was heard from the first of these by Guidobaldo del Monte and Bernardino Baldi among others,[91] both of whom contributed significantly to the non-university mathematical culture of Renaissance Italy, and, among other things, both fed back into the mathematical tradition culminating in Galileo.

The new mathematical culture of the universities is exemplified by the Sicilian Giuseppe Moleto(1531–88),[92] who taught the subject at Padua from 1577 until his death, at which time the position remained vacant until Galileo came from Pisa to fill it in 1592. Moleto's life was cut short and he was unable to complete the works which were in preparation when he died. The manuscript writings which he left behind to Gianvincenzo Pinelli and which are now in the Biblioteca Ambrosiana of Milan reveal clearly the range of his interests and teaching activities. Taken along with other evidence they provide a clear indication of the amplitude of mathematical interests at Padua inherited by Galileo. Already in his first published work Moleto showed his broad and scientific approach to geography.[93] In addition to teaching Aristotelian *Mechanics* which we have already noted, he also lectured on optics, anemography and hydrography, which probably refer to problems arising out of his geographical studies; and he left behind an unfinished treatise on fortification, setting a precedent at Padua for another interest of Galileo in later years.[94] Besides discussions of problems in mechanics, astronomy, spherical geometry and ballistics, Moleto's manuscripts also include two rather general treatments of the subject of mathematics as he understood it. One is a dichotomous table reminiscent of those published by Ramus, Dee and many others during the century. Starting from an Aristotelian organization of the sciences,[95] he rapidly fleshes out the section on mathematics in a way which goes far beyond Aristotle. Among the topics covered in his arrangement are included algebra, *optica*, *scenographia*, *gnomica*, 'fire and objects like the weapons of war which are today called bombs, cannon and other machines for breaking down walls, towers . . .',[96] hydraulic machines, rotary clocks, and the science of weights, along with many other things. A second and much fuller treatment of some of the same material in Italian, in a form nearly ready for publication, has an imposing title which fully explains his purpose in writing it:

> Discourse of Ms Giuseppe Moleto mathematician in which he shows what mathematics is, how many parts it has, what they are and how they are related to one another; he discusses each of these parts and teaches the way to study in order to be able to master them, he explains once again the many passages of the philosophers and mathematicians found in them, and at the same time resolves many doubts and uncovers many secrets.[97]

Here he shows himself aware of an extensive mathematical literature: ancient, medieval and contemporary. Besides Copernicus, he discusses other recent writers such as Cardano, Stifel and Tartaglia on algebra; Zarlino on music; and Alberti, Dürer and Daniele Barbaro on perspective.[98] A practical air pervades the whole treatise,[99] which includes brief discussions not only of fortification, but also architecture in general, as well as balances, which he brings down to an everyday example drawn from Venice.[100] Such was the state of mathematics at Padua before Galileo arrived there. This is not to say that Moleto was one of the most skilled or original mathematicians of the century, for, from all indications, he was not, but further work remains to be done on him.[101] What we can learn from his case, however, is that the Paduan mathematical tradition was a broad one and not confined to the rather restrictive diet of texts listed by the official statutes.

While it cannot be claimed that all of the universities of Italy were as progressive as Padua in this regard, it is nevertheless clear that more was happening than is often supposed. Even at Pisa, which was rather undistinguished in mathematics throughout the sixteenth century, we find a man such as Filippo Fantoni venturing into the field of natural philosophy.[102] In fact the interaction between philosophy and mathematics was perhaps more pronounced than we might at first glance suspect, given the rather strong views of Aristotle on this subject. It can by no means be claimed that Aristotelian logicians and natural philosophers made much use of mathematical methods in their work, but there are a few instances of interaction even there, for example in the discussions regarding mathematical certitude which formed the basis of a significant polemic involving mathematicians and philosophers alike.[103] Moreover, we know that the strong Platonic tradition of interest in mathematics found its way into universities to some degree as, for example, through the Paduan mathematics lecturer Francesco Barozzi, who published an edition and exposition of texts relating to mathematics drawn from Plato's *Republic*.[104] All in all mathematics in sixteenth-century Italian universities was not a blind alley as is often supposed, nor was it the most important seedbed of new ideas. From the hints we have come across it seems a subject worthy of further study.

TRADITION AND CRISIS IN THE UNIVERSITIES

One could object that the picture I have painted thus far is too optimistic a one. I would agree. It must be balanced against the conservative and even reactionary attitudes which we know pervaded the universities. There can be no doubt that, in spite of the new infusions of life into university philosophy by humanistic methods and the reintroduction of the Greek commentators, much sixteenth-century Italian university philosophy was moribund. For every well-trained and incisive mind such as a Cesalpino[105] or a Zabarella there were certainly a dozen time-servers who fitted themselves into the expected groove by lecturing on traditional subjects in the usual way. Yet it was really in the early seventeenth century that Italian universities – and other aspects of Italian cultural life – declined drastically. This statement might appear paradoxical, for there can be no doubt that the real blossoming of Italian science can be located in the seventeenth century, from the emergence of Galileo as a significant figure down to the death of Borelli, Malpighi and Redi.[106] During those years Italian science was living on borrowed time, and this time had been borrowed from the previous century.[107] It is easy of course to overestimate the degree of suppression by ecclesiastical and other authorities. The terrible cases of Bruno, Galileo and Campanella are well known, but it is also clear that many original and creative thinkers came to live with the situation and remained productive in spite of difficulties. Not only Galileo and Campanella, but a number of others including Severino and Malpighi had their important books published abroad where they could avoid the problems imposed by the Roman Inquisition.[108] There can be no doubt that the situation was very repressive – significantly more so after the Council of Trent than before – and certain topics such as Copernican theory were proscribed. Nevertheless, the contribution of Italian science during much of the seventeenth century, when the suppression was at its height, is indeed impressive.

Still, I feel that the seeds for the destruction of the rich Italian scientific culture lay, in large measure, with the Tridentine reforms, though not perhaps in the way normally thought. While there can be no doubt that the repression of freedom of thought and expression had a devastating effect, even more important was the active development and encouragement of theological and moral studies in the universities at the expense of scientific subjects. As is well known but not always remembered, theology was little cultivated in pre-Tridentine Italian universities.[109] Italians who wanted an advanced theological education almost inevitably went to the great northern European centres, throughout the Middle Ages and into the fifteenth century, when Giovanni Pico went to Paris for the purpose. Although the Jesuits never dominated Italian universities to the extent they did those of the Catholic countries of the north, a very tight rein was kept on the formulation of university courses.[110] While there was some development of new scientific subjects, it in no way compared with the expansion of those disciplines favoured by the Tridentine reformers. The most significant of the Jesuit institutions, the Collegio Romano, typifies this approach. Traditional scientific subjects were still taught, even by teachers as capable as Clavius,[111] but they were somewhat subservient to scholastic theology, philosophy and moral studies. There was a strongly apologetic tinge to the curriculum.[112] The same became increasingly true at Padua, Bologna and elsewhere. At Padua, for example, the Franciscan school of Scotism became more and more critical of modern developments in philosophy and science, increasingly nourishing itself on a degenerating tradition of inward-looking Scotist textbooks.[113] The *rotuli* of Bologna illustrate very well the progressive domination of the stifling recommendations of Trent.[114] Before 1550 the university had only one chair of theology and it was filled only irregularly. By 1580 there were three teaching positions in subjects related to theology, by 1600 there were six and by 1650 nine. Included were several chairs of scholastic theology, the first founded in 1588. Perhaps more than anything else this discipline typifies the

[314]

structured approach to theology encouraged officially by the Church after Trent. Examples could easily be multiplied; the first theology chair at Ferrara dates from 1569[115] and, at Pisa, new chairs in theological subjects were added in 1575 and 1589.[116] Such was the pattern throughout Italy. If a friend could write Malpighi to complain how badly Italian scientists were being treated as compared to English colleagues of the same period,[117] one is equally impressed at how well theologians were being catered to and how easy it was for them to get books printed, while the great Bolognese anatomist,[118] whose work was establishing a foundation for an important branch of modern science, had to send his writings abroad to be published.[119]

This was the period of the rise of neo-scholasticism. It came throughout most of Europe, perhaps less in Italy than in most other countries, both Protestant and Catholic. As we reach 1600 noticeably fewer new commentaries on Aristotle were being published,[120] but we find more textbook expositions of Aristotelian doctrine set out in a form often quite independent of the structure of the individual Aristotelian works themselves. Typical of these is the *De communibus omnium rerum naturalium* of Benito Pereira[121] which was repeatedly reprinted well into the seventeenth century. The fundamental Aristotelian textbooks for Catholic Europe during the first third of the seventeenth century were the commentaries prepared by the Jesuits of the University of Coimbra.[122] Each of the eight principal works in the series was reprinted between fifteen and twenty-five times, but rather less frequently at Venice than at Cologne and Lyons, the other two great centres for their production. Though the Coimbra commentaries contain the Aristotelian text – but not in Greek in the Venetian reprints[123] – they are much more theological in orientation than the commentaries of the sixteenth century coming from Italy, such as those of Nifo, Pendasio or Zabarella. Indeed the pattern emerging in Italy, already in the late sixteenth century, and certainly by the early years of the seventeenth, is for natural philosophical and scientific subjects to follow one of two paths. The first is the scientific, naturalistic way of Galileo and – in a somewhat more traditional Aristotelian way – that of Cremonini.[124] The second is the path of the theologically oriented neo-scholastic commentary, which can be associated not only with Pereira, and the Coimbra commentaries, but also with the many Scotist textbooks which proliferated during the period.[125] One's general impression is that the neo-scholastic tradition came rapidly to dominate the field, though the historical *value* of the other tendency was undeniably more important from the point of view of later developments.[126]

Even before the Council of Trent, however, there was a very clear withering away of certain traditions of medieval philosophy and science. Thus the great fourteenth-century developments in natural philosophy (e.g. *intentio et remissio formarum* and *de primo et ultimo instanti*) and especially in logic, which had such a brilliant *fortuna* in Italian universities during the fifteenth century, came to a rather abrupt end during the decade of the 1520s. The evidence for this is quite clear. In the case of the fourteenth-century writings on physical questions, emanating from Oxford and Paris, the making of new editions and new manuscripts cannot be traced beyond 1525 or 1530.[127] After that date it was only the older generation which remained aware of the intricacies of the problems treated in the *Liber calculationum*, for example.[128] Thereafter, knowledge was largely second-hand and confined to rather general points and not based on a detailed and thorough acquaintance with the major treatises which had been read and commented upon so avidly a few years before, not only in universities such as Pavia, Padua and Bologna, but also among those of a more humanistic orientation such as Girolamo Pico[129] or Domenico Grimani.[130] As Lewis has shown, by the time we get to the generation before Galileo the sort of knowledge which Pomponazzi still had of intention and remission doctrine is no longer to be found.[131] The same is true of logic. Jennifer Ashworth's work in this area shows that the great developments of fourteenth- and early fifteenth-century logic continued for longer than is generally realized, i.e. into the beginning of the sixteenth century, still being adequately understood, though not sympathized with, in Nifo's *Dialectica ludicra* (1520).[132] None the less she can name 1530 as the date for the decline of medieval logic.[133] It was replaced, partially by a purified Aristotelian logic championed by Nifo, which culminated in Pacius, and partly by a humanistic dialectic, rooted in the reforms of Valla and Agricola which led in turn to the rhetorically oriented Ramist handbooks of the seventeenth century.[134]

A major problem, yet to be faced, is why fourteenth-century traditions of logic and natural philosophy died what appears to have been a natural death at the time when the Reformation crisis struck throughout Europe, while other medieval traditions lived on. It is quite understandable – both from the social-organizational standpoint of the orders and from the intellectual perspective of a Catholic Italy attempting to defend herself from heresy – that Thomist and Scotist textbooks should have begun to proliferate. Less understandable, however, is the continued interest in the expository writings of Averroes. Not only were the medieval translations of Averroes' commentaries on Aristotle reprinted, but a great many previously unutilized works were newly translated and repeatedly printed.[135]

RENAISSANCE PHILOSOPHY AND SCIENCE

Between 1550 and 1575 there were no fewer than four complete multi-volumed editions of Aristotle–Averroes at Venice and many reprints of separate works as well. This came at a time when there was not only a strong political and religious reaction against Islam in general, but also an equally intense dislike on the part of humanists for the barbarous style and mode of expression associated with the Arabic language in all its guises.[136]

We are consequently left with a situation in which quite clearly some aspects of medieval philosophy and science were consciously and vehemently rejected during the middle years of the sixteenth century, while others – which seem to a twentieth-century interpreter, equally repugnant – continued to be accepted. Indeed, it is not only in this instance that the sixteenth century in Italy shows itself to be a strange blend of traditional and innovative elements. We have already mentioned some examples of the new developments within universities and we have also indicated some of the carry-overs from the Middle Ages, as well as some of the conservative reforms brought about through the implementation of the Tridentine decrees. The interaction of old and new could be discussed at some length and, I think, profitably, but there is not ample space to consider the matter very thoroughly here. Rather I shall briefly look at merely one facet of the situation.

PLATONISM VERSUS ARISTOTELIANISM

The question of the continuity of Aristotelianism with regard to its rival philosophies is one which must be faced by all who hope to understand the intellectual development of sixteenth-century Europe.

There can be no real doubt that Aristotelian philosophy, in one or another of its various Renaissance forms, continued to dominate throughout the sixteenth century. This is not to say that it was static and wholly resistant to change, for, as we have seen, there were a number of important internal developments. On the other hand, revived ancient philosophies (Platonism, Stoicism, scepticism and atomism) and the new philosophies of nature (Patrizi, Telesio, Bruno) gained little foothold within the universities. Platonism, perhaps more than the others, calls for particular comment. Even though it was never a serious rival to Aristotelianism during the sixteenth century, it made certain inroads, not only into the university curriculum itself in a direct way, but also in a number of indirect ways. By the end of the sixteenth century Platonic philosophy had gained institutional recognition in several universities and was represented in a more informal way in several other centres. If natural philosophy within the university – on the surface at least – remained steadfastly Aristotelian, there is good reason to believe that the eclecticism promoted by a Mazzoni or the neo-Platonic natural philosophy championed by a Patrizi had some resonance. What is more, it is clear that in philosophy of mathematics, especially with regard to those aspects increasingly discussed in relation to scientific methodology, there was a particularly strong Platonic streak by the end of the century. This can be seen in the discussion on *certitudo mathematicarum* debated by Piccolomini, Barozzi, Catena and others; in the mathematican Barozzi writing on the *Republic*; or in the work of Jesuit mathematicians such as Clavius or Bianchini, as Galluzzi's illuminating work so aptly shows.[137] While by no means the dominant tendency in sixteenth-century education, the Platonic tradition, nevertheless, was an important leavening agent, linking together mathematical speculation and empirical science in a way generally alien to Aristotelianism. All of this came to bear fruit in Galileo, who took something from both Aristotelian and Platonic approaches to knowledge, refined mathematical and empirical techniques, and produced a new vision of science as revolutionary as it was fruitful.[138]

It would be perhaps going too far to read too much into Platonic–Aristotelian tension, but it is quite clear that some of the more conservative Aristotelians saw the rising tide of Platonism as a genuine threat. This can partially be seen in economic and social terms, but it is also clear that Girolamo Borro felt intellectually threatened by some of the new tendencies. Indeed, Borro as well as anyone illustrates the contrasts and inconsistencies of the century. In his most narrowly Aristotelian work we find an earlier – and perhaps as sophisticated – version of the famous 'leaning tower experiment' usually considered to be one of the great achievements of Galileo.[139] On the other hand, in a recently published short treatise from his pen we find him openly scornful and critical of the eclectic and Platonic tendencies in natural philosophical thinking, which became the hallmarks of some of the most productive thought of the next century. Few of the key figures of the so-called scientific revolution from Galileo to Newton would say that '*amor . . . geometriae*' could lead one into grave ignorance in the study of nature.[140] Yet here we have it. Borro was far from the most intelligent of sixteenth-century Aristotelians, but still we find the root of the empirical, observational method later to become famous as the core of a modern science, which consciously turned aside from the Aristotelian approach. At the same time we find him rejecting in the clearest possible way the other key element in the new science, the application of mathematical methods.

[318]

RENAISSANCE PHILOSOPHY AND SCIENCE

GENERAL CONCLUSIONS

The sketch I have drawn is all too superficial. Many important elements have been omitted and even those discussed have not been considered in any depth. Nevertheless, I hope that my analysis has made it evident that the whole question of sixteenth-century university history must be reconsidered. Unlike many colleagues I do not feel that a significant historical phenomenon such as the scientific revolution – if that term has a real meaning – can be related to a particular historical strand, be it Platonism, Hermeticism, empiricism, the recovery of Greek mathematics, the rise of hedonistic secularism, or any of a number of other intellectual, mystical or intuitive movements. Rather I am increasingly convinced that the rise of modern science – and, similarly, humanism – can be linked to various intellectual traditions which blended together to provide the proper *ambiente* from which a particular mode of thought could emerge. Nor would I want to exclude social, economic or political factors, though I am once again convinced that such elements can never fully replace intellectual elements in historical explanation. The point at issue here is whether the universities had anything to contribute to the rise of modern science and philosophy. While I cannot claim to have presented compelling evidence in favour of the universities having had a central role in all of the more progressive tendencies of early modern thought, I hope that I have been able to provide some arguments in favour of them having had a more important position than normally admitted.

In conclusion I should like once again to emphasize a factor which I take to be central to the work of Eugenio Garin and his many students and followers, i.e. the close relation between philosophy and science during the Renaissance and early modern period.[141] It is far too easy for us in the twentieth century to make a sharp distinction between science and philosophy, following the influential tendency of Wittgenstein and the *Wiener Kreis*. Yet the intimate links between *scientia* and *philosophia*, forged in Antiquity and the Middle Ages, continued to play a central role at least through the seventeenth century and perhaps even later. It is most important to keep in mind the fact that during the whole period a sharp distinction cannot be drawn between *philosophia* and *scientia*. Thus, much of the modern scholarly tradition, which divides the field into 'history of philosophy' on the one hand, from 'history of science' on the other, seems to me to approach the problem in a curiously one-sided and distorted way. Once again Garin and his school have been at the very forefront in trying to maintain the necessary balance in studying medieval and early modern philosophy and science.

[319]

Logical and metaphysical issues (including theological ones) can in no way be separated from the problems of the empirical and theoretical sciences, not only in Albertus Magnus and Roger Bacon, but also in Galileo, Descartes and Newton.

NOTES

I should like to thank the Harvard University Center for Renaissance Studies, the American Philosophical Society, and the John Simon Guggenheim Memorial Foundation for grants enabling me to carry out the research upon which this paper is based. The following abbreviations will be used:

CTC   *Catalogus translationum et commentariorum* (Washington, 1960ff.)

DBI   *Dizionario biografico degli italiani* (Rome, 1960ff.)

DSB   *Dictionary of Scientific Biography* (New York, 1970-80)

IA   *Index Aureliensis* (Baden-Baden, 1965ff.)

1 The recent work of W.A. Wallace shows that even for a figure so well known as Galileo Galilei we still have much to learn about his sources. See especially his *Galileo's Early Notebooks: The Physical Questions* (Notre Dame, 1977) and 'Galileo Galilei and the *Doctores Parisienses*' in R. Butts and J. Pitt (eds), *New Perspectives on Galileo* (Dordrecht, 1978), 87–138. Nor has Galileo's relation to the previous Florentine tradition of culture and science been adequately investigated. Studies such as E. Cochrane, 'The Florentine background of Galileo's work' in E. McMullin (ed.), *Galileo Man of Science* (New York–London, 1964), 118–39, and T.B. Settle, 'Ostilio Ricci, a bridge between Alberti and Galileo', *XIIe congrès international d'histoire des sciences* (Paris, 1971) III B, 121–6, offer useful suggestions for further work. An effort to reassess the whole situation will be found in Settle's forthcoming paper in the *Atti del convegno internazionale: Firenze e la Toscana dei Medici nell'Europa del Cinquecento*.

2 'Philosophy and science in sixteenth-century universities. Some preliminary comments', in J.E. Murdoch and E.D. Sylla (eds), *The Cultural Context of Medieval Learning* (Dordrecht, 1975), 485–537.

3 This has long been accepted as one of the chief dichotomies useful for understanding the quattrocento. The more one looks at the situation in Florence (Argyropoulos, Poliziano, Bruni, Acciaiuoli, Palmieri, etc.), the more it is evident that there was a strong Aristotelian element continuing throughout the century. Further work is required to isolate the Aristotelian tradition at Florence at the end of the century. For some indications see A. Brown, *Bartolomeo Scala (1430-1497) Chancellor of Florence: The Humanist Bureaucrat* (Princeton, 1979), 310–11, especially n. 3.

4 For basic information and further literature see C.H. Lohr in *Renaissance Quarterly*, 32 (1979), 532–9, See especially P. Zambelli, 'I problemi metodologici del necromante Agostino Nifo', *Medioevo*, 1 (1975),

129-71; E.J. Ashworth, 'Agostino Nifo's Reinterpretation of Medieval Logic', *Rivista critica di storia della filosofia*, 31 (1976), 354-74; and A. Greco, 'Agostino Nifo nel V centenario della nascita', *Arcadia*, ser. 3ª, 6 (1975-6), 147-64.

5 Especially illuminating in this respect is Zambelli, ibid.

6 This is why it is essential that Nifo (and Pomponazzi!) must be seen whole and not merely as a writer involved in the immortality controversy, as the leading Nifo scholar of our time seems to see him. For this reason the work of Ashworth and Zambelli is important in counterbalancing such an interpretation. See also N. Jardine, 'Galileo's road to truth and the demonstrative regress', *Studies in the History and Philosophy of Science*, 7 (1976), 277-318, which has several important pages on Nifo.

7 From Ashworth's work we learn a good deal about this point. Nifo tried to put forward a refined or purified version of Aristotelian logic, consciously turning aside from certain medieval traditions. See also L. Jardine, 'Dialectic or dialectical rhetoric? A. Nifo's criticism of Lorenzo Valla', *Rivista critica di storia della filosofia*, 36 (1981), 253-70.

8 For Ghini see especially G.B. de Toni, in A.Mieli (ed.), *Gli scienziati italiani*, I (Rome, 1921), 1-4; L. Sabbatani, 'La cattedra dei semplici fondata a Bologna da Luca Ghini', *Studi e memorie per la storia dell'Università di Bologna*, 9 (1926), 13-53; and A.G. Keller *in DSB*, V(1972), 383-4 (with further bibliography).

9 See article by G. Stabile in *DBI*, XIII (1971), 13-7, now best general summary.

10 The literature on Mercuriale is very scattered and we still lack a comprehensive evaluation. See in general A. Simili, *Gerolamo Mercuriale lettore e medico a Bologna* (Bologna, 1966).

11 For the general situation at Pisa see C.B. Schmitt, 'The Faculty of Arts at Pisa at the time of Galileo', *Physis*, 14 (1972), 243-72; 'The University of Pisa in the Renaissance', *History of Education*, 3 (1974), 3-17; G. Cascio · Pratilli, *L'Università e il principe. Gli studi di Siena e di Pisa tra Rinascimento e Controriforma* (Florence, 1975); and P. Zambelli, 'Scienza, filosofia, religione nella Toscana di Cosimo I', in *Florence and Venice: Comparisons and Relations*, II: *Cinquecento* (Florence, 1980), 3-52. For the failure to get Alciati there see R. Abbondanza, 'Tentativi medicei di chiamare l'Alciato allo Studio di Pisa (1542-1547)', *Annali di storia del diritto*, 2 (1958), 361-403.

12 For Robertello the best general survey is still G. Liruti, *Notizie delle vite ed opere scritte da' letterati del Friuli* (Venice-Udine, 1760-80; reprinted Bologna, 1971), II, 413-83. Also see below n. 19.

13 For a brief survey of Zabarella's career, entirely at Padua, see W.F. Edwards in *Enciclopedia filosofica*, 2nd edn (Florence, 1967), VI, 1187-9, where further bibliography is given.

14 On this see F.E. Cranz, 'Editions of the Latin Aristotle accompanied by the Commentaries of Averroes', in *Philosophy and Humanism. Renaissance Essays in Honor of Paul Oskar Kristeller* (Leiden, 1976), 116-28, and C.B. Schmitt, 'Renaissance Averroism studied through the Venetian editions of Aristotle-Averroes (with particular reference to the Giunta edition of

1550–2)', in *L'Averroismo in Italia* (Rome, 1979), 121–42.

15 For Simplicius see B. Nardi, 'Il commento di Simplicio a *De anima* nelle controversie della fine del secolo XV e del secolo XVI', in *Saggi sull' aristotelismo padovano dal secolo XIV al XVI* (Florence, 1958), 365–442. For Alexander see F.E. Cranz, 'The Prefaces to the Greek editions and Latin translations of Alexander of Aphrodisias 1450 to 1575', *American Philosophical Society. Proceedings*, 102 (1958), 510–46; the same author's article in *CTC*, I (1960), 77–135; II (1971), 411–22; and E.P. Mahoney, 'Nicoletto Vernia and Agostino Nifo on Alexander of Aphrodisias: an unnoticed dispute', *Rivista critica di storia della filosofia*, 23 (1968), 268–96. The case of Philoponus remains to be studied, but see E. Garin, *Rinascite e rivoluzioni. Movimenti culturali dal XIV al XVIII secolo (Bari, 1975), 316.*

16 See especially E. Garin, 'Le traduzioni umanistiche di Aristotele nel secolo XV', *Accademia fiorentina di scienze morali "La Colombaria"*, n.s. 2 (1947–50), 55–104, and 'La fortuna dell'etica aristotelica nel quattrocento', in *La cultura filosofica del Rinascimento italiano* (Florence, 1961), 60–72; J. Soudek, 'Leonardo Bruni and his public: a statistical and interpretative study of his annotated Latin version of the (Pseudo-) Aristotelian *Economics'*, *Studies in Medieval and Renaissance History*, 5 (1968), 51–136, and my papers cited in nn. 14 and 42, among others.

17 L. Gargan, *Lo studio teologico e la biblioteca dei domenicani a Padova nel Tre e Quattrocento* (Padua, 1971) could be extended into the next centuries. See also F.E. Cranz, 'The publishing history of the Aristotle Commentaries of Thomas Aquinas', *Traditio*, 34 (1978), 157–92.

18 See especially the material collected in *Problemi e figure della scuola scotista del Santo* (Padua, 1966), and A. Poppi (ed.), *Storia e cultura al Santo* (Vicenza, 1976).

19 One good example is Robertello who taught Greek and Latin at the universities of Pisa, Bologna and Padua, besides at several schools (e.g. Lucca and Venice). His *In librum de arte poetica explicationes* (Florence, 1548) shows his method clearly. He edited the Greek text, gave a Latin translation and a detailed literary and philological commentary. See C. Diano, 'Francesco Robertello interprete della catarsi', *Atti del XII congresso internazionale di filosofia*, IX (Florence, 1960), 71–9; B. Weinberg, *History of Literary Criticism in the Italian Renaissance* (Chicago, 1960), *passim*; and A. Carlini, 'L'Attività filologica di Francesco Robertello' (Udine, 1967; also in *Atti dell'Accademia di scienze, lettere, e arti di Udine*, ser. VII, 7, 1966–9).

Robertello was, of course, not a philosopher strictly speaking, but taught rhetorical and philological subjects. Zabarella, on the other hand, was primarily a philosopher, but also had 'humanistic' interests and was well trained in rhetoric and poetics. See W.F. Edwards, 'Jacopo Zabarella. A Renaissance Aristotelian's view of rhetoric and poetry and their relation to philosophy', in *Arts libéraux et philosophie au moyen âge*, Actes du quatrième congrès international de philosophie médiévale (Montréal-Paris, 1969), 843–54.

20 The logical debates at Padua involving Zabarella, Piccolomini and Petrella are well known through the studies of Ragnisco, as are the psychological discussions of an earlier date involving Pomponazzi, Nifo, Vernia, Trombetta, etc. Several parallel situations at Pisa are discussed in my papers cited above in n. 11.

21 While in general this is true, at Bologna for much of the sixteenth century there were several lecturers in mathematical subjects, in addition to those who taught basic arithmetic as an elementary subject similar to *ars scribendi* and *grammatica*. See U. Dallari, *I rotuli dei lettori legisti e artisti dello studio bolognese dal 1384 al 1799* (Bologna, 1888-1924), II. In the year 1557-8, for example, there were two lecturers in astronomy and one in mathematics, compared to eighteen in medical subjects, twelve in philosophical subjects, and four in Greek and Latin (II, 141-2).

22 For example, when Galileo went to Padua in 1592 he was the only mathematics teacher and the lectureship in simples was vacant. There were four lecturers in theoretical medicine and four in practical medicine. See Galileo Galilei, *Opere*, ed. Favaro (Florence, 1929-39), XIX, 117-9.

23 For Ghini see L. Sabbatani, op. cit. For Aldrovandi see *Intorno alla vita e alle opere di U. Aldrovandi* (Bologna, 1907).

24 See C.B. Schmitt, 'L'Introduction de la philosophie platonicienne dans l'enseignement des universités à la Renaissance', in *Platon et Aristote à la Renaissance* (Paris, 1976), 93-104.

25 For a survey see A. Favaro, 'I lettori di matematiche nella Università di Padova dal principio del secolo XIV alla fine del XVI', *Memorie e documenti per la storia della Università di Padova*, 1 (1922), 1-70.

26 See, in addition to Schmitt, 'The Faculty of Arts', 255-63; also my 'Filippo Fantoni, Galileo Galilei's predecessor as mathematics lecturer at Pisa' in *Science and History. Studies in Honor of Edward Rosen* (Wroclaw, etc., 1978), 53-62.

27 See E. Bortolotti, *La storia della matematica nella Università di Bologna* (Bologna, 1947).

28 The key position of Aristotelian moral philosophy in fifteenth-century Florence has become increasingly apparent since Garin's important study on the humanist translations of Aristotle cited in n. 16. The results thus far of A. Verde, *Lo studio fiorentino 1473-1503. Ricerche e documenti* (Florence-Pistoia, 1973ff.) show that, though Florence was unusual in some ways (e.g. more rhetoric and poetry than was usual) there was no shortage of Aristotelians in the university. An interesting document from the fifteenth century is Giovanni Rucellai's *Zibaldone*, which contains numerous references to various works of Aristotle and his commentators precisely at the time when the Platonic Academy was in full bloom. See A. Perosa (ed.), *Giovanni Rucellai ed il suo zibaldone*. I. *Il zibaldone quaresimale* (London, 1960), 224-5. For Plato at Padua in the early quattrocento see E. Garin, 'Ricerche sulle traduzioni di Platone nella prima metà del XV', in *Medioevo e Rinascimento. Studi in onore di Bruno Nardi*, I (Florence, 1955), 339-77, at 345-6.

29 A detailed argument cannot be given here, but the case of Paolo Beni for

Padua (on whom see the article by G. Mazzacurati in *DBI*, VIII (1966), 494–501) and Lorenzo Giacomino Tebalducci for Florence (whose numerous vernacular translations of Aristotle are still in MSS and will be discussed in a subsequent publication) are samples. See also the next note and the text cited in n. 34.

30 For the case of Varchi see U. Pirotti, *Benedetto Varchi e la cultura del suo tempo* (Florence, 1971), 69–108 ('Nel solco dell'aristotelismo'). Vettori, of course, edited, translated and/or commented upon the *Nicomachean Ethics, Politics, Poetics*, and *Rhetoric*. For information see W. Rüdiger, *Petrus Victorius aus Florenz* (Halle, 1896), *passim*. See also R.S. Samuels, 'Benedetto Varchi, the *Accademia degli Infiamati* and the origins of the Italian Academic Movement', *Renaissance Quarterly*, 29 (1976), 599–633, especially 610–11, 613, 620–3, for the importance of Aristotle, and E. Garin, 'Aneddoti di storia della cultura del Cinquecento', in *Umanesimo e Rinascimento. Studi offerti a Paul Oskar Kristeller* (Florence, 1980), 155–72, especially 164–71 (on Varchi).

31 Though Verino held the first chair of Platonic philosophy at Pisa and championed the Platonic cause, he was also active in Aristotelian matters, albeit in a rather eclectic way. For example, he published *Trattato delle metheore di M. Francesco de' Vieri Fiorentino* (Florence, 1573), perhaps identical with Firenze BN Palat. 785 (not seen). In the prefatory letter to the work he writes: '. . . finally because everyone believes in this teaching as true, and certain, I shall follow Aristotle master of those who know, and his greatest interpreters, as are all the Greeks, and among the Arabs the great commentator Averroes, and among the Latins St Thomas Aquinas' ('. . . finalmente perche ogn'uno presti fede a questa dottrina come vera, et sicura, io seguirò Aristotele maestro di color che sanno, et i suoi migliori interpreti, come sono tutti i greci, et tra li arabi il gran comentatore Averroys, et tra i latini San Thomaso d'Aquino . . .') (fol. 4^v –5^r). On Verino see besides my papers 'The Faculty of Arts', 263–4, and 'L'Introduction', also P.O. Kristeller, *Studies in Renaissance Thought and Letters* (Rome, 1956), 292, and Francesco de' Vieri, *Lezzione d'amore*, ed. J. Colaneri (Munich, 1973), the most detailed modern study of him with further bibliography, including a list of Verino's writings (pp. 9–13).

32 *Francisci Barocii . . . Commentarium in locum Platonis obscurissimum et hactenus a nemine recte expositum in principio dialogi de Republica ubi sermo habetur de numero geometrico de quo proverbium est, quod numero Platonis nihil obscurius* (Bologna, 1566).

33 A Platonic tradition at Venice is not difficult to document with names such as Pietro Bembo, Francesco Zorzi and Agostino Steuco playing some role. For Platonic mathematics see P.L. Rose, 'The Accademia Venetiana, science and culture in Renaissance Italy', *Studi veneziani*, XI (1969), 191–241, especially the conclusion on p. 199. There was a strong Platonic thread running through the teaching of moral philosophy at the *Studio* of Padua, as is evident from A. Poppi, 'Il problema della filosofia morale nella scuola padovana del Rinascimento: platonismo e aristotelismo nella definizione del metodo dell'etica' in *Platon et Aristote*, 105–46.

34 This is evident from the often cited autobiographical letter to Baccio Valori dated 1587, which is worth quoting at length, since it tells us a good deal about what an apt eighteen-year-old might learn at a centre of Aristotelianism: '. . . and in May of the year 1547 he was sent to the *studio* at Padua. Where that first summer, having found a Greek and Latin Xenophon, without any guide or help he applied himself to the Greek language, of which he had had a few principles in Ingolstadt, and profited so much that at the beginning of November he burned to study the text of Aristotle and the commentaries on the Greek *Logic*. He went to listen to Tomitano, the famous logician, but he did not please him, without being able to say why, whence he studied logic by himself. The following year he began philosophy with a certain Alberto and with Genua and neither could these please him, whence he studied alone. At the end of his studies he heard Monte the physician, and he pleased him by his method of treating things, and likewise Bassiano Lando, whose scholar he was whilst he was in the *studio*. And after a long time, hearing a friar of St Francis upholding Platonic conclusions, he became enamoured of him and then made friends with him asking him to send him on the path of Plato. He proposed as the best way the *Theology* of Ficino, to which he applied himself with great avidity. And such was the beginning of that study which he was henceforth always to follow.' ('. . .e di maggio, l'anno 1547 fu mandato a studio a Padova. Ove quella prima state, trovato un Xenofonte greco e latino, senza niuna guida o aiuto si mise nella lingua greca, di che havea havuti certi pochi principi in Inghilstat, e fece tanto profitto che a principio di novembre e di studio ardì di studiare e il testo di Aristotile e i commentatori sopra la *Loica* greci. Andò ad udir il Tomitano, famoso loico, ma non gli pose mai piacere, senza saper dire perchè, onde studiò loica da sè. L'anno sequente entrò alla filosofia di un certo Alberto e del Genoa e nè anco questi gli poterono piacere, onde studiò da sè. In fin di studio udì il Monte medico, e gli piaque per il metodo di trattar le cose, e cosi Bassiano Lando, di cui fu scolare mentre stette in istudio. E fra tanto, sentendo un frate di S. Francesco sostenar conclusioni platoniche, se ne innamorò, e fatto poi seco amicizia dimandogli che lo inviasse per la via di Platone. Gli propose come per via ottima la *Teologia* del Ficino, a che si diede con grande avidità. E tale fu il principio di quello studio che poi sempre ha seguitato.') Francesco Patrizi da Cherso, *Lettere ed opuscoli inediti*, ed. D. Aguzzi Barbagli (Florence, 1975), 46–7.

35 In the influential and widely read textbook by Denys Hay one is at pains to find even a reference to what was taught in the arts faculties of Renaissance universities. According to him, 'The significant figures of the Renaissance . . . were neither for nor against physical science. They were as relatively indifferent to this particular aspect of traditional philosophy as to philosophy of the old kind altogether' (D. Hay, *The Italian Renaissance in Its Historical Background*, 2nd edn, Cambridge, 1976 , 138). Either Professor Hay understands 'physical science' in an exceedingly bizarre way or he has remained unaware of a vast area of important recent research on the Italian Renaissance. See P.O. Kristeller, *Studies*, 35–97 ('The

Scholastic background of Marsilio Ficino'); C. Dionisotti, 'Ermolao Barbaro e la fortuna di Suiseth', in *Medioevo e Rinascimento. Studi in onore di Bruno Nardi*, I (Florence, 1955), 219–53; E. Garin, *L'Età nuova* (Naples, 1969), 139–77 ('La cultura fiorentina nella seconda metà del Trecento e i "Barbari britanni"'), 449–75 ('Gli umanisti e la scienza'); C. Vasoli, *Studi sulla cultura del Rinascimento* (Manduria, 1968), 11–39 ('Pietro degli Alboini da Mantova "scolastico" della fine del Trecento e un'epistola di Coluccio Salutati'); and R.G. Witt, 'Salutati and contemporary physics', *Journal of the History of Ideas*, 38 (1977), 667–72, among others.

36 See L. Minio-Paluello, 'Attività filosofico-editoriale aristotelica dell'Umanesimo' in his *Opuscula. The Latin Aristotle* (Amsterdam, 1972), 483–500, and Soudek, op. cit., especially 85ff.

37 See I. del Lungo, 'Angelo Poliziano, il "greco" dello studio fiorentino', in A. Poliziano, *Le selve e la strega* (Florence, 1925), 231–41, and C. Vasoli, *La dialettica e la retorica dell'Umanesimo* (Milan, 1968), 116–31.

38 Credit for this is generally attributed to Niccolò Leonico Tomeo at Padua in 1497. The relevant document is printed in J.L. Heiberg, *Beiträge zur Geschichte Georg Valla's und seiner Bibliothek* (Leipzig, 1896), 19. Cf. I. Facciolati, *Fasti Gymnasii Patavii* (Padua, 1757), I, lv-lvi. See also D. de Bellis, 'Niccolò Leonico Tomeo interprete di Aristotele naturalista', *Physis*, 17 (1975), 71–93. See, however, also the texts quoted in C.B. Schmitt, 'Thomas Linacre and Italy', in F. Maddison *et al.* (eds), *Linacre Studies* (Oxford, 1977), 36–75, at p. 61, n.1, which attribute the first teaching of Aristotle in Greek to Francesco Cavalli.

39 I have been unable to consult the paper on this subject promised by E.P. Mahoney, 'A Note on Agostino Nifo', *Philological Quarterly*, 50 (1971), 125–32, at p.131, n.35. See also Zambelli, op. cit., 134, n.1. I am inclined to see this as more significant than does Zambelli. Let us hope that the intention of today's leading Nifian scholar to clarify this issue will eventually come to fruition. See E.P. Mahoney, 'Agostino Nifo and Saint Thomas Aquinas', *Memorie Domenicane*, n.s. 7 (1976), 195–226, at p. 202, n.38.

40 See especially E.F. Rice, 'Humanist Aristotelianism in France: Jacques Lefèvre d'Etaples and his circle', in A.H.T. Levi (ed.), *Humanism in France at the End of the Middle Ages and in the Early Renaissance* (Manchester, 1970), 132–49.

41 *In hoc libro haec insunt. Porphyrii introductio. Liber unus. Aristotelis praedicamentorum. Liber unus* . . . (Florence, 1521). This volume was published by the Giunta press and contains a prefatory letter of Antonius Francinus to Ignatius Squarcialupus. It is not listed in *IA*, but copies are to be found at Amsterdam, UB (copy used: 2334.G.10); Oxford, BL; Firenze, BN; and elsewhere. On the edition see A. M. Bandini, *De florentina. Juntarum typographia* . . . (Lucca, 1791; reprinted Ridgewood, NJ, 1965), II, 164–6.

42 The standard study on the fifteenth century remains E. Garin, 'Le traduzioni umanistiche'. On the sixteenth-century translations see my 'Renaissance Averroism'; 'Aristotle's Ethics in the sixteenth century: some

preliminary considerations', in W. Ruëgg and D. Wuttke (eds), *Ethik im Humanismus* (Boppard, 1979), and 'Some observations on the Renaissance translations of Aristotle', forthcoming. I hope to be able eventually to treat the matter more comprehensively in my section on Latin translations on Aristotle to appear in *CTC*.

43 Poliziano's *Dialectica* printed, for example, in *Angeli Politiani Opera*...(Basle, 1553), 517-28, is reprinted in many editions of the medieval translations of Aristotle's logic, including the following, which I have seen: Venice, 1541 (*IA*, 108.028; Paris, BN: R.9449); Lyons, 1546 (not in *IA*; Firenze, B. Riccardiana: XX.I.16620); Lyons (Paganus), 1547 (*IA*, 108.127; Kraków, BJ: Philol. gr. 220); Lyons (Gryphius), 1547 (*IA*, 108.126; Munich SB: A.gr.b.555); Venice, 1552 (not in *IA*; Oxford BL: Antq.f.I 1552/5); Lyons, 1553 (*IA*, 108.260; Munich SB: A.gr.b.557) and numerous others. The text was also reproduced in editions containing more recent translations as in *Aristotelis . . . opera omnia*. . .(Basle, 1563) (London, Warburg Institute: AKH 232), which contains the Perion-Grouchy translations.

44 See my 'Renaissance Averroism' and 'Some observations'.

45 See above, n. 15. Alexander, Theophrastus, Olympiodorus and Priscianus Lydus have now been covered in *CTC*.

46 Many examples could be given, but I shall cite merely two, one from an Aristotelian and one from an anti-Aristotelian. See Mahoney's article cited in n. 15 and my *Gianfrancesco Pico della Mirandola (1469-1533) and His Critique of Aristotle* (The Hague, 1967), 129, 138-56.

47 This subject requires much further study. Some useful notes and bibliography on the *Theologia*, for example, are found in G. Faggin, 'Pseudo-Aristotele', *Enciclopedia filosofica*, 2nd edn (Florence, 1967), I, 468-9, and E.P. Mahoney, 'Pier Nicola Castellani and Agostino Nifo on Averroes's Doctrine of the Agent Intellect', *Rivista critica di storia della filosofia*, 25 (1970), 387-409, at p. 389, n.8. See also Fabricius–Harles, *Bibliotheca graeca*, 4th edn (Hamburg, 1790-1809), III, 278-80, which seems better informed on the sixteenth-century *fortuna* of the work than do most twentieth-century scholars.

48 My as yet incomplete study of the *fortuna* of the Greek commentators on Aristotle during the Renaissance shows how dominant Venice was in the printing history of these texts. For the case of Alexander see Cranz in *CTC* (n. 15), where 27 of the 32 listed editions of the genuine and spurious commentaries are printed at Venice. For Philoponus I find that 45 of the 50 editions known to me are from Venice; for Simplicius, 21 of 24. The reprinting of all of the Renaissance Latin translations of the Greek commentators has begun as C. Lohr (ed.), *Commentaria in Aristotelem Graeca. Corpus versionum latinarum sexto decimo saeculo impressarum* (Frankfurt, 1978ff.). To date two volumes have appeared.

49 Flaminio Nobili translated *De generatione et corruptione I* anew and added a commentary. It was printed as *Aristotelis de generatione et interitu liber primus a Flaminio Nobilio in latinam linguam conversus et simplici primum verborum explanatione, deinde quaestionibus copiosissimis ad*

[327]

finem cuiusque capitis appositis illustratus (Lucca, 1567) (copies used Lucca B Governativa: Busdrago 0.22 and Göttingen Niedersächische S-UB: Auct. gr. IV.1132 = *IA*, 108.518). The printed version seems to be identical with MS Firenze, B Laurenziana 84.2, which I have also examined. It was reprinted at Padua in 1596 (*IA*, 108.750; copy used Oxford, BL:L.1.9.Jur(2)). A translation of the second book appeared as *Aristotelis de generatione et interitu secundus. A Flaminio Nobilio Lucense in linguam latinam conversus et publice in almo Gymnasio Pisano explicatus*. . . (Venice, 1598) (*IA*, 108.750; copy used Oxford, BL: L.1.9 Jur. (3)). Mainetti's new translation of the *De coelo* appeared as *Commentarii in librum I Aristotelis De coelo necnon in librum Averrois De substantia orbis* . . . *Auctore Maynetto Maynetio Bononiense in Pisana Academia primo philosopho* (Bologna, 1570) (not in *IA*; copy used Firenze BN: Palat. 29.3.7.17(2)). Both new translations are dedicated to Cosimo I. Further discussions of them must wait for another occasion.

50 This is true, for example, of the botanical writings of Theophrastus on which see *CTC*, II, 239–322. See also below, n. 53. For the case of Sextus Empiricus see R.H. Popkin, *The History of Scepticism from Erasmus to Spinoza* (Berkeley–Los Angeles–London, 1979), and C.B. Schmitt, 'The recovery and assimilation of Ancient Scepticism in the Renaissance', *Rivista critica di storia della filosofia*, 27 (1972), 363–84.

51 For a brief survey see R. Klibansky, *The Continuity of the Platonic Tradition During the Middle Ages* (London, 1938).

52 For the recovery of Ptolemy's *Geography* and its impact on Renaissance culture see Joseph Fischer, *De Cl. Ptolemaei vita operibus geographia praesertim eiusque fatis*, which is the *Tomus prodromus* to C. Ptolemaei, *Geographiae codex urbinus graecus 82* (Leiden–Leipzig, 1932), especially 171–208, and T. Goldstein, 'Geography in fifteenth-century Florence', in J. Parker (ed.), *Merchants and Scholars: Essays in the History of Exploration and Trade* (Minneapolis, 1965). I am indebted to Mr David Thomason for information.

53 See MSS Bologna, B Universitaria, Aldrovandi 78^1 and 78^2, which contain evidence of Aldrovandi's work on Theophrastus (accurate description in L. Frati, *Catalogo di manoscritti di Ulisse Aldrovandi*, Bologna, 1907). According to his *Autobiography* written in 1586, '[in 1560] per seconda lettura [Aldrovandi] lesse Theophrasto, *De causis plantarum*': *Intorno alla vita*, 1–27, at p. 11.

54 On this see below, p. 311.

55 In my view there were two basic reasons why Plato's writings were not more generally adopted for university instruction. First, the unsystematic nature of the *Dialogues* makes them difficult to use as teaching textbooks in philosophy, as opposed to literature. In spite of the neo-Platonic systematization of Plato (on which see E.N. Tigerstedt, *The Decline and Fall of the Neoplatonic Interpretation of Plato*, Helsinki, 1974), the Platonic system was not so easily amenable to classroom instruction as was Aristotle. Moreover, to try to introduce an approach to the study of philosophy via Academic Scepticism (i.e. another form of Platonism) could

have only limited appeal and required special circumstances. On this point see my *Cicero Scepticus: A Study of the Influence of the Academica in the Renaissance* (The Hague, 1972), especially. 81–91.

The second major reason for the failure of Platonism to gain more than a foothold in sixteenth-century universities is its restricted nature. Though quite broadly based in metaphysics and moral philosophy, the logic and, even more so, the natural philosophy are not very highly developed or well articulated in the available sources. Since the latter two branches of philosophy were the core of instruction in Italian Renaissance universities, Platonism had little chance of gaining ascendancy.

56 For further information see my 'L'Introduction de la philosophie platonicienne . . .'.

57 For the Mazzoni–Galileo link see F. Purnell, 'Jacopo Mazzoni and Galileo', *Physis*, 14 (1972), 273–94. For the place of Patrizi in Newton's background see J. Henry, 'Francesco Patrizi da Cherso's concept of space and its later influence', *Annals of Science*, 36 (1979), 549–73.

58 See especially C. Vasoli, 'Copernico e la cultura filosofica italiana del suo tempo', *Giornale di fisica*, 14 (1973), 79–107, and E. Garin, *Rinascite e rivoluzioni* (Bari, 1975), 255–95, which cite the previous literature. Among those whose considerations on Copernicus do not seem to have been adequately studied are Francesco Vimercato and Giuseppe Moleto. The MS Milano, Ambrosiana L.130, fols 283–5 by Vimercato discusses Copernicus. I have not seen the MS, but draw my information from N.W. Gilbert, 'Francesco Vimercato of Milan: a Bio-Bibliography', *Studies in the Renaissance*, 12 (1965), 188–217, at p. 215. Moleto took account of Copernicus in various places, including MSS Amb. D.235inf., fols 28–9; R.94sup., fol. 184; S.103sup., fol. 144.

59 See L.R. Lind, *Pre-Vesalian Anatomy* (Philadelphia, 1975), and H.B. Adelmann, *The Embryological Treatises of Hieronymus Fabricius of Aquapendente* (Ithaca, 1942).

60 This can be seen, for example, in R. Eriksson (ed.), *Andreas Vesalius' First Public Anatomy at Bologna 1540, an Eyewitness Report by Baldasar Heseler.* . . (Uppsala–Stockholm, 1959).

61 At Ferrara at the beginning of the sixteenth century there were only chairs of practical and theoretical medicine; later in the century other specialities developed, e.g. surgery (1540), botany (1543), anatomy (1570): A. Franceschini, *Nuovi documenti relativi ai docenti dello studio di Ferrara nel sec. XVI* (Ferrara, 1970), 236–51. At Bologna botany was added in 1534 and anatomy in 1570:L. Simeoni, *Storia della Università di Bologna*, II: L'Età moderna (Bologna, 1940), 34.

62 Paolo Bagellardo, *Libellus de aegritudinibus et remediis infantium* (Padua, 1472 = GW 3166), and Gabriele Zerbi, *Gerontocomia scilicet de senum cura atque victu* (Rome, 1489 = H 16, 284), were both published by Padua professors. The first book on plastic surgery is Tagliacozzo's *De curtorum chirurgia* (Venice, 1597), on which see M.T. Gnudi and J.P. Webster, *The Life and Times of Gaspare Tagliacozzo* (New York, 1950).

63 See R. Herrlinger, *Geschichte der medizinischen Abbildung*, I: *Von der*

Antike bis um 1600 (Munich, 1967). For the general impact of printing see E.L. Eisenstein, *The Printing Press as an Agent of Change* (Cambridge, 1979), 453–682.

64 See M. Bacci and A. Forlan, *Mostra di disegni di Jacopo Ligozzi (1547-1626)* (Florence, 1961), and U. Stefanutti, *Piante e animali nell'opera di Ulisse Aldrovandi* (Milan, n.d.).

65 Explorations such as those of Captain Cook and von Humboldt and the voyages of the *Beagle* or *Discovery* all took care to make accurate sketches of local flora and fauna.

66 See K. Reeds, 'Renaissance humanism and botany', *Annals of Science*, 33 (1976), 519–42.

67 For a brief sketch with further bibliography see C.B. Schmitt, 'Science in the Italian universities', in M.P. Crosland (ed.), *The Emergence of Science in Western Europe* (London, 1975), 35–56, especially pp. 39–44.

68 ibid., p. 40. See also G. Ongaro, 'Contributi alla biografia di Prospero Alpini', *Acta medicae historiae Patavina*, 8–9 (1961–3), 79–168, at pp. 117–18, 120–1, 156–8.

69 See above, n. 8.

70 The best study of Mattioli is J. Stannard, 'P.A. Mattioli: Sixteenth-century commentator on Dioscorides', University of Kansas Libraries, *Bibliographical Contributions*, I (1969), 59–81.

71 See G. Ongaro, op. cit.

72 Schmitt, 'Science in the Italian universities', 42–4. For a general consideration of Aldrovandi and his impact, especially at Mantua, see D.A. Franchini *et al.*, *La scienza a corte* (Rome, 1979).

73 In general see P.L. Rose, *The Italian Renaissance of Mathematics. Studies on Humanists and Mathematics from Petrarch to Galileo* (Geneva, 1975).

74 There is a large literature on this subject, but see J.A. Weisheipl, 'Curriculum of the Faculty of Arts at Oxford in the early fourteenth century', *Mediaeval Studies*, 26 (1964), 143–85, especially pp. 170–3, and C. Vasoli, *Profezia e ragione* (Naples, 1974), 405–75.

75 John Dee, *The Mathematicall Preface to the Elements of . . . Euclid*, ed. A.G. Debus (New York, 1975).

76 E. Bortolotti, op. cit.

77 See S.A. Jayawardene in *DSB*, II (1970), 279–81, with references to the more detailed literature.

78 See S.A. Jayawardene, 'Rafael Bombelli, engineer-architect: some unpublished documents of the Apostolic Camera,' *Isis*, 56 (1965), 298–306.

79 Especially in *Questiti e inventioni diverse. . .* (Venice, 1546). There is a convenient reprint of the more complete 1554 edn with a valuable introduction by A. Masotti (Brescia, 1959). Also see Masotti's *Studi su Niccolò Tartaglia* (Brescia, 1962).

80 Printed in Galileo Galilei, *Le opere*, II, 7–146. In fact there is a strong technological and practical component running through most of the works of Galileo, e.g. the rather unstudied First Day of the *Due nuove scienze*.

81 This is true for a number of universities. It is spelled out clearly for Pisa, on which see F. Buonamici, 'Sull'antico statuto della Università di Pisa:

alcuni notizie storiche', *Annali delle università toscane*, 30 (1911), 46, cited in Schmitt, 'The Faculty of Arts at Pisa', 257.

82 See, for example, *Medioevo e Rinascimento* (Bari, 1954), 188–9. The articulation of this view has been developed in the work of P. Rossi, C. Vasoli, P. Zambelli, P. Galluzzi and others.

83 In my view the more or less complete separation of the two strands of the history of mathematics by modern scholars has been most unfortunate. What is needed is a sympathetic – yet, at the same time technically competent – study of figures such as Cardano and Dee. Those who study the hard mathematics of such thinkers all too often have little sympathy for their mystical flights of fancy. Those who study the occultist and mystical strand too often tend to be 'enthusiastic', finding 'hermetic' symbolism behind every *locus communis*.

84 See Schmitt, 'Filippo Fantoni'.

85 In general see A. Favaro, op. cit., to be supplemented by P.L. Rose, 'Professors of mathematics at Padua University, 1521–1588', *Physis*, 17 (1975), 300–4.

86 See Schmitt, 'Science in the Italian Universities', 46, for documentation.

87 Ptolemy was listed in the statutes of virtually all of the universities of the time.

88 Details are given in Schmitt, 'Filippo Fantoni'.

89 Franceschini, op. cit. 263. On the question of the term *cosmographia*, see in general A. de Smet, 'Les géographes de la Renaissance et la cosmographie', in *L'Univers à la Renaissance: Microcosme et macrocosme* (Brussels, 1970), 13–29, which deals mostly with northern Europe.

90 P.L. Rose and S. Drake, 'The Pseudo-Aristotelian *Questions in Mechanics* in Renaissance culture', *Studies in the Renaissance*, 18 (1971), 65–104; Rose (op. cit.), 302.

91 ibid., 90, 93.

92 See especially A. Favaro, 'Amici e corrispondenti di Galileo Galilei. XL. Giuseppe Moletti', *Atti del Reale Istituto Veneto di scienze, lettere, ed arti*, 77 (1917–18), 47–118.

93 ibid., 51ff.

94 Amb. S.100sup. Cf. Favaro, op. cit., 89.

95 Amb. R.94sup., fol. 184 entitled 'Partitio mathematicarum scientiarum'.

96 ibid.; 'ignes et corpora ut tormenta bellica quae bombardas hodie appellant, trombae et reliquae machinae rumpendo parietes, turres . . . .'

97 Amb. S.103sup., fol. 122^r: 'Discorso di Ms. Giuseppe Moleto Matematico nel quale egli mostra che cosa sia Matematica, quante sien le parti di quella, quali sieno e come sieno insieme ordinate, si discorre intorno a ciascuna et insegna la via con la quale si debanno studiare per potersene impadronire, dichiara ancora in esse molti luoghi de'filsosofi et de'matematici et insieme volve molte dubitationi et scuopre molti segreti.' Cf. Favaro op. cit., 88.

98 ibid., 122^r–175^r. There is a certain practical orientation in all of this as when he says (fol. 127^r): 'And who does not know that in the arithmetic of Fra Luca and others all things dealt with can be dealt with and managed with two results, the one of which is in considering the force, and the power

and likewise the proportion of those numbers being dealt with, and the other is in accommodating those numbers to business . . .' ('Et chi non sa che nell'aritmetica di fra Luca edd'altri tutte le cose, che si trattano si possono con due fini trattare e maneggiare, l'uno de quali è nel considerare la forza, et la potenza, et insieme la proportione di quei numeri, che si trattano, et l'altro è di accommodare quei numeri al negotio. . .').

99 The final remarks of the treatise (ibid., fol.175^r) are as follows: 'From this whole discourse one can see for oneself, without my striving to demonstrate it, how much and in what way is useful that which can be extracted from mathematics at any time and in any place and how much mathematics is worthwhile to any class of man and particularly to princes' ('Da tutto questo discorso si puo vedere da se senza che io mi affati a mostrarlo quanto e quale n'a l'utile, che dalle matematiche si puo in ogni tempo et in ogni luogo cavare et quanto a ciascuna qualita di persone si convengano et particolarmente a principi').

100 ibid., fol. 165: '[scales] are used until this day both in Venice and all over Italy indiscriminately and at Venice they are sold publicly on the San Bartolomeo square, indeed I wish to say that Aristotle did did not allow scales of iron' ('[bilanze] s'usano fin al di d'hoggi et a Venetia, et per tutta l'Italia indifferentemente e publicamente a Venetia si vendeno su'l campo di San Bartolomeo, anzi mi movo a dire che Aristotele non concesse bilanze di ferro . . .').

101 The manuscripts are very disordered and often difficult to read, but a detailed study of his work would seem to be worthwhile and would undoubtedly shed light on some of the questions being discussed here.

102 The importance of this is emphasized by S. Drake, 'The evolution of *De motu*', *Isis*, 87 (1976), 239–50, at p. 240. I plan to publish a study of Fantoni's *De motu* in the near future.

103 See especially the following works of G.C. Giacobbe, 'Alcune cinquencentine riguardanti il processo di rivalutazione epistemologica della matematica nell'ambito della rivoluzione scientifica rinascimentale', *La Berio*, 13 (1973), 7–44; 'Il *Commentarium de certitudine mathematicarum disciplinarum* di Alessandro Piccolomini', *Physis*, 14 (1972), 162–93; 'Francesco Barozzi e la *Quaestio de certitudine mathematicarum*', *Physis*, 14 (1972), 357–74; 'Epigoni nel Seicento della *Quaestio de certitudine mathematicarum*: Giuseppe Biancani', *Physis*, 18 (1976), 5–40. See also G. Crapulli, *Mathesis universalis: genesi di una idea nel XVI secolo* (Rome, 1969), especially 33–62.

104 Cited above, n. 32. For further information on him see the paper by Giacobbe cited in the previous note (bibliography).

105 The empirical and progressive aspect of Cesalpino has recently been stressed by C. Colombero, 'Il pensiero filosofico di Andrea Cesalpino', *Rivista critica di storia della filosofia*, 32 (1977), 269–84, but the fruitfulness of such an approach has not yet been demonstrated.

106 The continued originality of Italian science until the end of the seventeenth century is perhaps best exemplified by Adelmann's magisterial studies, *Marcello Malpighi and the Evolution of Embryology* (Ithaca–New York,

1966) and *The Correspondence of Marcello Malpighi* (Ithaca–London, 1975). Borelli's significance is sketched by T.B. Settle in *DSB*, II (1970), 306–14. Also see E. Balaguer Perigüell, *La introducción del modelo físico-matemático en la medicina moderna. Análisis de la obra de G.A. Borelli (1608–1679). De motu animalium* (Valencia–Granada, 1974).

107 The physical sciences declined earlier and only Borelli and, perhaps, Tommaso Cornelio, can be considered figures of international significance from those active during the second half of the seventeenth century, but the whole question is in need of re-evaluation, perhaps along the lines pursued by Charles Webster, *The Great Instauration* (London, 1975). See W.E.K. Middleton, 'Science in Rome, 1675–1700, and the *Accademia fisicomatematica* of Giovanni Giustino Ciampini', *British Journal for the History of Science*, 8 (1975), 138–54.

108 The case of Malpighi is amply documented in the work of Adelmann (see n. 106). For Severino see L. Amabile, 'Due artisti e uno scienziato: Gian Bologna, Jacomo Svanenburch e Marco Aurelio Severino nel Santo Officio Napoletano', *Atti della Reale Accademia di scienze morali e politiche. Società Reale di Napoli*, 24 (1891), 433–503. A number of Severino's most important works – like those of Malpighi – were published abroad. See C.B. Schmitt and C. Webster, 'Harvey and M. A. Severino. A neglected medical relationship', *Bulletin of the History of Medicine*, 45 (1971), 49–75, especially 70–3.

109 A glance at the matriculation lists and *rotuli* for any of the universities shows that theological studies were little cultivated compared to law and medicine.

110 There is a large literature on this. For one study which cites much earlier literature see G. Piaia, 'Aristotelismo, "heresia" e giurisdizionalismo nella polemica del P. Antonio Possevino contro lo Studio di Padova', *Quaderni per la storia dell'Università di Padova*, 6 (1973), 125–45.

111 The standard study is R.G. Villoslada, *Storia del Collegio Romano dal suo inizio (1551) alla soppressione della Compagnia di Gesù (1773)* (Rome, 1954), but further work is needed on this subject. Clavius in particular should be studied. The article by H.L.L. Busard in *DSB*, III (1971), 311–12, is not very adequate. See also Galluzzi (n. 137).

112 Villoslada, op. cit., 84–115.

113 See the works cited above in n. 17, especially the papers by A. Poppi, P. Scapin, F. Costa and G. Panteghini. See also below, n. 125, and A. Poppi, 'Per una storia della cultura nel convento del Santo dal XIII al XIX secolo', *Quaderni per la storia dell'Università di Padova*, 3 (1970), 1–29.

114 U. Dallari, *I rotuli dei lettori e artisti dello studio bolognese dal 1384 al 1799*, 2 (Bologna, 1888–1924).

115 Franceschini, op. cit., 264.

116 A. Fabroni, *Historia academiae pisanae*. . . (Pisa, 1791–5), II, 123–7, corroborated by Pisa, Archivio di Stato, Univ. 177–80.

117 Adelmann, *The Correspondence of Marcello Malpighi*, 459–60 (G.B. Capucci to Malpighi, dated 19 May 1670).

118 This is one of the conclusions to be drawn from P.F. Grendler, *The Roman*

Inquisition and the Venetian Press, 1540–1605 (Princeton, 1977).

119 See Adelmann, *The Correspondence, passim*, for the exchange with Oldenburg in London concerning the publication of his work. Further study is required for a number of seventeenth-century Italian scientists who are not quite of the first rank. An approach such as that of M. Torrini, *Tommaso Cornelio e la ricostruzione della scienza* (Naples, 1977), seems to me much more fruitful than trying to trace 'Hermetic' strands through the major seventeenth-century scientists. On this see the incisive comments of E. Garin in *Rivista critica di storia della filosofia*, 31 (1976), 462–6; 32 (1977), 342–7.

120 I cannot now document this precisely, but I plan to deal with the question in a future publication.

121 The first edition was Rome, 1576, and it was reprinted frequently thereafter. On Pereira see M. Solana, *Historia de la filosofía española. Epoca del Rinascimiento (siglo XVI)*, III (Madrid, 1940), 373–400.

122 The first edition of these works appeared in the decade of the 1590s at Coimbra and were reprinted at Lyons, Cologne, Venice and Mainz. See the illuminating introduction by A.A. de Andrade to *Curso conimbricense, I. P°. Manuel de Góis: Moral a Nicómaco de Aristóteles* (Lisbon, 1957), i-cxiv, and C.H. Lohr in *Renaissance Quarterly*, 28 (1975), 717–19 (bibliography).

123 The printing history of the commentaries is quite complicated and there are various textual and bibliographical problems which have not yet been satisfactorily studied. I plan to deal with them more fully in a future study.

124 The tradition of Aristotelian biological thought in Italy must still be studied with care. Cesalpino and Cremonini are two of the key figures here. For this aspect of Cremonini see the various studies of Walter Pagel including *History of Science*, 9 (1970), 33–4.

125 See especially D. de Caylus, 'Merveilleux épanouissement de l'école scotiste au XVIIᵉ, *Etudes franciscaines*, 24 (1910), 5–21, 493–502; 25 (1911), 35–47, 306–17, 627–45; 26 (1912), 276–88, and J. Jansen, 'Zur Philosophie der Skotisten des 17. Jahrhunderts', *Franziskanische Studien*, 23 (1936), 28–58, 150–75.

126 For the case of Padua see M.L. Sopplesa, *Genesi del metodo galileiano e tramonto dell'aristotelismo nella scuola di Padova* (Padua, 1974).

127 See the evidence given in C.B. Schmitt, 'Hieronymus Picus, Renaissance Platonism and the Calculator', *International Studies in Philosophy*, 8 (1976), 57–80, for the case of the Calculator. A similar pattern can be found for the works of Heytesbury, Strode, Buridan, etc.

128 Of the important philosophers of the period only Achillini and Pomponazzi seem to deal with the issues in detail. For a survey with bibliography see the article on Swineshead by J.E. Murdoch and E.D. Sylla in *DSB*, XIII (1976), 184–213, especially 209–13.

129 Schmitt, 'Hieronymous Picus'.

130 P. Kibre, 'Cardinal Domenico Grimani, *Questio de intensione et remissione qualitatis:* a Commentary on the Tractate of That Title by Richard Suiseth (Calculator)', in S. Prete (ed.), *Didiscaliae: Studies in Honor of Anselm M. Albaraeda* (New York, 1961), 147–203.

131 C.J.T. Lewis, 'The fortunes of Richard Swineshead in the time of Galileo', *Annals of Science*, 33 (1976), 561–84, and *The Merton Tradition and Kinematics in Late Sixteenth- and Early Seventeenth-Century Italy* (Padua, 1980).

132 Ashworth, 'Agostino Nifo's reinterpretation of medieval logic'. Many other publications by the same author are also relevant to the same point.

133 'The eclipse of medieval logic', in *The Cambridge History of Later Medieval Philosophy*, ed. N. Kretzmann (Cambridge, 1982), 787–96.

134 In general see W. Risse, *Die Logik der Neuzeit*. 1. Band, *1500–1640* (Stuttgart–Bad Cannstatt, 1964), and H.-E. H. Jaeger, 'Studien zur Frühgeschichte der Hermeneutik', *Archiv für Begriffsgeschichte*, 18 (1974), 35–84.

135 See H.A. Wolfson, *Studies in the History and Philosophy of Religion*, I (Cambridge, Mass., 1973ff.), 371–401 ('The twice revealed Averroes') and 530–54 ('Plan for the publication of a *Corpus Commentariorum Averrois in Aristotelem*'); and the articles by Cranz and Schmitt cited in n. 14.

136 The view of Petrarch, Bruni, E. Barbaro, etc. is well known, but it continues down to the sixteenth century. Tommaso Giunta characterizes such a view accurately in the prefatory letter to the great 1550-2 edn of Aristotle-Averroes; 'But our age, which has scorned and virtually trodden under foot the learning of the Arabs, accepts and admires nothing except what it knows to have been brought here from the treasures of the Greeks. [Our age] worships only the Greeks . . .' ('Aetas vero nostra, contempta et quasi iam conculcata Arabum doctrina, nihil recipit, nihil miratur, nisi quod a Graecorum thesauris huc norit esse translatum. Graecos solos [aetas nostra] colit . . .') Aristotelis Stagiritae omnia quae extant omnia. . .Averrois Cordubensis in ea opera omnes qui ad nos pervenire commentarii (Venice, 1550-2), I,I, fol. 2. Cf. Schmitt, 'Renaissance Averroism'.

137 P. Galluzzi, 'Il "Platonismo" del tardo Cinquecento e la filosofia di Galileo', in P. Zambelli (ed.), *Ricerche sulla cultura dell'Italia moderna* (Bari, 1973), 39–79.

138 Consequently, I do not feel that Galileo's achievement can be reduced to the effect of Platonism, experimentalism, mathematics, Aristotelian logic, or any of the single elements which have been suggested. Many different traditions went into his mature thought. He selected from the possibilities available to him, reformulating where necessary, and showing not a small degree of originality.

139 Girolamo Borro, *De motu gravium et levium* (Florence, 1575), 125. Cf. Schmitt, 'The Faculty of Arts', 267–71, and W.A. Wallace, *Causality and Scientific Explanation* (Ann Arbor, 1972), I, 149–50.

140 C.B. Schmitt, 'Girolamo Borro's *Multae sunt nostrarum ignorationum causae* (Ms. vat. Ross. 1009)' in *Philosophy and Humanism*, 462–76, at p. 476.

141 Garin, *L'Età nuova*, 482: 'a significant portion of the early beginnings of "modern" science must be sought in scholastic works and courses of instruction commonly considered 'philosophical', but often in sectors

neglected by "historians of philosophy" because they are "scientific" and by historians of science because they are "philosophical" ' ('. . . una parte cospicua degl'incunaboli della scienza "moderna" deve cercarsi in opere scolastiche e in corsi d'insegnamento comunemente considerati di "filosofia", ma spesso in settori trascurati dagli "storici della filosofia" perche "scientifici", e dagli storici della scienza perchè "filosofici" ').